CAMBRIDGE TEXTS IN THE
HISTORY OF POLITICAL THOUGHT

═══

GEORGE LAWSON
Politica Sacra et Civilis

CAMBRIDGE TEXTS IN THE HISTORY OF POLITICAL THOUGHT

Series editors:
RAYMOND GEUSS, *Columbia University*
QUENTIN SKINNER, *Christ's College, Cambridge*

The series will make available to students the most important texts required for an understanding of the history of political thought. The scholarship of the present generation has greatly expanded our sense of the range of authors indispensable for such an understanding, and the series will reflect those developments. It will also include a number of less well-known works, in particular those needed to establish the intellectual contexts that in turn help to make sense of the major texts. The principal aim, however, will be to produce new versions of the major texts themselves, based on the most up-to-date scholarship. The preference will always be for complete texts, and a special feature of the series will be to complement individual texts, within the compass of a single volume, with subsidiary contextual material. Each volume will contain an introduction on the historical identity and contemporary significance of the text concerned, as well as such student aids as notes for further reading and chronologies of the principal events in a thinker's life.

For a complete list of titles published in the series, see end of book.

GEORGE LAWSON

Politica Sacra et Civilis

EDITED BY

CONAL CONDREN

Professor, School of Political Science, University of New South Wales

CAMBRIDGE
UNIVERSITY PRESS

Published by the Press Syndicate of the University of Cambridge
The Pitt Building, Trumpington Street, Cambridge CB2 1RP
40 West 20th Street, New York, NY 10011–4211, USA
10 Stamford Road, Oakleigh, Victoria 3166, Australia

First published 1992

Printed in Great Britain at the University Press, Cambridge

A catalogue record for this book is available from the British Library

Library of Congress cataloguing in publication data

Lawson, George, d. 1678.
[Politica sacra & civilis]
Politica sacra et civilis / George Lawson; edited by Conal
Condren.
p. cm. – (Cambridge texts in the history of political
thought)
Includes index.
ISBN 0 521 39248 9 (hardback)
1. Church and state. 2. Political science – Early works to 1800.
I. Condren, Conal. II. Title. III. Series.
JC510.L38 1992 322'.1 – dc20 91–40352CIP

ISBN 0 521 39248 9 hardback

Contents

Politica Sacra et Civilis

Contents

Preface

My first thanks are to the editors of Cambridge Texts in the History of Political Thought for inviting me to prepare this edition. This was done largely in Cambridge during 1990. Specifically my thanks to Richard Tuck for advice given despite the toils of bringing his edition of *Leviathan* to its conclusion; to Raymond Geuss; and especially to Quentin Skinner for help and much typical kindness. During my stay in Cambridge, solicited and unsolicited assistance saved hours of time.

Much of this help was given during lunch at Clare Hall and during random, if sometimes subversive, breaks in the University Library Tea Room. My thanks to the denizens of the latter and to the fellows and Anthony Low, President of the former – a college of surpassing friendliness.

In particular I am grateful to Hugh Williamson for transliterating Hebrew, Pascalis Kitromilides for advice on some of the Greek, John Kilcullen for helping with Lawson's non-citation of medieval texts. Additional thanks are due to John Morrill and Mark Goldie, and to Ian Maclean, who made me feel a little less foolish for being unable to trace a reference to Grotius; to Bruce Kaye (for more Hebrew); to Paddy Schreuder for all the hard work on Dr Carr's convoluted and misprinted poem; to Averil Condren for further help, sub-editing and the index; and to Libi Nugent for keyboard skills, intelligent attention to detail and her wry patience. My thanks also to Laurien Berkeley for copy-editing.

I am grateful to the University of New South Wales Faculty of Arts Research Grants Committee for financial support. To Dona Haycraft and John Chalmers, who turned casual neighbourliness into lasting fellowship, my part in this text is dedicated.

Editor's introduction

I

George Lawson's *Politica sacra et civilis* is a systematic treatise which traverses much of the conceptual terrain of seventeenth-century political discourse, and provides a critical accompaniment to many of the loudest catch-cries that echoed over it. Lawson's stated purpose is to facilitate a lasting civil and religious settlement. He conceives the church and the state as two broadly parallel and mutually informing structures of political, sovereign power and argues that an understanding of either requires an understanding of both. As Lawson provides an accessible synopsis of the volume in 'The arguments of the several chapters' (pp. 8–13), only the briefest outline of the work's theoretical structure is needed here.

Lawson begins by sketching in what he takes to be the nature of all forms of government under a supreme being, the very existence of whom is taken to limit all modes of human allegiance. From the outset, then, Lawson prefigures the central importance to him of authority and its limitations. In chapters two and three he introduces his notions of community and citizenship in civil and ecclesiological society respectively. Communities are divinely sanctioned, pre-political associations; they are comprised of citizens who, in a Ciceronian sense, are naturally free and equal fellows. A community of citizens, however, is not a mere aggregation of isolated individuals; it is a complex, incorporated society under natural law, whose full members represent the disfranchised. The community may lack nothing but the security afforded by the laws of a formal political hierarchy. When impressed upon a community, such a hierarchy creates a proper commonwealth. Lawson may be seen as suggesting something like the later sociological distinction between *Gemeinschaft* and *Gesellschaft*, though not as distinct types of society, but as complementary aspects of all political societies.

From chapters four to seven Lawson discusses in detail the imposition of political order upon communities of fellowship. This order turns a community of believers into a formal visible church and a society of fellows into a state. The rationale for the imposition is, in the case of a church, to aid salvation, and, in the case of a state, to secure the public good. It is clear that, for Lawson, the creation of a polity from a community requires the consent of the citizens, although it is not consent but living according to justice which principally legitimizes the community itself. The immediate consequences of the transmutation are that the citizen takes on a double identity by becoming a political subject; that a notion of office-holding now augments that of representation; and that sovereignty must also be seen in a dual light.

Sovereignty is divided into two species which, following the nomenclature of property law and its political application by Christopher Besold, Lawson calls personal and real. Personal majesty, or sovereignty, is the office constituting the rights and duties of the government and its officers to rule, administer and protect. It involves the distinguishable functions of legislation, execution and judgement; it is, however, not divisible into separate, balanced or shared powers. Although personal majesty is as such divinely ordained, its specific forms are mutable. Thus Lawson discusses the ways in which it is gained and lost, concentrating on the all too frequent phenomena of conquest and usurpation. By contrast, real majesty is largely immovable; it is the underlying authority of the community. It comprises the rights of real majesty is often unproblematic; but acute ethical problems do arise where personal majesty is illegitimately transformed rights of real majesty are often unproblematic; but acute ethical problems do arise where personal majesty is illegitimately transformed through tyranny or usurpation. At such times, Lawson insists, it is particularly important to understand the competing claims of subjection, entailing political obedience, and of citizenship, which is characterized by freedom from human authority.

Chapters eight and nine specify the manifestations of personal majesty in state and church. Lawson shows relatively little interest in the pure forms of monarchy, aristocracy and democracy, regarding them less as types than as administrative tendencies. These two chapters largely prepare the ground for a discussion of the Power of the Keys. This expression refers figuratively to the human power to facilitate salvation. It is taken broadly to stand for the ultimate authority within a visible church, and is seen by Lawson as directly analogous to real majesty in the commonwealth.

From chapters ten to fourteen Lawson discusses a range of arguments concerning the proper location of the Keys. He deals in turn with the claims of the papacy and monarchical Erastianism, episcopacy and Presbyterianism, and with Congregationalism. Each is considered in terms of the conventional Aristotelian categories used for secular institutional forms – monarchy, aristocracy and democracy. Throughout this group of chapters Lawson insists that this power is properly located in no specific form. Rather, he concludes, it is found in the whole community of believers, or, with qualifications, their representatives, constituting a church. Although, for example, episcopal and Presbyterian churches are seen as permissible forms of aristocratic government, Lawson argues that they are not divinely sanctioned but are only contingent modes of personal majesty.

With this conclusion it becomes necessary for Lawson to say more about the nature and limits of a particular church. A national church, he concludes in chapter fourteen, is both permissible and desirable as a mean between the illegitimate extreme of papacy and the untenable one of Congregationalism.

In chapters fifteen and sixteen Lawson returns to the matter of subjection in church and state, dealing again with the tensions between the requirements of subjection to a political form and the rights of the community. He explicates a hierarchy of loyalty, placing loyalty to a prior community above allegiance to the person of a ruler. Between these extremes lie obligations to the laws and to the forms of government which have been impressed upon the community. The work ends with a specification of the orders of subjection within the commonwealth and their value in promoting the common good.

Throughout, both to clarify abstract concepts and to show his understanding of Britain's condition, Lawson illustrates with extensive reference to recent history. Thus in chapter four he uses the notions of real and personal majesty to discuss the English Constitution and assess the claim that it is a 'mixed monarchy'. The institutions of monarchy and parliament, he concludes, are but components in an incorporated personal majesty. In dealing with the loss and acquisition of power, in chapter five, he canvasses the issues of conquest, usurpation and forfeiture of power, all of particular relevance to Interregnum Britain. In chapters eight and fifteen he explicitly discusses the Civil War and Interregnum in order to show how his theories and distinctions can make sense of what has seemed so confused. In chapters ten, eleven, twelve and fourteen he explicitly ties his arguments to the problems surrounding the English Reformation and the form that a Church of England should take.

Strictly speaking, Lawson's work is unfinished, for there was to be a second volume dealing with the details of administration which was already written when the *Politica* was published. What we have in book one, then, is a general conspectus dealing, *inter alia*, with the concepts of representation and office-holding as functions of communal empowerment and political accountability; with the nature and limits of obligation to a polity and loyalty to community; with the acquisition and loss of political power and with its varieties of institutional form. Each of the work's principal categories: subject, citizen; church member, believer; real and personal majesty; church, state; officer, representative; are understood as rather abstract binary pairings. These are all of a distinctly ramist and nominalist nature, in that they are to be understood in mutually defining relationship. As meaning is thus apt to reside in formal contrasts, the misunderstanding of any one term is taken to have an immediate consequence for the use or meaning of its opposing term. Lawson recognizes that, in practice, several of his abstract categories will be applicable to an individual at any given time, so involving patterns of potentially conflicting injunctions. But this, in a sense, is the point; the principal distinctions are made in order to delineate the moral and prudential cruxes of political life, so that the individual may discourse rationally and face them squarely.

II

Lawson claims that his work was written for ordinary people; his persona is that of a minister tending a flock in need of guidance and reassurance. Appropriately, his idiom is at times casuistic, and to carry conviction he variously displays the credentials proper to his office: modesty, integrity, even a repetitive and didactic informality. His renowned learning should also be seen partially in this light. The complex citation of texts, and the use of Latin, Greek and Hebrew, seem not merely to convey knowledge. Indeed, his specified audience could not have taken full advantage of such learning. Rather, much of the erudition seems to reinforce his authority. This would be doubly necessary if, as becomes manifest at times, his intended audience included the clergy. Regardless of the precise audience sought, then, Lawson's citations and allusions should be seen not as incidental to his argument but, as it were, a text function within it, providing the means of creating a public space in which to be heard. This was no easy task when Lawson had his first volume printed.

The publication dates of the *Politica*, 1660 and 1689, are of obvious significance, each marking the beginnings of a new regime and a new attempt at settlement. On each occasion a monarch waited off-stage and was conditionally invited to ascend the throne. On each occasion, much depended upon the movements and compliance of armed forces, which especially in 1659–60 had held massive if uncertain sway. Each juncture required that people think carefully about the nature of the polity, its generation and potential shape, and about the moral difficulties attendant upon extreme political action. There is an added significance in that together the two editions of the *Politica* frame the House of Stuart's final attempt at absolutism. It was a form of rule Lawson considered deeply un-English.

Yet, in 1680, a high point of fear about the restored monarch's absolutist drift towards France and Rome, the Nonconformist John Humfrey commended Lawson's *Politica* as having strewn the way for the return of Charles II and his bishops (*A Peaceable Resolution of Conscience*); and within a few years of this, he and others would use the same work to strew the way for William III or a republic after the speedy exit of James II. The *Politica* proved to be a protean text, and its importance in the seventeenth century stands in marked contrast with its later obscurity.

To an extent Lawson's own obscurity has been rather artificially maintained. Richard Baxter, for example, lavished praise on him in his autobiography, but this was edited out of later editions. Baxter claimed that, more than anyone, Lawson had shaped his own political thinking and, over a long friendship, shown him the value of rigorous conceptualization. Too little is known of Lawson's life for an account of it to act as a firm context for the *Politica*, but biography can provide something, and I want briefly to turn to it as the first of a series of overlapping contexts which can be constructed to illuminate and explicate further aspects of the *Politica*.

III

Lawson was born into a yeoman family in Lancliffe, Yorkshire, probably during April 1598. He had a younger sister, who did not survive childhood, and his mother died in 1610. He attended Emmanuel College, one of the most zealously reforming in Cambridge, and claimed to have an MA from there. He was ordained in 1624, but comes to notice only after William Laud became Archbishop of Canterbury in 1633. Lawson, allegedly a supporter of Laud, certainly had the archbishop's help in his unsuccessful attempt to obtain a disputed position in the important church of St Chad's in Shrewsbury, 1637. By this time he seems to have been living in the village of More, twenty miles south of Shrewsbury. There Lawson would spend the rest of his life, for shortly after his failure at St Chad's, he was appointed to the rectory of More, the advowson of which belonged to Richard More of Linley. Thereafter, Lawson was involved in Church government in Shropshire and was probably tutor to the More family. Like the Mores he was prepared to work with the Presbyterian system of church government established by the Long Parliament; when Shropshire was divided into six classes (1648–9) he was judged a minister fit to serve. He was prepared, like the Mores, to work with that which followed the partial breakdown of English Presbyterianism during the Interregnum. Yet Lawson was not a Presbyterian, let alone an Independent, although he had friends who were both. With the Restoration and re-establishment of the episcopal Church of England, he kept his living, despite his suspicions of episcopacy and the rigours of the Act of Uniformity (1662). This cost many of his previous colleagues their livings and it hardly presaged the comprehensive religious settlement advocated in the *Politica*. He died in July 1678, still working in his parish, and was survived by his wife Anne (d.1680) and their son Jeremiah (1635–1705). Lawson left a comfortable estate, which included fine linen and a hair shirt; and above all a substantial library, which was sold after the death of Anne.

All his writings suggest an intense piety, but only an indifferent commitment to the church forms through which he worked. Whether his institutional scepticism was typical, an accommodating attitude throughout this troubled period certainly was; and whatever his motivations for compliance, his *Politica* fits with a willingness to opt for less than perfection. As such, it may be said to give theoretical expression to a widespread clerical and gentry sentiment which explains what an exclusive emphasis on the divisions of the civil wars cannot, namely the marked continuity in ecclesiastical office-holding.

Lawson's long association with the More family may also cast light on the more secular aspects of the *Politica*. Lawson's patron, Richard More, was a man of noted Calvinistic piety, serving on Long Parliament committees and giving plate to its cause before his death in 1643. His son Samuel (d. 1662) succeeded Richard as head of the family. Having been a principal parliamentarian commander in Shropshire, Samuel More was excluded from Cromwell's last Parliament and retained his offices at the Restoration. Again, the pattern suggests a widespread capacity to compromise around 1660. From this scrappy evidence we do find, however, pretty well what we would expect in the *Politica*: a residually strong if critical commitment to Parliament, especially to the Commons (8.14, 22); and intimations of a willingness to accept a re-established monarchy. With respect both to church and state, the *Politica* adopts an irenic tone and emphasizes the need for accommodation, though never at any price. The ends of government in both orders of power thus function as criteria for circumscribing the terms of a settlement. Casuistry is discredited without curtailment (8.11, 19).

IV

The initial publication date also provides a clarifying context for the *Politica*, helping to explain its tone. Between 1659 and 1660 there was a burgeoning of politico-religious literature, reflecting and addressing a heightened instability following the death of Oliver Cromwell in 1658. In the nine years since the execution of Charles I, the country had remained unsettled; and in the months following Cromwell's death, changes of government achieved an almost Italianate frequency. In such circumstances, only hindsight makes the eventual restoration of Charles II look inevitable; only a remarkable propaganda campaign has left the impression that it was universally popular. Few could have thought the regime was securely restored. Indeed, some believed that, after Cromwell's death, the long-awaited republic might be established; others, that the way forward lay with Richard, or with one of Cromwell's generals. Of those who supported Charles's restoration, some did so because he looked the least of available evils, or because there was hope of his improvement with a little impounding. None of this was lost on Charles or his advisers, not least the fact that as king he was initially the creature of his old enemy's armies. The Restoration was a true crisis – a well-perceived point of danger and opportunity.

One major response to this common perception was to put faith in some fixed, legitimate set of institutional arrangements. In part the *Politica* is a commentary on such beliefs. Lawson argues that traditions and what suits the country must be respected; yet, he insists that all political forms are variable structures. As they can be corrupted, so they can be adapted to circumstances. Such views about the contingency of governmental organization had intermittently been aired since John of Paris in the fourteenth century; more recently they had been associated with Presbyterian theories of government. The crucial point was the distinction between the necessity of some form of government and the contingent nature of all governmental structures. On this basis, Lawson is able to argue that what matters at present is not a perfect order, on which there is bound to be much dispute, but some order. In an imperfect world 'where we cannot do what we will, we must do what we can' (15.10). The relatively little time he spends discussing ideal forms of government reinforces this sceptical pragmatism. Even the Ancient Constitution, which he sees as encapsulating natural right and as standing for the abstract principle of constitutional law, he treats more as a general goal than a binding model.

With respect to the church, unlike Presbyterians, Congregationalists, Episcopalians or Catholics, Lawson is intent on showing that all churches are also political organizations and are thus like state structures, legitimately adaptable. This, partly, seems to be the point of using secularizing terminology in discussing their respective claims to the Power of the Keys. In arguing that none can claim a divinely sanctioned status, he maximizes the area of negotiability in reaching a religious settlement. Those who insist on their own church or state institutional models as uniquely legitimate multiply their enemies and minimize the chances of a settlement by marrying intransigence to theoretical error. A settlement, then, depends on knowing where one can give way; this is to presuppose that one understands the few necessities of politics.

If the contexts of the Restoration crisis and the remnants of biography help explain the ameliorating tone of the *Politica*, they may account also for some of its specific equivocations and use of litotes; that is, Lawson's tactic of writing something even in the process of distancing himself from it. For example, he urges the reduction of the episcopacy to an ancient form in the idiom of James Ussher, yet he explicitly accepts, on apostolic evidence, that no precedents need be binding in an emergency. A parallel to this casuistic reason of church is found in his view that monarchy provides a suitable basis for a settlement, but might prove to be otherwise (8.22). Again, he quotes extensively from John Sadler, *The Rights of the Kingdom*, 1649, a work of Miltonic antimonarchical vigour, but refuses to endorse Sadler's judgements. Such an air of evasiveness may have arisen from genuine doubts; it certainly exhibits the appropriate rhetorical credentials of moderation and charity. And such a display may also have been part of a strategy to make others doubt more and judge less glibly. Censorious political judgement was certainly one of the barriers Lawson saw as inhibiting a lasting settlement (8.21).

Lawson's choice of vocabulary and his treatment of the dominant myths of the civil wars also seem designed to exercise a settling force in 1660. He is reluctant to apply the highly inflammatory terms 'resistance' and 'rebellion' to the Civil War, preferring instead the less charged 'failure' or 'dissolution' of government. Even Charles I, who is held to be largely responsible for the 'dissolution', is not paraded as the tyrant of parliamentarian myth. Indeed, in the context of discussing the issue of legitimate resistance to tyrannical governments, Lawson argues that there was neither resistance nor rebellion, as both terms are predicated on the prior existence of a governmental form, an order of subjection, which had broken down. This may now seem like a mere semantic quibble; but one needs to keep in mind the instability of the English language in the mid-seventeenth century. Hobbes had hardly been alone in recognizing a relationship between a stable political order and the precise signification of words. Along with tracts on language, dictionaries and even legislative proposals, definition and distinction were regarded as important. It was, for Lawson, part of an under-labouring task that might clear the way for rational discussion. To be trapped in 'curious distinctions' (15.8) and to have only inadequate 'notions' had a deleterious effect on understanding and action. He also saw words as weapons, believing that firing off such terms as 'rebellion' hindered settlement. The *Politica* was published to spike the guns of recrimination and to isolate the last bastions of intransigence, if not 'to quench at least (to) abate the flames of dissension' (1.3; 8.22). It is only when placed in such a context that one can see the rhetorical care with which it was written.

To leave the matter there, however, is to ignore Lawson's somewhat recalcitrant resources and to give the impression that the *Politica* was simply *un livre de circonstance*. In its overall shape the work pre-dates 1660, the published text being probably the incompletely revised version of a work drafted around 1657. Although settlement was a theme of discourse throughout the Interregnum, this long gestation suggests we broaden the context by placing the *Politica* alongside Lawson's earlier works.

V

Lawson's first known writings date from *c.* 1649, when he responded to Baxter's controversial *Aphorisms of Justification* (1649). The gist of Lawson's reply is contained in the manuscript 'Amica dissertatio', a one-sided dialogue between Lawson and Baxter's propositions. The work is with the unpublished Baxter Treatises in the Dr Williams's Library. Its predominant theme is abstrusely theological, concerning the nature of sin and divine punishment, and the definition of theological terms.

Three points are of informing significance for the *Politica*. First, Lawson writes as a theologian. Even in the *Politica*, his most secular work, he maintains that all politics must be seen as a branch of divine providence (1.1; 4.1). And while he is only intermittently confident about recovering the ancient Constitution, he never doubts the Bible's relevance. Israel in the Old Testament is something of a model of political relationships; the early Church of the New Testament legitimizes a diversity of ecclesiological ones. Secondly, in dealing with the question of how to define or establish the necessary attributes of God, Lawson shows a pointed awareness of the necessity to use tropes. His reliance on metaphor in particular underpins the conceptual structure of the *Politica*. Not only is the work organized around the time-honoured analogical images of church and state, but, as I have indicated, the nomenclature of political activity is consistently used to describe God and ecclesiological relationships. Thirdly, Lawson's characteristic way of understanding the political individual as existing simultaneously under the auspices of contrasting abstract categories of subjection and citizenship may have been adapted from the definitional strategy he employs in the 'Amica dissertatio' in order to attempt the impossible, the definition of God. In the early work Lawson argues that God must be seen as *duplex* rather than *simplex*. He is both judge, which entails an obligation to carry out a law, and lawmaker, which carries a status above the law. There is a striking logical analogy between this and Lawson's later *duplex* understanding of the individual as subject and citizen. Further, the individual is presumed to be a member of both a state and a church; and at the same time, the individual is also a member of the community of England and a Christian community. The individual may be seen, in short, as formed by roles, to be a complex of offices. In this light the *Politica* can be seen as an elaborate doctrine of office. It is little wonder that Lawson is apt to see a world full of moral difficulties, in which clarifying the individual's options is important, but impossible without an adequate battery of 'notions'.

Lawson published two known works before the *Politica*, the *Examination of the Political Part of Mr. Hobbs, His Leviathan* (1657); and the *Theo-politica* (1659). The critique of Hobbes is broadly consistent with the line of argument taken in the *Politica*. It attacks *Leviathan*'s Erastianism, which is seen as leading to, or being a form of, atheism; it dismisses Hobbes's legal positivism as a *simplex* understanding of law and inveighs against his authoritarian notion of sovereignty, which is seen as leading to slavery. All this would be consistent with Lawson's having drafted the *Politica* by around 1657. Nevertheless, there are changes of emphasis and a more systematic order of exposition in the *Politica* as printed. The rights of the individual in the face of tyranny and usurpation are more cautiously handled, being more obviously balanced by an emphasis on the prudent exercise of rights, and by stress upon the rights of government. The tonal difference may be explained by the *Examination*'s need to counteract the extremity of *Leviathan*, or by the special requirements of putting the *Politica* on the market to urge a settlement. Here, too much talk of tyranny, right and the infringement of property as a criterion for resisting a tyrant (all evident in the *Examination*) would not have been obviously assuaging. But there is a further difference. The principal concepts are, by and large, dealt with more abstractly, less as empirical generalizations than as defining aspects of the political world.

In a number of respects, Lawson's views in the *Politica* are not so far from Hobbes's in the excoriated *Leviathan*. Their attitudes to the problem of predicating anything of God, to the political nature of a church, to the identity of bishop and presbyter and to the perceived need to control ecclesiastical externals in the interests of peace are all much the same. Lawson was acutely aware of the leading role of secular rulers in the English Reformation (12.10) and may seem to us closer to Hobbes's Erastianism than he would be happy to admit. For all his reliance on history, like Hobbes he believed that history teaches matters of fact not right (8.13).

With respect to the state, Lawson, like Hobbes, will have nothing to do with shared sovereignty or mixed monarchy theory as it was widely understood; and, as has sometimes been said of Locke, he places sufficient emphasis on the need to govern by the sword to allow a Hobbesian sovereign in at the back door. Also like Hobbes, he recognizes the dependency of the sword upon the purse (4). Again, as for Hobbes and Locke, an element of consent is central to the foundation of the state.

Finally, there are passages in the *Politica* which suggest a view of representation close to that of *Leviathan*. Both Hobbes and Lawson worked within the ambit of medieval adaptations of Roman Law theories of corporation. In *Leviathan*, the sovereign as representative takes on the persona of the individuals in need of its protection and so is not accountable to them. There are times when Lawson writes in a similar vein (e.g. 14.5, 14.12); there are even occasions when the personal sovereign is depicted as the representative of the community (8.14, 17; 13.2). Such notions of representation require a distinction between officers and representatives; and, for the most part, Lawson is careful, like Hobbes, to keep these concepts distinct. Lawson's officers are like Hobbes's public ministers (*Leviathan*, 23), agents accountable to a sovereign body. Overall, for Lawson, both officers and representatives have a derivative power and must not be confused with the whole from which they derive. Yet officers are directly accountable to a prior authority, be it state or church, whereas the representatives are sometimes depicted as acting for it, perhaps being accountable only to later representatives (14.12; 15.5). It is a distinction reinforced by Lawson's metaphor of the eye or the ear for the representative (13.6). The eye is not the whole but, as no other organ can do its work, the eye is the whole's way of seeing. Lawson does not treat the distinction between officers and representatives with total consistency (4.9, 12; 13.2). For sometimes he suggests that representatives are also accountable to a larger whole (13.6). The consequence is to cast a shadow of ambiguity over the sovereign as representative.

The *Theo-politica* (1659) is designed to advise the individual on moral duty to God in the light of the Ten Commandments. It essays for the world of private morality what the *Politica* attempts for the individual confronted by the vicissitudes of public life. Perhaps the principal light it casts upon the *Politica* is with respect to the distinction between the Fifth Commandment ('Honour thy father and thy mother') and Christ's injunction 'love thy neighbour' (Matt. 19.19).

For Lawson, the notion of honouring parents is essentially hierarchical; the commandment legitimizes subordination. As Dr Johnson was later to believe so firmly, politics is above all a matter of subordination, and so the Fifth Commandment is a political one. Neighbourliness, in contrast, is a matter of fellowship, of freedom and equality (4.1). In short, as the Fifth Commandment legitimizes political, as it were vertical, orders (5.1); so, Christ's injunction legitimizes communal, horizontal ones. The self-conscious expansion from the Fifth Commandment may have consequences with which Lawson would not have been happy; for, in taking it as a text from which to elaborate an understanding of political relationships, Lawson suggests a patriarchalism to which he is explicitly opposed. He did not hold that the family provides the model for political society, any more than he believed that there is one legitimate form of political arrangement. Consequently, as Gordon Schochet has noted, Lawson is ambivalently located in a context of patriarchal thought.

One further work needs brief mention. According to Baxter, Lawson wrote an Engagement tract. No such work appeared under his name, although Julian Franklin has suggested that the anonymous *Conscience Puzzled* (1650) might be Lawson's work (*John Locke and the Theory of Sovereignty*, Cambridge, 1975). The matter cannot be decided, but the possibility does valuably point to two further contexts necessary for understanding the *Politica*.

VI

The Engagement controversy, 1649–51, and the pamphlet war a decade earlier noticeably inform the *Politica*. The pamphlet war had concerned the proper form of English government and had established an important agenda of discussion throughout the Civil War. The Engagement controversy arose precisely because, however it had been understood, the proper frame of government was no more. In its place stood an army requiring obedience. This possibility had hardly been a cloud on the conceptual horizon in 1640. The importance of the army was made doubly difficult to digest because many believed that soldiers were not properly members of a political society. In 1659–60, when another army was in process of restoring a monarch and a parliament, it must have seemed as if the same issues of engagement had come again.

Lawson's belief that absolute monarchy is un-English (8.17) is directed against all those who held that Parliament had no traditional role to play in government. 'The Grand Remonstrance' of 1640 had forcibly claimed such a role. One view arising from this was that Parliament, or even the Commons, was an ultimate locus of legitimate authority. Another, more ecumenical, one was that Parliament shared rule with the monarch in a 'mixed' monarchy or constitution. This latter notion was to become particularly popular. Concepts of mixed constitutions enjoyed an august lineage. In variant forms they had been praised by Aristotle, Polybius, Cicero and Machiavelli. Aquinas had attributed such a constitution to Israel under Moses; and with such impeccable credentials it is not surprising to find such writers as Thomas Starkey and Sir John Fortescue attributing mixed government to England. From the 1640s, its cachet was augmented; it had plausibility if one looked at some of the workings of government; appeal if one sought a compromise between the King and his enemies, or if one sought to guarantee some role for everyone with a serious stake in government. But its diplomatic lack of specificity was also a theoretical drawback.

In so far as the sovereignty disputes from 1640 provide a context for the *Politica*, Lawson can be seen as attacking on a wide front; he believed that most people were confused about the nature of sovereignty, the character of England and the terms of the debate (15). Parliament on its own was no more sovereign than the King; the Commons, though ascendant, also had no claim to sovereignty. But this did not mean that sovereignty was a balance of shared separate powers. It was rather a single corporate identity (4.14; 8.9). If any part moved beyond its sphere, then the whole of this edifice of personal majesty collapsed. In this way, Lawson attempts to cauterize the earlier debates on sovereignty by restricting them to the sphere of personal majesty, the functional domain of legislative, executive and judicial. The dissolution of this preceded the civil wars but did not affect the locus of real majesty. This remained in the community (4.8), the bloodied but unbowed victim of governmental failure. Sovereignty debates had missed the mark, partly because, being informed by an inadequate nomenclature of sovereignty, they could not hope to locate it clearly, nor identify the underlying authority which could authorize a settlement.

Although Lawson's universalist notion of citizenship does not exclude soldiers from society, at no point does he embrace the army as representative of the people; and he shows no marked love of Cromwell, whose rule had been illegitimate and whose achievements were mixed. The country continues to thrive, but still awaits a settlement. The Engagement controversy, which brought Cromwell's ascendancy into discomforting focus, raised a host of painful issues concerning moral integrity and judgement during a time of usurpation, the sanctity of oaths, the role of providence and contingency in politics, and the purpose of government itself. In the sixteenth century Bodin, in Augustinian style, had remarked that most governments had their origins in violence. It was a maxim of state that had a resounding immediacy by 1650.

Such matters are so apparent in the *Politica* that, in discussing usurpation, Lawson might well have been reworking his Engagement response. He seems also to have been doing so in elaborating his hierarchy of loyalty, designed to put obligations and loyalties to persons and specific forms of government into perspective. Ultimately, it is the theological perspective announced at the outset, that unqualified allegiance is due only to God (1.1; 16.1). Lawson's insistence on the priority of loyalty to a community may have been intended to ease scrupulous consciences still feeling heavily obliged to past promises

(15.4–7) and to ruined forms and former rulers. That Lawson could argue in this way in 1660 indicates how deeply impressions of the past could pattern perceptions of the present. That John Starkey could reprint the work in 1689 reinforces the point.

VII

One major reason why some had wanted to share in the government of Charles I had been to redirect his religious policies. For many clerics, and the fervent amongst the gentry and aristocracy, the nature and direction of the English (or Scottish) Reformation was the central issue – the one issue amongst a host of grievances which could justify extreme action against the legitimate monarch. Yet this was no straightforward matter. Since the sixteenth century the Reformation in England had been principally an aspect of royal policy, as Lawson knew full well; and for this there had been precedent enough in the policies of Henry II and Henry V and the theology of Wyclif. By the seventeenth century, such a tradition made the relationships between church and state particularly difficult to disentangle.

On such matters, the *Politica* is at its most incisive and ingenious, exhibiting a telling ability to play one position off against another. Lawson shows a masterly grasp of the major themes of English ecclesiology, church–state relationships, discipline, authority and judgement. To these he brings a knowledge of late medieval conciliar theory which he uses to refine the problems of representation and church authority; and a sympathy with Grotian beliefs in accommodation. Indeed, as I have indicated, it is central to his settlement strategy to push as much as possible into the realm of the biblically indifferent, for to do this is to expand the area of political negotiability. It is precisely in such a context of argument that one should see his insistence that no particular church form is required by the Bible, and that, regardless of church form, the ultimate earthly authority of the Keys belongs to the whole community of believers. Lawson goes so far as to describe the church as a free state (13). Although there may be, as with a classical republic or 'free state', a monarchical element, it is constrained within the polity. The designation is a corollary for him of Christ's being the only legitimate claimant to absolute power in any visible church. Lawson thus accommodates a traditional monarchical control over the Established Church which stops short of a Cesaro-papism analogous to political absolutism. Here, as elsewhere, ecclesiology parallels the secular dimension of his settlement theory; for in a civil context of argument Lawson also co-opts the notion of a free state, associating it with England's traditional government, and so loosening its usual moorings to Italianate republicanism (8.9, 17).

Parallel taxonomies under the complementary notions of the Keys and the Sword date at least from the time of Alcuin (730–804), although, in the persistence with which they are developed, Lawson seems to be following Marsilius of Padua. In order to keep church and state distinct Lawson even goes so far as to favour masculine pronouns for the state, feminine ones for the church. This pattern of ramist anaphora provides a decorous corollary for the militaristic imagery of the sword and the time-honoured images of the church as bride and mother. But although Lawson also offers the reader the option of ignoring the organization of the work, and reading all that is said about church and state separately, it remains the case that each has to be read in order that the other be fully understood.

VIII

Hitherto, I have suggested a series of contexts which have been restricted to seventeenth-century England. But Lawson's orchestration of texts makes this inadequate. The importance of a classical and medieval inheritance itself renders a notion of English political thought somewhat artificial. Lawson illustrates, for example, just how well Machiavellian casuistry and theories of contingency and corruption could be blended with traditional and scholastic understandings of natural law and with conciliar ecclesiology. Two streams of continental Reformation discourse, however, are additionally important for understanding the *Politica*: monarchomach literature and post-Bodinian sovereignty and public law theory, each of which drew extensively on earlier materials.

Monarchomach theory developed in the French Wars of Religion of the sixteenth century and was largely associated with names such as Beza, Duplessis-Mornay and Buchanan. It was comprised principally of apologetic pamphlets justifying resistance and even tyrannicide. It was the work of threatened Protestant minorities and had its cognate in Jesuit political theorizing on behalf of Catholics under similar circumstances (such as those of late sixteenth-century England). Both repaired to a casuistic rhetoric centred on the notion of the integrity of the (religious) community which, usually through its representatives, retained a right to resistance *in extremis*. A weighty counterpoint was provided by post-Bodinian sovereignty theory. This effectively confined political options to those allowed by public law under the auspices of a sovereign (regardless of the form it took). It also explored the attributes of sovereignty and the conditions necessary for its maintenance.

Lawson probably saw each of these traditions of discourse as having an immediate relevance to England not simply because other writers drew on them, but also because he saw the English Civil Wars as episodes in Europe's wars of religion (8.18). With respect to his theory of the state, Lawson may be seen as standing at the junction of these two bodies of Reformation theory, showing a clear awareness of their medieval and classical antecedents, to which he occasionally goes directly. He is critical of both, and uses each against the other in order to attempt some synthesis.

These traditions give an augmented resonance to the distinctions between real and personal sovereignty and are most noticeably coalesced in chapter 15.2. Lawson's writing here is redolent of a contract between the fellows of a community who divest themselves of unlimited liberty in order to form or consent to a personal sovereign; but it is a sovereign morally limited by its duty to rule for the common good under divine dispensation. The result of this implicit, or displaced, contract is called a representative in a way that sits ill with Lawson's earlier understandings of sovereignty. Nevertheless, the general shape of his theory is clear. In a sense, Lawson confines the themes of post-Bodinian sovereignty theory to the realm of personal majesty, whilst the monarchomach inheritance is given some legitimacy as one expression of real majesty. Resistance, however, is never seen as the only alternative to obedience, for Christians may suffer or censure. Moreover, the main emphasis Lawson places upon the community, is upon its capacity to sanction more than subvert political forms. This was to use for constructive and ameliorating purposes what had been reduced largely to a rhetoric of violent destruction.

IX

Lawson's orchestration of a diversity of often discordant voices had considerable appeal and explanatory power precisely at a time of settlement in 1660 and in 1689. On both occasions, something like a parliament was called in a constitutional vacuum that robbed it of some authority; and its role was formally to invite a monarch to rule. Thus, it appeared both as an efficient cause of a sovereign, something difficult for kings to accept, and as an alienator of its own position. If, however, the Parliament could be designated a special convention representing the community rather than a parliament (4.8), then the uncertainty of the authority resulting from the political system's self-legitimization might be overcome. At the Restoration and the Revolution, the Parliaments called to authorize the new regime were designated conventions. There is no doubt that in 1688–9, in particular, a Lawsonian reworking of sovereignty theory and its nomenclature had considerable appeal. It seems even more likely, however, that the principal attraction of his work between the first and second editions lay with those reluctant Nonconformists in search of a concept of a national Church settlement which might accommodate without compromising them. This Lawson had certainly set out to provide, and one can only imagine his disappointment at the eventual severity of the ecclesiastical settlement of 1662.

X

The specification of a number of contexts for the *Politica* shows it to have been a rich if variously exploitable work. These characteristics have proved central to the difficulty of locating Lawson's political thought, which has been variously, if anachronistically, styled, 'left', 'radical' and 'moderate'. Some final bearings, however, can be provided indirectly by using Lawson's printer to intimate a further context.

John Starkey was responsible for both editions of the *Politica*, and presumably for the timing of, and alterations to, the second edition. Together the editions virtually frame his career. Like many seventeenth-century printers and booksellers, he was apt to specialize, and within his fields of interest to produce works of similar political and religious colouring. The specification of a family resemblance between the volumes he helped market goes some way towards refining the politico-religious location of Lawson's work. Although it will probably not permit us to judge the man by the company he was made to keep, it will suggest why the *Politica* is unfinished.

Starkey's main interests seem to have been at the nexus of common law, Nonconformity, and Italianate, republican political theory. He printed the works of legal figures such as John Selden, and Justices Croke and Coke; he printed Nonconformists such as Baxter and John Howe; and more Independent dissenters like Henry Stubbe and John Milton. He brought out works by Harington and Tasso; and was creatively involved in Henry Neville's famous translation of the works of Machiavelli. Lawson's *Politica* hardly looks odd in such company, exhibiting as it does a great respect for common law, a sympathy for Nonconformity and a well-digested knowledge of Italianate political theory. Lawson, then, may with some justice have been perceived as a crypto-Nonconformist and 'commonwealthsman' fellow traveller. Such a perception, however, would only have been partially justified, for Starkey felt it necessary to gloss the second edition to give it a more activist twist than the text will really allow (5.7, second edition, p. 93). Be this as it may, Starkey's output confirms Lawson's place towards the edge of the politico-religious establishment of Restoration England. When the first volume of the *Politica* appeared in 1660, a sense of establishment was so fluid that Lawson could hardly have felt marginal; but the strident cavalier tone of settlement politics between 1660 and 1662 must have made Lawson feel his voice was out of tune with the times, and in a way that may well have made his fellow clerics in the Church of England sense a dissonance in his words. They seem to have ignored him, and Lawson, relying on the reception of the first volume to gauge the timing of the second, seems never to have offered it to his printer. The marginalized latitudinarianism Lawson represented would gradually become more central only after he had died, as a settlement was shaped from the receding threat of war and a diminishing suspicion of dissent. And with this his theories faded like intricate descants on a noisy past.

A note on the text

There is no known manuscript of the *Politica*, the work surviving only
through the badly printed first edition of 1660 and the partially corrected one of 1689. I have worked principally from the first, attempting to make it more accessible. This has involved some silent editorial
intrusions. I have spelt out ampersands and modernized dates, punctuation and spellings. Capitalization has also been modernized, thus
'parliament' and 'king' are lower case unless a specific parliament or
monarch is mentioned or directly implied. I have retained capitalization for 'the Power of the Keys'. 'Sword', however, has a more diverse
resonance than Keys and I have retained its capitalization only when it
seems to be in direct opposition to the Power of the Keys. Thus the
sword of war, justice or the length of a monarch's sword are lower
case. All texts have their particular problems and those of the *Politica*
have required some additional changes from the original. These are
contained in square brackets or are indicated in footnotes. They fall
under the following headings:

Diagrams

The most substantial deviation from the previous editions concerns
the ramist diagrams. Lawson showed a particular delectation for them
in Latin and English. They were used as headings or summaries for
arguments. On occasion, he provides them only to admit their
inadequacy; and sometimes the parts of the larger diagrams are
repeated as subheadings. I have taken the liberty of dispensing with
this format. Instead, I have generally changed the diagrams into

continuous sentences in square brackets and if they have been omitted altogether, because they are repeated as subheadings, this has been indicated in the text.

Syntax, grammar and vocabulary

These have been left largely intact although sometimes the modern equivalent of an obscure or obsolete word has been added in square brackets. The odd word seems to be missing from the text, and sometimes the wrong word was typeset. If the second edition did not repair the damage I have added the words needed to make complete sense, again in square brackets.

Numbering

Lawson had a pronounced habit, scholastic or catechistic, of numbering his points and of putting nests of numbers within main sequences without in any way distinguishing sets from subsets. Often the numbers operate as words. Sometimes series do not add up. All this can be distracting and confusing. Depending on context, I have left the text untroubled, spelt out numbers, for example '[First]' for '1.'; or I have omitted the numbers, especially where a minor punctuation change will serve the same purpose. For example, 'This is either $1.x$ or $2.y$ or $3.z$...' becomes this is either 'x, y, or z' with square brackets indicating the omissions [...]. This too may seem distracting, but the departures do need signalling, and it seems better to do this than to use a calculator to follow the prose. Sometimes, when dealing with a long sequence of numbered points, I have replaced the numbers with lubricating words such as '[further]', '[moreover]'. In all cases, I have been guided by what makes the text seem to flow best without sacrificing the distinctiveness of Lawson's points.

Translation

Lawson's text is strewn with Latin, Greek and Hebrew, the purpose of which, as I have suggested, seems by turns to impress and teach. It is important to maintain this rhetorical dimension of the text as far as possible. Where Lawson translates or makes the meaning of a phrase clear in the context of argument, it has been left. Where necessary I have translated in square brackets. Sometimes the translation is slightly shorter than the original as the quotation overlaps with Lawson's English. On occasion it is slightly longer; for, at times, Lawson appears to have been quoting or paraphrasing from memory, and clarity seems to require that one go to the original source. Again, I have been guided by what seems to make Lawson's argument clearest and least cluttered. All Hebrew is transliterated, as is the Greek where it has not been translated.

Footnotes

These are largely restricted to providing details of the texts and figures to whom Lawson alludes. His citations of the Bible are in round brackets in the text, his numerous unattributed allusions and quotations are footnoted. Paraphrases that appear as biblical quotations have been left as such. Where a work is best known by an English title (e.g. Aristotle, *Politics*) I have preferred this. Where possible, and if a work is not readily available in a standard modern edition, I have filled out the details from texts that would have probably been available to Lawson. As it has proved possible to construct an extensive though indeterminant bibliographical context for the *Politica*, sometimes one can be reasonably sure that Lawson owned a copy of a particular edition. The Forsterus, *Dictionarium Hebraicum* (Basle, 1557) and the Marsilius, *Defensor pacis* (Frankfurt, 1592) listed in Edward Millington's *Catologus librarum* (London, 1681), were probably Lawson's. Sometimes, however, his references are of such a generalized nature that a precise textual location would add a spurious air of precision, even if one could tie it down. I have not been able to trace every specific reference. For example, one to Grotius seems not to refer to anything he wrote, while the only indication I have been able to find of a pseudonymous, and misprinted M. Camillus, *De Anti-Christo*, is in Millington's *Catalogus*, p. 28, item 370, but it is one of the few entries that carries no date or place of publication.

Bibliographical guide

Biography

There is a brief, old and partially inaccurate account of Lawson in the *Dictionary of National Biography*; Lawson is also entered, with improved inaccuracy, in R. Greaves and R. Zanner, eds., *A Biographical Dictionary of British Radicals in the Seventeenth Century* (Sussex, Harvester, 1982). The fullest account of Lawson's life is in Conal Condren, *George Lawson's* Politica *and the English Revolution* (Cambridge University Press, 1989), on which I have drawn above.

Background to the Politica

There is a superabundance of fine work on British politics in the seventeenth century; in particular see: Blair Worden, *The Rump Parliament* (Cambridge University Press, 1974, corrected 1977); useful alike for its detailed discussions of the background to the Engagement controversy and for the treatment of the Rump Parliament's last moments; G. E. Aylmer, *The Interregnum: The Quest for a Settlement* (London, Macmillan, 1972), a valuable collection on the years leading to 1660; Richard Hutton, *The Restoration: A Political History of England and Wales, 1660–67* (Oxford, Clarendon, 1984); and especially Paul Seaward, *The Cavalier Parliament and the Reconstruction of the Old Regime, 1661–1667* (Cambridge University Press, 1988). The introductory sections of these works are valuable with respect to the period in which the *Politica* was printed. More specifically on ecclesiology see George Yule, *Puritans and Politics: The Religious Legislation of the Long Parliament* (Oxford, Sutton Courtney, 1982); Ian Green, *The Re-Establishment of the Church of England, 1660–63* (Oxford University Press, 1978), for the immediate and Civil War context of religious dispute; more broadly Patrick Collinson, *The Religion of the Protestants* (Oxford University Press, 1982).

Intellectual context

Quentin Skinner, *The Foundations of Modern Political Thought*, 2 vols. (Cambridge University Press, 1978); J. G. A. Pocock, *The Machiavellian Moment* (Princeton University Press, 1975), the sections of the work on seventeenth-century England are particularly suggestive; and *The Ancient Constitution and the Feudal Law* (Cambridge University Press, 1957). These are all deservedly standard works. See also, for a general coverage of political writers during the Civil War and Interregnum, Perez Zagorin, *Political Thought in the English Revolution* (London, Routledge, 1954); C. C. Weston and J. R. Greenburg, *Subjects and Sovereigns* (Cambridge University Press, 1981), for substantial information, though conceptually to be treated with caution.

The Politica *in the context of broader concerns*

A number of fine studies have touched on the *Politica* or looked at only aspects of it in the context of much wider concerns. In particular see: Gordon Schochet, *Patriarchalism in Political Thought* (Oxford University Press, 1975); J. W. H. Salmon, *The French Wars of Religion and English Political Thought* (Oxford University Press, 1959); Richard Tuck, *Natural Rights Theories: Their Origin and Development* (Cambridge University Press, 1979); William Lamont, *Richard Baxter and the Millennium* (London, Croom Helm, 1979); see also Mark Goldie, 'The Roots of True Whiggism', *History of Political Thought*, 1:2 (1980), pp. 195 ff. There are also some not entirely reliable comments in Richard Ashcraft, *Revolutionary Politics and Locke's* Two Treatises of Government (Princeton University Press, 1986).

Substantial studies of the Politica

The first substantial study was A. H. Maclean, 'George Lawson and John Locke', *Cambridge Historical Journal*, 9:1 (1949), pp. 72 ff.; the claims for Lawson's seminal role in the development of English constitutional thought were taken further in Julian H. Franklin, *John Locke and the Theory of Sovereignty* (Cambridge University Press, 1978). The chapter on Lawson is the centre-piece of the whole volume. For critical comment see Conal Condren, 'Resistance and Sovereignty in Lawson's *Politica*', *Historical Journal*, 24: 3 (1981), pp. 673 ff.; and James Tully, 'Current Thinking on Sixteenth and Seventeenth Century Political Theory', *Historical Journal*, 24: 2 (1981), pp. 478 ff. Brian Tierney, *Religion, Law and the Growth of Constitutional Thought, 1150–1650* (Cambridge University Press, 1982) uses Lawson's *Politica* as the concluding example of the themes of the work and is valuable for pointing to the continuity of medieval arguments in the seventeenth century. To date, the most extensive treatment of the *Politica* is Conal Condren, *George Lawson's* Politica; this deals *inter alia* with the work's principal concepts, its inheritance, reception and use in the seventeenth century, and with its relationship to the theories of Hobbes and Locke. More specific aspects of the work are discussed in Condren, 'More Library Salop' (Appendix with F. Carlton), *Library History*, 7 (1987), pp. 141 ff., dealing with the immediate bibliographical context for Lawson's work; 'George Lawson and the *Defensor Pacis*', *Medioevo*, 5–6 (1980), pp. 595 ff.; on Lawson's use of Marsilio of Padua; and 'Sacra before Civilis', *Journal of Religious History*, 11: 2 (1981), p. 534, which also carries misleading biographical baggage. John Bowle, *Hobbes and his Critics* (London, Frank Cass, 1952), first discussed Lawson's critique of Hobbes; this has more recently been discussed by Condren, 'George Lawson's Reactions to Hobbes's *Leviathan*', *Political Science*, 40: 1 (1988), pp. 67 ff.; and see especially Mark Goldie, 'The Reception of Hobbes', in J. H. Burns ed. with the assistance of M. Goldie, *The Cambridge History of Political Thought, 1450–1700* (Cambridge University Press, 1991), a work which has much valuable background material. Unfortunately it has appeared too recently for it to be used as it deserves in the preparation of this text.

Biographical notes

The basic details of the lives of figures such as Cicero, Augustine and Aristotle are so much in the public domain that they are given minimal space here, but are included for the sake of completeness. For the other figures, important in the context of Lawson's work, I have drawn on the following: *Allgemeine Deutsche Biographie* (Leipzig, 1875); *Allgemeines Gelehrten Lexicon* (Leipzig, 1750); *La Nouvelle Biographie universelle* (Paris, 1852); *Il dizionario biografie degli Italiani* (Rome, 1960); F. L. Cross, ed., *The Oxford Dictionary of the Christian Church* (Oxford, 1971 edn.); *The Dictionary of National Biography; The Encyclopaedia Catholica*; J. and J. A. Venn, eds., *Alumni Cantabrigiensis*; B. Hanbury, *Memorials of the Independents* (London, 1839–44).

Ailly, Pierre d', or Pietro de Alliaco, *c.* 1350–1420/5?

He is cited by Lawson as Cameracensis. d'Ailly was a French ecclesiastic and scholar, a friend of Jean Gerson, with whose works some of his were printed. Early in his career he was involved in attempts to heal the Great Papal Schism, was a papal legate to the Emperor Sigismund; and in the Council of Constance, 1414, he argued against ecclesiastic infallibility and in favour of the control of the papacy. He was a powerful and lucid theologian and philosopher, in many ways a follower of William of Ockham. In all the above respects he was clearly congenial to Lawson, who cites his commentary on Peter Lombard's *Sentences*, as he was to other Protestant thinkers. According to the *Dictionario de historia de Portugal*, he was also a great influence on Columbus, arguing in his geographical writings that the Indies could be reached from the west.

Andrewes, Lancelot, 1555–1626

He was educated at Pembroke Hall, Cambridge where he became a fellow in 1576 and Master in 1589. Elizabeth I offered him two bishoprics which he declined, becoming Dean of Westminster in 1601, a most influential position. He was a renowned and highly ornate preacher, who is now widely regarded as one of the major theologians of what only later became known as High-Church Anglicanism. Andrewes was also one of the principal translators of the *Authorised Version of the Bible* and died as Bishop of Winchester. Lawson seems to draw on and approve only of his *Tortura Torti*, 1609, an attack on Bellarmine's pseudonymous discussion of the Oath of Allegiance following the Gunpowder Plot, 1605. Much of Andrewes's ceremonial episcopal style was institutionalized with inflammatory effects by William Laud, Charles I's ill-fated Archbishop of Canterbury, and early supporter of Lawson. Long after, Andrewes was made something of a mythic figure of Anglican piety and traditionality by T. S. Eliot, who dedicated a series of essays to him, not just to his memory.

Aristotle, 384–322 BC

Often cited as 'the Philosopher' (as Cicero was 'the Orator') or the 'Stagyrite', from his birthplace in Thrace, northern Greece. He spent many years as a pupil of Plato, a while as tutor to Alexander the Great, and opened his own school, the Lyceum, in competition with Plato's Academy. His works, surviving in note form, were lost to the West, but many of his doctrines were mediated by Roman writers such as Cicero and Boethius. In the latter part of the Middle Ages, Aristotle's work assumed a huge authority in all domains of intellectual life. This was retained until well into the seventeenth century. By the time Lawson was writing, Aristotle's significance was shrinking to something like its present-day confines in the domains of political and moral philosophy, metaphysics and rhetoric.

Arnisaeus, Henning, 1580?–1636

He was born in Halberstadt, studied medicine and travelled to France and England and eventually settled in Frankfurt. When in England he seems also to have studied English history, which provides a prominent and, for Lawson, improper illustration of his learned and carefully presented neo-Aristotelian sovereignty theories. His principal work was in medicine and he was appointed as Chief Physician to King Christian IV of Denmark. He died in Copenhagen.

Augustine, St, of Hippo, 354–430
He was educated in Rome and, according to his *Confessions*, converted to Christianity by St Ambrose. He became perhaps the greatest, certainly the most magisterially severe and reverenced, of the patristic theologians. He fought sin and heresy on all fronts, producing a prodigious number of works. In his most famous work, *The City of God*, he attempted to locate the whole of Roman experience within a providential frame, incorporating, criticizing and remodelling much Roman political thought, especially that of Cicero. Prior to Aquinas he became the major theological authority for the Roman Church, and the Reformation in no way diminished his standing. It is perhaps ironic that, with accusations of heresy being so rife from Augustine's day to beyond the years in which Lawson read 'Austin' and his *City of God*, Augustine's name should be used so ecumenically.

Besold, Christopher, 1577–1638
Besold was a distinguished and extremely prolific academic writer. He took his doctorate at Tübingen and in 1630 became Professor of Jurisprudence. His writings span politics, international and canon law, jurisprudence and imperial history. He was also employed by the Duke of Württemburg as a diplomat and was converted to Catholicism in 1635. This opened further career prospects for him, which were unrealized because of his death in Ingolstadt. For one so productive and eminent he seems to have been remarkably little used in England, although Philip Hunton as well as Lawson seems to have been familiar with some of his work.

Bodin, Jean, 1530–1596
Having studied law at Toulouse, Bodin became a successful Paris advocate, although his early published writings were on the sixteenth-century price spiral. He was appointed attorney to Henry III in 1576 and in 1581 secretary to the duc d'Alençon when the duke went to England in quest of the hand of Elizabeth I. Bodin's *Six Livres de la république*, 1576, was a major piece of French vernacular political theory and it set an agenda for discussions of sovereignty well into the seventeenth century. Less discussed was the work's emphasis on

political geography and climate. The work was translated into Latin and, when he saw the result, into Latin again by Bodin himself. It was probably one of Bodin's versions that Lawson knew, though there is a good English translation by Knolles, an indication of Bodin's significance. He also wrote on witchcraft and died of the plague.

Bracton, Henry de, d. 1268
He was a judge and ecclesiastic and is most famous as the name attached to the *De legibus et consuetudinibus Angliae*, of which he was thought to be the author until recently. He was probably only the last of its compilers and arrangers. His name was one to be conjured with from the fifteenth to the eighteenth century, for *De legibus* was an extremely ambitious attempt to codify English law and its principles. The first full edition was by Richard Tottell, 1519. This was reprinted in 1640, a political as much as a legal act.

Bucer, Martin, 1491–1551
He was a Dominican monk born in Alsace and open to the ideas of Erasmus. In 1518 whilst studying at Heidelburg, he converted to more thorough reform on hearing Luther. In 1521 he left his order and like Luther married an ex-nun. In 1523 he settled in Strasburg, becoming the city's principal leader of religious reform. He made various attempts to bring the reforming groups together, co-operating with Luther and later Calvin. He fled the Continent for England in 1549 in the face of Imperial forces and was appointed Regius Professor of Divinity at Cambridge by Edward VI. He was much consulted during the Edwardian phase of the English Reformation; his tomb, destroyed by Mary I, was rebuilt during Elizabeth's reign.

Buchanan, George, 1506–1582
His appears to have been one of the more densely packed lives and less violent deaths of sixteenth-century Scottish politics. Educated at the University of St Andrews, MA 1528, he spent some time at large in Paris, and some time in prison for his Calvinist views. He escaped, however, and spent a while in London, after which he returned to France in the service of the maréchal de Brissac. He was back in Scotland by 1562 and became much involved in Church government. He was a moderator of the Kirk in 1567 and also became embrangled in some of the more dubious aspects of Tudor/Stuart policy through

the affair of the casket letters. He was a tutor to James later VI and was appointed Keeper of the Privy Seal, 1570–8. He was perhaps a typical Calvinist humanist, no contradiction in terms, being much interested in the *studia humanitatis*. He wrote poetry as well as political theology and history. Most of his work was in Latin, a little in Scots. He wrote a much-cited history of Scotland and a widely disseminated piece of political theology and jurisprudence in many ways at one with French monarchomach theory, the *De jure regni*, 1579. It offered an uncompromising theory of limited monarchy, monarchy limited by the subject's right to tyrannicide. As a sign of future success it was suppressed in 1584.

Camden, William, 1551–1623

He was born in London and initially educated at St Paul's School and Pembroke College, Oxford and then at Christ Church under the patronage of Dr Thomas Thornton. From *c.* 1571 he began to amass materials which were to lead to the publication of his famous *Britannia*, 1586. In the ten years it took him to write the initial version he travelled widely in Britain when he was not earning his living as a schoolmaster at Westminster School (from 1575). He became part of a closely knit antiquarian circle including Cotton, Seldon and Spelman (q.v.) in England, Brisson in France and Ussher in Ireland. Having become headmaster of Westminster in 1593, he became Clarenceaux King-of-Arms at the urging of Fulke Greville. This seems largely to have been a result of his antiquarian fame, for *Britannia* was highly successful and was perceived as a great moment in antiquarian studies; and it is upon this work which Lawson relies. Camden also produced a more contemporary history or annals of England and Scotland under Elizabeth, which enjoyed a similar success. He founded a lectureship in history at Oxford in the year before his death.

Carr (Car), John, 1630?–1675

Lawson's encomiast was born in Lawson's village of Lancliffe, Yorkshire, *c.* 1630, the son of William. The parish records are incomplete and I have been able to find no precise record of birth. The Lawsons and Carrs had been maritably entwined certainly since the mid-sixteenth century, so Lawson and Carr were related, though it is impossible to say how closely. Carr attended Giggleswick School and

Christ's College, Cambridge as a sizar, as Lawson had attended its adjacent foundation, Emmanuel, as a sizar thirty years earlier. He took an MB in 1652 and his doctorate in 1657; he was a fellow from 1662 to 1665 and was a Fellow of the Royal College of Physicians, 1669–70.

Cicero, Marcus Tullius, 106–43 BC

Sometimes cited as Tully or just 'the Orator' he was one of the richest and most brilliant of Roman lawyers. His own greatest claim to fame was the unmasking of the Catiline conspiracy when consul, 63 BC. In the Civil Wars which finally destroyed the Roman republic, he reluctantly sided with Pompey, but was pardoned by Julius Caesar after his victory. After Caesar's death Cicero was particularly outspoken against Mark Anthony, who was not so forgiving. He was beheaded as he tried to escape the carnage of civil war and his head presented to Anthony. His significance is manifold. He was a major conduit for Greek and Stoic thought and was Christianized by patristic writers, such as Ambrose and even the critical Augustine. He later became the principal model for Latin style; and in his own right is probably, after Aristotle, the greatest theorist of rhetoric. Like Aristotle his political and moral doctrines became so widely disseminated that, by Lawson's day, it is impossible to assess precise and direct use of them.

Coke, Sir Edward, 1552–1634

A common law judge of surpassing authority. He was educated at Trinity College, Cambridge and from 1571 at Clifford's Inn. He was called to the Bar in 1578 and became a very successful lawyer. With additional leverage provided by Lord Burghley, he rapidly rose in public office, becoming Chief Justice of Common Pleas and, in 1613, Chief Justice of the King's Bench. In the former role he clashed with Archbishop Bancroft over the jurisdiction of ecclesiastical courts, and so indirectly came into conflict with royal authority. He was above all vehemently jealous of the domain of common law. Coke was suspended from the council and from the exercise of his duties in 1616, but was recalled in the following year. His was a major voice in the Parliament of 1620, being particularly precise over the impropriety of forced loans. His main works are the prodigious *Institutes*, which are a compilation, translation and commentary on England's written law; and his even more daunting and incisive *Reports*, judgements on case law and their implications. His oddest yet most telling epitaph is the mind-boggling reduction of the *Reports* to verse, ed. J. Worrall, 1742; it was a popular work but did stop short of the limerick.

De Dominis, M. A., 1566–1624

He is cited by Lawson as Spalatensis, having been Archbishop of Spaleto from 1602 to 1616. Before then he had been a Jesuit and Professor of Mathematics at the University of Padua. However, like Paolo Sarpi, he fell out with his Church over its strained relationships with Venice, of which Padua was a part. Unlike Sarpi, he formally joined the Church of England, in 1617, much to the delight of James I. He was rewarded by being made Dean of Windsor and in the same year produced the first part of his *De respublica ecclesiastica*, an important defence of national Churches against the claims of Rome. He edited Sarpi's significant if inflammatory *History of the Council of Trent*, 1619; but a national Church also proved irksome. In 1622 he left England and its Church, reconverting to Catholicism, and then naturally attacked national Churches in the name of Rome. This did not stop his excommunication and incarceration at the hands of the Inquisition. He died in the Castel Sant Angelo, Rome, as a relapsed heretic.

Duplessis-Mornay, Philippe, 1549–1623

Born in Normandy to a Protestant family, fought under Condé and after a stay in England joined the future French King Henry IV as a diplomat and adviser. He was made Governor of Saumur, 1589, and later started the first Protestant academy there, in 1599. He was probably the author of the anonymous *Vindiciae contra tyrannos*, 1579, and remained a Protestant after Henry's conversion to Catholicism.

Fortescue, Sir John, 1394?–1476

Probably educated at Exeter College, Oxford and later at Lincoln's Inn, he became a governor of the Inn, 1425–6 and 1429. In 1422 he became Chief Justice of the King's Bench. During the Wars of the Roses he was a staunch Lancastrian, allegedly being at the battle of Towton, 1461. He went into exile in Scotland and then Flanders with the egregious Queen Margaret. Towards the end of this period, *c.* 1471, he wrote his little dialogue *De laudibus legum Angliae*, a dialogue between a prince and a Chief Justice on the nature of English law and the ruler's responsibility to it. He returned to England and remained on the hapless Lancastrian side at the battle of Tewkesbury, 1471, where he was taken prisoner. After recanting some of his more extreme Lancastrian views he was pardoned by Edward IV and later admitted to the young king's council. *The Governance of England*, which may be called the first vernacular political theory in English, was also probably written around 1471. Both Fortescue's political works were known in whole or part before publication. *De laudibus* was published in 1537 and then produced in an English–Latin parallel text by Mulcaster. The work gained considerable authority. *The Governance* had to wait until 1714 before publication but was certainly in circulation before then, as John Selden's preface to his edition of *De laudibus* attests. Fortescue is a major part of the common law tradition of political speculation, or tradition that reduces politics to common law problems and perspectives, and which places the monarchy within the ambit of the law. He associates such a monarchy specifically with England and with a distinctly political rule. Lawson identifies an incipient communitarianism in this, but overlooks the intimations that government is shared between king and people.

Gerson, Jean, 1363–1429
Major French theologian, born in Rethel, he studied under Pierre d'Ailly (q.v.), with whose work he is strongly associated. He became a doctor of theology in 1394, and 1405 Chancellor of the University of Paris. His early writings were much preoccupied with reform and the healing of the Schism that had proliferated popes. Eventually he advocated a general council to this end. He became a leading figure in the Council of Constance, 1415, where he argued that the papacy had to be subordinate to a council. His conciliarism and Gallicanism were central to the development of the Sorbonne school, for whom Protestants like Lawson had sympathy, not least because of the secular resonances of a theory which advocated the control of a pope through council and through law, and which emphasized the integrity of a national Church. Gerson lived for some years in seclusion at Melk Abbey, near Vienna, but eventually returned to France, and died at Lyons.

Grotius, Hugo (Huig van Groot), 1583–1645
A jurist and theologian, Grotius came from a prominent Delft family

and was educated at the University of Leiden. He became Advocate-General of Holland and Zealand, 1607, and in the same year appointed historian to the States-General, and was an envoy to England in 1613. However, he was assisted into prison in 1618 by his public sympathy for the theology of Arminius, whose party was destroyed by Maurice of Nassau and the Synod of Dort. He only avoided life imprisonment by escape and he settled in Paris in 1620. In 1622 he published his *On the Truth of the Christian Religion*, an attempt to prove the harmony between nature and Christianity, and in 1625 published *On the Law of War and Peace*, the work for which he is now most famous. He returned to Holland in 1631, was banished and went to Germany, was employed by Christina of Sweden as an envoy to Paris and died on the way from Sweden to Paris at Rostock. His is a name much cited in the context of biblical criticism and exegesis; his views deeply worried Baxter as being crypto-Catholic, though Grotius was not a Catholic. He is one of the most cited names of the seventeenth and early eighteenth century. Often he is called 'the father' of international law, which he was not, as his theories derived very largely from Suarez and Gentillet.

Hobbes, Thomas, 1588–1679

Born in Malmesbury in Wiltshire and educated at Magdalen College, Oxford, one of the most important of English philosophers and the most important political writer in the English language. His work had as great an impact on the Continent as it did in England. He was widely travelled and was sometime mathematics tutor to the future Charles II, but spent most of his later life as friend and tutor to the Cavendish family. His theological Erastianism caused as much distress as his authoritarian views, and this together with a form of materialism got him branded as an atheist. Lawson was amongst his earliest critics, though perhaps the only one to go on and develop a systematic political vision of his own.

Hooker, Thomas, 1586–1647

He is cited by Lawson as 'of New England', presumably to avoid confusion with Richard Hooker, d. 1600, although rational grounds for confusion would be difficult to find. Hooker was educated at The Queen's College, Oxford, MA 1611. He left England for Holland in *c.* 1630 under pressure from the Church of England. At various times he preached to what were clearly difficult congregations in Amsterdam, Delft and Rotterdam and finally left the Old for the New World in 1633. He settled at first in Cambridge, Massachusetts but left there, taking his congregation with him, for Hartford, Connecticut. He was a prolific defender of independency and reforming Calvinism, though he is best known now for advocating a permanent confederation of the American colonies, although he was unable to set a confederative example.

Horne, Andrew, d. 1328
He was a successful London fishmonger, and was Chamberlain of London from 1320 to his death. In his will he left the Guildhall, *inter alia*, his manuscript of the *Speculum justiciarorum*, written in Norman French. Like much manuscript material of the early modern period, it was well known before publication. Whether it was written by Horne, amended or compiled by him is uncertain; but in any case, it purports to be a summation of English common law, with a strong focus on criminal law. As such it has since been regarded as misleading by authorities such as Maitland. This perhaps is to miss the work's force, which implicitly was to warn against the corruption of the common law by justices and to limit monarchy by placing it within the context of the common law, à la Fortescue and Coke. These at least were the points of emphasis seized upon by Lawson, who refers to the work through its English, and timely, translation of 1642 and 1646, *The Mirrour of Justices*.

Irenaeus, St, 130?–200?
Irenaeus was probably a native of Smyrna and was partially educated at Rome. Around 178 he became Bishop of Lyons. He was involved in requests to tolerate the Montanist sect, with whom Tertullian (q.v.) was associated. Regarded as a man of peace he was less tolerant of gnosticism, against which he wrote his *Adversus omnes haereses*, a work emphasizing the traditional elements of the Church, monotheism and the co-ordinate authority of the four Gospels. As such it is both a major work of early Church theology and a thoughtful theory of interpretation. Lawson is quite unspecific in his references to Irenaeus in the *Politica* but he did know more than just the name.

Machiavelli, Niccolo, 1469–1527

Machiavelli was a Florentine diplomat and administrator forced into exile after the fall of the republic, 1512. After his fall from grace his life was divided largely between farming, writing and attempting to get re-employed. He managed only a little *ad hoc* work, but his written output was considerable. It spanned military theory, of which he was most proud, history, poetry, dramatic comedy and what we now call political theory. In the sixteenth and seventeenth centuries there was a fluid line between history and political theory. His *Prince* became the most notorious piece of political casuistry of its age and was publicly castigated on all sides; his *Discourses* was amongst the most respected of histories, and it is in this capacity as historian that Lawson uses him and cites him with approval.

Marsilius, Marsilio, Marsiglio of Padua, 1279?–1342?

He was born into a notarial family in Padua and went from university there to Paris. His education is thought initially to have been in medicine. In 1312 he was Rector of the University of Paris but fled the city when his name was associated with the *Defensor pacis*, finished on John the Baptist's Day, 1324. He went to the court of Lewis (Ludwig) of Bavaria, then in deadly dispute with Pope John XXII. Marsilio remained at Lewis's court for the rest of his life, in the company of that other notable exile William of Ockham. He wrote a number of tracts for the Emperor and more pointedly against the Roman Church, and he marched with Lewis when the Emperor descended on Italy and chased the Pope out of Rome in 1329. *Defensor pacis* remained Marsilius's most important work; it is the most brilliant and systematic attack on the Roman Church written before the Reformation, orchestrating Aristotle, Cicero, the Church Fathers, law, Franciscan theology and New Testament history with remarkable panache and authority. Marsilius was regarded as a proto-Protestant and Luther was called a Marsilian. The work was as widely translated and adapted by those hostile to the papacy as it was condemned by the papacy, Clement VII cataloguing 250 heresies in it. Writers such as Locke and Hobbes have both been thought to have been influenced by it; some have claimed it to have been the informing ideological document of the Henrician Reformation, though to such an end it would have needed severe editing. Lawson is probably the work's principal transmitter in the seventeenth century; it is now established

as the most important piece of political theory from the later Middle
Ages.

Owen, Sir Roger, 1573–1617

Roger was the son of Justice Thomas Owen, d. 1598. The family was
a Shropshire one and was almost certainly known directly by Lawson's patrons, the Mores, and perhaps to Lawson himself. Roger
Owen was educated at Christ Church and by 1613 was a barrister at
Lincoln's Inn. He was member for Shrewsbury in 1597 and for
Shropshire in 1601, 1605, 1610 and 1614. He was Sheriff of Shropshire, 1603–4, and was knighted in 1604. In Parliament he is alleged
to have spoken out strongly against King James's methods of raising
money and was eventually dismissed from the Commission of Peace
for Shropshire because of his hostility to the King and his support for
the clergy. I have not been able to trace what Lawson refers to as his
manuscript.

Parker, Robert, 1564–1614

Parker was a protégé of the Earl of Pembroke and also a fellow of
Magdalen College, Oxford. He was associated intellectually with such
firmly reforming Calvinists as Ames and Perkins. Consequently, he
had a pronounced hostility to episcopacy and ceremony. In 1607,
after writing *A Scholastic Discourse against Symbolising*, he felt obliged
to leave England for Holland. He settled initially in Leiden but find-
ing no peace there moved in turn to Amsterdam, Delft and to
Doesburg, where he died. The *De politeia ecclesiastica*, 1616, is one of
the principal statements of Tudor/Jacobean dissenting theology. It is
a work both learned, as Lawson accepts, and polemical, which he
loftily ignores; and with as many passages taken up in castigating and
abusing bishops such as Downham and Bilson as it has passages of
argument. Parker's son, a man of similar ecclesiastical leanings, was at
the Westminster Assembly, having settled in New England, where he
died in 1677. Tudor Calvinism lived long.

Sadler, John, 1615–1674

Sadler came from Lawson's adopted county, Shropshire, and was a
fellow of Lawson's college, Emmanuel, before becoming Master of
Magdalene. In 1653 he was elected member for Cambridge. He is
mentioned in the Ordinance of March 1653–4 as a Commissioner

appointed for the Approbation of Public Speakers. He was First Commissioner under the Great Seal, 1659. A committed parliamentarian and an outspoken critic of Charles I, he lost all office at the Restoration, but in a sense had the last word, for which he became famous, by prophesying the plague and fire of London. He should be better known for his now rare work *The Rights of the Kingdom*, 1649, on which Lawson clearly relies. It is a rambling but learned account of English monarchy with a clear message for any who would be King of England. It seems to lie behind some of Milton's uncompromising views of monarchy.

Spelman, Sir Henry, 1564?–1641

Spelman came from a gentry family in Norfolk and reminded himself of this until his seventies by always wearing a sword. He attended Walsingham Grammar School and Trinity College, Cambridge, taking a BA in 1582–3 and then attending Lincoln's Inn, 1585–6. He greatly increased his estates by marrying Elenor L'Estrange and was thus able to devote much of his time to antiquarian studies. He was a member of the original Society of Antiquaries, 1593. He was member for Castle Rising in 1597 and High Sheriff of Norfolk in 1604, though eventually he moved from Norfolk to London, apparently to gain easier and greater access to the materials for his studies.

He produced a pioneering and hugely valuable *Glossary* of Latin and Anglo-Saxon legal terms intended as prefatory to a history of English law. The first volume was finished in 1626 and the work completed in 1638 though it did not appear until 1664. Lawson relies upon the first volume. In 1625 Spelman was elected to the first Parliament of Charles I and although a firm royalist was sympathetic to the Petition of Right. Five years later he finished his *Councils, Laws, Constitutions of the English Church*, the first volume of which was published in 1639. Much of his work was unfinished or published posthumously. Its significance in the context of the history of English law, common and especially ecclesiastical, was great; its wayward impact on the myth of Britain's Ancient Constitution was also considerable. Consequently, his name or his works are central to many political disputes in the latter part of the seventeenth century. He was also partly responsible for establishing a lectureship in Anglo-Saxon at Cambridge.

Tertullian, Quintus Septimus, 160?–220?

He was a Carthaginian Roman lawyer who converted to Christianity, *c.* 195. For a short while he was a member of the ascetic apocalyptic sect called the Montanists, whom Irenaeus (q.v.) wished to have tolerated. The sect, however, had been condemned by the time Tertullian joined it, *c.* 207, but he left, forming his own group. The Tertullianists survived into the fourth century. Tertullian's theology is infused with the categories of Roman law and is regarded as amongst the most important of early Church writings. He may have been the first explicitly trinitarian theologian and seems to have been the first to write in Latin rather than Greek. He is the third of the patristic trinity with Irenaeus and Augustine that Lawson cites with approval.

Principal dates

Date	Lawson	Other
1598	Born, Lancliffe, Yorks.	Edict of Nantes; *Much Ado About Nothing.*
1599		b. Oliver Cromwell; James VI, *Basilikon Doron.*
1600		b. Charles Stuart, later Charles I.
1603	b. Margaret Lawson.	d. Elizabeth I.
1610	Death of mother.	Henry IV of France assassinated; d. Archbishop Bancroft.
1615	At Emmanuel College, Cambridge.	
1616		Cromwell at Sidney Sussex, Cambridge; Horn rounded; d. Shakespeare.
1618		Outbreak of Thirty Years War; Bacon Lord Chancellor.
1619		Harvey's circulation theory made public.
1625		d. James I; accession of Charles I.
1632	Licensed to serve.	Wentworth Lord Deputy of Ireland; Gustavus Adolphus killed.

1635	Curate at Mainstone, Salop; birth of son, Jeremiah.	First inland post service; b. Robert Hook; Académie française founded.
1637	St Chad's dispute; appointed to rectory at More.	Hampden's Ship Money Case; Scottish prayer-book.
1640	Richard More member for Bishop's Castle.	Long Parliament; Laud, Wentworth impeached.
1642		Civil Wars begin.
1643	d. Richard More.	Westminster Assembly; alliance with Scots; censorship imposed; d. Louis XIII.
1646	Samuel More commander Ludlow.	Charles I surrenders to Scots; end first Civil War.
1647	More commander Hereford.	Levellers emerge; Army takes Charles I.
1648–9	Fit to serve in sixth Salopian classis.	Second Civil War; Pride's Purge; execution of Charles I; abolition of monarchy and Lords; Engagement controversy.
1650	'Amica dissertatio'? Engagement tract?	
1651		Hobbes's *Leviathan* published.
1654	Minister assisting 'Triers'; Samuel More a 'Trier'.	Ordinance for Ejection of Scandalous Ministers.
1656	Samuel More elected to Parliament, ejected.	Harington's *Oceana* published.
1657	*Examination of Mr. Hobbs.*	Humble Petition and Advice; Anglo-French Alliance.
1658		d. Cromwell.
1659	*Theo-politica.*	Richard Cromwell succeeds Oliver; Rump restored; end of Protectorate; Rump redissolved; threat of civil war; Rump restored again.

1660	*Politica.*	Monck's march south; return of secluded members; dissolution of Long Parliament; Convention Parliament, Charles II, House of Lords restored.
1662	d. Samuel More; *Exposition of Hebrewes.*	Church of England settlement.
1665	*Magna Charta universalis.*	Plague; Clarendon Code in operation.
1678	Death of Lawson.	d. Andrew Marvell; Popish Plot; Danby impeached; *Pilgrim's Progress* published.
1679		d. Hobbes.
1680	d. Anne Lawson; Richard More donates library to More church; elected to Parliament.	'Exclusion' Parliament; Halley's Comet.
1681	Lawson's library sold; *Magna Charta* republished.	Persecution of Nonconformists intensified.
1689	*Politica* republished.	'Glorious Revolution'.

POLITICA SACRA

&

CIVILIS:

OR,

A Modell of Civil and Ecclesiasticall

GOVERNMENT.

WHEREIN,

Beſides the poſitive Doctrine concerning
State and Church in general, are debated the
principal Controverſies of the times.

CONCERNING

The Constitution of the State and Church of
England, tending to Righteouſneſs, Truth
and Peace.

The first Part:

By George Lawson Rectour of More, in the
County of Salop.

LONDON

Printed for John Starkey at the Miter, neer the
middle Temple Gate in Fleet ſtreet. 1660

Politica Sacra & Civilis:
Or, A Model of
Civil and Ecclesiastical

GOVERNMENT.

WHEREIN,
Befides the pofitive Doctrine concerning
STATE and *CHURCH* in general,
Are debated the principal Controverfies
of the *TIMES* concerning the

CONSTITUTION

OF THE
State and Church

OF

ENGLAND,

Tending to Righteoufnefs, Truth,
and Peace.

By *GEORGE LAWSON*, Rector of
More in the County of *Salop*.

The Second Edition.

LONDON,
Printed for *J.S.* and are to be Sold by *T. Goodwin* at
the *Maidenhead* over againft *St. Dunstans* Church in
Fleet-ftreet. 1689.

The epistle to the reader

Reader,

In the time of our divisions, and the execution of God's judgements upon the three nations, I set my self to enquire into the causes of our sad and woeful condition, and to think of some remedies to prevent our ruin. Whilst I was busy in this search, I easily understood, that the subject of our differences was, not only the state but the church. This gave occasion to peruse such authors as write of government, and to study the political part of the holy Scriptures, wherein I found many things concerning the constitution, the adminstration, the corruption, the conversion and subversion of civil states and kingdoms, with much of church-discipline. There I observed certain rules of government in general, and some special, and proper to civil, or else to ecclesiastical polities. All these, accourding to my poor ability I reduced to method, and applied them to our own church and state severally. I further took notice of our principal differences both civil and ecclesiastical, and did freely deliver mine own judgement concerning the particular parties, and their opinions, yet so that I endeavoured to be of no party, as a party. And though in some things I differ from them, yet it was not out of singularity, or a humour of opposition, but out of an unfeigned desire of truth; which in many things I found so evident, that whatsoever should not acknowledge it, must needs be willful, and blinded with partiality or prejudice. Whilst I go on in this work I easily perceived, that as our sins and impenitency brought God's judgements upon us,[1]

---

[1] An almost universal explanation: 'But our sins being ripe, there was no preventing of God's Justice, from reaping that glory in our Calamities, which we robbed him of in our prosperitie,' *Eikon Basilike* (London, 1649), p. 4.

3

so our ignorance and errors in matters of government, with prejudice, partiality, pride, obstinacy and want of charity were the causes of our divisions, which gave great advantage to our enemies and foreign politicians who, as formerly, so now especially at this time, fear our union and agreement more than ever, because we are become a warlike nation, and furnished with gallant men both by sea and land. Therefore their great work is to continue our differences amongst ourselves, as subservient to their interest. These causes once discovered, the remedies were obvious, if men were in any capacity to make use of them. For, sincere repentance and a real reformation private and public, with the punishment of crying sins are very effectual to avert God's judgements: and to renounce our errors, to be informed in the truth; to lay aside all pride, partiality, prejudice, obstinacy, self-interest; to put on humility and charity, which is the bond of perfection, and to let the peace of God rule in our hearts are the only way to quench the fire of contention, and firmly to cement us together. Yet, though good men may propose clear truths, dispel the mists of error, persuade the repentance, and pray, yet there seems to be little hope of peace and settlement. For, after so many fearful judgements executed upon us, and severe admonitions given us from Heaven, pride, covetousness, injustice, oppression, malice, cruelty, and abominable hypocrisy continue, and nothing is reformed. This is the reason why God's hand is stretched out still: many persons have suffered, many great families have been ruined, many feel God's heavy hand to this day: but who shall suffer most and last no man knows. Men of the same English blood, and of the same Protestant profession continue obstinate in their errors, rigid and high in their opinions, resolved in their different designs, admire their own models of government in church and state, will not abate of their confidence, and refuse to recede from their supposed principles. Some are for a boundless liberty, and will not be confined by the rules and dictates of reason or the common faith revealed from Heaven; these have no principles, but seem to have abandoned not only Christianity, but their own reason. Some are for peace, yet only upon their own terms, though not so reasonable as they should be. Some complain, they are wronged and must be satisfied: others are very high, and must be revenged. Every party must reign, or else they will be enemies. Many men of great estates and excellent parts, who as yet have suffered little or nothing, look on as strangers, and will do nothing, whilst church

4

and state lie a bleeding, ready to breathe out their last. And what can be the issue, but that either we shall be brought very low, made a poor and base people, and willing of peace upon very hard terms, and yet hardly obtain it; or we shall be made a scorn and derision to the nations round about us, a prey unto our enemies, and they, who hate us, shall rule over us. To prevent so sad a condition, my humble request to all true hearted English Protestants, is, seriously to consider. 1. What our condition was before the Scots first entered England with an Army. 2. What those things were, which then the best and wisest desired to be reformed both in church and state. 3. What reformation we are capable of at this present time. 4. Where the guilt of so much blood as hath been shed, especially in Ireland, doth principally lie. 5. What our duty is as we are English, as we are Christians, as we are Protestants, which amongst other things is to deliver the gospel to our posterity, as we received it from our fathers. 6. What may be the most effectual means according to the rules of reason and divine revelation, to promote the public good without respect of persons or parties, that so no wicked men, but only such as fear God, may have cause to rejoice. This is all I thought good by this Epistle to signify unto thee at the present, for the rest referring thee to the book, and remaining

Thine, to serve in the Lord,

George Lawson.

For the political work of a most distinguished man, my compatriot, George Lawson[1]

Which author's work lends system to the ancient art of ruling,
And gives endurance to the sceptre's sway?
His simply written page has taught great nations,
Giving peace to peoples and to princes, trust.
Public office is defined by the exertions of the private hand;
Behold how one man labours at the public weal,
So well he settles kingdoms, it seems he might have ruled,
Oh how much greater than his station he was!
Houses built upon this concisely written page stand firm,
Nor would such states easily falter at that juncture
When the monarch is removed.
For this page gives laws to peoples and strength to law;
It arms you, Themis, who alone should punish wrong;[2]
You, Regulus, would fear nothing and be no longer feared,[3]
For the power to harm you or to be harmed is now erased.
This page would have succoured infant Rome,
Sufficient for Numa without Egeria's counsel.[4]

---

[1] This is a less than literal translation as I have tried to keep something of the encomiastic cadence and rhythm to the whole, but without going so far as to versify the English.
[2] Greek goddess of law, mother of Dike, goddess of justice.
[3] Marcus Regulus, third century BC, sacrificed himself rather than have the Senate accept the Carthaginian peace terms he had been released to negotiate.
[4] Numa Pompilius, religious founder of Rome, sought the advice of the goddess, or nymph, Egeria in establishing Rome's religion. Paddy Schreuder suggests that the printed line 'Ne vacet Egeriam consuluisse Numae' might be a misprint for 'ni vacet...'. The English would then read 'Should Numa not have time to consult Egeria'.

And had Sparta, ruled by stern Lycurgus, gleaned wisdom from
   this same page
She would have stood for as many centuries as she lasted days.[5]
Nor, I tell you, Parthenope, would the fickle masses
So often have changed masters in so few years;[6]
Nor would the infamous Angle so selfishly have defiled the
   calendar,
Wandering in a thousand aimless alterations.[7]
How well, Lawson, so apt an heir to such a lustrous name,
Do you make laws from your own disinterested wit.[8]
Behold, gladly we concede the power of the pen to you,
Who teaches us how to rule, how to obey.
So great a man a tiny village bred,
Lancliffe a corner of the world that knew me from my birth,
Let York, or even Athens envy.
I owe more now on your behalf, my country,
and on my country's behalf to you.[9]

J. Carr, M.D.

---

[5] Lycurgus, mythical lawgiver to Sparta, first mentioned in Herodotus, *Histories*.

[6] Parthenope, nymph washed ashore at Neapolis (Naples), hence associated with the city. The text carries the marginal gloss to Philippe de Commynes, *De Carolo Octavo Galliae rege et bello Neapolitano commentarij*, bk. 5.

[7] Obscure but presumably an allusion to the controversies surrounding the Gregorian calendar reforms, although 'fastos' may not mean calendar here but consular registers; hence it may be history that is defiled, not dates.

[8] This is a somewhat metaphorical reading of a line which translates more literally as 'You are he who provides laws on the sea (*salo*) with you on the land.' A literal reading has no bearing on the text.

[9] Reading 'patria' as dative 'patriae' as suggested by Paddy Schreuder.

The arguments of the several chapters

Chapter 1

[Of government in general and the original thereof]

The propriety of God acquired by creation, and continued by preservation, the ground of God's supreme dominion and power, which is universal over all creatures, more particular and special over men and angels, who are capable of laws, rewards, punishments, not only temporal but eternal: the exercise of this power over men immediate, or mediate. Mediate in his government by men over men, is either temporal and civil, or spiritual and ecclesiastical. Of the government spiritual before Christ's incarnation and after his session at the right hand of God. Of the church Christian, triumphant, militant, mystical, visible, universal, particular. The particular parts of the universal church, as visible, the principal subject of the following discourse. Of our differences and the causes thereof: of hope of better times, and the author's disposition and intention.

Chapter 2

Of a community civil

What *Politica* is, what a commonwealth, the subject of *Politica*: what the parts of a commonwealth: what a community in general, which is the subject of a commonwealth; the name and nature of it. Of a community civil, the matter and the form thereof, the original of civil

communities; the members both natural and naturalized, whether
they be imperfectly, or formally, or eminently such. The capacity of
this association to receive the form of a civil government. Liberty,
equality, propriety, adjuncts to this community.

Chapter 3

Of an ecclesiastical community

The definition of it; the explication of the definition. The distinction
of the members, less or more perfectly such: the manner of
incorporation; liberty, equality, and an aptitude to receive a form of
discipline. Properties of this society. Where, something concerning
children born of Christian parents, whether they be members of the
church, or no.

Chapter 4

Of power civil

The parts of *Politica*, constitution and administration: what constitution is, and what the parts of a commonwealth both civil and
ecclesiastical, which are two: 1. Sovereign. 2. Subjects. What power
in general, what power civil, what supreme power or majesty civil; the
branches thereof, which are called *Jura Majestatis*; the multitude of
them reduced to order by several writers, and by the author. The
properties of majesty, which is real or personal. What sovereign real
and personal may do. The subject of real majesty in England; the
personal majesty of the parliament, and of the King.

Chapter 5

Of the acquisition of civil power, and the amission thereof

Civil power, not essential, but accidental to any person. It's acquired
in an extraordinary, or ordinary way. In an ordinary way by consent or
conquest; justly or unjustly, as by usurpation. Usurpation no good
title. The person usurping power at the first, by subsequent consent
may acquire a good title. Succession, and the several ways of

succession. Amission of power by violence, or voluntary consent, or death. Whether any can be made sovereign by condition. Whether sovereign power once acquired may be forfeited: how, and to whom the forfeiture may be made.

Chapter 6

Of power ecclesiastical

The power is spiritual, not civil. Why it's called the Power of the Keys, as different from that of the Sword. Binding and loosing, the same with shutting and opening: and both belong chiefly to legislation and jurisdiction. This power is supreme and independent in every particular church constituted aright according to the rules of the gospel. The branches and several acts of it: as, making of canons, the constitution of officers, jurisdiction, disposing of the church's goods. Of the extent, and also the bounds of the power. Certain distinctions of spiritual government: as internal, external, universal, particular, formal, material, or objective.

Chapter 7

Of acquiring or losing ecclesiastical power

The just acquisition of this power extraordinary in the highest measure, as in Christ, or in an inferior degree, as in the Apostles. How ordinary churches derive it from Christ by the gospel-charter in an ordinary way. The power of the church, and church officers unequal. The several ways of usurping, and also of losing this power.

Chapter 8

Of the disposition of power civil, from the several manners of which arise the several forms of government

General observations premised. The several ways of disposing majesty, or supreme power in a state. *Pure forms.* Monarchies, despotical and regal. Pure aristocracies and democracies. Mixed governments, when the power is placed in the several states jointly.

The constitution of England, our king[s] and their title. Peers, commons, parliaments, and the limits of their power. The limits of the king's personal majesty. Our late divisions and confusions. Whether king or parliament as separate, could be justified by the fundamental constitution of England. By what rule the controversy must be tried. Whether [either] party at the first was more faithful to the English Protestant interest. How the state of the controversy altered. The high and extraordinary actings of all parties. The good that God hath brought out of our disorders and confusions. Whom God hath hitherto most punished. What is to be done, if we intend a settlement of state and church.

Chapter 9

Of the disposition of power ecclesiastical, and whether the bishop of Rome be the first subject of it under Christ

The many and great differences about the first subject of the Power of the Keys: the pope, the prince, the prelate, the presbyter, the people challenge it as due unto them by a divine right. Their several pretended titles examined. Whether that of the bishop of Rome be good or valid. His greatness, state, and pomp. The opinions of some authors concerning him. The power he challengeth is transcendent. The reasons to prove his title taken from politics: ancient writers, the Scriptures. The insufficiency of them: though some may seem to prove the possession, yet none make good the title.

Chapter 10

Whether civil sovereigns have any right unto the Power of the Keys

Their power and advantage to assume and exercise this power. Their power not spiritual, but temporal. The power of ordering matters of religion, what it is, and how it differs from the Power of the Keys, *Jus Religionis ordinandae* rightly understood, belongs to all higher powers. The kings and queens of England, though acknowledged over all persons, in all causes both civil and ecclesiastical supreme governors, yet had not the Power of the Keys. What [is] meant by those words of the Oath of Supremacy. Erastians worthy of no answer, because they mistake the state of the question, and do not distinguish between the Power of the Sword, and the Power of the Keys.

Chapter 11

Whether bishops be the primary subject of the Power of the Keys

The different opinions concerning the definition and essence of a bishop, as also concerning the first institution of episcopacy. St. Jerome's opinion in this point. Spalatensis his arguments to prove the divine right of bishops, as invested with the power of ordination and jurisdiction examined and answered. Dr. Andrewes' judgement in this point. After the primitive and also the hierarchical bishop, which differ much, the English episcopacy different from both the former; in some things proper to itself is examined. Though some episcopacy be grounded upon a divine general precept; yet it's not the primary subject of the Power of the Keys: neither is episcopal government proved to be necessary by any special evangelical precept of universal, and perpetual obligation.

Chapter 12

Whether presbytery be the primary subject of the Power of the Keys

The abolition of episcopacy and surrogation of presbytery in several reformed churches. The nature, institution and distinction of ecclesiastical presbyters. The places of Scripture, whereon the divine right of lay, or ruling elders is grounded, examined. The reasons why presbyters cannot be the primary subject of this power. The arguments of the authors of *Jus divinum, regiminis ecclesiastici* insufficient to prove it. The English presbytery, as intended and modelled by the Parliament, with the advice of the [Westminster] Assembly of Divines inquired into; the perfections and imperfections of the same, as modelled by the Parliament without the King. Certain reasons which may be imagined, why the Parliament would not trust the ministers alone with this power.

Chapter 13

Whether the Power of the Keys be primarily in the people

The opinion of Morellius and the Brownists, of Blondel, of Parker; and his mistake in politics, applied to the church to make it a mixed government. The judgement of the author concerning the Power of the Keys to be primarily under Christ in the whole church, exercised by the best and fittest for that work. The explication of his meaning concerning the power, the subject of the power, and the manner how this power is disposed in this subject. The confirmation of the proposition; that the Power of the Keys is in the whole church, both by the institution and exercise of this power. Where is premised a confutation of Mr. Parker's opinion, grounded upon two several places, as he understands them. The principal places of Scripture concerning church government *in foro exteriori* explicated, to find out where this power is by institution, for legislation, jurisdiction, and making of officers.

Chapter 14

Concerning the extent of a particular church

The several extensions of the church in excess, according to the opinions of such as subject all churches particular to that one church of Rome: of such as subject all to a general council. Whether Mr. Hudson is justly charged by Mr. Hooker and Mr. Ellis, and divers others, as guilty of popery in asserting the unity of the universal church. The congregational extent: what congregations are? How they are gathered? Whether the primary subject of an independent power. The arguments of Mr. Parker and the dissenting brethren from Scripture and politics, answered. A national extent examined. What means to be used for to compose our differences, and to settle peace amongst us.

Chapter 15

Of subjection civil

What subjection in general is, the degrees of it. What a subject in a civil state is: the definition explained. What the duties of subjects be. What offences are contrary to this subjection; what rebellion and treason: the several degrees of treason. What usurpation is; whether any subjection be due to usurped powers. When a power is dissolved. How far the Oaths of Supremacy and Allegiance bound the English subject. Whether the civil war did dissolve the government. Whether the late warlike resistance made against the King's party and his commissions was rebellion, or no? Something of the question: whether upon any cause it be lawful for the subjects to resist, or take up arms against their lawful sovereign as it's handled by Arnisaeus. Whether after the war said to be between King and Parliament was commenced, there was any ordinary legal power which could induce an obligation to subjection. Whether the Act of Alteration, or any other form since proposed could introduce an obligation. Whether it be lawful to submit unto an extraordinary power, when no legal power according to the fundamental constitution can be had. The distinction, division, and education of subjects.

Chapter 16

Of subjection ecclesiastical

What ecclesiastical subjection is. The distinction of ecclesiastical subjects. The qualification of a church member. Something of separations from a church. The alterations, divisions made, and the errors, blasphemies professed in the Church of England in these late times. The manner of admission of church members. The ancient and also the modern division of ecclesiastical subjects, and their subordination. The hierarchical order. The education of church members.

Book one

CHAPTER I

Of government in general, and the original thereof

I.

Propriety is the ground of power, and power of government; and there are many degrees of propriety, so there are of power. Yet, as there is but one universal and absolute propriety, so there is but one supreme and universal power, which the most glorious, blessed and eternal God can only challenge as his due. For he contrived all things by his *wisdom*, decreed them by his *will*, and produced them by his *power*, and to this day 'worketh all things according to the counsel of his will' (Eph. 1.11). In this respect he is 'worthy to receive glory, and honour, and power, because he hath created all things, and for his pleasure they are and were created' (Rev. 4.11). By creation he began, by conservation he continued to be actually the proprietary of all things: for he made them of nothing, and gave them being and existence, so that they wholly always depend upon him, and are absolutely his. Therefore he hath power to dispose of them as he pleaseth, and to order them to those ends he created them. This ordination of them, which began immediately upon creation, continueth and shall continue to the end, and is either general of all things, or special of some special, more noble and more excellent creatures: such are men and angels, endued with understanding and free will, and capable of laws, rewards and punishments, both temporal and eternal. The ordination of these is more properly and strictly called government, which is a part of divine providence. The government of angels no doubt is excellent and wonderful, though we know little of it, because not revealed.

2.

That of men is more fully manifested to us as men, in that book of books, we call the holy Scriptures, the principal subject whereof is the government of man, as ordered to his final and eternal estate. This government is twofold: [...] That of strict justice, [and] that of sweet mercy in Christ. For it pleased the eternal sovereign to bring man fallen back again, and raise him up to an estate of eternal glory; this was his great design, wherein he most gloriously manifested his divine perfections of wisdom, justice, power, and especially of free mercy. This man we find in a twofold capacity; the first is temporal, confined to this mortal life, the second is spiritual, and in both he is subject to his maker and eternal king, who doth not always exercise his power himself immediately, either in the constitution or administration of these earthly states, but as he useth the ministry of angels, so he makes men his deputies and vicegerents [viceregents], these are called higher powers ordained of God,[1] who are trusted with, and bear the sword to protect the good, and punish the bad, according to certain laws and rules of wisdom and justice. This power may reach the persons and the goods of mortal man, but not the soul and conscience, which are exempted and reserved to the Tribunal of God, who cannot only kill the body, but cast both body and soul into Hell, and reward men with spiritual and eternal rewards, which the powers of the world cannot do. Of this government by the temporal Sword something shall be said in the following discourse, but with some reference to that which is spiritual, that the generals wherein they do agree, the particulars wherein they differ, the subordination of the one unto the other may be the better known. All men should be of this spiritual society, but are not many excluded through their own fault and just judgement of God? This separation was made betimes, for

---

[1] Rom. 13; Heb. 13.17.

we read of Cain cast out of God's presence, and excommunicate, of the sons of God, and the sons of men before the flood; of Jews and Gentiles, after that the world was peopled by the sons of Noah, and family of Abraham, Isaac and Jacob singled out of all other nations, and this before the incarnation and the glorification of the Messiah. And since then we may observe that there are Christians opposed to pagans and idolaters, which do not acknowledge [the] one [and] only God; to Mahometans, who acknowledge the true God, who made Heaven and earth, but not God [the] redeemer by Jesus Christ; to Jews, who confess God the creator, and Jesus Christ in general, but as yet to come; to apostates, who first professed the truth, but afterwards denying it, are excommunicated by a sentence and decree of Heaven. Though these be many, and of several and different sorts, yet they are reducible to two societies or cities, the one of God, and the other of the Devil, as the learned Augustine did well observe in his excellent treatise of *The City of God*; this spiritual society was governed by God, as sole monarch from the beginning without any vicar or deputy universal, till such time, as Christ having finished the great work of expectations, was set at the right hand of God, and made the adminis- trator or general of the church Christian, for now that is the name of this spiritual society. This church, and especially as Christians, may be considered under several notions, and distinguished into that which now triumphs in Heaven, and is secure of everlasting bliss, and that which is militant aiming at a final victory, and expecting a perpetual peace. [...] This militant church may be conceived to be, either as mystical, consisting only of real saints, and such as by a lively faith have fellowship with Christ, and are living members of his body; or visible, of such as acknowledge and profess their faith in God, and in his son Jesus Christ already exhibited and set at the right hand of God; and because the sincerity of this profession is known certainly to God alone, therefore in this visible society we find Judas amongst the Apostles; Simon Magus amongst Christians, Pharisees and Saddu- cees, though a generation of vipers, amongst the disciples of John [the] Baptist, yet these are but chaff, upon the floor mingled with the wheat, and by the fan in Christ's hand to be separated, and burned with the unquenchable fire.[2]

---

[2] Matt. 3.12–13.

3.

This visible church militant may be considered either as universal or particular. The universal is the number of all Christians living on earth, who by their profession of faith in Christ already come, signify that subjection to Christ, and their relation one to another as brethren. In this respect the government of the church is monarchical under one head Jesus Christ, who never appointed any one vicar universal, or supreme independent judicatory visible on earth with plenitude of power over all Christians of all nations. The word, sacraments, ministry and the outward means of conversion belong to this church, as considered under this notion; and every particular person therein is first admitted into this society, and made a member thereof before he can be a member of any particular church. Though one baptized in a particular church under a form of external government may be solemnly received both as a member of the universal, and also that particular body at one and the same time; yet in order of nature he must be conceived as a member of the universal, before a member of that particular. For, we are first Christians, and subject to Christ, before we can be subject to the power of any particular church. For we are baptized into one body universal, and in the name of 'God the Father, Son and Holy Ghost', not into the church of Rome, Corinth, Ephesus, Jerusalem, or into the name of any of the governors or officers of these churches. Particular visible churches are parts of the universal, and are first so many several communities denominated usually from some place, and after that by association and consent receive a form of government visible and external. This kind of spiritual visible policy, and the government thereof is the principal subject of the ensuing discourse, wherein I aim at peace and truth, desiring not to kindle, but to quench, or at least abate the flames of dissension, which so long and so violently have ranged amongst us.

4.

The government of these particular churches at this present time is the subject of so many disputes amongst us, that some doubt whether there be any such thing or no; some presuppose it, but know not what

it is; some make it to be the same with civil government, and put all
the power in the civil magistrate's hands, and only except the word
and sacraments, which they grant to ministers; some take those from
the ministers, and make this administration common to others with
them; and because there is no certain order established amongst us,
therefore many are our divisions, and fanatic sects are multiplied.
Some are subtle and politic agents, and divide the church that they
may disturb the state; these care not much what the doctrine is, so
they can separate those which should be united. Some desire to
propagate their own opinions, though false, unprofitable, blasphemous, and their design is to draw disciples after them. These
prevail the more, because they find the minds of many so ready to
receive any impression. For some have 'itching ears', and every new
and strange opinion doth affect and much take with them.[3] Few are
well grounded in the principles of Christian saving truth, so as to have
a distinct, methodical knowledge of them, with an upright humble
heart disposed to practise what they know; for a distinct knowledge of
fundamentals, with a sincere desire and intention to practise and live
accordingly, are excellent means to avoid errors, for such God will
guide in his truth; some aim at an higher perfection than this life can
reach, and boasting of their high attainments insolently censure
others, or look upon them with scorn and contempt, as far below
them. Some design to make men sceptics in all matters of religion,
that then their minds being like matter ready to receive any form, they
may more easily imprint upon them what they please; yet in the issue
many of them prove atheists and enemies to all religion. The grand
politicians and chief agents, who do least appear, animate the design,
take all advantages, watch all opportunities, single out the fittest
persons, and make men even of contrary judgements, and of a temper
quite different from themselves, instrumental and efficient to their
own ruin. Yet I hope that God in the end will not only discover, but
disappoint them. All these bandy together, and do conspire to destroy
the Protestant English interest, and it's a sad thing, that orthodox
Christians take little notice of these things, but fearfully wrangle
about matters of less moment, to the great prejudice of the necessaries and substantials of religion.

[3] 2 Tim. 4.3.

5.

All this is come upon us for our neglect and abuse of a long continued peace, and the light of the gospel shining so gloriously amongst us. We are guilty but God is just, and also merciful and wonderfully wise. For he is trying of us to purge away the tin and dross; and he expects that we should search more accurately, pray more fervently, and more humbly depend upon him, whose wisdom is such as that he can and will bring light out of darkness; good out of evil; and a far more excellent order out of our confusions. The prayers of the upright for this end are made and heard in Heaven already, and what we desire in due time shall be effected. For he will comfort Zion, he will comfort all her waste places, and he will make her wilderness like Eden, and her desert like the garden of the Lord.[4] This indeed is a work to which man contributes little, hinders much, retards long, that God's hand and wisdom may the more appear, and that he may have the glory. In the meantime, Christ takes care of the universal church and the parts thereof, converting some, confirming others, and directing all true believers to eternal glory; and though a storm be raised and the same very terrible, yet it is nothing, but we may be confident, when we consider the skill and miraculous power of our Heavenly pilot.[5]

6.

My intention is not to instruct the learned, who are more fit to be my masters, yet to these endued with far more excellent gifts I would give occasion, and also make a motion to exercise their improved parts and learning in this subject, and do this poor distracted church of ours, a part of the universal, some far more glorious service. God may make me, though very unworthy, an instrument of his wisdom to inform the ignorant, and remove their errors, and correct their mistakes. It may also through God's blessing, contribute something unto peace by uniting well-affected minds. I am enemy to no man, yet professedly bent against errors; and that not only in others, but also in myself, if once I know them. I am not pre-engaged to any party, but a servant unto truth, and devoted unto peace. I wish I may not be prejudicate,

[4] Isa. 51.3.   [5] Matt. 8.23–6.

or partial, or precipitate as many do [are], who contend to maintain a party or a faction, but do not care to search out the truth; these do not close up, but open the breaches among us, and make them wider, and leave others unsatisfied. Our differences be so many, and so great, that we seem to be uncapable of any peace; yet God can do wonders, and we may trust in him, who in his time will give us peace, if not on earth, yet certainly in Heaven, the place of our eternal rest.

CHAPTER 2

Of government in general, and of a community civil

I.

Church government presupposeth the rules of government in general, therefore he that will know the latter, must understand the former: for he that is ignorant of government, must needs be ignorant of church government; and this is the very case of many in our days, and this is one cause of many differences amongst us at this time. To give some light in this particular, I will say something of government in general. The government of God, whereby he more immediately orders man to his final and immortal estate, I have according to my poor ability declared in my *Theo-politica*,[1] or divine politics, therefore I will con- fine my discourse to the government of man by man, or rather the government of God by men set over men. For God communicates some measure of his power to mortal men; and such as are entrusted with it, become his vicegerents and bear his name according to that of the psalmist, 'I have said ye are Gods' (Ps. 82.6). My design in this treatise is not to deliver an exact system of politics, yet I will make use of those rules I find in political writers of better rank, but with a reservation of a liberty to myself to vary from them, as I shall see just cause. To pass by the distinction of government monastical and eco- nomical; I will pitch upon that which is political. The subject whereof is a community and society larger than that of a family, and may be sufficient to receive the form of a commonwealth.

[1] London, 1659.

21

2.

To this end we must observe [1.] what (*Politica*) which some call the rule of government of a polity is. 2. What [is] a polity or commonwealth. 3. What the parts of (*Politica*) be.

> [*Politica*, or politics is the act of well ordering a commonwealth.
>
> A commonwealth is the order of superiority and subjection in a community for the public good.
>
> Of politics there be two parts, the constitution [and] administration of a commonwealth.][2]

These rules are the foundation of the following discourse, and inform us [1.] that (*Politica*) is an act, that is a rule of divine wisdom to direct some operations of the creature: for so I understand it here. 2. That the object of this rule is a commonwealth. 3. That the proper act is to direct how to order a commonwealth aright, so that it may attain its proper end. 4. That the subject matter of a commonwealth is a community or common and public society of men. 5. That that form is an order of superiority and subjection established in this community. 6. That the end of this order is the common good or benefit of the whole and every part. 7. That seeing a commonwealth must first be made by establishing the order of superiority and subjection, and being once made must act according to the order determined; therefore *Politica* must have two parts, the first must be the rule of the constitution, the second the rule of administration. For the more orderly proceeding in this particular, I will begin with the constitution, which will take up the first book of this treatise; then I will proceed to the administration, the subject of the second book.

3.

The constitution is the settling of an order of superiority and subjection in a community, whereby it becomes a commonwealth. And we may be allowed to say that a community is the matter of a commonwealth; and a commonwealth, as some understand it, the form of a community. These two, [...] a community, [and] a commonwealth are chiefly to be handled in this first part.

[2] This is expressed as a ramist diagram in the text.

A community may be considered in general [or] special.

In general I will examine the name [and] nature.

The name in Hebrew is [*'am*] in Greek [*polis*] and that may come of [*polus*] because the matter of a community is a multitude, in Latin, *civitas, populus,* and here observe, that [*polis, polus*] *populus, publicus* seem to have some affinity; yet we must distinguish between *civitas* and *urbs.* For the former signifies the people, the latter the place, buildings, habitations of the people. The Romans promised the Carthaginians not to destroy, *civitatem Carthaginis,* to make good their word, they brought out the people, which was *civitas,* and then ruined *urbem,* the place, buildings, walls, houses. Though *plebs* and *populus,* as *civitas* and *respublica,* are sometimes taken for the same, yet more properly *plebs* signifies the meaner and inferior part of the people, and *populus* the whole body, both the highest and lowest. *Civitas* also differs from *respublica,* as the matter from the form, the body from the soul in many writers of politics. The Hebrew word [*'am*] is turned by the Septuagint most frequently, [*laos*] *populus,* the people, yet sometimes [*ethnos*] a nation, sometimes [*ochlos*] a confused multitude, sometimes [*synagogue*] a congregation, sometimes [*plethos*] a multitude, sometimes [*genos*] a generation. All these signify a multitude of persons, some ways united and combined together, which agrees always unto a community. Forsterus tells that [*'am*] is a multitude of people or society, which being joined together have the same name, language, laws, religion, polity.[3] Though this is true sometimes, yet it is not always so; and to have the same polity, is not only to be a community, but a commonwealth. It's true that Israel not long after their coming out of Egypt, had the same name, language, laws, religion, polity, both civil and ecclesiastical.

4.

This is the name, the nature follows, and we may learn it out of (Augustine, *City of God,* 19, 21–2), as he did from the Roman orator, [Cicero, *De republica,* 1.25] according to both these, [a republic is the people's concern. A people is an assemblage of a multitude associated by consent to law and community of interest], in another place, [a people is a rational multitude bound together by common agreement

---

[3] Johannes Forsterus, *Dictionarium Hebraicum*(?) (Basle, 1557).

as to the objects of their love]. Arnisaeus out of Aristotle describes it to be a perfect society of *Vicinities*, having all things necessary to a happy life.[4] Yet because these definitions are not perfect, I will first enquire further into the nature of a community, as it is the subject of a commonwealth; [second] discover the original of communities; [third] declare who are members of a community. A community is a society of persons immediately capable of a commonwealth; or it is a society fit to receive a form of public government. This is the general nature of a community, which may be considered under a civil, or ecclesiastical notion.

5.

A community civil is a society of families and vicinities fitted for, and capable of a commonwealth civil. And here I will take occasion more distinctly to explain what is a community in general. [Second] what this community civil is. In a community there are men; for the matter of it is rational, not irrational creatures. [...] There must [also] be a multitude of them. [Further] this must be a multitude of families and vicinities to distinguish it from a college, a university, an army and other occasioned multitudes. [Finally][5] these must associate and be united together; for they make up this body, not as severally considered, but as joined together in one; for the *Genus* is a society. This society [first] presupposeth union, and is a communion, whereby they communicate in something common to the whole; as in an organical body, there are many members. [Second, these] are united to make one whole body of many parts. [Third, from] this union ariseth a communion and participation in some things which agree and belong unto the whole body as a body. This union doth not arise merely from some accident or cohabitation, or natural instinct, but from a rational and just consent, *ex juris consensu* saith Cicero;[6] for till they be thus united, they cannot be immediately capable of, or *in proxima potentia* to a commonwealth, therefore, this union must be rational, according to that of Augustine, ['a people is a rationally associated multitude']. [Further it] must be free and voluntary, for it is by consent. [Moreover because] thieves, pirates, conspirators, murderers, seditious persons,

---

[4] Henningus Arnisaeus, *Opera politica omnia* (Strasburg, 1648), 1.6–7; Aristotle, *Politics*, 1252b28.
[5] The text misnumbers these points.　　　　[6] Cicero, *De republica*, 1.25.

yea devils may be united by a rational consent, and yet cannot make a commonwealth, neither can be any fit subject thereof; it must be just, for so the learned father [Augustine] understands the words of the great orator, *ex juris consensu*, though all multitudes of men by the light of nature, or by the Laws of God revealed, if they enjoy divine revelations are bound to associate and unite so far as God shall direct and enable them, yet they cannot associate unjustly. For they are bound to observe certain rules of eternal justice, so that both the things wherein they unite, and the manner of uniting must be just; and the more just the association, the more excellent and perfect the commonwealth and ordination may be. From this union ariseth a communion or common union; for as they are one common body, so that have some things, acts, rights, which are common; wherein all jointly have a share or part: for a community is one person morally considered, and whatsoever is not private is public and common. These common things may be few or many: and as the persons united have one common reason, will, and power, so they all communicate in these things, and do certain common acts as a society, which are acts not of a part but of the whole. Yet these things, acts, rights, privileges, interests, differ from those which are common either unto other creatures or mankind in general. This society was ordained of God for the benefit of mankind and tends much unto their good and happiness temporal at least. For God saw at the first creation, that it was not good for man to be alone, therefore he created woman, who together with man was the root and original of all human societies (Gen. 2.18). Two saith the preacher are better than one, and 'woe be to him that is alone' (Eccles. 4.9, 10). Where his principal intention is to show the excellency and benefit of society, yet he presupposeth love, humanity, and a nearer affection to those of one and the same society than to all mankind in general; as in this civil society there must be families to distinguish it from single person, and vicinities to difference it from families. And [further an] association [must be] both rational and just, so [also] there must be in them thus associated an immediate capacity and fitness to receive a commonwealth or form of government. For though this association conduceth much unto their safety, help, comfort, and furnisheth them with many things not only necessary, but convenient, which without association they could not so easily enjoy, yet without a form of government, these advantages could not be so firm and lasting. This fitness, capacity, and immediate disposition to a form of civil government doth not arise so much from the multitude of the persons, or extent and goodness of the place of their habitation, as from their good affections one towards another, and the number of just, wise and eminent persons amongst them, who are fit, not only to be the matter of a state, but to model it, and order it once constituted; experience here of sufficient we have at this day in this nation; for so many and great are our differences both in judgement and affections, and our several interests so contrary, that the same language, laws, religion, common country cannot firmly unite us together; but we are ready every moment to fly asunder and break in pieces, if we were not kept together rather by the sword of an army, than by any civil power and policy, or good affection. This is a sad condition, and a just judgement upon us for our sins.

6.

This is the first thing whereof I thought to inform the Reader, that he might the better understand the nature of a community, before I said anything of the original thereof, which is the next in order. The original is either natural or accidental. The natural source is that which hath some principles in the creation of man, who though fallen retains something of the creation, whereby he continues not only a reasonable creature, but also sociable. For man by nature, as the Philosopher [Aristotle] observed is, [*zoon politicon*]⁷ a sociable creature, because he hath not only reason, but speech, without both which there can be no human society, as human amongst us. This natural propension to society presupposeth mankind actually existing and multiplied; therefore it pleased God at the first to make man and woman the foundation of a family, and families of vicinities; this is the reason why the authors of politics, following the Philosopher, speak so much of economical relations, as the foundation of a community.⁸ The first relation is of man and wife, the second of parents and children, the third of masters and servants. God at the beginning did give men not only reason and language, but a power of generation, with a blessing, so that one man and one woman joined in the sacred bond of matrimony become husband and wife first, and then parents of children, and of children's children, till they multiply to a numerous posterity. Thus God blessed our first parents before, and

⁷ Aristotle, *Politics*, 1253a.   ⁸ *Ibid.*, 1252b10.

Noah's family after the flood, that they replenished and peopled the earth, and became not one, but many communities. And it was a strange providence and wonder to divide their multiplied posterity of Noah by dividing the language into several companies, and disperse them into several parts of the earth; and hence the many societies of the world, and their different communities. God promised Abraham to 'make him a father of many nations', that is, not only of many civil, but spiritual societies (Gen. 17.5), and he said to Rebekah, 'two nations are in thy womb' (Gen. 25.23). Thus Jacob's family multiplied in Egypt to a great community; so that the original of societies civil are from God, the cause of all things, 1. As making men and enduing them with reason and speech. 2. As multiplying and blessing them. 3. As dividing them into several parts and portions of the earth, where they may cohabit and have communion one with another. 4. Besides all these, he so creates them, and orders them in the very first moulding of them, when they are multiplied, that they have need one of another, and one may be beneficial and helpful unto another, so that their subsistence and their well-being depends upon society; for as he hath made the body to consist of many members, so that they have their several offices and ministrations all useful one for another, so that the body cannot be a body without many members, nor subsist without some necessary parts, nor well continue or be perfect and entire without all and every one, so in like manner hath he composed these great bodies and communities; some by his providence are rich, some are poor, some wise, some ignorant, some strong, some weak, some bold, some timorous, some fit for learning and more noble place, some of inferior quality; some fit for husbandry, some for trade; and some fit for one trade, some fit for another. Though we, who have our houses, stocks, trades, fairs, markets, towns, cities, villages do not understand this so well; yet they, who make new discoveries, and begin new plantations, are very sensible of the necessity and benefit of society civil. This was made evident by that policy of the Philistines, who by taking away from Israel their smiths, and depriving them but of one trade, disarmed the great body of that nation; for we read there was no smith found in all the land of Israel, so that it came to pass in the day of battle, that there was neither sword nor spear found in the hand of any of the people that were with Saul and Jonathan;[9] and when God intended to ruin not only the state, but the community of

[9] 1 Sam. 13.19–22.

Judah, he threaten[ed] to take away not only 'the mighty man, the man of war, the judge, the prophet, and the prudent, and the ancient, the captain of fifty, and the honourable man, and the counsellor, but the cunning artificer, and the eloquent orator' (Isa. 3.2, 3). Though God alone can be fully happy by himself alone without man or angel, or any company, yet man cannot. Man solitary is very imperfect, and like a body which wants some necessary parts. God knows this full well, therefore he so orders multitudes of vicinities, that he inclines them by their very constitution to society; for by it they are not only stronger and more able to defend themselves, and provide for their safety, but also they are better supplied with necessaries, and commodities, what one hath not, another hath; what one cannot do, another can, what few are not able to effect, many may, and all much more. But that whereby God is the immediate cause of society is voluntary consent, to which he inclines their hearts, when he hath once multiplied them and cast them together. This consent whether tacit or express is grounded upon love and good affection, with an intention to do good and just things one for another, according to the work of the eternal law written in their hearts. The accidental original is when by divine providence many from several countries are cast together in one place or part of the earth, and that upon several occasions, or for several causes; these in time grow familiar, and acquainted, one with another, and for mutual help, safety, benefit, cement into one body, and according to the dictate of natural reason join, in one common interest; this some say was the original of the state of Venice at the first. [Thus] the several distinct communities upon the division of languages at Babel had their beginning. Thus one part of a community seeking some new place for their habitation, becomes a distinct community of themselves.

7.

The third thing to be considered is, who are members of a community. To say nothing of municipal societies, colonies, plantations, provinces, titular members, who are only *cives honorarii*, this is a general rule, that after a form of government once introduced, whosoever are subjects, are *cives*, members of that community, and continue such, though the form of government be altered or dissolved. For there are degrees of them; for some are *virtualiter et diminutè*, some *formuliter et plenè*, some *eminenter cives*, members of a community, that is, they are either imperfectly or perfectly such. The lowest rank of such as are not [themselves under the law, but are under another power, are not] free and in their own power. To this form are reduced women, children, servants, strangers, whether sojourning, or inhabiting out of their own commonwealth. Some kind of tenants or vassals do so much depend upon others, that they are not competent members; all these are virtually included in others upon whom they depend. Formally and fully members are all such, as being males of full age, free, independent, have the use of reason, and some competent estate; such freeholders seem to be with us.

[These become such by birth, election, or manumission. Or they are natural, or naturalized.]

Being once such, they have *Jus suffragii in publicis*, as our freeholders have a vote in choosing their knights for the parliament, and they virtually give their suffrage in that assembly by their representatives. *Eminenter cives* are such, who by reason of their descent, estates, parts, noble acts, are not once members, but somewhat more, as being fit for honour, offices and places of power, if once a commonwealth be constructed.

8.

There be amongst others three inseparable adjuncts of a community, as a community, propriety of goods, liberty of persons, equality of the members. Propriety there must needs be, and the same absolute and independent: the reason hereof is, because, what a man hath justly acquired, is his own by the law of nature, which a community doth not take away; and further, there is no *dominium eminens*, as in a commonwealth there must necessarily be. Liberty of persons there is, because every complete member is *sui juris*, and no ways bound by the rules of a civil supreme power; and this is more than can be in a state once constituted, wherein this liberty is bounded by allegiance and laws. There is equality, for there is no superior or inferior in respect of government, because there is no government, no sovereign, no subject, all are fellows, [and fellows are fellows in so far as they are equals]; inequality of superior and inferior civil ariseth from a form of government, which is sometimes so despotical, that it is destructive both of liberty and propriety. This inequality is consistent with an imparity of births, parts, estate, for [or?] age: for this is from nature or providence. These civil societies may be less or greater both in respect of the number of persons, and extent of place. Neither can the certain number of persons, nor the particular bounds of place be well determined. If it be too large, it cannot so well unite, if too little, it is insufficient to protect or provide for itself, and so fall under the protection of others.

9.

This community civil considered abstractively and antecedently to a form of government not yet introduced, or upon a dissolution of a former model, or upon a failer [failure] of succession in a time doth virtually contain a supreme power, and hath a liberty and right to determine upon what form they please, so that it be good; though it's true, that this power may be taken from them by a potent invader, or some other way; and here it is to be noted, that when a form of government is altered or dissolved, any community may remain, nay, under a government it retains the nature of a community, as the matter and subject of the commonwealth, wherein every subject must be considered, first as *civis*, a member of the community, before he can be conceived, as *subditus*, a member of the commonwealth. This stricter association of a multitude, to make a particular community, doth no way hinder their society or communion with other communities, or with all mankind upon the earth so far as is possible, in things which may add unto their happiness.

CHAPTER 3

Of an ecclesiastical community

I.

Hitherto of a community in general, and of a community civil, that which we call ecclesiastical follows. This in opposition to that which we call temporal and civil is spiritual, and is such in respect of religion; for as there are matters of this life, which concern us as mortals with relation one unto another, so there are matters of God, spiritual, divine, and of a far higher allay [alloy]; there is no nation or people, though rude and barbarous, but profess some religion, by the observation whereof they acknowledge their dependence upon a superior power and providence far above that of mortal man; yet many, contrary to the very light of nature, either worshipped that which was not truly God, or with the true God a false deity; or the true God alone, without any certain rule and direction from Heaven, after the invention of men, or the suggestion of the devil. Of these there have been many communities, which I will no further mention; for these were never called churches, or the people of the living God; for the true church is a community of such as worship the true and living God, according to certain rules of truth revealed from Heaven, and now contained in the holy Scriptures. And these direct us to worship God, not only as creator, but as redeemer by Christ. Such a kind of society there hath been ever since the fall of Adam, and the first promise of Christ; and all these societies of all places and all times might be called Christian,[1] because all the members thereof professed faith in Christ, either as to come, or already come. Yet because these believers and worshippers of God the Redeemer began to be called Christians after Christ's exaltation at the right hand of God in the Apostles' times, I intend principally to speak of this community Christian in the times of the New Testament; therefore to pass by the churches before the flood, and after till the time of Christ's exaltation. I will confine myself unto the communities Christian in the latter and stricter sense.

2.

These things premised, a community ecclesiastical is a society of Christians in an immediate capacity to receive a form of spiritual external government. The principal parts of this chapter shall be 1. The explication of the definition. 2. A declaration of the manner how we become members of this society. 3. The determination of the several and distinct degrees of these members. The first thing in the definition is the matter, and that as Christians, and especially in the

---

[1] Text has 'Christians'.

stricter sense. I do not say it is a society of families as formerly was expressed in the definition of a civil community. For though the churches of Jerusalem, Antioch, Rome, Corinth, Ephesus and other places, might in their several divisions and precincts contain some whole families, and perhaps vicinities Christian; or because their habitation was in the same city or place, they might be called vicinities, in which sense all particular churches should be vicinities. Yet our Saviour tells us, that upon the preaching of the gospel, there should follow such a division in religion, even in the same family, that 'there should be five in one house divided, three against two, and two against three' (Luke 12.52). So that there might be several religions professed and exercised in one family, and the persons of several societies. Thus it is with us since our unhappy divisions: for the husband sometimes is of one church, the wife of a second, the children of a third or fourth. Yet sometimes a whole family might come in together: as the nobleman or ruler of Capernaum believed and his whole house (John 4.53). Lydia and her whole household were baptized at one time.[2] The gaoler and his whole house believed, and was baptized the same night (Acts 16.33, 34). As in families, so much more in vicinities, not only several but also contrary religions have been practised. So that the first thing to be considered in the definition, is persons as Christians. And here I might take occasion to enquire, whether a parish may be a congregation Christian, and a multitude of parishes in the same vicinity may be a community spiritual. Mr. Hooker gives occasion of this enquiry.[3] A parish may be considered under a civil or ecclesiastical notion. Under a civil, as first made by the power civil, and also a civil society [it may be considered] as a part of an allotment for civil ends, and under civil officers. In an ecclesiastical action it's a society and body politic spiritual, appointed for worship and discipline. In which respect it consists as a vicinity of such persons as within the precincts thereof profess the same religion, and join in the same worship, have one and the same pastor or pastors, and usually frequent the same religious assemblies. In this respect, if either Jews, or heathens, or Mahometans, or heretics, or pagans died within the same precinct, they are not of the same society,

---

[2] Lydia, the seller of purple, Acts 16.14–15.
[3] Of *The Laws of Ecclesiastical Polity* (originally printed London, 1593), bk. 3.1. 13–14(?). See the Folger Library edn. of *The Works of Richard Hooker*, ed. W. Speed Hill (Cambridge, Mass., Harvard University Press, 1977–82).

yet are bound to pay their tithes, for the maintenance of God's worship in that place. And these tithes, as determined by the civil magistrate, to be paid in that place, and to be recovered by civil laws, may be called a lay-fee: but as they are due to Christ for to maintain the gospel and divine worship, they come under another notion. Further, though the pastor of such a parish may, as opportunity is offered and occasion requires, do Christ service in other places, yet he is in a special manner bound to that place, and not only to edify the converted, but to convert the unconverted in that place.

3.

Because any kind of persons are not fit to be of this society, therefore these persons must be Christians, and such as profess their faith in Christ, and in Christ already exhibited and reigning in Heaven. If they be adult, they must not only believe but profess in their own persons. And this profession must be such as a rational Christian may judge to be serious, as being unable clearly to prove the contrary. The inward faith should be sincere, and the outward profession should agree with it, yet it proves often otherwise. Therefore we find a Judas in the College of Apostles, a Simon Magus, a Demas amongst Christians:[4] for there hath been and will be tares amongst the wheat, and chaff on Christ's floor, which none can separate but he that hath his fan in his hand.[5] And let no man doubt, but that such as Christ and his Apostles admitted and retained in the visible church till they were openly discovered, that man might judge of them. Such we must admit and retain, and may do it.

4.

1. As they must be Christians, they must be a society of Christians, not single persons by themselves. This implies there must be a multitude. 2. A union of this multitude. 3. A communion. Yet as the multitude must be Christian, so the union and communion must be even in holy spiritual things. [First they] must be a multitude, yet not a little number or a few as will appear afterwards [ch. 14]. The power and right of a college may be preserved in one, and exercised in three;

---

[4] Acts 8.9–24.   [5] Matt. 3.12; 13.30.

33

and a small number may make a family society, yet here in this particular it is not so. As there must be a multitude: so [second they] must be united in a sacred bond of Christian religion. For, as in a natural, so in a spiritual political body, there must be not only many members, but they must be all united in one to make up the body. This union as the civil, is not merely from vicinity of place, but from voluntary and free consent directed, not only by right reason, but the rules of God's word. For that must be united not merely as men but as Christians. This consent may be tacit or express, and must make them one, not only when they make and assemble in one place, but when they are parted asunder. For by reason of this bond, a fraternity spiritual continues amongst them. And the more solemn, serious, regular, deliberate and agreeable to the gospel it shall be, the more effectual, comfortable, lasting it will prove. This union is not made either by baptism or profession but it presupposeth both. And though it be made by a free and voluntary consent, yet all vicinities of Christians, who by divine providence have an opportunity to associate, are by a divine precept bound to unite and consent to such a union. And this union is so firm, not because of man's consent, but God's precept and institution, to which it shall be conformable. From this a multitude of Christians become morally one person spiritual: and as such may act and do many things. And every particular member of this body is bound to seek the good of the whole and every part, and the good of this particular society, more than of any other, though he must endeavour the good of all, so far as God shall enable him. Upon this union therefore follows a communion. For as they all partake in all things and privileges, and rights, which are common to all, so they must communicate their gifts, cares, labours, for the promoting of the general good of all, and particular good of everyone. As by this union they become one person, so they receive a power and ability to act as one person for the special good of themselves. Yet it doth not give them power to separate either from the universal church, or from other communities in anything God hath made common, either to the universal church, or other particular communities.

5.

By this time you understand that a community Christian is a society of Christians, yet this is not all: it must be a society of Christians fitted for and immediately capable of an external form of government spiritual, and the same independent. For in a commonwealth of necessity there must be a supreme and independent power, otherwise it hath not the essence and being of a commonwealth. Therefore in politics both civil and ecclesiastical, we speak of a community, as it is actually the subject of a form of government, or fitted immediately to be such, otherwise we shall be heterogeneous, or at least exorbitant. Take notice therefore that [first] this community is not a civil society, nor the society of all Christians living at the same time on the earth, which make up the body of the church universal or visible, as subject to Christ, nor of a family, or congregational, or any petty Christian society, but of such a society Christian as is immediately capable of an independent discipline. [Second though] some acts of discipline may by a paternal spiritual power be performed, and so likewise in a congregation some degrees of power ecclesiastical may reside and be exercised, yet this is not sufficient to make them such a society as we speak of. [Third in] this community an independent power of discipline is virtually contained. [Fourth this] cannot be except it consists of such members as are fit both to model a commonwealth and manage a supreme Power of the Keys. [Fifth this] community, before a form of government be introduced, is but like a homogeneal or similar body, and then becomes organical, when it's the actual subject of a commonwealth, and a formal visible polity. And besides the consent required to the constitution of a community, there must be another consent to make it a polity: and the latter is distinct and really different from the former. For a multitude of Christians as such, are not the immediate matter of a spiritual visible state, but a community and a sufficient community, as such is the subject of this political form. [Sixth that] company of Christians which is not sufficiently furnished with men of gifts and parts, and yet presumes to set up an independent judicatory, must needs offend. For where God gives not sufficient ability, he gives not authority. That every petty congregation, which enjoys word, sacraments, ministry have an entire, intensive, independent judicative power in itself, and therefore may refuse to associate with others, is the opinion of some, which can hardly be proved out of the word of God.

6.

Thus I have explained the definition, and in the next place proceed to show the original of this community, and how particular persons become members of the same. Whether any are incorporated by election or birth, yet both the matter and form of this society is from God. For we read in the books of the New Testament, that the first original of societies of Christians was this. [First the] Apostles indued with the Holy Ghost from above preached, that Jesus of Nazareth was crucified at Jerusalem for our sins, rose again, was made Lord and King, and that remission of sins and eternal life was granted to all such as should repent and believe in him. Such as heard the doctrine, believed it, professed their faith, and promised to live accordingly, were baptized, and so admitted as visible subjects of Christ's kingdom. So they were made Christians, and remote materials of this community. [Second when] they were once multiplied, so as to make several congregations for worship, and there were found fit men to be pastors, pastors were ordained and set over the flocks: and these became societies for Christian worship. [Third when] there was a competent number of such in a vicinity as were able to manage a supreme independent power, they associated and combined together in one body for to introduce a form of external government. If any after, they became a community or a polity, were converted within their precincts, and did manifest his conversion so far as man might judge of it, he was baptized, and was admitted a member of their community. This was the manner of entering into and being incorporated into this body. And now if any pagans, Jews, Mahometans by the doctrine of the gospel be reduced to the Christian faith, then they must enter, in this manner they must be admitted. This association and incorporation is not from the laws, decrees, and mere consent of man, but from the power or commandment and institution of God, who requires that such, as are once made Christians, should associate, and that others, in whose power it is, should admit them. These are like branches ingrafted, not natural, but are made members by allection [attraction]. And whosoever is thus incorporated, he is first made a member of the universal church, and a subject to God the Father, Son and Holy Ghost, before he can be a member of any particular society. For he must of necessity be first a Christian before he can be a member of a Christian society; for the matter is before the form. If his profession be sincere, presently upon his conversion he is made a living member of Christ, and an heir of glory, far greater privileges, than to be a visible member of any visible spiritual polity. And though there is a certain priority of order, yet one and the same person may be made a living member of Christ, a member of a Christian community, and of a visible spiritual polity at one and the same time.

7.

As[6] there be ingrafted, so there be natural branches of these communities, as well as of the great and universal society, for such there have been, and that by divine ordination; and never any yet could evidently prove out of Scripture, that this law and ordinance, which made the children part of the parents, and one person with them in matter of religion, was abrogated or reversed to this day. Therefore children born of Christian parents, who were members both of the universal and particular communities, and not disfranchised, are members of a Christian community by birth, at least in charity; and they must needs be presumptuous dictators, who exclude them. It's true that infants born of man as men, are men, of such as are free, are free, of such as are noble, are noble. And so, such as are born of Mahometans, are Mahometans; and such as are born of Jews, are Jews; such as are born of heathens are by their birth heathens, and aliens to the commonwealth of the Christian Israel, and strangers from the covenants of promise (Eph. 2.12). And shall not such as are born of Christians be Christians? That covenant which God made with Abraham though accidentally different, is essentially the same with that of the gospel, as appears (Rom. 4 and Gal. 3). Yet in that covenant, God promised to be a God to him and his seed after him, and this part, of it which includes the children with their parents, must needs remain in force, if there be no clause of exception in the New Testament. If there be, where is it? As for the example and instance from the Apostles baptizing only such as professed their faith. [First it] doth not follow that only such persons were baptized, because that none but such are expressly named. [Second when] it's written, that whole houses were baptized, no wit of man can prove, that none of

---

[6] The second edition carries the marginal gloss 'A good ground of children's right to baptism'.

these were infants. [Third those] expressly mentioned were adult, *et sui juris*, such are not children: and their baptism was but matter of fact, not of law; shall the children be first seminally and virtually in their parents, then after extraction by birth part of their parents, and one person with them both by the laws of God and men, even so far, as they may be punished for the sins of their parents? And shall their parents be bound for them, and they bound in their parents in matter of religion? And shall not God's promise extend so far as their obligation? Surely it must. This manner of incorporation by birth is from God, who [...] by his divine providence brings them forth into the light of the world within the bosom of the church so that they are born of Christian parents, who are members of a community Christian; and [...] from his institution. For though an infant should be born of Christian parents, members of a Christian community, yet he could not be a Christian, and have any privilege spiritual, except it had been God's will and pleasure to account and judge him to be such. For it's the decree, the promise, the covenant of God that makes him a Christian. For as born of his immediate parents, or by them of Adam, or of them as godly or ungodly, he cannot be a member of the church. And to be so, is not to have actual faith, or to be justified and sanctified as believers at age, but to have a right unto the promise, which no heathen or any other born out of the church can have. And as part of his parents and included in the covenant by the will of God, he hath this privilege. 'The promise (saith Peter) is to you and your children, and to all afar off, even to as many as the Lord our God shall call' (Acts 2.39). Where observe, that the promise was not only to them at age, but also to their children. Again, 'You are the children of the prophets, and of the covenant, which God made with our fathers, saying unto Abraham, in thy seed all the nations of the earth be blessed' (Acts 3.25). Where note, 1. That the covenant was concerning everlasting bliss by Christ the seed of Abraham. 2. That this covenant includes all nations, not only Jews but gentiles. 3. That this is the covenant of the gospel for substance. 4. That the present Jews were within this covenant by birth, and that both for the obligation to duty, and the right unto the promise. For they were the children of the prophets and of the covenant, which neither the heathens, nor their children could be before they were called, and their children in them. From all this it appears, how the original of these communities are from God: for he 1. makes them Christians; 2. multiplies them in the same vicinity; 3. inclines their hearts to associate, and stirs up some eminent persons to motion and endeavour the association; 4. by his divine providence brings some into the world in the bosom of the church, and includes by his gracious covenant infants with their parents in this spiritual society.

8.

After the explication of the definition, [and] the declaration of the original of these societies, it remains we consider the degrees and distinction of the members. For though the community in respect of a form of outward government be an homogeneal body, yet considered in itself, and in the qualities of the several members, there is an imparity, and something organical in it. For they are so qualified, and the gifts of God so variously disposed in them, that they are several ways disposed for to contribute according to their several graces, something to the benefit of the whole and one another. This the Apostle makes clear (1 Cor. 12 and 14). These distinctions and degrees are like those in the members of civil society. For [...] some are *virtualiter et diminute cives* incomplete members, as women, children, and many weak Christians. [...] Some [however] are so gifted and qualified, as they are fit to act and give suffrage in business which concerns the whole. These are *formaliter cives* complete members. [And some] are endued with more than ordinary knowledge, wisdom, grace above the rest, and most fit to introduce a form of government, and act in the highest business of administration. These are *eminenter cives*, eminently members. Such as being members of another church, and yet sojourn or inhabit in a community distant from their own, before they are incorporate, though upon certificate and letters communicatory, they may partake *in sacris*, yet they are but *diminute cives* members incomplete and for a time. For, as such, they can have no vote or suffrage of any power in things public. They may indeed advise and declare their mind, and their counsel may be liked and accepted.

9.

This community ecclesiastical hath the same inseparable adjuncts with the civil, except propriety of goods, which they have in another respect. For the members have liberty and equality, and an immediate capacity of a form of government. For, [...] they are free from any subjection either to any other communities, or one unto another, till a form of government and discipline be settled. Yet [they] are subject to Christ as the head of the universal church visible: subject to God as supreme Lord; subject to their pastors if they have any. For they are commanded to obey them, who rule over them, and to submit unto them, etc. (Heb. 13.17). For ministers are officers and representatives of Christ, and therefore must needs have power [in internal matters of conscience], as the schoolmen speak. Yet ministers as ministers have no Power of the Keys [in matters external]: they are only eminent members of the community, otherwise the government external of the several congregations in one community should be purely aristocratical in them, and monarchical in a single congregation.[7] [...] They are [also] equal as members of the community in respect of power and government, which is not yet introduced, or at least considered as not actually brought in, they cannot command or judge one another: neither can the whole sentence any single member. For that were to act as a commonwealth, which yet it is not. [Moreover the] whole is in an immediate capacity to form a government as you heard before. This may be done immediately by the eminent and complete members, or by a delegation of a power of modelling the government by a few of the principal and fit for such a work, and afterwards approved and ratified by all. And though the general rules of discipline are plainly delivered in the Scriptures; yet few will understand them, or apply them right, and it's a hard thing to abolish the corruptions of former governments; so that many times a discipline is settled and perfected only by degrees and in a long time.[8] Not only the constitution but a reformation of a church meets with many difficulties. One reason is, there is so little of Christianity in many, and none in some, that yet profess their faith in Christ, which either they do not understand or refuse to practice. This hath given occasion to some to gather churches out of churches, and to separate. How justly or wisely this hath been done, something may be said hereafter. [Chs. 12, 14, 16.]

[7] The first clear intimation of Lawson's dissent from the Nonconformist tradition of Robert Parker, *De politeia ecclesiastica* (London, 1616), see below, ch. 12. Richard Baxter, *A Treatise of Episcopacy* (London, 1681), ch. 2, takes up this issue against Lawson, whom he sees as diminishing the proper authority of ministers.
[8] The second edition carries the marginal gloss 'What hinders reformation'.

CHAPTER 4

Of a commonwealth in general, and power civil

I.

The subject of a commonwealth being a community, which is twofold, civil and ecclesiastical. It remains, and order requireth, that I say something of a commonwealth. You heard before that the subject adequate of politics, was a state or commonwealth, and that the parts of this act are two: [...] the constitution [and] the administration. The constitution, as you may remember, is the first part of politics, whereby an order of superiority and subjection is settled in a community; wherein three things were principally to be examined: [...] what a community in general, [...] what a community civil, [and] what a community ecclesiastical is: and all this is done. Therefore to proceed, observe, that a community is like a matter without form in respect of something that it must receive, yet a matter and a subject disposed and *in proxima potentia* to receive a form to perfect it: and this form is that we call a commonwealth, a polity, a state, wherein we may observe four things. 1. That it is an order. 2. An order of superiority and subjection: this is the general nature of it. 3. An order of superiority and subjection in a community. 4. Such an order tending to the peace and happiness of a community. [First] it's [*taxis*] an order, or as some understand the philosopher (an ordination) which is a disposing of things in their proper place. For as the learned father observes, ['Order is the disposition of disparate parts, each allotted to its proper place', *The City of God*, 19.13]. It's *inter plura*, which may be equal or unequal. For there may be an order of priority and posteriority in time or place amongst equals. Therefore [second], it's an order of superiority and subjection in respect of power. Yet [third] because there is a superiority and subjection in a family, a college, a corporation, therefore it's an order of superiority and subjection in a community, whether civil or ecclesiastical. [Fourth] because there may be such an order in a community of wicked men and devils, if that might be called a community, where the association is unjust, as properly it cannot; therefore it must be such an order as tends and conduceth directly to the peace and happiness of the community. This an unjust order cannot do. To understand this the better, you must know that all communities spiritual and temporal are grounded upon that commandment of God, 'Love thy neighbour as thyself': where that word neighbour may signify indeed a single person, yet it includes a notion of society: and the Hebrew word *Re 'a H* signifies [associated]. This neighbour therefore is either a single person, yet as in society, or collective as in a family, kindred, congregation, corporation, community. This love is the true cause of all association, and is the special duty of all parties associated. A commonwealth is grounded upon a branch of that great love, the fifth commandment, which presupposing superiority and subjection, in respect of power, requires certain duties of the parties superior and subject both in a greater and lesser society. And because these duties cannot be peformed in great societies except this order be settled, therefore by that commandment all communities are bound so far as they are able, to erect a form of government. In which respect polities are from God, not only allowing and approving them, nor merely as enabling men, but commanding them enabled to establish and preserve them established, for the better manifestation of his glory and their own greater good both temporal and spiritual. From hence it's evident, that politics both civil and ecclesiastical belong unto theology, and are but a branch of the same.

2.

In this commonwealth two things are most worthy of our consideration, [...] the superiority [and the] subjection: for it consists of two parts.

> Which are *imperans et subditus*, the sovereign and subject.
> And because the sovereign is civil or ecclesiastical, I will begin with the civil, and so proceed to the ecclesiastical.
> And seeing that *imperans* the sovereign, is a concrete, and therefore signifies the power and the subject of this power, I will first speak of power, then of the subject of this power.
> The power must be considered what it is in general [and] special.

> In respect of the subject, I will declare the manner [in which it is acquired and disposed.][1]

This is the method which I intend to observe, and wherewith I acquaint the reader. My observation of it will make the discourse more clear and distinct. The reader's knowledge of it will help both his understanding and his memory.

3.

Pars imperans, the sovereign civil, which is the first part of a commonwealth, is one invested with majesty civil. Where observe: [First] that it is a part of a polity and that's the general nature of it; and is an essential or integral part, which together with the subject gives essence to the state, and constitutes it in being and existence. [Second] it's the first part; for though as superiority and subjection, and so sovereign and subject are relates, and in that respect simultaneous; yet the sovereign is not only the first in dignity, but in some sort by origination, if not as a cause. For as paternity in some respect is before filiation, so it is in this particular. For subjection doth rather follow upon sovereignty than the contrary. And therefore in moulding a state, they first determine upon a sovereign, whereupon instantly and at the same time follows without anything intervening, subjection. [Third] this party that is sovereign is invested with majesty civil. Where we have two things: [...] majesty as an adjunct, [and] the subjection invested with it. And as power is the very essence of a superior, so majesty is of a sovereign.

4.

Majestas est maxima in civitate potestas; majesty is the greatest power in the community. It's [1.] *potestas*, power. 2. *Maxima in civitate, potestas est ius imperandi*, power is a right to govern. It's *ius*, a right and in itself is always just; and is from some propriety. And as the absolute propriety so the absolute power of all things is from God, and there is no power but derived from him. It's not physical but moral, and so *nomen iuris*, and may be considered as a faculty or habit, which qualifies the subject to do something, which one that hath no power cannot do.

[1] The text is spaced eccentrically in a semi-diagrammatical form.

The proper act of it is to govern and in governing to command, so as to bind the party subject to obedience or punishment. This *imperium* or command is an act of the will, and presupposeth some act of the understanding and must needs be ineffectual and vain without a sufficient coactive force. And because the understanding may be ignorant or erroneous, the will unjust, the coactive force act accordingly; therefore the understanding of a superior as such, ought to be directed by wisdom, his commanding will by justice, and his executive force by both. And that act of power which is not thus directed is not properly an act of power, nor any such command binding. Therefore the Apostles refused to obey the charge and command of the Jewish rulers, when it was devoid both of wisdom and justice, and it was so much the more invalid, because contrary to an express command of a superior lord and master, even Jesus Christ. This power is an excellency, and makes the party invested with it like unto God: and the greater it is, the greater the excellency of him that hath it. Though it is in itself good and just, as being from God, or rather the power of God in the creature intellectual, yet it may be exercised either too little or too much. For one that is invested with it may do less or more than his power doth warrant him; nay, he may act contrary to the rules of divine wisdom and justice. And such is the imperfection of man, that there is no perfect government in the world, but that God doth supply all defects and aberrations. 'For the judge of all the world will do right';[2] and in the final judgement will complete all justice, and reward every man according to his works, so that nothing in any person, man or angel, but shall be judged.

5.

This is power in general, and may be distinguished many ways, as into the power of God, or of angels, or of men. Here we speak of the power of men, which is the power of a father, or a master, or an officer of peace or war by sea or land. Again, it's civil, ecclesiastical, and both supreme or subordinate. The subject now in hand is majesty civil, which is the greatest power in a civil community; the power of a sovereign, whereby he is able to bind the whole community and every member thereof. It's an act of the public and universal will, directed by the universal judgement, made effectual by the universal and

---

[2] Gen. 18.25 (read 'earth' for 'world').

general coactive force: and all this is done according to the rules of justice and wisdom. And that the best, wisest and most just, are most fit to govern, to know it the better, we must consider: 1. the principal and several kinds of acts; 2. the qualities of it. The particular acts of this power in one community are numberless, yet all reducible to one. And that is the wise and just government and ordering of the community. Yet this is divided and subdivided by the authors of politics. And the several branches of this power, are called *jura majestatis*, *praerogativa regalia*, &c. The distinction of these rights, are made according to the several acts of majesty conversant about several different objects, and according to the diversification of the objects, is the diversity and difference of these rights. I might here relate both the number and the method of these rights of majesty, as delivered by Angelicus, Bodin, Clapmarius, Grotius, Besoldus, Arnisaeus, and others, if it were either needful or useful. The civilians, and sometimes though seldom, the casuists mention them. Yet hardly two of them agree either in the method, or the number, or the particular names of them.

6.

Yet not to neglect them all, attend how handsomely and briefly *Grotius* reduceth them to a certain order.

> [The supreme government in a city rules by maintaining and repealing general and particular laws; directing the actions of peace and war and the matters of taxation, power and rank; and should through other magistrates and guardians maintain public and private order for the sake of peace.][3]

Yet this is far short of some others, and indeed no ways accurate. The civilians, some of them reduce them into order, according to the several acts of this power, which are [acts of grace or justice.] *Besoldus* [Besold] doth distinguish of majesty, and informs us, [that it is real or personal.] Real [is] in the people, personally [it is] in the prince.[4] He

---

[3] The text carries a diagram which I have not been able to find in any text of any edition of Grotius, father or son. The ramist formulation would in any case be uncharacteristic. The views are general enough to be in agreement with Grotius, and Grotius might be a misprint.

[4] The second edition carries the marginal gloss 'majesty in the people really &c.' Although Lawson derives the political use of the distinction between real and personal from Besold, Julian Franklin has suggested that it was first developed by Hermann Kirchner,

understands by the people the community, and under God, that is the primary subject of it, wherein it virtually resides, and out of which by the constitution it is educed. It hath power to form a state, where there is none, and if after a form once introduced, the order be not good, they may alter it. What the rights of personal majesty is, he tells us; but what those of real sovereignty be, he saith nothing.[5] Majesty so naturally belongs unto the community, that upon a failer [failure] of succession, or a dissolution it devolves to them: and that people is not wise, which parts wholly with it, and absolutely alienates it, as the Romans are said *lege regiâ* to have done, if necessity or some very weighty cause required it not.

7.

We might in this particular expect much from Arnisaeus, who hath composed a whole treatise of this subject, in which he informs, [...] of the name, [and] of the nature of majesty. The name may be given to such as have nothing of the thing, and so be a mere title. [...] It may signify dignity or honour without any power. The nature of it consists in power, which hath several branches, concerning which he relates the opinion and judgement of the Philosopher of historians, of the writers of politics, of lawyers, and in the end delivers his own mind, and reduced them to certain heads: in this manner.

> [The major rights of sovereignty consist in the defence of government and maintenance of law; the minor in the gathering of public money and the appointment of magistrates.][6]

The first division is taken from the inequality of these prerogatives and rights. The second he seems to ground upon these words: 'That

Respublica, 1608, Marburg, 1614 who wrote in the same post-Bodinian public law tradition. See 'Sovereignty and the Mixed Constitution: Bodin and his Critics', in *The Cambridge History of Political Thought, 1450–1700*, ed. J. H. Burns, with the assistance of Mark Goldie, Cambridge University Press, 1991, p. 316.

[5] Christopher Besold, *De magistrate in genere* (Strasburg, 1625), bk. 1, chs. 1, 3–4. Uncharacteristically, this is unfair to Besold, who makes it clear that real majesty establishes fundamental laws and resides in the community. Only in a democracy, suggests Besold, are real and personal majesty as one, 1.1.5, although sometimes he does intimate that the community shares in personal majesty. See Conal Condren, *George Lawson's* Politica *and the English Revolution* (Cambridge University Press, 1989), pp. 100–1.

[6] Henningus Arnisaeus, *De jure majestatis, libri tres* (Frankfurt, 1610 and 1635).

our king may judge us, and go out before us, and fight our battles'
(1 Sam. 8.20); where to judge, seems to signify to govern by laws, and
officers: to go out before us and fight our battles, presupposeth in his
judgement the power of the militia. To these he adds [an]other two,
concerning the ordering of religion, and coining of money. Under
these general heads he reduceth many other particulars: and so proceeds to handle, 1. the greater, 2. the lesser prerogatives severally,
and that largely. This, with the salving of some doubts, and confuting
some errors, is the scheme and substance of the whole treatise,
divided into three several books.

8.

Leaving everyone to his own method, I will, with submission to better
judgement make bold to deliver my own.

> [Majesty is real which is the power to constitute, abolish, alter,
> reform forms of government: and it is personal which concerns
> foreign affairs, peace, war, treaties, embassies; and the regulation
> of religion and human law.]

This, though not exact, may serve the turn, and in some measure
declare the several branches of this great power, which in itself is but
one, yet hath many acts, and the same different, in respect of several
and different objects and subjects. I only mention the chief heads, to
which the rest may be reduced. For the better and more distinct
understanding of it, I will more particularly explain myself.

> [1. Therefore majesty is real or personal.]

Real is in the community, and is greater than personal, which is the
power of a commonwealth already constituted. For, as you have heard
before, this form of a commonwealth is virtually in it before it be
constituted, and their [its] consent is the very foundation of it. And
this consent whether mediate or immediate, tacit or express is so
necessary, that though a people be conquered, yet the victor cannot
govern them as men without their consent. Nay more: when God
designed [designated] immediately, first Saul, then David, yet the
election and consent of the people did concur with and follow upon
the divine designation. As this real majesty is a power to model a state,
so it's always inherent and can never be separated; insomuch, that

when a form of government is dissolved, or there shall be a failer of succession, the power of the sovereign doth devolve unto them by the law of nature, or rather it was always in the people. As this community hath the power of constitution, so it hath of dissolution, when there shall be a just and necessary cause. Hence appears the mistake of Junius, Brutus,[7] Buchanan, Heno and others: when they say, [those who may constitute may set aside] if they meant it of the multitude and body of the subjects, as subjects under a form of government; it can only be true of a community where they have just and necessary cause. Subjects as subjects cannot do it, because of their subjection and obligation, whereas the community as a community is free from any obligation to any particular form, either from the laws of God, natural or positive, or from their own consent or oaths. And though the people in this consideration are bound both by the natural and positive laws of God to constitute a government, if they can, yet they are not bound to this form or that. Another act of this majesty in the community is, when they see it necessary and just, and they have not only power but opportunity to do it, to alter the form of the government. This act as with us, is above the power of a parliament, which may have personal, yet cannot have this real majesty. For a parliament doth necessarily presuppose a form of government already agreed upon, whereby they are made the subject of personal sovereignty. Therefore they cannot alter or take away the cause whereby they have their being, nor can they meddle with the fundamental laws of the constitution, which if it once cease, they cease to be a parliament. If the government be dissolved, and the community yet remains united, the people may make use of such an assembly as a parliament, to alter the former government and constitute a new; but this they cannot do as a parliament, but considered under another notion, as an immediate representative of a community, not of a commonwealth. And thus considered, the assembly may constitute a government, which as a parliament [it] cannot do, which always presupposing the constitution, as such, can act only in and for the administration. That community is wise which doth, and happy which can keep their majesty so due unto

---

[7] The comma after Junius is probably a printing error. If so, Lawson is referring only to Junius Brutus, alleged author of the *Vindiciae contra tyrannos* (Basle, 1579), copies of which are in the Millington *Catalogus* (London, 1681); if not to François Junius, 16th-century religious leader of the Low Countries, possibly his *De politia* (Lyons, 1593), a copy of which was in the More Library. The ambiguity is repeated in ch. 5, see n. 37.

them, as to limit their personal sovereigns, so as not to suffer them to take it from them, and assume it to themselves.

9.

As there is a real, so there is a personal majesty so called, because it's fixed in some persons, who are trusted with the exercise of it, and may, and many times do forfeit to God, and in some cases forfeit it to the community or the people.[8] For, when it is said it may be forfeited to the people, we must understand, that the people is not plebs, the meanest and the lowest rank, and but a part of the community, but the whole community itself as a community, otherwise, we may lay the foundations of all kinds of tumults, confusions, seditions and rebellions. The person or persons trusted with the majesty and power, are bound to seek the good of the whole people, and for that end are they trusted with it, and no otherwise. Hence the saying, [the supreme law is the safety of the people]. The acts of this power, which it hath a right to exercise, are many, and that in respect of those without, or those within the commonwealth. For *agit cum exteris*, it dealeth and acteth with those without. This is not the first, but rather the last kind of acting. It ariseth from the relation which it hath to other states, with which it may have some society, though it hath no dependence upon it. The rules of this acting, as it respects themselves and the states, with whom they deal, are the laws of nations. Yet the particular laws of every several state may determine the rules, according to which it will act with, or against another state. Because one state may wrong or benefit or strengthen and help another, hence it comes to pass that sometimes there is a cause of war. For when by ambassadors or other agents, the state wronged demands satisfaction or justice, and cannot be heard, then there remains no way but to hazard a war, and defer the cause to God to decide it by the issue, which he shall give. Sometimes a state may be unjustly invaded, in which case there is no remedy but a defensive war: 1. To judge and determine of this war, whether offensive or defensive, to have the chief command, to grant commissions, to press men, provide for arms, and money; to denounce and proclaim the war by heralds, belongs unto the

---

[8] The notion of forfeiture here takes on an uncharacteristically aggressive connotation, which is qualified later as only a loss of right, not possession, ch. 5.10.

sovereign, who is trusted with this militia, not only against foreign states, but against seditious and rebellious subjects. 2. After a war begun and continued a peace may be concluded, and this is another act of majesty personal. 3. Because one state may strengthen, help and benefit another, hence leagues of peace and amity; and also for mutual offence or defence, or for protection, or for commerce. Yet none of these are valid by the very law of nations, but as made, concluded, continued by the supreme powers personal. 4. The sovereigns of several states cannot in their own persons, except very rarely, meet together and act personally face to face one with another, neither is it convenient or expedient so to do. Therefore a way and means dictated by the light of nature hath been invented to act by others, who are their deputies and representatives, and these are [called] ambassadors. To send these, whether ordinary or extraordinary, and to give them power and commissions, with instructions and letters credential, that their acts may be valid, is the right of majesty personal. To this head may be referred to sending of heralds and agents or envoys.[9]

10.

This personal majesty and sovereignty acts within the commonwealth, and with the subjects as subjects. With these it acts 1. in matters of religion. For [the magistrate is the guardian of both books], where by magistrate, we must not understand officers, but supreme governors, as the word is taken largely by many authors, especially such as profess theology. For it is the duty, as it is the right of civil sovereigns to order matters of religion, and that in the first place, so far as it tends unto or concerns the peace and happiness of a state, which depends much upon the establishment, profession and practise thereof. As they must order it, so they must not only constantly and sincerely profess, practise it themselves, but as sovereigns protect and defend their subjects in the profession and exercise of the same, so far as their coactive force and sword may justly do it. This should be their first and principal work, which they should do, not only for the good of the people, but their own happiness, success and establishment in the throne. They are not to associate as priests or presbyters, nor

---

[9] Lawson still seems to be commenting on Arnisaeus here, *De jure*, bk. 2, ch. 5.

arrogate the power of making canons, ordination, excommunication, absolution and such like acts, which are purely spiritual; yet they may make civil laws concerning those things, and execute the same, and also ratify by civil acts the ecclesiastical canons; and punish such as shall violate the same. Yet this right doth presuppose the religion, which they establish and maintain to be true and instituted from Heaven. It's true, that the consciences of men are subject only unto God, and to him alone are they answerable for their secret thoughts and opinions, which men can have no certain cognizance of. Yet if they broach errors in religion, and blasphemies, and seek by communicating them by word, or writing to seduce, pervert, infect others, they disturb the peace of the state, offend God, and bring God's judgements from Heaven upon themselves, who are guilty of such sins, and upon the sovereign and the subject of that state where they live. And in this case, though the consciences cannot be forced, yet their estates, persons, lives, are liable to the sword, and, in that respect they may and ought to be punished by the sword of justice. This is so [much] a right of civil sovereigns, that we never read of any state of civilized people without laws concerning religion and the worship of a deity. I confess, this branch of civil power is not rightly placed, nor is the method exact, because it comes in under the heads of legislation and jurisdiction, the matter of both which are religion, men's persons, estates, and lives.

II.

After matters of religion, which are more spiritual and divine, follow such as are temporal and humane. Concerning these we have two acts of majesty: [...] legislation, [and the] execution of laws made, hence these two, *Jura Majestatis*, [...] a right to make laws, [and a] right to execute them. This power of making laws is the principal and most necessary, and doth inseparably adhere unto the sovereign once constituted. It was Jethro's counsel to Moses, which with God's approbation, he followed, to teach the people laws, that all subjects and officers might know their work and duty, and the rule which must direct them in all actions of officers and subjects as such, this was God's order.[10] For, after that he became their sovereign, and the

---

[10] Exod. 18.18–25.

people of Israel his subjects, he proceed[ed] to make laws moral, ceremonial, judicial; yet the personal sovereign hath no power to make fundamental laws concerning the constitution, but only for the administration. This our parliaments, if rightly constituted and duly acting for the public good, I honour as much as any man, may take notice of. Yet I may not presume to teach them, much less correct them. This power is given by the consent of the people in the constitution, who upon their submission become their sovereign's subjects, and are bound thereupon, either to obey his laws once made, or suffer. This is not merely a power to teach and direct them, but to bind them. To this head, are brought the power of repealing, interpreting, altering laws, with dispensations, reservations, naturalizing, granting privileges, conferring honours, founding colleges and corporations, legitimation, restoring the blood tainted, and all acts of grace, as giving immunities, exemptions, tolerations, indulgences, acts of oblivion.

I2.

After legislation follows execution, which in this place is not the execution of the judge's sentence, for that follows as a distinct act of jurisdiction. This right of majesty is of far greater latitude, and reacheth all acts that tend to the execution of the laws, which are in vain, if not put in execution. And because this cannot be done without officers and judgement, therefore this comprehends under it:

[The right of making officers and the administration of justice.]

The making of officers, as without which the laws cannot be put in executions, is the first of these two. By officers, I understand all such as are used by the sovereign, for to put in practise the law, and perform any public act. These may be either ordinary or extraordinary, temporary, or standing; for peace or war, for to deal with foreign states. Such are all dictators, viceroys, regents, treasurers, counsellors, judges, sheriffs, constables, captains and commanders by sea or land, in time of peace or war. To these may be referred heralds, ambassadors, public agents with the rest, which shall be mentioned in the second book of this treatise. And because he is no officer, which hath not some public power, and this he cannot have of and from himself, therefore all officers are made such by the sovereign; who by granting commissions, and other ways derives their power unto them. And as he gives them power, so he may remove them and revoke their power or translate them, or call them to account. To choose, nominate, propose them may be an act of the people or some of them, yet to constitute them and give them their political being, is an act of majesty, either mediate or immediate. And because the personal sovereign and his officers cannot do their duty and discharge their places without sufficient maintenance, therefore in this respect, there is a right to command the purse. For, as they say, he that bears the sword, must have the purse. And, if there be not a sufficient standing revenues and treasury determined in the constitution, the sovereign must have a power to raise monies to defray the public necessary charges. Hence, that *universale et eminens dominium* of majesty in every state, so much mentioned in the authors of politics. The reason of this is clear in the very light of nature, that the people maintain their governors, because the benefit of the government redounds unto them, according to that of the Apostle, 'For this cause pay ye tribute also, for they are God's ministers, attending continually upon this very thing. Render, therefore to all their dues, tribute to whom tribute is due, custom to whom custom' (Rom. 13.6, 7.) It's true, that sovereigns may have their private purse: therefore some distinguish, *inter aerarium et fiscum*. *Aerarium* is the public treasury, which is maintained by tribute, custom and other impositions: and this is to be raised and disposed of by the supreme for the preservation of the public. *Fiscus*, as some tell, is the sovereign's private purse, whereof he may dispose at will and pleasure. This public propriety presupposeth every man's several propriety, and no ways prejudice it. This right is reckoned by some amongst the lesser prerogatives, but there can be no *minora Jura Majestatis* in [the] proper sense. For, because *majestas* is *maxima potestas*, therefore all the essential parts and rights are so too.[11]

13.

The last is the power of jurisdiction, whereby justice is administered: and it's over all persons in all causes both military, civil, and ecclesiastical, so far as they fall under the sovereign's cognizance.

---

[11] *Contra* Arnisaeus, *De jure*, bk. 3.

Under this head I comprehend, not only the power of those acts of judgement, more strictly so called, as convention, discussion, decision of the cause upon evidence of the merit or demerit, but the execution. To which last, may be referred all penalties as well capital as not capital, with dispensations in judgement, suspension of execution, pardons. To this of jurisdiction also belongs all reservations of certain causes: the receiving last appeals, the final determinations, and irrevocable sentences. By virtue of this power, commissions for judicial proceedings, courts, the order of trial from first to last, all calling of assemblies general and provincial, civil and ecclesiastical, are determined. From all this it's evident, that all *Jura Majestatis* may be reduced to the legislative, judicial, and executive power, if we understand judicial and executive in a larger sense, than they are commonly taken.[12] And here it's to be noted, that majesty real is before and above all majesty personal. And by personal majesty or personal sovereign, I do not mean only one single person as a monarch, but all aristocratical and polyarchical sovereigns who are many physically, but considered as one person morally, as jointly invested with one power sovereign.

14.

Thus far concerning the nature of majesty, after which follows some epithets given to majesty by authors, to signify the properties thereof. These are either included in the essence, or flow from it. For [first], it's absolute and so arbitrary, absolute, *soluta legibus*. It cannot be bound by any laws, nor judged, because the sovereign is the lawgiver himself, and the fountain of jurisdiction. He may bind himself by oath to govern, and judge according to the laws, not to be governed or judged by the laws. Yet no sovereign personal is free from the obligation of the natural and positive laws of God in force: and how far he is inferior to the real sovereign, who is subject to the same laws, I will not here discuss. [Second] it's universal, not only in respect of all acts of government, but of all persons within that territory. For it must be

---

[12] The distinction between legislative, judicial and executive, so often associated with Montesquieu, was quite familiar to 17th-century writers, e.g. John Sadler, *The Rights of the Kingdom* (London, 1649), pp. 86–7. According to Brian Tierney, it dates back to the Middle Ages; see his *Religion, Law and the Growth of Constitutional Thought, 1150–1650* (Cambridge University Press, 1982), p. 45.

coadequate to the whole body, which it must act and animate, it's neither greater nor less. No persons, things or actions within, can be exempted from this power, nor can it extend to any thing, person, action without, but *per accidens*. [Third] it's supreme, not in respect of God, nor of the power of other states, but in respect of the power of fathers, masters, officers, corporations, and societies within every several state. For by virtue of majesty it is that sovereigns are equal in respect of themselves, superiors in respect of their subjects; and inferiors unto God, whose servants and subjects they are, trusted with a particle of his power, and accountable unto him. [Fourth] it's independent (yet not in respect of God) upon whom all sovereigns do not only chiefly but wholly depend, but in respect of all subordinate powers within, but coadequate to them without. For all power civil within the territory is derived from majesty. Fiduciary princes therefore as such are not sovereigns, though they may have the title of sovereignty; yet a sovereign may be fiduciary for some part of a country within, and part of the dominions of another sovereign. Neither can the chief magistrate of a commonwealth, trusted at certain times with the general exercise of the power be such. Protection and vassalage are conceived by some not to destroy independency, neither doth confederation. For though the League between several states, as in Switzerland, and the United Netherland Provinces may be strict, and commissioners may be made and trusted with great power in things, which concern the several states jointly (such the States-General of the Low Countries be); yet this is thought to be no diminution of majesty.[13] For it remains entire in the several republics. [Fifth] it's indivisible, for though it hath several branches, which may be distinguished, yet they cannot be separated. For if you take away but one, much more if you take away more, you make it imperfect and essentially defective, and insufficient to govern. For as in philosophy, [essence is indivisible: so in politics sovereignty is indivisible and the rights of sovereignty inseparable from it]. As these rights are indivisible in respect of themselves, so they are in respect of the subject. For divide and separate some of them, even but one from the sovereign, he is an imperfect sovereign, take away all he ceaseth to be a sovereign. Again, the subject of majesty and of all the rights and

---

[13] Lawson is here alluding to major themes of continental public law theory to be found in writers like Arnisaeus, Besold and Althusius, *Politica methodica digesta* (Herborn, 1614), ed. C.J. Friedrich (Cambridge, Mass., Harvard University Press, 1982).

parts thereof must be only one, either physically or morally. If you divide the subject, you destroy them. For if in this commonwealth we give part of these to the king, part to the peers, part to the commons, we make it a Babel and destructive of itself. For, suppose the king have the militia to himself, he may command the purse, make void the laws, revoke judgements, reject parliaments, and none can hinder him, because neither peers nor commons have any right to the sword whereby to defend themselves. Therefore little need is to be given to that book, or bitter invective, entitled *Elenchus motuum nuperorum*, which informs from the lawyers, if we may believe him, that these sovereign rights were thus divided.[14] [Sixth] from this, that it's indivisible follows it, that it is incommunicable. For, to whomsoever they are communicated, they cease to be subjects, and the sovereign to be a complete sovereign, and this communication tends to the dissolution of the government. [Seventh] it's perpetual, that is, fixed in a certain subject, to continue in the same according to the fundamental laws of constitution. Therefore the temporary or occasional power, though very great of a dictator or regent, or protector, who are but trusted with it for a time in extraordinary cases, and upon occasion, cannot be majesty when there is an interregnum, or suspension of the government, by reason of sedition, faction, rebellion, civil war or some other cause, it's good and expedient for the safety of a state, to set up some extraordinary governor or governors, trusted for a time with transcendent power, till the state disturbed and not capable of any union be settled; which done, that power doth cease, and majesty is fixed in his proper, primary and constant subject, that the government may run in the old channel, except they intend to make an alteration of the constitution.

15.

There is another kind of personal majesty inferior to and different from the former. We find it in some princes of Europe, as in the

---

[14] G. Bate, *Elenchus motuum nuperorum in Anglia* (Edinburgh, 1650, 1658), republished and extended during the Restoration. A translation (as *A Short Narrative of the Late Troubles in England*) was printed in 1902, introduction by Edward Almack (London, Robinson). See pp. 16–17 for the notion of mixed monarchy Lawson is attacking. Such a widespread notion is intimated in Sir John Fortescue, *De laudibus legum Angliae*, printed in London, 1567, with English translation by R. Mulcaster, later available in a version edited by John Selden. Lawson shows more respect for Fortescue than for Bate.

Emperor of Germany, the kings of Denmark, Sweden, Poland and England. For our kings had not only the title of majesty, but some power with the title. For in the intervals of parliament, he was sovereign alone, and all and every one, yea the greatest were his subjects. He called and summoned parliaments, made all officers by sea and land, sent and received ambassadors, conferred all honours, the subjects swore allegiance to him. His dignity was eminent, his state great, and so many advantages he had, that if he should have used them all, he might easily have undone his subjects, and so have undone himself. Yet he had not the power of the purse. He was sworn to corroborate the just laws and customs, which the people had chosen. In the parliament he made a third party, yet so, that neither in acts of laws or judgement, could he do anything without the peers and commons, and as Sir Roger Owen in his manuscript observes together with them, he was greater than himself.[15] Yet, as kings have sometimes curbed parliaments, so parliaments have kings, and disposed of the militia, the navy, the ports, the chief offices. Nay, they have sometimes judged kings, accusing them of acting against the fundamental constitution, and challenging such power as tended to the dissolution of the same, and have deposed them. But of this particular something may be said hereafter [chs. 5, 8, 15]. These kinds of sovereigns have so much power, whether more or less, as the constitution gives them, yet it will be a difficult thing to keep them within their bounds.

CHAPTER 5

Of the manner how civil power is acquired

I.

What the nature of power in general, and majesty civil is, hath been declared. The next thing to be considered, is the subject who from it is denominated a sovereign, and we must enquire first, how this power is acquired; [and then] how disposed in a certain subject. As for the acquisition it's certain, man as man, or as a member of a community, cannot have it from himself, but it must be communi-

---

[15] I have failed to trace this manuscript; for Owen see Biographical notes.

cated to him from God, who being the universal sovereign is the
fountain and original of it, and derives some part of it unto man, and a
greater measure unto mortal sovereigns than other men. Yet he doth
not this immediately, but mediately for the most part. It's extrinsical,
and comes [from elsewhere], not only unto men but angels. A
paternal power, which is more natural, is acquired by generation,
though sometimes by adoption. This generation from divine benedic-
tion is the seminary of all societies, which as societies and communities may be so disposed and complete, as virtually to contain in them a
power of a commonwealth, and by a general consent constitute an
actual sovereign. The sovereign before he was made such, was not
invested with majesty, but it was extrinsical unto him. And here that
distinction between the power itself, the designation of the persons
governing, and the form of government is worthy taking notice of.
The designation of the persons, and the form of government is from
God, leaving man at liberty, but not so the power, which is more from
him than the other two. Though the parties justly possessed of power,
may be thought to have the propriety of it, yet they have not any: for,
let it be never so firmly conveyed upon them by designation and
submission, yet they are but trusted with it. Princes tell us, they hold
their crowns and kingdoms, *per Deum et gladium*. If they mean that
they derive their power from God, so as that they neither receive, nor
hold it from the bishops of Rome, or the emperor, or any other
mortals, it may be true; yet they have their power so from God, that
they are invested with it by human designation. As for their sword, it
may by a conquest make way for a government, but it cannot constitute it. *The fundamental charter of all civil majesty, is the fifth commandment*, taken in a large sense, and understood by other Scriptures,
which speak more expressly and distinctly of civil government. In this
commandment, including much more by analogy than is expressed,
we may observe [1.] that there is a power of superiority and excellency, as in fathers, so in the princes and rulers of the world, and that
from God, who made them men, fathers, princes. 2. That all government should be paternal. Not that the first-born of the most ancient
family in every tribe, kindred, nation, should be a sovereign; for that
we seldom find, but that they should as fathers love their subjects, and
seek their good, and tender them as fathers do their children.[1] 3. That

---

[1] Aristotle, *Politics*, 1259b, citing Homer; Cicero, *De republica*, 1.35.54, expressed as a
characteristic of kings, not as an injunction.

by virtue of God's command, so soon as they are actually governors, honour and subjection are due unto them. 4. That all vicinities, as far as they are able, ought first to associate, and then establish an order of government and observe it, that their days may be long in the land, wherein God hath placed them, and that it may go well with them.

2.

But to return to the acquisition of power, the designation of persons, as it is from man, so it is from God, who ruleth in the kingdoms of the world, and sets up one and puts down another, so that this power may be communicated from him, and so acquired by man, that it may be taken away, and lost again. [. . .][2]

[*The extraordinary acquisition of power through divine dispensation*]

Power may first be acquired, and that several ways, as justly or unjustly, in an extraordinary or ordinary manner. This extraordinary way, and more immediate from God we find in Scripture. For thus Moses, Joshua, and many of the judges, Saul, David, Jeroboam, Jehu were designed to their places of government. Some of those, as Saul, David, Jehu were anointed by God's appointment, and the sceptre entailed upon David's family in the kingdom of Judah. Yet two[3] things are remarkable in the designation of Saul and David. 1. That after the divine unction the people assemble[d], and in a general assembly by their votes, freely chose them, and voluntarily submit[ted], and without election they could not actually and effectually reign. This doth signify, that there can be no orderly or lasting government without consent tacit or express of the people: for men must be governed as rational and free, for such they are as men. This was the manner of investing the kings of England. For at the coronation amongst other things this is done. The King being before them, one doth ask the people, 'Will you have this man to be King, or reign over you?' This is more fully expressed in the form of [the] coronation [oath], which at present I have not by me, and doth signify, that they should have the voluntary consent of the people. 2. That if we may

---

[2] The text carries a large ramist diagram which has been omitted here as its principal headings are repeated separately. These have been abbreviated slightly.
[3] Under the first are three numbered points.

believe Fortescue, the kings of England had not [regal power but political, issuing from the people].[4] 3. That they did not derive that power from the first investiture as hereditary, but in another way. The second thing to be noted is that those kings thus designed of God, were bound to govern according to the moral, judicial, ceremonial laws of God. This implies that no princes should govern by an arbitrary power, but according to laws, and them so wise, so just, as that they may be truly said, to be rather the laws of God than of men.

3.

[*Ordinary just acquisition of power through election or just war*]

God doth seldom use this extraordinary and more immediate designation; for his usual way is by ordinary providence, and that first in the beginning and constitution of a government, the foundation whereof may be laid in peace or war. In peace, power is acquired by a free election of a sovereign, and singling out some person or persons, to whom they will submit themselves. Sometimes it is determined, that all jointly should be sovereign, and every single person a subject. This is the best, most just, and the wisest way, and most agreeable to man as a rational creature.[5] The parties, whether one or more, before their designation had no civil power at all, but upon the designation, when they are once agreed upon, declared and submitted unto, they must by divine institution of necessity have so much power as is necessary for the government and general good of the people. This power which is now acquired, is *majestas*, and is more from God than man: because it is a power to do such things as God commands, or such as are not contrary to his will. In the first modelling of a state, they may either compose one of their own invention, or take example from some other commonwealth, and take the whole or some part and make it their own. Thus the foundation of the Roman state was first laid by Romulus, who in his work followed the Greeks in many things, as Halicarnassus tells us, *Antiq. Rom. lib.* 2.[6] In this case, whatsoever

[4] Sir John Fortescue, *De laudibus legum Angliae* (London, 1567), 9, 13; trans. R. Mulcaster (1567). See also below, ch. 8.22, where Lawson paraphrases slightly differently.
[5] Cf. Aristotle, *Politics*, 1284a. Lawson later backs away from this participatory enthusiasm.
[6] Dionysius of Halicarnassus, *Roman Antiquities*, bk. 2.13–14, cf. 16, 17 for contrasts between the Greeks and Romulus.

kind of state is constituted, there must be some invested with majesty personal, which by the free election and voluntary submission of the parties who are free, and have power to make this election and submission, it is communicated, and so acquired. But if upon a victory obtained by a just and necessary war, a people is reduced under the power of the party conquering, and they upon certain terms submit, the power is acquired by the sword, and their voluntary submission, which they would not have made, if they had not been conquered. And they who formerly were a free people, and would have chosen another, or continued under their own personal sovereign, if before the war they were under a form of government, do submit, because neither they nor their sovereign can protect them. And if they be brought so low that they must either subject themselves or do worse, or perish, they willingly come under the protection of the conqueror, if he be willing to protect them, and take them as his subjects. Majesty acquired in this manner for the most part, is more despotical and absolute. And that princes are divested of majesty and people of liberty, and fall under the power of strangers: it's from the just judgement of God, punishing them for their crimes.[7] And this is a most common title of most sovereigns in the world. Yet it may be said, that the inward motives of the conquerors of the earth are ambition, or covetousness, or cruelty, therefore this kind of title is not good. The answer is that, in respect of any one, or more of all these motives it's unjust. Yet, if we consider this title as given by God, in making them victorious, and rewarding them for the execution of justice, which they seldom think upon, and also the consent of the people and their submission, when they can do no better, it's certainly just. What strange instincts from Heaven, what commands from God, what suggestions from angels or God's messengers, or prophets, conquerors might have we know not. Jehu was anointed and designed by God to cut off Ahab's family, and had a promise afterward. Judah also and many nations were persuaded, and in some sort commanded by the prophet Jeremy, as sent from God to submit unto the King of Babylon, and come under his protection.[8]

---

[7] An echo of Henry de Bracton, see *De legibus et consuetudinibus Angliae*, 'addicio de cartis', ed. G. E. Woodbine (Cambridge, Mass., Harvard University Press, 1968).
[8] 2 Kgs. 10; Jer. 38.

4.

[The continuation of sovereign power through free or restricted election and hereditary succession]

After a title is once established by the fundamental charter, and the first investiture, care is taken how this title may be continued, that so not only the present, but the future sovereign and subject of personal majesty may be determined, and not only the state, but the sovereign thereof may become perpetual and immortal. This can no way be done but by succession, and this depends upon election at least of the first constitutors of the state, which determines the successive sovereigns to acquire their title by election, or birth, or both. If by election only, that many times is left free to the electors, to choose out of what family or country they please. Thus the Roman and also the German emperors and the kings of Poland, acquire and receive their power. Sometimes the election is confined to a family or line. In this respect the title is said to be hereditary, which is not to be understood, as though the personal sovereigns were absolute proprietaries of the crown, or had power of alienation, but because they are like those, who in civil law are called *heredes sui* heirs natural, by law and birth who succeed into, and by birth acquire the right which their predecessors justly had. This succession is sometimes tied to the males, as in France; sometimes is indifferent to male or female children. Thus it is in England, where the kings and queens are said to have their heirs: which, if we may believe the great lawyer Sir Edward Coke upon *Magna Charta*, are nothing but the successors; for heirs, saith he, are successors.[9] Yet surely he means successors not only by election, but blood. In this kind of succession, sometimes the present sovereigns, if they have children, may determine and declare, which of them shall succeed them. Thus David chose Solomon.[10] Sometimes it's otherwise, because by the constituion it's entailed upon the first-born or next of blood. This seems to be the ancient right and custom of this nation. This may be the reason, why King Henry VIII though he took upon him much of an absolute prince, would not presume of himself to define his successor, but desire[d] an

[9] Sir Edward Coke, *The Second Part of the Institutes of the Laws of England* (1642 edn.), p. 7.
[10] 1 Kgs. 1.37, 43.

act to be made in parliament for to enable him by will to dispose of the Crown. Yet such an act could not make void the election used at the coronation, which hath something of the constitution in it, though it was made a mere formality.

5.

[The unjust acquisition of power, usurpation, by grievous injury, through money,[11] *murder, or in some other way]*

As power may be justly so it may be unjustly acquired, and this is usually called usurpation, which is the taking and keeping possession of that which is not our own, or which we have no right unto. It's true that in civil law it's defined to be *praepossessio juris controversi*. Yet in this manner of usurpation, that right is seldom doubtful, but for the most part clear enough. The power is always good, because from God, and the act thereof, which is government, is good, yet the manner of acquiring may be bad. And it's observable, that many who have ill acquired, have well used their power.[12] It's generally held, that usurped right and power is no right or power, because it's not in his proper subject. Therefore it's conceived, that *tyrannus in titulo* (such every usurper is said to be) cannot command and bind the people; nor do any acts of government which is valid, and may justly be removed before the people acknowledge him, or swear fealty to him. And many think it unlawful to submit unto or act under a usurped power. Sometimes it may be so, yet there are cases, when we may, nay we must submit and act too. If Christians under the heathen emperors had stood upon such terms as some do in our days, their condition had been far worse than it was. For, though they liked not usurpation, and the cursed means whereby many acquired their power, yet this was their principle, ['It is of no great matter under which rule a man

---

[11] The text has 'pecunia', which, though not explicitly discussed, would in context seem to embrace extortion, bribery, peculation and robbery.

[12] Lawson here introduces the distinction between tyranny by title and by rule. It is associated with the medieval jurist Bartolus of Saxoferato and the Florentine humanist Coluccio Salutati. See e.g. Salutati, *De tyrannia* (1400), trans. E. Emerton, *Humanism and Tyranny* (Cambridge, Mass., Harvard University Press, 1925, reprinted 1964). Lawson, however, may be following more immediately Henningus Arnisaeus, *De auctoritate principum* (Strasburg, 1635), ch. 4, sects. 11–12; or even monarchomach literature.

lives who is soon to die, if those ruling do not force him either to impiety or iniquity.']¹³ Blood, bribery, treason, rebellion, unjust invasions, they abhorred as abominable, and detested them as unfit means to ascend an imperial throne. Yet it was not in their power to dispossess them once possessed, and to establish better. They knew God had reserved this unto himself. Neither did they think, that by submitting unto their power, though unjustly gotten, yet justly exercised, that they were guilty of their sinful and unjust manner of usurpation. Concerning this unjust acquisition of personal majesty, many things may be observed. [First] there are few titles now, especially such as are successive in a line, which did not at first begin in usurpation. [Second] that the power itself with the just exercise thereof, is a different thing from the manner of acquiring it. [Third] that one that hath the right in reversion may unjustly prepossess it: and with us, as the lawyers tell us, if the heir apparently by murder or some other way remove the present just sovereign; yet so soon as he is possessed of the crown, he cannot be questioned, an indemnity presently follows upon the possession. Richard III is called an usurper, and was so at the first, yet his laws and judgements, and other acts of government were, and are judged valid, after the parliaments received him. Henry VII [could not] be acquitted from usurpation till the parliament acknowledged him. Neither his victory nor marriage with the right heir could give him a good title: though this might conduce to his quiet possession. He did never stand upon that marriage as the foundation of his right unto the crown; for he knew well enough, that if that had been his best and only title, that though it might make the power good unto his children, yet while she was living¹⁴ he must hold the crown in her right, not in his own, and if she died before him, it was lost. [Fourth] many princes have invented oaths for to secure not only the form of government but the crown unto their own posterity and family. And here it's to be considered, whether these oaths do not necessarily presuppose a higher obligation of fidelity, not only unto God but their own native country, to which they are bound to be faithful under any form of government or personal sovereign what-

---

¹³ St Augustine, *The City of God*, bk. 5, ch. 17. The text carries the misprinted reference *Aust. de l.D.* Lawson, working presumably from memory, slightly misquotes the original, rhetorical question, 'What matters it under whose rule a dying man lives if those who rule force him not to impiety and iniquity?'
¹⁴ Elizabeth, d. 1502/3, daughter of Edward IV.

soever. If their present allegiance cannot stand with this universal good, it's surely unlawful and unjust. For the good of the whole is to be preferred before the good of a part: and we are bound to love the whole body of the community more than any family, or some particular persons.[15] Again, it may prove sometimes impossible to be actually faithful and perform our oaths, either to the persons to whom they are taken, or their heirs and successors, and then it will be unreasonable. [Fifth] we must distinguish between the human positive laws and constitutions, and the laws and rules of divine providence: for that may be usurpation in respect of the former, which is a just possession in respect of the latter. [Sixth] as for removing a usurper, or refusing to submit unto him, or act under him, we must consider [...] how far God hath any hand in dispossessing one and giving possession to another, least [lest] we be found to resist God; [also] what means we resolve upon to remove and reject the usurper, and whether the remedy will not be worse than the disease. [And we must consider] what may be the bad and miserable consequences of this refusal of submission and acting. [Yet] some will say, we will live peaceably and not meddle, neither will we own the present power nor act against it. But do such think, that any person or persons, which have the sword in their hands, to which their lives and estates are subject, will suffer men within the bowels of the state to be neuters, and yet give them protection?[16] [Seventh] such as justly acquire their power at the first may be the greatest usurpers, because they will challenge more power, than either God will, or man can give: or more than by constitution is due, or the necessity of the state and public good require. [Eighth] God may justly give to Nebuchadnezzar, Alexander that power, which they did unjustly seek, and this for reasons best known unto himself; as for executing his judgements upon other nations for their sins: when he hath once given, the possession continued is lawful. [Ninth] it's a heavy judgement upon a people, when the title to personal majesty is doubtful and liable to usurpation, as it often falls out upon a dissolution, civil wars, a failer [failure] of

---

[15] From here until the end of the section Lawson is probably rehearsing the substance of his lost engagement tract (see also ch. 15), the existence of which, in MS, is attested by Richard Baxter, *Reliquiae Baxterianae*, ed. Matthew Sylvester (London, 1696), bk. 1, p. 107.

[16] Cf. Anthony Ascham, *A Discourse Wherein is Examined what is particularly Lawfull During the Confusions and Revolutions of Government* (London, 1648), p. 51. 'Neuter' was a key term in the Engagement controversy.

succession, which is certain and clear, or in other cases. And happy is that people, whose nobles shall be of themselves, and their governors shall proceed out of the midst of them (Jer. 30.21). And also when these governors enter quietly, according to the laws of God and the just constitution of men.

6.

[Loss of power through natural causes, death, failure of succession, and through moral ones, voluntary resignation, desertion and violent invasion]

As power may be acquired, and one that had it not may have it, so it may be lost and he that was possessed of it may be dispossessed, for it is no inseparable adjunct to any person or persons. And it's God's will it should be so. Therefore crowns and sceptres with imperial power, cannot be so entailed, or anyways made sure by any constitutions of man as not to be cut off from any families or persons. They are like unto estates, which for want of heirs or the extinction of families, or some other ways may pass to strangers. It may be lost in a way which is orderly and not from any unjust cause. And that first naturally upon the death of the sovereign or a failer of succession. For all sovereigns especially personal, are mortal, and as they live and reign, so they die and lay aside their majesty, and leave it unto others. This is a common and a usual way. And let no man take up a crown but with a purpose to lay it down, when it shall please God to require it: only the crown of Heavenly glory shall abide upon our heads for ever. Death itself shall never be able to shake it off, it fits too close. Therefore, it were wisdom for to aim at an eternal kingdom; for that's God's command, as it is his promise to give it to them that seek it. Ambition is base and far below the excellency of that noble creature, which was made and redeemed for eternity. Yet there is old catching at these earthly crowns, which are a bait wherewith the most noble spirits are taken. This was Satan's reserve and last temptation, wherewith he thought to overcome our Saviour.[17] As persons, so families may fail, and the supreme power may return unto a community, which then hath liberty either to alter the form of government, or if they retain the former model, to design another sovereign, and the same eligible either at random with a latitude, or in a certain family.

[17] Matt. 4.8–10; Luke 4.6–7.

7.

This is a natural way of losing this power, though always directed by a divine special providence. There is another way, and the same moral, and voluntary, as by [...] resignation [or] desertion. For in some cases a sovereign may resign his power to another even in his lifetime. Thus Charles V resigned his hereditary dominions unto Philip I of Spain, and others have done the like. Some desert the charge either to take a better or a greater, as the Duke of Anjou deserted Poland to succeed his brother in the kingdom of France,[18] or out of discontent, or upon some other cause. And usually in a vacancy, either upon the issue failing, or a desertion there follows a competition amongst pretenders. For as they say, no man that hath an estate can want heirs: so in this case there will be pretenders, and many times competitors. Thus it fell out in Portugal upon the death of Sebastian and Henry the Cardinal his uncle. For Anthony's legitimation could do him little good, his sword was not long enough; the King of Spain's was.[19] Therefore his title, though not the best, was yet the strongest and most effectual. As this power may be lost, or rather voluntarily laid aside, so it may be violently invaded by a just war, either of the people defending themselves, and their rights unjustly denied them or taken from them, which according to the fundamental constitution, they may and ought to maintain even against a personal sovereign; though not as their sovereign, but as one that usurps greater power than is due unto him, and doing the people wrong.[20] For some tell us, that is no right which may not be defended. The final issue of such a war may be the overthrow of the sovereign and his party, and a deposing of him, or a rejection, or death, with the exclusion of his family. Whether these things be done justly or no, must be known by the laws of God written or natural, and the laws of the constitution of that state, where any such thing is done. Some of our barons' wars seem to be reducible to this case: as likewise the late difference between King and Parliament and the Civil War following thereupon. Yet even in that difference, if the Lords and Commons have [a partial power] and participate the power jointly with the King, then they seem to have the

---

[18] Henry III (1574–89).

[19] Sebastian (1557–78), killed fighting the Moors, succeeded by his great-uncle, Cardinal Henry, and the last of the Avis line. Philip II of Spain became king by force in 1581.

[20] The second edition carries the marginal gloss 'subjects may defend their rights'.

advantage: because, according to their own profession, the war being
undertaken by them in their own just and necessary defence, and
ending in a clear conquest of the King, this not only preserved their
own rights; but if we may believe Grotius, and the case be, as he puts
it, or the same with his, the King plainly lost his right.[21] Yet if it was a
war between sovereign and subject as such, it was rebellion on the
subjects' part, and so the King could lose no right. But the war was
said to be, as some express it, between the King and Parliament: yet
the Parliament declared they fought for King and Parliament. And so
the King as King was not the enemy, yet it fell out that the person who
was King was conquered and confined, and in the end put to death.
But in these difficult points, it's not easy either to have true and
perfect information, or if we had, to meet with an impartial judge.
Sovereignty may be taken away by a foreign invasion, upon a just war,
whether defensive or offensive. For, if the unjust party be conquered,
the right of sovereignty is lost, and this is a usual case.

8.

[*Irregular loss of power by dissolution or maladministration*]

The dissolution of a state, must needs destroy and take away all
personal majesty. And except this dissolution be from a mutual consent of all parties, sovereign and subject for to erect a better frame; it
must needs be inordinate or disorderly. And if the personal sovereign
be the cause and begin this dissolution without just reason, he must
needs forfeit. For, whosoever holds any power from the constitution,
and yet acts against it, he must needs lose. And if he once lose his
power, and through his own default, his subjects are freed from their
allegiance. This was the reason why the Parliament passed so high a
judgement upon the King.

> For, upon his withdrawing from Parliament, refusing to return,
> and setting up his standard, both the Houses proceeded jointly
> together in adjudging it treason against the state, or kingdom, in
> deserting his Parliament, betraying his trust and people, setting
> up his standard, and levying war against the Parliament and
> kingdom, that is against his own peace, crown and dignity.[22]

[21] Hugo Grotius, *De jure belli ac pacis, libri tres* (Paris, 1625), bk. 1, ch. 4, on internal wars.
[22] John Sadler, *The Rights of the Kingdom* (London, 1649), p. 82 (irregular pagination).

Thus the author of *The Rights of the Kingdom*. This he takes to be peremptory sentence, and that the latter general's commission for to take the King was a strong *capias ut legatum*. These things are out of and beyond my sphere. Yet it's certain, that so far as the King's proceedings were against the fundamental constitution, so far they tended to a dissolution and a forfeit of the power regal. And when the militia and the array did so fearfully clash and dash the people in pieces, there was a plain dissolution of the government for the present. And upon a victory followed an act of alteration and not only the present sovereign was dispossessed, [first] by a judgement, then by death, but his family disinherited, and continues so to this day. Whatsoever men in this particular have done, yet God hath judged justly. And it deeply concerns that family seriously to consider what the guilt is, for which God hath so severely punished them. There is another cause whereby, and for which sovereignty is often lost; and that is *maladministratum*. For as wisdom, justice, judgement are the establishment of the throne, and that by virtue of God's institution and promise: so is negligence, imprudence, injustice, oppression, and other such like sins, a cause of dethroning and divesting the governors and princes of the world. For these offend God, abuse the power wherewith they are but trusted, provoke the people. Therefore, God either stirs up their own people against them, or makes use of foreign power to invade them, and delivers them into their hands. The highest degree of this ill administration is called tyranny, and such wicked governors are said to be *Tyranni in exercitio*. For though their title may be good, yet their power is so abused, as that they for the most part are worse and more wicked than usurpers. These in their administration violate both the written and natural laws of God, the law of nations, the law of the constitution of that state, where they govern, and the laws of justice and equity: the violation of all which tend directly to the ruin of the commonwealth.[23] Arnisaeus, who together with Bodin, is so much for absolute princes, doth confess that such a tyrant doth *exidere jure suo et si haereditario*.[24] And there is great reason for it: because his manner of administration is against the

---

[23] It may be significant that Lawson does not directly associate Charles with this accusation but rather alludes to him and his family as tending to dissolve the commonwealth. For Lawson, quite conventionally, *tyranni in exercitio* evokes the rhetoric of armed rising which he is at pains to keep at a distance from the Civil War.

[24] Arnisaeus, *De auctoritate* (?), ch. 4; see below, ch. 15.

very fundamental rules, and the very end of all government. For God never did, man never can give any power to be unjust.

9.

Before I conclude this chapter, the reader must know, that this scheme of acquisition and amission of power is not exact. [First], for there may be more ways both of acquiring and keeping, as also of losing power: and to this head may be reduced those *arcana imperii et dominationis*, handled more at large by Clapmarius and Angelius,[25] whereof some are prudential rules for the acquisition, and conservation of the form of government, and also for the continuance of power in the hands of the persons or families possessed of it. Some of them are but sophisms of state, used too much by many statesmen in these days, who separate religion and policy to their own ruin. For as the learned Fitzherbert hath made it evident, God will never prosper such courses.[26] Hitherto also might be referred the causes of corruption, conversion and subversion of states. Whereof something shall be said in the chapter of disposition [ch. 8].

[Second] the right may be lost, and the possession continue, or the possession may be lost, and the right may remain for a time.

[Third] that a bare title is no power. For as the sword in possession without wisdom and justice is insufficient, so wisdom and justice with a title without the sword cannot actually govern: because it cannot protect and punish.

[Fourth] no man can acquire and receive any power except God give it, nor keep it any longer than God is willing to continue it. For he hath reserved it in his own hands to dispose of it to whom, and how long, and in what measure and manner he pleaseth: yet he seldom doth communicate it immediately, or in an extraordinary way. He gives it for the most part mediately by man to man. Therefore that *sovereigns hold their crowns from God, and that they are supreme next under God* admits of some limitation and explication, otherwise it may prove an error. For I am sure few of them receive their sovereignty immedi-

---

[25] Arnaldus Clapmarius, *De arcanis rerumpublicarum, libri sex* (Frankfurt, 1611); Nicholaus Angelius?, 16th-century commentator on Cicero.

[26] Thomas Fitzherbert, *An sit utilitas in scelere* (Rome, 1610); and *A Treatise concerning Policy and Religion* (Douai, 1615), for explicit attacks on Machiavellian policy.

ately from God as Saul or David did.[27] The immediate foundation of
it is some human constitution and agreement made, not immediately
by God, but men. This, to such as understand the fundamental laws
of states, is clear enough.

[Fifth] the greatest power of any mortal man is but very little, and
he is but trusted with it for a while: and such is his frailty, that he
cannot well manage that little which is committed to him. Therefore
all defects of human government are supplied by the universal and
eternal King, who punisheth all offences, not punished by man, and
rights all wrongs, not righted and rightly judged by the rulers of the
world. And he makes use of angels, men, armies, all creatures to
execute his righteous judgements.

[Sixth] majesty hangs very loosely upon such as do profess it, they
have no strong hold of it. It's easily separable from man, and man
from it, and it's more easily lost than acquired, and acquired many
times more easily than kept. Therefore it is that a sceptre is so easily
turned to a spade, and a spade unto a sceptre.

[Seventh] here is the proper place to examine, [...] whether
majesty can be conferred upon any person or persons upon condition;
or [...] whether once conferred and received, it can be forfeited. Not
to be conditionally given and received; not to be liable to forfeiture,
are not *Jura Majestatis*, as Mr. Hobbes improperly calls them,[28] but if
they anyways agree to majesty (as it will be hard to prove they do) they
are rather adjuncts than anything else. For the first, whether they be
given upon condition or no, cannot be well determined, except we
distinguish of this power as given by God, and as given by man; [...]
between majesty real and personal; [...] between personal of the first,
and of the second degree; [and] between the sovereign, materially and
formally considered.[29] [...] God never gave any power or majesty real
or personal but upon condition, [...] that the receiver use it well; [...]
that he may take it away at will and pleasure. [...] Real majesty cannot
by man be given upon condition to a community as free, and such in
proper sense. [...] A community may give personal majesty upon
condition: and by the laws of God cannot give it otherwise. And the

[27] 1 Sam. 9.16.
[28] Hobbes, *Leviathan* (London, 1651), pt. 2.18; cf. Lawson, *An Examination of the Political part of Mr. Hobbs, His Leviathan* (London, 1657), pp. 20–1.
[29] That is, as subject-matter and as definition.

condition is, that they use it well and for the good of the people, according to the eternal laws of divine wisdom and justice; for that very end for which God ordained all higher powers and civil government. And no good sovereign will desire it upon any other terms. Hence the oaths solemnly administered to the sovereigns of the world: which the people impose upon them, not as subjects, but as members of a free community, and this imposing refers to the first constitution and the fundamental law of government. This is clear enough in the first institution of a King in England, as *The Mirrour* tells us.[30] The conqueror received the crown upon the same terms. And some good lawyers inform us, that before the king had taken his oath to the people, he could not require an oath of allegiance from them. Therefore Sir Edward Coke must be warily understood, when he makes the coronation but a formality. For though the setting of the crown upon their heads, which is but a sign of dignity and honour, be but a ceremony, yet the matter of his oath is essential to the making of him king; and if that, being the substance of the fundamental contract, be not presupposed, as first consented unto, he cannot be a king. Bracton, who advanceth our kings, as high as any ancient lawyer, saith,

> [Moreover, the king himself should not be under man, but under God and the law, because law makes the king. Therefore the king is to assign to the law that which the law assigns to him, namely dominion and power. For there is no king whenever will dominates, not law.][31]

And here he seems to understand, not only the law of constitution but administration. That he means the latter is plain, when he saith, ['There should be no one in his kingdom greater than him in the exercise of legal right.'] He formerly asserted that ['The king has no equal in his realm,'][32] which is true in respect of every single person, otherwise we know the king may be judged. With this agrees that of *The Mirrour*, that it was the great abusion [perversion] of all, to say,

---

[30] Andrew Horne, *Speculum justiciarorum*, trans. 1642 as *The Mirrour of Justices* (London), ch. 1.2.

[31] Henry de Bracton, *De legibus et consuetudinibus*, 5.2, fol. 5b, p. 33. I am following a translation by Cary J. Nederman. The passage was much cited in the 17th century. See generally, Cary J. Nederman, 'Bracton on Kingship: The Idea of Sovereignty and Bractonian Political Thought', *Political Science*, 40: 1 (1988), pp. 49–66.

[32] Bracton, *De legibus et consuetudinibus*, p. 33.

the king was above the laws, to which he ought to be subject. And we know who makes these laws. Arnisaeus, who is so zealous for absolute monarchs, confesseth with the Philosopher, that [where the laws are predominant], the king cannot be absolute. He observeth three kinds of oaths which princes take: The [first] is to maintain religion; the [second] to do their duty; the [third] whereby they subject themselves to the laws.[33] Such are the oaths to be taken by the kings of Poland, Sweden, Denmark and England, whose coronation oath includes all the three. Yet this very man having no better author than Holinshed is bold to affirm, that our kings were absolute hereditary monarchs. Bodin and Besoldus seem to be of the same mind. And if they be such, then saith Arnisaeus, they are kings before they take their oaths, and hereditary too. But, who told him so? How will he prove it? We know for certain it's otherwise, and our antiquaries in law will say that he is very ignorant, and yet very bold, if not an impudent flatterer. That Bodin with him and others, should make the king of France absolute, there may be some colour, if we look upon their practise, for they act very highly as absolute princes. Yet if Hotman a better lawyer, and a far greater antiquary than either Bodin or Arnisaeus, be true, the kings of France are made kings and receive their crowns from the first investiture, and that upon conditions?[34] Neither is there any government, which hath a rational and just constitution, which may be known by ancient records or unwritten constant customs, but will manifest that the sovereigns thereof receive their crowns, and keep them upon certain conditions, different from the written and natural laws of God. And it's remarkable, that no constitution can be good or allowable, which is not agreeable to those laws. It's true, that if a people design one or more persons to be their sovereign, and promise absolutely to acknowledge them, by that designation and promise, they are bound to grant him or them all the power whereby he or they may be an absolute sovereign: and if they will keep their promise, they must not, they cannot put any conditions upon him or them, which may tend to the diminution of the power already given. And they may give it so, as that he may as absolutely transmit it and derive it to his

---

[33] Arnisaeus, *De jure majestatis* (Frankfurt, 1635), bks. 1.7; 2.6; 3.3. *De auctoritate* draws extensively on English history, the significance of which is clearly at issue here. (See also below, ch. 15 n. 24.)

[34] François Hotman, *Franco Gallia* (Geneva, 1573); cf. Jean Bodin, *Les Six Livres de la république* (Paris, 1576), trans. *De republica, libri sex* (Paris, 1594).

posterity. Yet if any shall do thus, and set up such an absolute
sovereign; that very person or his successor may be considered
materially as such, or such men, or formally as such sovereigns.
Materially considered, especially as such as not yet invested, they may
be bound to such conditions as upon the non-performance of them,
they may forfeit. But, consider them as actually and absolutely
invested, there can be no such obligation: neither can any conditions
or oaths be imposed upon them, except they be willing to accept of
them. Yet, if any people constitute such a sovereignty, it's to be
examined how justly and wisely they have done, and whether they
have not enslaved both themselves and their posterity, and laid the
foundation of their own misery and ruin. And if this constitution be
neither just nor wise, I cannot see how it should bind posterity. And I
would gladly know, whether those authors, who are so zealous for
absolute, hereditary powers, can give us an instance of any wise and
just people, that at the first constitution did give their free and full
consent to such a government. They never did, nor I think ever can
instance in this particular.

10.

The second question is, whether majesty acquired can be forfeited.
Where you must note, that to forfeit anything is to lose the right unto
it. For, it's one thing to lose the right, another to lose the possession.[35]
For as before, one may lose his right and retain the possession, and
lose his possession, and yet retain his right. Therefore the question is
not [the possession but the loss of right]. [...][36] The question is not,
whether they may forfeit to God, for that they undoubtedly may; but
whether they may forfeit unto men; [and] who those men are, to
whom it may be so forfeited, so as they may take the forfeit and that
justly. For solution of this question [...] this I take as a certain rule,
that whatsoever is given and held upon condition, that may be lost and
forfeited. [...] A right once forfeited falls to the party who gave it, and

---

[35] Forfeiture here is not a mere euphemism for the overthrow of a government, it is more
of a moral sanction, a theme John Humfrey (1621–1719) was to associate strongly with
Lawson; see *A Peaceable Resolution* (London, 1680). Lawson, however, also intimates a
more aggressive notion of forfeiture below, and above, ch. 4.9.
[36] The numbers to the points under 'The first' question (5.9) were left out because the
sequence was confused. For the sake of consistency, I have left out the nine numbers to
the points concluding this chapter under the heading of 'the second question'.

set down the conditions. [...] They, who from God give majesty to any person or family at the first, before they had any right unto it, are the people and community to be governed. [...] There is no rational and intelligent people in the world will bind themselves to subjection, but upon condition of a just protection. No, a people conquered will not yield to be the subjects of the conqueror, but upon this condition. And, though his sword may take away their lives, yet it cannot make them his subjects without their voluntary submission. [...] No wise people, if they can do otherwise, will so submit themselves as to lose the propriety of their goods, the liberty of their persons, the enjoyment of their religion, or to be governed by an arbitrary power without just laws. [...] Princes, kings and conquerors, may either by themselves or their ministers of state, insensibly encroach and usurp, yet these encroachments and usurpations, cannot constitute a right contrary to the fundamental laws. And there can hardly be found any other way, whereby many become absolute and arbitrary lords, but this way. [...] The party to which the forfeiture is made, is not the subjects as subjects, but the people and community, who only can invest one or more with majesty, and constitute a government. Neither can magistrates as magistrates, nor any officers, as such, take the forfeiture. Neither can parliaments, except such as participate in the personal majesty, do any such thing. Yet if the sovereign once forfeit, the subjects cease to be subjects. Nor can a great multitude of these, if they make not the whole body either actually or mutually, though they cease to be subjects, challenge the forfeiture. By this you may easily understand how loosely the question between Arnisaeus and his party, and Buchanan, Arthusius, Heno, Junius, Brutus and their adherents, is handled.[37] [...] It's certain that sovereigns by law, who have not the legislative power in themselves solely, and are bound by oath to govern according to laws, which they themselves cannot make, may forfeit. [...] Such personal sovereigns, as constantly act, not only against the laws of God and nature, but against the fundamental laws, by which they receive and hold their power, may and do forfeit. And this is one reason why all tyrants in exercise do *excidere jure suo et si haereditario*, which Arnisaeus himself affirms.[38]

---

[37] Arnisaeus, e.g. *De jure*; George Buchanan, *De jure regni apud Scotos Dialogus*(?) (Edinburgh, 1583); Arthusius/Johannes Althusius?, *Politica methodica digesta* (Herborn, 1614), ed. J. Friedrich (Cambridge, Mass., Harvard University Press, 1932); Heno, possibly the Dutch scholar Nicholas Hoeniger. 'Junius Brutus', see above, ch. 4 n. 7.

[38] Arnisaeus, *De auctoritate*, ch. 4.

Yet as he wisely observes, it's not safe always to take the forfeiture. For it is better by petitions, prayers to God, or patient suffering for a while (so that they suffer not the state in the meantime to come to ruin) to seek and expect a redress, than suddenly to involve the people in blood, and hazard the commonwealth, and put it in such a condition, as that it shall not be able in any due time to settle. Yet a real necessity of defence doth alter the case. Hitherto concerning the manner how majesty may be acquired or lost.

CHAPTER 6

Of power ecclesiastical

1.

The former rules may easily be applied to a particular church, for it's a spiritual commonwealth, and must as such, have governors, and them invested with a supreme power, yet such and of the same nature as the church is: that is, spiritual and ecclesiastical. This power, as all other in civil states, is derivative from Heaven, and of a very narrow scantling. And, that I may be more perspicuous and direct the reader by some line or thread of method, I will say something of the power: [...] as it is spiritual; [...] as supreme; [and] as divisible into several branches.

2.

In the first place it's spiritual, and that in many respects, as the authors of *Jus divinum regiminis ecclesiastici* have sufficiently demonstrated.[1] For the person's rule, actions and end are to be considered, not under a civil, but a spiritual notion. As styled by divines, and that according to the spirit's language, and the phrase of Holy Writ, to be *potestas clavium*. And the acts thereof are opening, shutting; or which are the same, binding, loosing. These are metaphorical terms, taken out of the Old into the New Testament. For our Saviour did love to

---

[1] *Jus divinum regiminis ecclesiastici, by sundry ministers within the City of London* (London, 1646).

use the spirit's words.[2] The first and chief place where we read these words in a political sense with reference to government, is that of the evangelical prophet. 'And the key of the house of David will I lay upon his shoulder, so he shall open and none shall shut, and he shall shut and none shall open' (Isa. 22.22). Where by key is meant *dominatio*, or *potestas gubernandi*. So Fererius, Schindler, Mollerus according to the former use do understand it.[3] For there it is said, 'I will commit thy government into his hand' (Isa. 22.21).

3.

It's not material to enquire, whether the power or key of the house of David, was a power over the family or of the family over the kingdom; nor whether Eliakim was a priest or a prince over the palace or the temple.[4] It's certain, David was a type [figura] of Christ; his house and kingdom of the church, and his regal power of Christ's regal supremacy (Rev. 1.18). For he hath the keys of Hell and death, even that key of David which bindeth the soul and conscience, and disposeth of man's spiritual and eternal estate, and that by an irrevocable sentence (2 Cor. 3.7). This power signified by key or keys is not civil, but that of the kingdom of Heaven, which he (Matt. 16.29) promised first, and (John 20.22, 23) conveyed afterward upon the Apostles. As for the acts of these keys being exercised, they are said to be sometimes shutting and opening: sometimes binding and loosing. And though these seem to differ, yet they are the same, and are acts of government. For [*pt.h*] to open is to loose, as Psalm 102.20, where it is turned by the Seventy Two [*Luo*] and not only there, but in other places, which I forbear to mention.[5] And [*'mr*] to bind, is sometimes to

---

[2] Cf. Bunyan, *Author's Apology to the Pilgrim's Progress*. The stress on metaphoricity in this context is something which has been strongly associated with Nonconformity. See N. H. Keeble, *The Literary Culture of Non-Conformity in Later Seventeenth Century England* (Leicester University Press, 1987), at length. On the conceptual significance of Lawson's metaphoric style see Conal Condren, *George Lawson's* Politica *and the English Revolution* (Cambridge University Press, 1989), ch. 16.

[3] Fererius, not Montanus Ferrerius, *De republica* (Basle, 1556), copy in Millington's *Catalogus*, but Franciscus Forerius, *Iesaiae prophetae . . . cum commentario* (Venice, 1563), copy in More Library; Schindler is possibly Valentin Schindler, author of the *Lexicon pentagloton* (Frankfurt, 1653); Mollerus could be Henricus, d. 1589, Fredericus, *fl.* late 16th century, or Martinus, d. 1606.

[4] Cf. 2 Kgs. 23.34–6; 2 Chr. 36.4–13.

[5] The Seventy Two (the Septuagint) are the early translators of the Old Testament into

govern or exercise the acts of coercive power. So Psalm 105.22 to bind his princes, compared with Psalm 2.3 where bands and cords are the laws and edicts of Christ. And the same word in the [Chaldean], is *obligavit ad obedientiam aut pœnam*, ['*mrh*] Daniel 6.7, 8, 9, is translated by the Seventy Two [*horisma*] a decree, *obligatio, interdictum*.[6] It's also remarkable, that [*mkr*] to shut up, signifieth [*paradidomai*] to deliver into the hand of enemies, or to destruction (Job 16.11; Ps. 78.48). Hence that phrase of delivering up to Satan (1 Cor. 5.5; 1 Tim. 1.20) and also [*aphorizo*] to separate or exclude lepers out of the holy camp, as Numbers 12.14, 15 and in other places: which was a typical adumbration of that act of jurisdiction, which we call excommunication.

4.

This Power of the Keys is spiritual, because exercised within a spiritual community. 'Do not ye judge them that are within,' saith the Apostle (1 Cor. 5.12): I have nothing to do to judge them without. 'For what have I to do to judge them also that are without?' (*ibid.*). God hath reserved them to his own tribunal. 'But them that are without God judgeth' (*ibid.*, 13). Yet these without the pale of the church, are not exempted from the civil jurisdiction of the Christian magistrate, if within his territories. The power of Hell and death is not the Power of the Sword. The power given to the church was not given to the state. The power of the Kingdom of Heaven is not the power of the kingdoms of the earth. The power promised unto, and conferred upon the Apostles, was not estated upon the civil magistrate, though Christian. This power opens and shuts the gates of Heaven: binds and loosens sinners as liable to eternal punishments, which no civil sword can do. Therefore it's spiritual.

5.

As it is spiritual, so it's supreme: for a particular church being a commonwealth or spiritual state, must needs have a spiritual tribunal independent within itself: except we will divest it of the very essence and soul, wherewith it's animated. Yet it cannot be such in respect of

Greek. The version included Apocrypha and was not superseded until St Jerome's *Vulgate*, completed around 404. The Greek is misprinted in the second edition.
[6] A boundary, misprinted?

him, whose throne is Heaven, whose footstool is the earth. Or, if by the divine prospective of faith, we pierce into the Heaven of Heavens, and approach that sparkling throne, where Christ sits at the right hand of God possessed of a universal and eternal kingdom; every particular and all particular churches must bow and waive the title of independent. In a word, in all imperial rights which God and Christ have reserved, and not derived by the fundamental charter of the Scripture, all particular churches, with all their members, nay, all their officers, even ministers are but subjects governed, in no wise governing. Supreme therefore it is, both in respect of its own members within, and also of other churches, enjoying equal power within themselves: and are not queens and mothers, but sisters in a parity of jurisdiction with it, but no superiority of command over it. For the parity of them without, is not destructive of her sovereignty over her own within. The universal vicarage and plenitude of monarchical power, arrogated by the patriarch of Rome, cannot justly depress or take away the rights of any particular church. This power was first challenged, then usurped, after that in a great measure possessed, exercised and pleaded for. The pretended right and title was invented after they had possession, and with a fair colour did for a long time gull the world: which at length awaked out of a universal slumber, and found it to be a dream.

6.

As this power is […] spiritual; […] supreme; so [also] it's divisible, and may be branched into divers particular *jura* or rights, which are four: 1. of making canons; 2. of constituting officers; 3. of jurisdiction; and 4. of receiving and dispensing of church goods. Thus they may be methodized.

> [The rights of the church are two-fold: concerning the making of laws and their execution by officers within the ambit of the constitution; and the management and distribution of church property.]

There may be other petty *jura*, yet easily reducible unto these. And this division, though grounded evidently upon Scripture, and will by the ingenious be easily granted, yet it may seem new to some, upon whose understanding the old perhaps hath made too deep an impression. For I find the old distinction of this power into two parts (the [first] of order; the [second] of jurisdiction) to be retained by many unto this day. Yet they do not unanimously define what this *Clavis* or *potestas ordinis* is. Some will have it to be the same with *clavis scientiae*, which the schoolmen understood of that juridical knowledge, which was antecedaneous and subordinate unto the decree or definitive sentence. Others say, it is the power of ordination and making of ministers. Others take it to be the power of a minister ordained to preach the word and administer the sacraments; in which respect it cannot belong to the external government of independent churches. For a minister, as such, is so a deputy of Christ, as that in the due execution of his office he is above any particular church, and above the angels. And his power in this regard is rather moral than political. As under this notion, some give him jurisdiction [in the court of internal matters], which the papists call [the place of penitence]. But [the court of external matters] he cannot challenge it as a minister: for then it could not be communicated to any other with him, as to ruling elders representing the people. This the bishops formerly assumed to themselves, with a power to delegate the same to others.

7.

These keys or powers in the root, are but one and the same power supernatural, which is a principle of supernatural acts; the first branch whereof is the legislative. This ever was, and doth still continue in the church, and is most necessary for to regulate, and determine the acts both of government and subjection. For without a certain directive and binding rule, no state could ever long continue, and God himself (whose power is absolutely supreme) did limit himself by a certain law, before he began to require obedience from his creatures, and exercise his power *ad extra*. For it's his will and pleasure, that neither men nor angels should be subject unto him, but according to a certain rule. This the Apostles, elders and brethren put in practice (Acts 15). And the *jus Canonicum Novi Testamenti* issued from this power. Unto his head are reduced the forms of confession for doctrine, liturgies for worship, catechisms for instruction in the principles of religion, and canons for discipline in every well-constituted church. In this legislation ecclesiastical, they either do declare what God before hath determined, or determined in things which God hath left indifferent, what is profitable and expedient according to the general rules of order, decency, unity and edification: according to that distinction of laws into declarative and constitutive.

8.

After laws are made and established, they must be put in execution: otherwise, though they be both wisely and justly enacted, and in themselves very excellent, yet they are in vain and to no purpose. This cannot be done without officers. Therefore, there must needs be a power of making church rulers. Under this head, we must comprehend election, examination, ordination, suspension, degradation, and whatsoever concerns the making, reforming or disposing of offices. When canons are made, officers with power of jurisdiction be constituted: yet all is to no purpose except they proceed to hear, and finally determine all causes and controversies within their spiritual jurisdiction. Therefore there must be [a court of highest appeal]. Hitherto appertain all ecclesiastical tribunals, judges, judicial proceedings; the discussion of all causes within their cognizance, sentences of authoritative admonition, suspension, excommunication, absolution and execution of all. Besides all these, because the church, whilst on pilgrimage towards her Heavenly city, hath need of these earthly and temporal goods; neither can the public worship of God, or her officers be maintained, nor her poor saints relieved without them. Therefore, every particular church should be furnished with a revenue and have a kind of [public treasury] of her own, which is not to be disposed of according to the will and pleasure of any private person or persons. But there must be a power, as to make officers for other things, so for this particular to receive, keep and dispense the church's treasure; this of themselves without public consent they cannot do. Therefore, though the making of deacons belong unto the second part of this independent power, yet [the right to manage the public property of the church] is a distinct power of itself. Christ and his Apostles had a common purse (John 13.29), so had the church (Acts 6.1, 2, 3, etc.). For this end they had their collections at set times (1 Cor. 16.1, 2). This treasury belonged to the church, not to the state, and did arise from the free gifts of such as were of ability and well disposed, before there was any tenure in frank almoigne,[7] as afterwards there was.

[7]Free alms bestowed on the Church in perpetuity.

81

9.

Before I conclude this point concerning power (lest instead of a well-composed body, I make an indigested lump of heterogeneous stuff) I will enquire how far it doth extend, what be the limits wherewith it's bounded, what measures and degrees thereof a particular church, as such by Scripture charter may challenge. For this purpose we may take notice of the subject of power, which is primary or secondary. In the primary, it's primitive, total, supreme: in the secondary, it's derivative, partial and subordinate. The power in both is the same essentially; yet in the one as in the fountain, in the other as in several channels. This seems to be intimated by that submission required by the Apostle unto the king as supreme, or unto governors sent by him (1 Pet. 2.13, 14). The king is emperor, who was the immediate subject of supremacy; governors were presidents and [vicars of the magistrate]; who are the instruments of the supreme as principal in government. Coincident with this seems to be that distinction (so frequent with Mr. Parker) [between condition (i.e. constitution) and exercise]. According to which he defines the government of the church [with respect to its condition] to be democratical, because the Power of the Keys is in the whole church (which with him is a congregation) as in the primary subject; but [with respect to its exercise] to be aristocratical in the rulers who derive their power from Christ by the church. This shall be examined hereafter.[8] This difference of the primary and secondary subject is to be observed, lest we make everyone who hath power, and is trusted with the exercise thereof, the prime and immediate receptacle of church power from Christ, which is not to be done.

10.

In the second place we must repeat a distinction, taken up in the beginning of this treatise, which may briefly be contracted in this manner: [A church government is internal or external; universal or particular; formal or material.] The internal is God's. The external universal, as such, Christ doth justly challenge. The external particu-

---

[8]Robert Parker, *De politeia ecclesiastica, libri tres* (London, 1616). Lawson provides an extreme summary of a hugely long and learned anti-Episcopalian polemic, see esp. bk. 3. For discussion see below, chs. 12, 13, 14.

lar formally and properly ecclesiastical is committed to particular churches. The external particular materially considered, is the Christian magistrate's due: because the matters of the church in this respect are an object of his civil power. That distinction of Camera-censis, *potestas est ordinis aut regiminis*, the same with that of Biel and many other schoolmen, hath some affinity with this.[9] For, the power of order with them is the power of a minister, as an officer under Christ of the universal church, and is exercised [in the penitential or internal court]. The power of government and prelation (which *Defensor pacis* saith, the bishops had *per accidens*)[10] is the same with this external government of the church, as exercised [in the court of external things] (Matt. 18; 1 Cor. 5; Rev. 2.2), or *judiciali*, as they term it. All the power of a particular church, is confined to matters ecclesiastical, as such in that particular community, and is exercised only [in the court of external things]. This must needs be so, because the internal government of the church, which by the word and spirit immediately rules the conscience, so, as to cast the impenitent both soul and body into Hell, belongs to God as God.[11] The external government of the universal church as universal, is purely monarchi-cal under Christ; in which respect all particular churches are merely subjects; and no way independent, no nor governing.

II.

Yet in the third place, if this be not so manifest and satisfactory, the point may be illustrated, if we parallel the government of the church with that of Israel. As that was [a theocracy] so it is [a christocracy]. In

[9] Pierre d'Ailly (Pietro de Alliaco), Cardinal Cameracensis, *Questiones magistri Petri de Alliaco ... super libros sententiarum ... Lombardus ... et questionibus de potestate ecclesie in suis verperiis disputatis* (Lyons, 1490, 1500). The distinction is made in *Questio vesparium*, L.; Gabriel Biel (1410?–95), conciliar theorist and commentator on Peter Lombard's *Sentences*. There is a conciliarist tone to this whole section possibly derivative of Jacques Almain (1480–1515). See J. H. Burns, 'Scholasticism: Survival and Revival', in *The Cambridge History of Political Thought, 1450–1700*, ed. J. H. Burns with the assistance of Mark Goldie, Cambridge University Press, pp. 132–55. Lawson's text carries an unhelpful marginal reference to Alliaco.

[10] Marsilius of Padua, *Defensor pacis* (completed 1324), ed. C. W. Previté-Orton (Cambridge University Press, 1928). Lawson possibly used the Frankfurt edition, 1592. Lawson is alluding to a principal theme of *Dictio* 2, esp. chs. 4–7, 22, 23.

[11] The distinction between internal and external, intimated in Marsilius, *Defensor pacis*, ch. 1.4 as transient and non-transient acts, had become central to the Protestant Reformation.

the theocracy of Israel God was *pars imperans*, and the absolute monarch, and reserved to himself the *Jura Majestatis*. For he made their laws, appointed their chief officers, generals, judges; he anointed their kings, proclaimed their wars, concluded peace, and received last appeals. Yet in many petty causes and matters of state, and that often he trusted their elders, officers and princes, and committed to them exercise of power and actual government. And their kings were but a kind of *Vicarij Magistratus* under him. So Christ hath retained to himself the government of the universal church as such: as also the legislative power of particular churches in all essentials and necessaries, and hath enacted general statutes for accidentals and circumstantials. He hath the principal power of making officers, for he determines how many kinds of necessary officers there should be: limits their power, prescribes their qualification, sets down their duty, and gives them their commission. Their judicial proceedings run in his name, and their sentence is so far valid on earth, as he shall ratify it in Heaven. Yet in making of canons they have power so far, as to declare in essentials, to bind in positive laws and in circumstantials. In ordaining of officers the designation of the persons is theirs. In jurisdiction, they have power to hear, examine, take witnesses, apply the controversy or cause to the canon, determine and see the sentence executed, and all this in a sovereign and independent manner within the circuit of their own church. And, whereas it may be said, all this power amounts but to a little, and is confined to a narrow compass, it's true, it's but a particle: yet the church is more happy and the government more excellent, because it depends so little on man, so much on Christ. And this power, though diminutive, yet through God's blessing is effectual, and tendeth much unto the preservation of purity, piety, unity and edification: and if well managed, is an excellent means to enlarge Christ's kingdom, and further our eternal salvation. The result of all this is that particular churches are not supreme but subordinate, both in respect of the internal government which is purely divine, and also in respect of the external universal, which is purely monarchical under Christ. The church of Rome doting upon her universal head and vicar-general, presupposed and took for granted, that the community of all Christians in the world were but one visible church under, and subject unto one and the same supreme independent judicatory. This no question is an error. For, though there be a universal visible church, yet it's subject only unto one supreme consistory in Heaven, but not on earth, either in a monarchical, or aristocratical, or democratical form, as shall be hinted hereafter.[12] And, suppose the Pope had been an ecclesiastical monarch, because the patriarch of the first See in the imperial city: yet he could not be universal, but only in respect of the church within the confines of the empire, which did enclose all the other patriarchates, and was but a little parcel of the world.

CHAPTER 7

Of the manner of acquiring ecclesiastical power

I.

Having manifested, what ecclesiastical power of discipline is, I must search how it's acquired: for this as well as civil is derivative and that from Heaven, and in a more special manner. It's not natural but acquired. It's also continued by succession, not hereditary but elective; not in a line, as the sacerdotal power confined to the family of Aaron.[1] It's first in God the fountain of all power, and from him derived to Christ as man and administrator general. For so after his resurrection, he said unto his disciples, 'All power in Heaven and earth is given me.'[2] Some measure of this he by commission delegate[d] unto the Apostles. Yet that power of theirs as extraordinary, was not successive, or to be derived to those who followed them as ordinary officers of the church: for it expired with them. Yet there was an ordinary power of discipline derived to them, and they never except in ordinary cases, did exercise it but with the church. This, some say was acquired, by those words of Christ to Peter, 'to thee will I give the keys of the Kingdom of Heaven', etc. (Matt. 16.19). This power was given to Peter, many of the ancients say, as representing the church; others think it was given him as head of the church; others as representing the Apostles, from whom it was derived to the bishops; or else, as others tell us, to the elders of the church. But of

---

[12] See below, chs. 8–12.   [1] Lev. 8; Ps. 115.12.   [2] Matt. 28.18.

this hereafter [chs. 11, 12]. But whatsoever power the Apostles might have either severally or jointly considered, it's certain that Christ derived it to the church, whereof the Apostles were members, yet extraordinary officers. The church acquired it, therefore by free donation from Christ, when he said, 'Tell the church', and afterwards, 'whatsoever ye bind on earth shall be bound in Heaven' (Matt. 18.17, 18). By this church is meant no Utopian, aerial or notional body, but such a society of Christians brought under a form of government, as may and can exercise this power, as the church of Corinth, Ephesus, Antioch, Jerusalem, or any of the churches of Asia.

2.

But, though I intend in this to be brief, yet I will observe some order, and this in particular it is: [ecclesiastical power is acquired by the immediate designation of Christ or the Apostles; and is lost by mediate institution and that justly or unjustly.]

Seeing none hath this spiritual power, except given from God, therefore it must needs be acquired as it is derived:

[It's derived immediately to Christ as man; to the Apostles as his delegates.]

Christ as man by his humiliation unto death, the death of the Cross, acquired an universal power over all persons in all causes spiritual. And he received it upon his resurrection, and upon his ascension, being solemnly invested and confirmed, began to exercise the same. The Apostles being extraordinary officers under Christ, received their extraordinary power, which was both intensively and extensively great from Christ. And, [first], for the lost sheep of Israel before Christ's death, [second], for all nations after the resurrection. [Third], more fully and solemnly invested after Christ's ascension, they began to act, and that both in an ordinary and extraordinary way, and that in discipline as shall appear hereafter. As they were extraordinary, they could not, as ordinary they might, have successors.

3.

As the power is derived in an ordinary way, so it's acquired by the church mediately. This church did first consist of the Apostles, the seventy disciples, and other believers of the Jews. After that we find several churches consisting of Jews and gentiles. After that a church, as taken from a Christian community, is once made up of persons, a multitude of persons associated, and endued with a sufficient ability to manage the Power of the Keys, in that visible body politic; presently it acquires this power by virtue of Christ's institution in these words: 'Tell the church, &c.' as before. For in that very rule, he gives to direct us how to deal from first to last with an offending brother; he institutes the external government of the church, and both erects and also establishes an independent tribunal. After a church is once constituted, and this power acquired, it's exercised either by a general representative, or by officers: both these must be invested with power before they can act. And these acquire their power by delegation, or by being constituted Officers. By these means the power may be acquired justly.

4.

Yet it may be possessed or exercised unjustly. It's usurped when any arrogate it, or take upon them to exercise it without just warrant from the gospel. Therefore; [...] When a multitude of Christians, who have no ability to manage it, shall erect an independent judicatory, they are usurpers. [...] When one church challengeth power over another [it also usurps]. When presbyters alone, or bishops alone engross the whole power ecclesiastical, both of making canons, and of jurisdiction and constituting officers [they usurp]. Magistrates, [usurp] who as such, take upon them spiritual power. [...] But the greatest usurper is the Pope, who usurpeth a power both intensively and extensively far greater than is due.

5.

As the power may be acquired, so it may be lost. For 1. when a church is so far decayed, as not to be able to exercise an independent jurisdiction or order, as their association, so their power is so much abated. 2. When a church doth wholly cease to be a church, then their power is wholly lost. Yet when it's hindered either by the magistrate, or by schisms and rents in itself, so that it cannot exercise it, yet it's virtually in them. And many times such is the neglect of Christians, that they will not associate nor reduce themselves into order when they might do it: this is a great sin. 3. When representatives turn into a faction and betray their trust, they lose their power as representatives. 4. All officers are divested, when for some just cause, they are deposed or degraded, but this belongs not to this part.

CHAPTER 8

Of the disposition of power civil, and the several forms of government

I.

After the acquisition both of civil and ecclesiastical power, follows the disposition of both, which will take up a great part of this first book. And first of the manner of disposing civil power. This disposition seems to be the same with acquisition, because it cannot be acquired but by a certain subject. Neither can it be said properly to be actually acquired, but at the very same time, and by this very act it's placed in that subject. Yet because power civil may be so communicated and acquired, [...] it may be disposed of several ways: and from these several ways of disposing, arise several distinctions and differences of commonwealths. I thought good to make disposition a distinct thing from acquisition, and so handle it for the better understanding of this particular. I will [first] premise some general observations; [then] briefly declare the several ways of disposing majesty, and the several forms of governments. [I shall then] enquire into the constitution of the commonwealth of England; [and finally] deliver some things concerning our condition in these late times.

2.

The observations are these: The [first] which belongs unto that of acquisition, is that no power can be fully acquired, till it be accepted of as well as communicated. For, no man can be bound to be a sovereign against his will.

[Second], that majesty is then disposed, when it is placed and ordered in a certain constant subject, which thereby may be enabled and bound to protect and govern.

[Third], that to be disposed in this or that subject, in this or that manner, is accidental to majesty, though to be disposed is essential to a commonwealth.

[Fourth], from the different ways of disposing this power arise the different kinds (as they call them) of commonwealths. For from the placing of it in one or more, arise monarchical, aristocratical and popular states.

[Fifth], majesty being the same in general in all states, it may be disposed several ways and in several degrees, in one or more. Hence arise the difference of one monarchy from another: one aristocracy from another: one popular state from another.

[Sixth], though it may be a question, whether the disposing power is one or more can make a specifical difference, yet monarchy and polyarchy are taken for different species of commonwealths essentially different.

3.

> [Sovereignty disposed in its pure forms is found in the one or the many. Invested in one it is despotic or else regal, hence monarchical power is despotic or regal. Invested in a plurality of plebs or optimates it is aristocratic or democratic. Sovereignty may also be a mixture with all or many hence a popular state.][1]

The knowledge of this scheme depends upon the difference and distinction of the parts and members of a community. For besides those which are but virtually members, there are such as are *sui juris*, independent upon [of] others: and these are divided into three ranks. As 1. Such as are only free. 2. Such as are of the nobility. 3. Some that are super-eminent. The two former are called in Latin, *plebs et optimates*. And amongst these *optimates* there may be very great difference: as we find a Pompey or a Caesar amongst the Romans: a Duke of Braganza amongst the Portugals, who inherited a vast estate

[1] Lawson's inelegant ramist reduction is rooted in the traditional Graeco-Roman notions of pure and mixed constitutional forms, though the popular state (*status popularis*) seems closest to the familiar Machiavellian image of republican Rome (*Discourses*, 1.2) out of Livy, Polybius and especially Cicero, *De republica*, 1.26–8.

in lands. These are called the *tres ordines,* the three states or ranks of the whole body of the people, with us, king, peers and commons. The super-eminent are few, the peers more in number, yet not very many: the commons are the greatest multitude by far, and make up the main body of the society. Yet with us, of these there be several degrees and subdivisions. Amongst the commons, we find the freeholders and the gentry, and a great disparity in both. Amongst the peers there is a difference. In respect of the manner of acquiring of this dignity: and so some of them are such by ancient tenure, amounting to so many knights-fees: some by writ, some by patent. These are called in Latin *Barones Feudatarij, rescriptitij, diplomatici.* There is another distinction with us of lords; for some are temporal, some spiritual. The highest of these amongst us are those of royal extraction: in France the princes of the blood. In some countries, as in Denmark, and some say in Poland, there be peers and lords, which hold *in allodio,* and these are independent upon [of] the king in diverse respects: such also the princes of Germany be for the most part. And in those states where such are found, the government usually is aristocratical. These kings, dukes and monarchs became such at first, either for the antiquity of their family and their great estates, or for their super-eminent wisdom and virtue, or for their rare exploits in war or peace. For such as are generals and great commanders in wars, prudent and successful, much beloved by soldiers, may do much: dethrone princes, set up themselves, and if it will not be fairly given, they will forcibly take the crown and sometimes they may deserve it, and prove the fittest to wear it. These are the three ranks and orders of the people.[2]

4.

These being known well, will give some light to that which follows, concerning the disposing of majesty whether real or personal, though all majesty, actually ruling, must be in some sense personal. First this super-eminent power may be placed.

[Purely in one or more.]

In one, and then that the state is called a monarchy. Yet it may be disposed in one [of] several ways; more absolutely, [or] more strictly

---

[2] In adapting inherited categories to English circumstances Lawson treats kings both as constituting a separate category and as pre-eminent aristocrats.

limited. An absolute monarch, whether elective or hereditary is such, as hath a full power over his subjects' goods and persons as his own: so, that the people have neither propriety in their goods, nor liberty of their persons. They are but his servants and little better than slaves: such Pharaoh's subjects, when Joseph had purchased their stocks, their lands, their persons for the crown, seem to have been.[3] This government is *absolutum dominium*, and therefore termed *despoticum et herile imperium*, and such a monarch seems to be that which by Aristotle is called [*pambasileus*, all ruling].[4] There be princes invested with majesty, who challenge the legislative power unto themselves, will by a proclamation or edict command the goods of their subjects, and imprison their persons at will and pleasure. These though they be limited by the fundamental constitution, and their oaths, are in the exercise of their power as absolute as the former. This kind of government may do well where the subjects are turbulent, insolent and unruly, or of a base and servile spirit, or rude and savage. But where the people are ingenuous, tractable, and of a better disposition, it's very unreasonable: for, it will either cause rebellions, and seditions, or much debase their spirits. This kind of monarchy is apt to degenerate into a tyranny of one person. Yet if this kind of sovereign be wise, just and virtuous, the people may live happily under his protection. Yet such a power, and so unlimited is not fit to be trusted in the hands of every one. And if it be hereditary, woe to the people that live under it.

[5.]

Yet this power may be trusted in the hands of one, yet so as that it may be allayed, limited, and justly and wisely poised, and the sovereign as a king. The word [*melek*] in Hebrew signifies a governor in general, [*basileus*] in Greek is a word of great latitude, and so is *rex* in Latin, and also *sultan* in the Arabic and Mauritian language. Yet some are such imperious dictators and masters of words, that the word king must needs signify an absolute monarch. That it often signifies a monarch and one that hath the title of majesty, there is no doubt. But the bare word or title [does] not distinctly inform us of the power, or the manifold differences of kings; which must be known another way, as by the constitution of those particular states, where

---

[3] Gen. 47.15–17.   [4] Aristotle, *Politics*, 1285a15–25.

the chief and most eminent governors have that title. For there is a great difference and that in respect of power, between the kings of Spain and France, and the kings of Poland, Sweden and Denmark. Neither doth the King of England in this respect exactly agree with any of them. But if the word cannot, the definition surely of a king should determine his power. Yet neither will the common usual definition do it. For thus he is commonly defined. *A king is a monarch, who governeth free men justly according to the laws, to the good of the commonwealth.* The genus is, that he is a monarch. And if such in strict sense, as such, he can have neither superior nor peer in his kingdom. The specifical difference is taken from the subject, the rule, the end of his government. For his proper act is *regere*, to govern. The subjects of his government are free men. The rule is just laws. The end the public good. Abstract the specifical difference, and lay the words king and monarch aside, and it agrees to all governors civil whatsoever. For civil government being grounded upon the eternal moral law, *love thy neighbour as thy self,* and more particularly upon the fifth commandment, no person or persons invested with sovereign power can be defined any other way; and neither their power nor the exercise thereof is good, further than it agrees with this definition. And the more their government swerves from this rule, the more of the tyrant is in them: and if the violation of it be more than their observation, and that habitually too, then they are really tyrants, *in exercitio.* For *denominatio sit a parte praedominante.* But I have wondered, why authors have made this the specifical difference of a king, which certainly it cannot be. Yet this definition leaves many things doubtful. For, it determines not what liberty is, and whether it can be perfect without propriety. Nor doth it tell us, what these laws are according to which he must govern: whether the laws of God only, or the laws also of men: and if of men, whether the laws of constitution or administration; if of administration, whether they must be made by himself alone, or by some others without him, or with him. For, if the laws be made by him alone, he is an absolute despotical sovereign; if by others, either with him or without him, he is not such. For there may be a king, at least in name above law, and a king by law, and such as cannot command or bind the meanest subject, nor judge him, but according to law. Such a king is not a pure monarch, which I now treat of. Therefore a king that is a pure monarch differs from a despotical sovereign in respect of his subjects, and the measure of his power, and according to this definition in the exercise of it. The subjects of the one are free, and have propriety of person and goods, the subjects of the other have neither. The power of the one is more absolute, and of larger extent, or rather more intensive. The exercise of the power of the one is bounded by just laws; the power of the other is not limited or directed by laws, and so tends not so much to advance the weal of his subjects as his own greatness. And in this respect [he] can be no lawful and good governor, if he act according to his absolute and arbitrary power, which God never gave him. And despotical sovereigns, if wise and just, will do as Trajan did,[5] that is, act according to the rule of justice and of a limited power, though they be not bound by man to do so.

6.

An absolute and pure monarchy is a very dangerous form of government, and very inclinable and propense to tyranny; and such a sovereign, as is invested with such transcendent power, degenerates and turns tyrant. Experience in all times and places makes this evident. Monarchy indeed in some respects is the best government, yet such is the imperfection and corruption of man that it proves not to be so.[6] If monarchs were like God, or saints and angels, it might be better. But in a succession, whether elective or hereditary, we find in tract of time few good, many bad, and very wicked. In Israel the first king was not right, the fourth too bad:[7] and after the kingdom was divided into the tribe of Israel and Judah, in Judah we find few like David, many very wicked: in the kingdom of Israel not one good.[8] Yet the laws both civil and ecclesiastical were made to their hands, and that by God himself. Sovereign power is a weighty burden, and requires much strength, and excellent abilities. Moses himself cannot bear it alone: he hath need of one hundred and seventy elders, and the same endued with the spirit of government to be his assistants. If a sovereign be imprudent, or weak of understanding, not able to judge of good counsel, or negligent, or timorous, or wilful, or destitute of good agents and instruments for administrations, the government begins to decline even in most peaceable times, and the subjects become suddenly unhappy. But if he be wicked, vicious, insolent,

---

[5] Roman emperor, 98–117, a standard assessment possibly mediated by John of Salisbury, *Policraticus*, for whom he is a symbolic contrast to tyranny.

[6] Cf. Aristotle, *Politics*, 1289b40; Cicero, *De republica*, 1.28.

[7] David and Jeroboam, respectively.   [8] See 1 Kgs., at length.

impetuous, cruel, he instantly becomes a tyrant, and then both church and state begin to suffer much, religion is corrupted or suppressed and persecuted, the wicked are predominant, and the best under hatches. Yea, though the prince may be of a good disposition, yet facile and flexible, devoid of wisdom and courage, and also destitute of good and faithful counsellors, and beset with wicked men, how easily is he misled, involved in many troubles, and in the end brought to ruin. Sometimes a few cunning politicians act him as a child, drive on their own interest, and neglect, yea pervert the public good. How much more if the monarchs be children, or idiots, as some be? If in such a model God raise up a David, a Solomon, a Jehosaphat, an Ezekiah, a Josiah, the people may be happy, and have great cause to be thankful for so great a blessing.

7.

There is another way of disposing majesty than the former, and that is, when it's fixed [purely in more than one and that is twofold in the optimates or in the plebeians].[9] When it is disposed in few, and the same more eminent, it's called an aristocracy, so called from the quality of the persons who govern. For they are [*aristoi*] *optimates, primores, praecipui*, the most eminent in the community and above the common sort of plebeian rank; for they are not only *formaliter*, but *eminenter cives*, as you heard before. Their eminency ariseth from their noble extraction, as being descended from noble and ancient families, or from their great estates, or from both, or from their excellent virtues. And such, as in whom all these concur, are the fittest for government. Amongst the Romans these were called *Patricii*. This order of peers, which may be so called, in relation of one unto another amongst themselves, is sometimes confined to certain families, as they say it is in the Ragusian and Venetian states, and with a permission or prohibition to marry in inferior families; or there may be way made open for the adoption of other persons for their eminent virtues, though of meaner rank. For *virtus vera nobilitas*. Such were the *Patricii minorum gentium* amongst the Romans. And though political virtues, as wisdom and justice do best qualify them for the place, yet it's requisite they have good estates, or sufficient allowance, otherwise

---

[9] The discussion continues in the terms established by Aristotle, *Politics*, and Cicero, *De republica*.

they will oppress the people, or be unfit to attend the public service. Yet such as are born of noble and ancient families have some advantage, because they many times inherit great estates, are more honoured by the people, have the benefit of the best education, sometimes participate some measure of the noble spirit of their ancestors, whose rare examples may do something to[10] [inspire them]. These, though physically many, yet morally are but one person collective. They may have a president; and such as the Duke of Venice and his privileges, honour, state and dignity may be paramount, and he may have the precedency, yet no negative voice nor power above the rest. For the power, and all the particular rights of majesty are in them all jointly: and when they in any business of state do differ, the major part carries it, and the rest submit. This may be an excellent government, when all or the greater and predominant party are wise and just, and follow some certain rules of the constitution, and seek the public good, as all other sovereigns should do. If there be not care taken in the succession, that the best may succeed the best, the body will corrupt and degenerate into an oligarchy, which is then done, when either they agree to advance their own private interest, to the neglect of the public; or if they be divided, one party bears down another, and a few prevailing engross the power, and usurp far more than is due, and oppress the people, and so prove a number of tyrants. When the richest engross the power to themselves, it's called a timocracy. If the succession into places vacant, either by death, or some other way be by election, an excellent qualification prerequired, some strict order for the admission should be observed, least [lest] unworthy persons enter by favour, money or some indirect way; and in this particular the state of Venice seems to excel. Neither must any of them be suffered to swell and rise above the rest, as many ways they may do: especially if they be men of excellent parts and successful, and be trusted with too great a command in the administration. For some wise men have observed, that the unlimited commission granted Pompey at the first, for the Pyratic war, laid the foundation of those bloody civil wars which followed.[11]

---

[10] Second edition has 'too'.

[11] Cnaeus Pompeius, 'The Great' (106–48 BC), given large forces to combat piracy in 67 BC; enlarged to fight King Mithridates before the final breach with Julius Caesar, 49 BC. Lucan's *Pharsalia* gives an important account of Pompey and the Civil Wars. After May's translation of Lucan the Civil Wars became something of an analogue for Britain's own.

8.

[*Sovereignty invested purely in the plebeians*]

This is the last and basest kind of the pure models. For *plebs* signifies the inferior rank of people, which for number far exceed the rest. Among these, besides artificers, husbandmen, and such as are for trade and traffic, there may be some merchants of the great estates, some of more noble descent and competent revenue, yet far short of such eminency as is required in peers or princes: which this kind of government cannot brook. Yet it may be so ordered, as that the exercise of the power may be trusted in hands of some just, wise and experienced persons, which either must govern by course, or be removed, least [lest] trusted too long, they engross the power to themselves, or to some few families, or to a faction predominant. For this kind of government is very subject to faction, disorder and tumults. The name of it is a democracy: in which there is the greatest liberty; not only because they are free from peers and princes, but because every one may be a magistrate and [proceed in such][12] a way as opens to that end. Yet because in such a state there be a few men of learning, wisdom, experience in matters of state, most of mean education, and many so taken up with their own private affairs, it can hardly continue long without some alteration, if not ruin. It presently degenerates into an ochlocracy, and when such, there it cannot stay long before it become an anarchy. It's a curse and heavy judgement of God to live in such a government, according to that in the prophet.

> And the people shall be oppressed, every one by another, and every one by his neighbour: the child shall behave himself proudly against the ancient, and the base against the honourable. (Isa. 3.5.)

The Philosopher reckons up four several kinds of this democratical form:[13] and there may be many more, some better, some worse. Of the tumults and intestine dissensions amongst these plebeians histories tell us much. But this is a subject, which is not very profitable, and I list not to enlarge upon it.

---

[12] Corrected in second edition.
[13] Aristotle, *Politics*, 1291b–1292a.

9.

[Mixed sovereignty: with sovereignty in all or many]

There is another kind of disposition different from the former, and
it's called a mixed government. The reason of the name few know,
because they little understand the thing. It's not called so, as many
think, because the *Jura Majestatis* are divided and given some to the
peers, some to the people, and some in some states to the prince.[14]
For this tends to confusion, and doth not well suit with the nature of
sovereign power. Therefore it's the cause of many quarrels and dissensions. But it's called mixed, because either three or at least two of
the states are mixed together, so as that the sovereignty is jointly in
them all and in the whole; and of these there are two sorts. For
sometimes there is no prince in the administration, and then it's in the
commons and the peers; not in peers and in commons severally; but
in both jointly. Sometimes it's *in omnibus*, in prince, peers, commons.
Yet these in the administration may have their several parts and
different manners of acting. Therefore we must not judge of states
according to the manner of administration, though the administration
will give great light and help us to understand the constitution. This
kind of government is called a free state, a popular state, a republic, or
the republic, and may be the best state of all others, where *majestas* is
tota in toto, yet there may be several kinds of this manner of government, which by the Philosopher, as some think, is called [the pre-
eminent polity], *the politie*.[15] Machiavelli informs us, that experience
of the inconveniences of pure states put men on work to find out this,
and for the most part it may be so.[16] If either of the two, or any of the
three states [estates] be predominant in the administration, the state is
denominated from the prevailing part. For where the prince hath the

---

[14] *Contra* G. Bate, *Elenchus motuum nuperorum in Anglia* (Edinburgh, 1650), see above, ch.
4.13; also *His Majesties Answer to the XIX Propositions of Both Houses of Parliament*
(London, 1642); Christopher Besold, *De majestate in genere: de statu reipublicae mixta*, chs.
1–3, in *Opera politica* (Strasburg, 1641).

[15] Aristotle, *Politics*, 1293 ff., for a discussion of the *politeia*, but the precise expression
Lawson uses (*politeia kat exochen*), seemingly from the expression *oi kat exochen*, 'the chief
men', I have not been able to find in the text. The nearest is at 1295a29–30.

[16] Machiavelli, *Discourses*, bk. 1, ch. 2. In some respects Lawson's discussion here seems to
be following Besold, *De majestate in genere*, chs. 1–3, whose starting-point is also
Machiavelli on pure forms. Machiavelli is following Cicero, Polybius and Livy on Rome.

title of king, and is predominant in the exercise of the power, it's
called a kingdom or monarchy; where the peers, it's an aristocracy;
where the commons, a democracy. And yet if it be a right mixture, it
can be none of these: and in this particular many are deceived. For
where the whole power is wholly in the whole, there *populus*, that is,
king, peers and commons, are the proper subject of majesty in the
constitution; by and in which if any be predominant, it cannot be a
free state. Such a government the German empire and the state of
Venice seem to be. Yet in this latter, the Great Council, which, some
tell us, consists of peers, is counted and judged to have the supreme
power. Yet if we may believe Machiavelli, the families out of which
they are chosen, were, at the first constitution, the whole people. The
Lacedaemonian state is thought by many to be mixed, and some say
the mixture was [principally democratic and secondarily aristocratic],
yet this is very improper and cannot be true.[17] The state of Rome
seems in the time of the kings to be a monarchy. After that an
aristocracy in the senate, and the *Patricii*. But when *plebs* did [pre-
scribe the laws],[18] then it was a democracy in the judgement of many.
Yet upon diligent search it will be found otherwise. For though the
king was the chief pontiff, and did call the assemblies, had the chief
and sole command in war [...][19] yet Halicarnassus lets us know, that
this form was taken from the Lacedaemonians, where the kings had
not absolute power, they were not [*autocratores*] but were limited by
their [*boulen*] or great council, and amongst the Romans by their
[*gerousian*], that is their senate.[20] They must not do what they will, but
what the senate did determine. Yet, we shall often find this mixture
very imperfect or very much altered in tract of time from what it was
at first. To say nothing of Platonic and Utopian commonwealths,
which are not practicable, nor people capable of them. The sum of all
this head is this: that God hath given to men in their several communities a power to protect the just and punish offenders according to
wise laws and just judgements; and also a power to preserve themselves, and justly maintain their own right against all enemies and
invaders. Yet he hath left them at liberty to dispose of it several ways,

---

[17] Aristotle, *Politics*, 1265b.
[18] Lawson has *jubere*, which in context could mean 'ratify', or the much stronger 'prescribe'.
[19] Lawson quotes Dionysius of Halicarnassus, *Roman Antiquities*, 2.14.2, repeating that the king as hegemon had complete command in war. [20] *Ibid.*, 2.14.

and trust it in the hands of one or more who, if they once take it upon them, must exercise it and be just. For he that ruleth over men must be just, ruling in the fear of God (2 Sam. 23.3).

10.

After [. . .] the generals [having been] premised; [and] the several ways and manners of disposing majesty in a certain subject handled, I proceed to say something of the constitution of the state of England, which hath long been governed by kings and parliaments. There was indeed a time, even after the Saxons were settled in this nation, when there was no king, but forty lords, who at length chose a king, which should have no peer: and there was a time when there were many kings. And after that we find one king and parliaments, and this before the Conquest. For this model of ours began in the time of the Saxon kings, and was brought to perfection, some say before; some say, in Edward the Confessor's time. What the power of these parliaments, and of these kings were, is the great question. For that once known, the constitution will be evident. There was a power of kings, and also of parliaments severally, and power of them jointly considered, we find the real majesty in the people, and personal majesty in king and parliament jointly; and a secondary personal majesty, sometimes greater sometimes less in the kings, in the intervals of parliament. But to observe a method and proceed more distinctly, I will [first] presuppose some things. [Second] I will say something of the kings; [third] something of the parliaments severally; [fourth] something of them both jointly [. . .] Therefore, I will suppose the government of England to have been by king and parliament before the conquest, and to have continued so till our days: and whosoever will not grant this, must either be very ignorant, or very partial. I will [further] take for granted, that there hath been extraordinary cases, wherein the rules of the constitution either have not, or could not be observed. [. . .] This is also true, that sometimes when they might have been followed, yet either the constitution of the parliament, or the carriage of kings was such, as that they have violated the same. [Moreover] wise and intelligent men will not deny, but that in our days the government was so altered and corrupted, that the first constitution was hardly known, and it was a difficult thing either to reform it, or reduce it to the ancient form.

II.

These things supposed in the second place, I will examine: [first] how the king acquires his power; [second] what his power acquired is; [and third] how far it's short of a plenary personal majesty. [First] the manner of acquiring this power and title, is either by deriving it from the first investiture, or by inheritance, or election. For the first investiture, I find none to insist upon it, though the rule of investing, if there be any, should be sought in the fundamental charter. If the crown be hereditary to the kings, and they have it as their own fee, they may dispose of it, and of themselves, appoint their successor whom they please: and King Henry VIII might without any act of parliament, have designed by will which of his children should succeed him. And Queen Elizabeth might have nominated either the King of Scots, or any other besides him for her successor. Some may demand, what right she had to nominate, or any other after her death to proclaim her successor. One answer to this demand may be, that her wise council did foresee, that this was an effectual, if not the only way to prevent greater mischiefs and effusion of blood, which in all probability might have followed, if this course had not been taken. And in an extraordinary case, some extraordinary thing, tending to the public good, may lawfully be done. Yet this is not to be made an ordinary rule, and followed as an ordinary example. A third way of acquisition is by election and consent of the people. Thus the first king, as *The Mirrour* tells us in express words, was elected.[21] So were the Saxon kings till Edward the Confessor, the last king of the Saxon race. So was William II, Henry I, Stephen, John. The manner and form of the coronation, which contains in a few words much of the constitution, determines the succession to be by election. Those words of Fortescue to the prince, [there is no royal power held but for that which flows from the people], imply so much.[22] The conqueror himself, who, as a bastard could not inherit the crown, confesseth, that he possessed not the crown *jure haereditario*. To this purpose the old book of Caen is alleged.[23] These things are above me, and out of

---

[21] Andrew Horne, *The Mirrour of Justices* (London, 1642), ch. 1.2.
[22] Sir John Fortescue, *De laudibus legum Angliae* (London, 1567), ch. 13, slightly paraphrased in the text.
[23] Sadler, *The Rights of the Kingdom* (London, 1649), pp. 68–9, on whom Lawson is relying here.

my element, therefore to be judged of by the learned antiquities in
law. But suppose it be granted to be elective, yet it's elective in a
certain line; for such hath been the practice for a long time, which is
conceived to be more convenient. Yet the author of the [...] *Rights of
the Kingdom*, saith, 'that if a King had such children, so qualified, and
so educated; that they were above others in virtue, wisdom, and true
worth (or at least *caeteris pares*) they were the most likely candidates for
the crown'.[24]

12.

But let the manner of acquiring this regal power be either by and from
the first investiture; or by inheritance, or by election. The second
point, and the same of more importance, is to know what this power
once acquired and possessed is. For the Roman emperors acquired
their power by election, and yet it was absolute, as is pretended and
very great. And, here I do not intend to say anything of his excellent
dignity; his sceptre, sword, throne, crown, robe, titles, the honour due
unto him; for these are not so material as the prerogatives of the King
of England. Prerogatives, saith Sir Roger Owen, are the flowers,
which by time immemorial the commons of this realm have granted
the kings thereof. If this be true, he hath no prerogatives, but such as
are granted him, and that by the commons of England. But Judge
Crook is no flatterer, he speaks plainly, and saith, he knows no
prerogatives the king hath but this, that he cannot do wrong.[25] This
may be understood either as it agrees to all sovereigns, or as to the
kings of England in a more special manner. It's true, that no
sovereign, though absolute and despotical can do wrong. For, *Id
quisque potest, quod jure potest.* The meaning is, they ought not to do
wrong; for to do wrong is contrary to the laws of God: whereby they
hold their crowns, and also to the very end, for which God instituted
civil government. Yet there is a more special reason why the kings of
England can do no wrong, because they are kings by law; they cannot
bind by their personal commands, but by their regal, which are not
regal, if not legal.[26] Again, he doth all things like an infant in his
minority by his ministers of state, to whom he can grant no power or

[24] *Ibid.*, p. 70.
[25] Sir George Croke, d. 1642, who came down strongly against Charles I in the Ship
Money Case (1637). [26] Sadler, *The Rights of the Kingdom*, pp. 76–7.

commission to act but according to law. Therefore if any wrong be done, as much is, it's done by them, and they, not the king, are chargeable with it, and questionable for it. Yet he hath power, and great power, and it's not the less, but rather the greater and more like unto God's because it's limited by law. He summons parliaments, makes officers, confers honours, sends and receives ambassadors, and gives them answer, makes leagues with other states, and other things formerly mentioned, when I spake of the second kind of personal majesty. Yet, if we may believe Bracton, he hath all this from the law. For *Lex facit Regem*, and he is but trusted with the exercise of it for the protection of the people, and the execution of the laws:[27] in which respect it seems to follow, that if the law be above him, they who make the laws must needs be above him.

13.

But in the third place, though the king hath great power, yet there is some power in the kingdom, which he hath not. For he cannot abolish parliaments, he cannot refuse to call them, either when the laws, or the *ardua regni* require them, he cannot exercise the militia but according to the laws, neither can he make or repeal laws without the parliament; he cannot command the purse, he cannot alienate the crown or the crown-revenue, nor dispose of the crown as his own hereditary fee; divers other things there are above his power. Yet the kings of England have challenged and exercised far greater power, than the laws and constitution gives them. But that was matter of fact and cannot found a right. We read that King Richard II was charged, as with other things, so with these two: 1. that he said the laws were in his head and his breast: that is, he had the legislative power solely to himself; 2. that he denied to approve the laws made by the parliament, that is, he challenged a negative voice. In both these, Arnisaeus undertakes to maintain his cause as just, and that he did but challenge his due. (*De authoritate principum...*, 4.) Yet all his whole answer is but *petitio principii*. For presupposing the King of England to be an absolute monarch, which we know he is not, he takes upon him to answer the whole charge, which he might easily do, if he take for granted, that which he can never prove, nor Englishmen, especially

---

[27] Henry de Bracton, *De legibus et consuetudinibus Angliae*, ed. G. E. Woodbine, trans. E. Thorne (Cambridge, Mass., Harvard University Press, 1968), 5.2, fol. 5b, p. 33.

antiquaries in law, will never grant him. That he wrote against rebellion and treason, and maintained the just and lawful authority of princes, he did well, but that he should write as a pensioner to the king,[28] and so presumptuously judge of the constitution of a foreign state, whereof he was sufficiently ignorant, we Englishmen cannot well brook. So Bodin being informed by Dellus (who I think, was Sir Thomas Dale, a prudent and experienced statesman, and far better acquainted with the government of his own country than he was) that the kings of England could not make or repeal a law without, but only by the parliament, he wondered, and notwithstanding his information, he presumptuously determines the kings of England to be absolute monarchs. So much he doted upon his imperfect notion of majesty and absolute power.[29] Mr. Camden, though a learned antiquary, yet not in the common law, speaks doubtfully in this point, and doth not well, though perhaps prudently, express himself. His words are, [the king has sovereign power and absolute command among us.] Yet afterwards, speaking of our courts, he gives to the parliament the supreme and sacred power in making, conferring, repealing and interpreting the laws, and in all other things, which concern the good of the state. If he meant that the king had it jointly with the two houses, it's tolerable; yet if so, [...] his former expression was not good, and [...] neither is that latter assertion of his, when he saith, the parliament is summoned *ad arbitrium Regis*, when the king pleaseth.[30]

14.

But let's go to the parliament, where we shall find the king again: and when we come there, we must consider: 1. what it is; 2. what power it hath; 3. what power it hath not. [First], to give a perfect definition of it is above my skill, neither is it within the sphere of my profession; ancient parliamentmen, and especially learned antiquaries in the common law know it best. Mr. Camden gives a tolerable description of it. 'It's a representative of all England, invested with the highest power of legislation, and all other acts that concern the common

---

[28] Christian IV of Denmark.

[29] Jean Bodin, *Les Six Livres de la république* (Paris, 1576), trans. *De republica, libri sex* (Paris, 1594), bk. 1, ch. 8; the translator, Richard Knolles, *The Six Books of the Commonwealth* (London, 1606), calls Dale an English ambassador.

[30] William Camden, *Britannia* (London, 1586), 'Ordines Angliae', pp. 59, 63. Camden's text has *principe* for Lawson's *regis*.

good.' This is the substance of the matter, though not given in his express terms.[31] And here I will not say anything of their election, incorporation, manner of proceeding after it's once constituted, and begins as a formal parliament to act. Some have conceived it to be one of the most orderly assemblies in the world, which is an argument of the great wisdom of our ancestors, who first moulded it, and brought it to perfection, yet it may be corrupted and ill-constituted, and then [the corruption of the best is the worst]. The election in our times is not well ordered: for if it were, the very quintessence of the wisdom and virtues of all England might be extracted, united, and act in that convention. But men are ready through want of understanding to undo themselves, by choosing insufficient and unworthy persons. The first constitution certainly required a qualification in the persons to be elected. For we trust them much, even with our estates, liberty, lives and religion for the outward profession. It's not fit to trust these in the hands of any sort of men, but such as shall be wise, faithful, just and sincerely affecting the public good. The Saxon name Witena Gemot [Witan Moot] implies this: for it signifies the meeting of wise men, and is the abridgement of all the folk-moots in England and of the wisdom of all England: and now of all England, Wales, Scotland, Ireland. If they should be wise men, wisdom includes all virtues. If we consider this great body as distinct from the king, it's said to consist of two houses, which some call the upper and the lower. This the commons did not like, did not acknowledge. The two houses, or the House of Commons, and the House of Peers may be tolerable: and I do not know they ever excepted against the expressions. Many ungrateful and unworthy persons, to their own wrong and prejudice, have much depressed the House of Commons, and are not ashamed to say, such is their ignorance, that it is but of late standing. Yet it's the chief part, and almost the whole representative: the Peers to them are but inconsiderable. Whatsoever is concluded there doth most concern them, and the heaviest burden lies on them. And though by Commons, some may understand only the plebeian rank, yet there we find in that house men of good birth, estates, and as eminent virtues, as many of the Lords be. What the House of Commons is may be more easily known, but the nature of the House of Lords is somewhat hidden. For in it we find lords spiritual, as abbots, bishops, and these

---

[31] *Ibid.* (*tribunalia*/courts), p. 63.

by tenure; we find in it also lords temporal, as dukes, marquesses, earls, viscounts, barons. And all these under the name of lords, peers, barons, though *barones, proceres, nobiles* do sometimes signify other persons. For we read of the Barons of the Cinque Ports, Barons of the Exchequer, the eight Barons of Cheshire, and the Barons of Burford in Shropshire. We find peers sometimes taken in another sense: and to include the Commons. And the truth is, if the whole assembly be considered as one representative, they are all peers, and in all acts should be taken so to be. These peers become such three ways, as I observed in my answer to Mr. Hobbes. For they are *aut Fœdales, aut rescriptitii, aut diplomatici*, barons by tenure and ancient prescription since the time of William the Elder, or by writ, or by patent.[32] It is not for me to debate, much less to determine the controversies about these Lords, as [first], whether they be essential parts in a distinct House from the Commons of the parliament or no (seeing acts and ordinances and the same valid, are said to be made without these Lords, not any by the Lords without the Commons). [Second], what these Lords may do, or for what end they are called. For some say, they sit there as judges of the king together with the Commons. For though the king in his politic capacity cannot do wrong, yet in his personal he may. This Horne and Bracton, with other of the old lawyers will tell us: in whom we may read of the torts and wrongs done by the king, and of judging him, as also the queen and the prince.[33] [Third], seeing by the writ of summons they are called to deliberate and consult, *Consilium impensuri*, not *ad faciendum at consentiendum*, as the Commons are, whether they be there only as the king's counsellors. [Fourth], suppose them to be the king's counsellors, whether they be such without or with the Commons. [Fifth], whether they have any share in the legislative power, or if they have, whether in the same House or in a distinct House and body with a negative to the Commons, or not. [Sixth], when this transmitting of bills to the House of Lords began, which some say, to be after the barons' wars. For it was not so from the beginning. [Seventh], whether the Lords, and not the Commons have power to administer

---

[32] *An Examination of the Political Part of Mr. Hobbs, His Leviathan (London, 1657), pp. 133–4.*
[33] See e.g. Horne, *The Mirrour*, ch. 1.3; cf. 'The Declaration of the Houses in Defence of the Militia Ordinance, June 1642', in R. S. Gardiner, *The Constitutional Documents of the Puritan Revolution, 1625–1600*, 3rd edn. (Oxford University Press, 1979), pp. 254 ff., and below, ch. 15.

an oath. We read in Sir H. Spelman's *Glossary*, in the word *Baro*, that no barons were called to the parliament, but such as held of the king in *capite*.[34] [Also] that all these were not called, but the chief of them, as earls who possessed twenty knights' fees, and barons which had to the value of thirteen knights' fees, and a third part of one; [and] that because these were too many, some of them were called to parliament, some omitted, and only such as were called were counted barons, the rest not. [...] This being taken ill, the barons caused King John [to be compelled] to covenant under the Broad Seal, to summon severally by so many writs, the archbishops, abbots, earls and the greater barons of the kingdom. [...] Yet Henry III so little regarded that compact, that he called and kept a parliament, with one hundred and twenty spiritual, and only twenty-five temporal lords, though he had numbered two hundred and fifty baronies in England. [Moreover], Edward I omitted divers of those, whom Henry III had summoned. So that it will be a very difficult thing to rectify or reduce unto the first institution this House, as distinct from that of the Commons. For it should be known; [...] what kind of persons must constitute this other House; [...] what their privileges be; [and] what they must do, which the House of Commons may not, must not do.

15.

By all this, something of the nature of the parliament may be known. But then what is the power of this assembly, either severally considered without the king, or jointly with the king? And that they may make orders and ordinances *pro tempore* will be granted, and also, which is far more, if the king have no negative voice, the legislative and judicial power is in them, and their ultimate resolves and dictates in all matters of counsel must stand. And if so, then reason will conclude that if the king refuse to be personally or virtually present, and to act with them, they may do anything for the good of the kingdom without him, which they may do jointly with him. Yet because laws and judgement are ineffectual without execution, therefore the king, being trusted with the execution, was required to give his consent, that he might take care of the execution. For to that end he was trusted with the sword of justice and war, that he might protect

---

[34] Sir Henry Spelman, *Glossarium archaiologicum* (London, 1626), entry under *baro, barus* (London, 1687 edn.), pp. 64 ff.

the people, and see that laws and judgements be executed. If we consider the parliament as consisting of king, peers and commons jointly, it is the first subject of personal majesty, and to it, and it alone belongs all the *Jura Majestatis personalis*. They have the power legislative, judicial, executive, to exercise it in the highest degree; and may perform all acts of administration as distinct from the constitution. They are the highest assembly for legislation, the highest council for advice, the highest court for judicature.

16.

This is the power of the parliament, which can do many and great things, yet some things they cannot do: for they are limited not only by the laws of God, but also by the laws of the constitution. Sir Roger Owen tells, that the parliament cannot do all things. For, many acts are voted for errors in matter of fact, and for contrariety in words, and sometimes they have idle and flattering provisos. [...] A parliament hath not power to ordain that a law shall not be abrogated for the space of twenty years, for a latter parliament may repeal their acts. [...] A parliament cannot enact, that, if there were no heir to the crown, that the people should not be able to choose a new king. [Further] it cannot change the form of our policy [polity] from a monarchy to a democracy. It cannot take away divers prerogatives annexed to the crown of England, or that the king should not be able to dissolve the parliament at will and pleasure. Yet in another place he tells us, that he [the monarch] cannot dissolve the parliament at will and pleasure; and again, he is not above the parliament, because he cannot be above himself: and in parliament he is *maxime Rex*. [Owen] further informs us, that the common law is the king's inheritance, and how the parliament may wither away the flowers of the crown.[35] The true reason, why the parliament cannot do some of these things (nor others not mentioned by him) is, because they have not real but personal majesty. They cannot alter the government, nor take away divers things belonging to the crown, because they did not give the prerogatives of the crown at the first; the commons of the realm gave them, as he confesseth. The form of government was first constituted by the community of England, not by the parliament. For the

---

[35] Presumably the manuscript referred to above, ch. 4.15.

community and people of England gave both king and parliament
their being: and if they meddle with the constitution to alter it, they
destroy themselves, because they destroy that whereby they subsist.
The community indeed may give a parliament this power, to take
away the former constitution, and to frame and model another, but
then they cannot do this as a parliament, but as trusted by the people
for such a business and work: nay, they may appoint another assembly
of fewer or more to do such a work without them. They may set up a
Concilium sapientum, which may determine what matters are fit to be
proposed to the parliament, and in what order, and also contrive a
Juncto for all businesses, which require expedition and secrecy, which
may act without them. Whether the parliament itself can do such
things or no, may justly be doubted. What may be done in extraordinary cases is one thing, what may be done in an ordinary way another.
When he [Owen?] saith, that the parliament cannot change the form
of policy from a monarchy, he presupposeth our state of England to
be a monarchy. Yet if he distinguish not between the constitution and
the administration, he may be guilty of an error. For it's not a
monarchy, but only in respect of the executive part in the intervals of
parliaments. Our ancestors abhorred absolute and arbitrary
monarchs: therefore before they did establish a king, they made bridle
to keep him in, and put it upon him. This is plain from Bracton,
Fortescue, the Coronation Oath, and *The Mirrour*.[36]

17.

From all this we may conjecture what the constitution of England was.
It was no absolute monarchy, that's plain enough. Neither was it a
state of pure disposition but mixed. Neither were the *Jura Majestatis*
divided, some to the king, some to the lords, some to the commons, it
was of a far better mould. The personal majesty primary was in king,
peers and commons jointly: in the whole assembly as one body. This
may appear several ways. [First] from this, that it was a representative
of the whole nation, and as it was a general representative of all

---

[36] The image of the bridle (*frenum*) seems to be taken explicitly from Bracton, *De legibus*,
the 'addicio de cartis' passage already cited by Lawson (ch. 5.9). The underlying contrast
is between rationality and will. See Cary J. Nederman, 'The Royal Will and the Baronial
Bridle: The Place of the *Addicio de Cartis* in Bractonian Political Thought', *History of
Political Thought*, 10 (1989), pp. 415 ff.

England and no ways else, was it invested with this personal sovereignty. It must represent the whole community, all the members thereof, of what rank or condition soever, not only the laity but the clergy too: these are words used in our laws and good enough, though disliked by many. The clergy and ministry of England were never represented by the knights of the counties before our times: neither could the parliament, without the personal presence of some of themselves impose subsidies, much less ecclesiastical canons upon them. They are as free Englishmen as any other, and by the laws of the land have their privileges and immunities distinct from those of other men, which are now taken from them: and it's a hard case that they may have none of their own faculty and capacity, as their proper representatives to maintain them and speak reason for them. They are willing enough to part with anything formerly they had, if not agreeable to Scripture. [Second] to prove this mixture, the king's Coronation Oath might be alleged, for he swears to corroborate the just laws and customs, *quas vulgus elegerit*, where two words require some explication [. . .] *Vulgus* [and] *corroborare*, that we may know what they mean. *Vulgus* some thing doth signify the Commons, and then the Lords, as of a distinct House, can have no share in the legislation, except as some tell us, they were represented by the knights of the counties, whom with the rest of the freeholders they did anciently elect, and contribute to their charges whilst they sat in parliament. *Vulgus* in Latin is the same as *Folk* in Saxon, and now remains in English; from whence *Folk-moot* the city or shire meeting, as the parliament is the great meeting of all the counties in England. In this place it must be the representative of the whole community of England in one body, all the members of the Witena Gemot [Witan Moot], as united, and distinct from the king. The word *Corroborare* doth not signify to give the essence to the law, as though it were not a law before, or not a custom; but it signifies to guard, keep, defend, observe the just laws and customs in the administration, and to see them executed according to judgement. It may be the same with [to validate] in Greek; which doth not give the being to a will and testament, for it must be a will before it be confirmed and so made effectual. Confirmation is extrinsical and accidental, not essential to the will or testament. The reason why the kings did swear to corroborate the just laws and customs made, approved, chosen by the people, was because that upon the dissolution of the parliament, the sword remained in his hands for to see the laws executed, which were ineffectual, would lie dead, be in vain without execution. These words explained, the matter to be observed is, that if by laws and customs we understand the rules of administration, not only as including a binding force, but also as to be made effectual, then it follows by the tenor of that oath, that the legislative power, which is the foundation and rule of all acts of administration, was in king, peers and commons jointly: this is a mixture, and a free state. [Third], this mixture will further appear from the manner of enacting. For this was the manner in our days. 'Be it therefore enacted by the King's most excellent Majesty, by and with the assent and consent of the Lords spiritual and temporal, and the Commons in this present Parliament assembled, and by authority of the same.' Neither is this new; for the substance of it is ancient, as Sir Edward Coke doth manifest in the cause of the Prince as Duke of Cornwall.[37] The collection of the statutes will manifest it for four hundred years. For what if other terms were used, yet they were in sense the same. Neither did this begin in the reign of Richard II, or Henry III, King Edward the Confessor's *Modus tenendi Parliamentum* will confirm the same, to which my Lord Chief Justice Coke tells us, the conqueror bound himself. Though Sir Roger Owen thinks this book but a pamphlet, yet my Lord Coke, as good a lawyer, and Sir Henry Spelman as good an antiquary as he, were of another mind, and thought better of it.[38] Nay, it's not only thus in making laws, but also in judgements which pass into an act. And this kind of judgement is the highest, from which there lies no appeal. This is the nature of the constitution so far as my poor understanding is able to judge.

18.

It remains I add something of our present condition since the times of our sad divisions. After a long-continued peace, the light of the glorious gospel, many blessings and great deliverances from Heaven;

---

[37] Sir Edward Coke, *Reports* (London, 1658), *Declarations* (bound in) . . ., trans. W. Hughes (London, 1659), pp. 280–1.

[38] The *Modus tenendi* was in fact late 13th or early 14th century. Widely circulated and cited, it was published in London 1660, 1671, ed. W. Hakewill. Sir Henry Spelman, *Of Parliaments* (n.d.), in English, and *Posthumous Works* (republished London, 1727). He refers to Coke in a way that makes it likely that Lawson had access to some version of this work. But see also Sadler, *The Rights of the Kingdom*, pp. 66–9. See also below, ch. 15 n. 42.

such was our unthankfulness, so great the corruptions of church and state, that when God expected better fruits, our sins were ripe for vengeance; so that some fearful judgement, if not the ruin of the three nations, did seem to approach; or rather to be fatal and unavoidable. And some of our teachers and watchmen, seriously considering the eternal rules of providence and divine proceedings with the world in former times, and knowing our present distempers, did foresee this, and gave us warning from those words of our Saviour, 'Except ye repent, ye shall all likewise perish' (Luke 13.3). Yet no warning given, either by our watchmen from the Scriptures, or the judgements of God upon Germany and the neighbour nations round about us, whom from our own shores we might behold wallowing in their own blood, would be taken. And even then when there was no danger from any enemy without, and we were secure, as enjoying the sweetest and most happy peace that could be expected on earth; God looked down from Heaven with indignation, and as though he had sworn to be revenged on such a nation, and so ungrateful a people, he sent a spirit of giddiness amongst us, and set the Egyptians against the Egyptians, and made us executioners of his own judgement upon ourselves: for from ourselves our miseries did arise.[39] For after a first and second pacification between England and Scotland, the long-continued Parliament began to reform both church and state, but found the corruptions so generally diffused and deeply rooted in the whole body, that there was a greater fear of ruin, than hope of reformation; and this some of our wise statists had formerly observed, was likely to be the issue. They acted vigorously at the first, but, as some wise men thought, too hastily and too high, and seemed somewhat to incline to an extreme. In the meantime no man suspecting, no man fearing it, break out that bloody barbarous massacre in Ireland [1641], wherein two hundred thousand English Protestants are said to be murdered in one month. In this the actors were Irish Papists, and the sufferers English Protestants. This could not quench the fire of dissension in England, which began to manifest itself in the Parliament's militia opposed to the King's array, which proceeded to a bloody battle at or near Kineton [Edgehill, 23 October 1642], which continued till the

---

[39] Isa. 19.2. The sense of surprise and an idiom of providential explanation were widespread. See e.g. The Solemn League and Covenant, Sept. 1643, sect. 6, para. 2, in Gardiner, *The Constitutional Documents of the Puritan Revolution*, p. 270; *Eikon Basilike* (London, 1649), esp. p. 53.

King's party was wholly subdued in England [1647], himself put to death, his posterity dispossessed of the crown [1649], Ireland reduced with the ruin of almost all the chief and ancient families of the same, and Scotland vanquished [1650–1]. In all our sad divisions which happened from first to last, and are not wholly yet ended to this day, two things are worthy the serious consideration of wiser men than I am: [...] What party for time past hath been most faithful to the English interest; [and] what course is to be taken for to settle us more firmly for time to come. For the first, we must understand what the English interest is. The interest of England is twofold, civil and ecclesiastical; for we are Englishmen and Christians. The civil interest is *salus populi Anglicani*, there is no doubt of that, for the peace, safety, liberty, happiness of our dear country is the end, whereat we are all bound both by the written and natural laws of God to aim. The interest ecclesiastical is the Protestant religion and the preservation of the substance thereof. Prelacy, Presbytery, Independency, much less Antipaedobaptism and other sects, are not essential, but accidental to it. This being the interest of England, we cannot judge of the faithfulness either of the King's or Parliament's party by the quality of the persons of either side. For there were both good and bad on both sides, who had their several grounds of adhering to this or that party, and their several ends: and neither their grounds nor ends good. Nor can any man justify all proceedings and actings of either side: both had their errors. Nor must we judge of them according to their protestations, for both could not by such contrary means attain the same end; as both sides protested to maintain, the King, the Parliament, the liberty of the subject, the laws and the Protestant religion. Neither in this particular must the laws of the English constitution and administration be the rule: for both acted not only above the laws, but contrary to the letter of them at least. For no laws could warrant the Parliament to act without the King, or the King without the Parliament. Much less was it justifiable that there should be in one kingdom two, not only different, but contrary commands supreme, and from different heads and persons. This was directly against the very nature of all commonwealths which have only one first mover, and one indivisible supreme power to animate and act them.

19.

The rule therefore must be the laws of God as above the laws of men, and we must consider according to these divine rules, what was the state of the controversy, the justice and equity of the cause made evident, and the just necessity of doing that which was done. Neither must we look at the cause only, as just in itself, but also how it's justly or unjustly maintained. For men may use such means as shall never reach the just end intended, but also such as may be destructive of the cause itself, and raze the very foundation of it. Besides all this, before a perfect judgement can be made, the secret counsels, contrivances, designs, hidden actings of the chief actors should be known, yet these many times lie hid and are not known, or if known yet to very few, and some of these few cannot sound the bottom. Many things are charged upon the king, as acting against the English interest as civil:[40] as that he dissolves parliaments without just and sufficient cause, that he intermits parliaments for sixteen years together; that having signed the Petition of Right, he acts contrary to it, imposeth ship-money, calls a parliament, signs the act of continuance, deserts it, calls the members from it, calls another parliament at Oxford, challengeth a negative voice to both the Houses, raiseth a war against it, though he was informed that this tended to the dissolution of the government, that whosoever should serve or assist him in such wars, are traitors by the fundamental laws of this kingdom, and have been so adjudged in two acts of parliament (Richard II [1388] and Henry IV [1399]); and that such persons ought to suffer as traitors. These with other particulars charged upon him, seem directly contrary unto the civil interest of the kingdom. Again, to marry a popish lady, upon articles directly contrary to the laws of England, and the Protestant religion established by law; to entertain twenty-eight popish priests with a bishop, to tolerate mass in the court; to receive three agents from the Pope one after another, Pisano, Con, Rosetti; to maintain the Queen Mother, to engage the generality of the people of England, to retard the relieving of Ireland; to admit divers of the popish Irish murderers and rebels into his army; to call our English forces, sent to relieve the poor distressed Protestants of Ireland, out of that nation, and employ

---

[40] Lawson is commenting here on The Grand Remonstrance, and the charge levelled against Charles at his trial. See Gardiner, *The Constitutional Documents of the Puritan Revolution*, pp. 202 ff. and 371.

them against the Parliament of England; to suffer some of the heads of the Irish rebels to be so near his person, to endeavour to bring in the Duke of Lorraine with his forces into this nation; to contract with the Irish rebels upon condition to enjoy their religion; to furnish him with ten thousand Irish rebels; to strengthen his party in England, with divers other acts, like unto these, is conceived to be, not only inconsistent with, but plainly destructive of the English Protestant interest. And if this be true, it must needs be so. Yet it might be said, that the King endeavoured to maintain his own regal power, the episcopacy and liturgy established by law, and that he did not oppose the Parliament, but a seditious party in the Parliament and other sectaries, whose principles were destructive both of all civil and also ecclesiastical government; and without the judgement of able lawyers and learned divines, he did not undertake the war, either against Scotland, or England, or any other. It's true, that of those who adhered to the King, and liked not the Parliament's proceeding, there were some conscientious persons, who judged the King an absolute monarch, and did not like many things done by that party, yet they thought it the duty of subjects to suffer, and that it was no ways lawful to resist. But the casuists say, that [ignorance excuses so much, not all], their ignorance might make their crime less, yet no ways free them from all guilt. It was not invincible; they might easily have known that the King of England was no absolute monarch, seeing he could not impose any subsidy upon the subject, nor make or repeal a law without the parliament; neither could he by his letters or personal command revoke the judgement of any court. And though they might be civilians, [civil lawyers] or read foreign writers, which take our kings for absolute sovereigns, yet no ancient lawyers, no parliaments did declare them to be such. Nay, they might have known, that they themselves, obeying the King's personal commands, disobeyed him as King, and that serving him in the wars, they were guilty of high treason against the kingdom and the King's crown and dignity. Of these royalists, some have been high and cruel against their brethren the parliamenteers, and have censured them, and do yet condemn them both in words and writing, as guilty of most horrible treason and rebellion, which others will undertake to prove the censurers themselves deeply guilty of. Wise and learned men, no whit inferior to them, do certainly know, that as they could not maintain their cause by dint of sword, so neither can they make it good by dint of argument. One of their learned casuists delivers this as a positive truth; 'that to disobey a lawful sovereign is such an act, as that no circumstances can make it lawful, no not the glory of God, nor the saving of many souls, nor preventing the ruin of a nation'.[41] This is high. Divers, who read this in his books, conceive, that in this he toucheth the cause and controversy between King and Parliament: I cannot charge him with any such thing. But let his application be what it will, I will consider his proposition in itself, and will suppose it to be grounded upon that divine maxim, we must not do evil that good may come. For that which God hath made sin, nothing can make lawful. But then the question is, what he means by sovereign, what by disobedience to a lawful sovereign? If he mean by sovereign one invested with supreme power, and an absolute monarch, it's clear enough the kings of England were not such. For [...] they had no legislative power which is the greatest without this Parliament; [...] his personal commands bound no man: for he could command nothing but according to the just laws and customs, *quas vulgus elegerat*; [and] the late King himself in his answer to the Nineteen Propositions confessed that the parliament had a share in the legislative power.[42] It's true, they had the title of sovereign and majesty, but in another sense than many take it. As for the second term disobedience, it might be twofold; in respect of absolute sovereigns; and in respect of the kings of England. In respect of the former, a lawful sovereign may command unlawful things, and contrary to the laws of God, and in this case, their commands may, nay, must be disobeyed. If they command things lawful in themselves, yet they may command them so, as to be unlawful. A man is bound to love father and mother by the law of God, and to do so is not only lawful but necessary. Yet if this love come in competition with the love of Christ, it's plainly unlawful. Therefore, I will be so charitable as to think, he understood the proposition of disobedience to lawful commands of lawful sovereigns, otherwise he saith nothing, but his proposition is false. [...] In respect of the kings of England, their commands are personal or legal. His legal commands, if agreeable to the laws of God ought to be obeyed, and his subjects are bound to submit unto his legal power, for other power, as king, he hath none. But as for his personal commands, they

---

[41] The unsourced quotation remains obscure.

[42] *His Majesties Answer to the XIX Propositions* was written largely by Lucius Cary, Nicholas Culpepper; it was the *locus classicus* of conventional mixed monarchy theory.

bind no subject as a subject, and if they be contrary to the law, in obeying them, we may be guilty of disobedience to the law, nay of disobedience to the king as king, nay guilty of treason against the kingdom and the king's crown and dignity. And methinks such learned men should not be ignorant of these things.

20.

As for the Parliament it was charged with taking upon them the militia, seizing upon the navy, securing the ports, making of a new Broad Seal, creating of officers, abolishing of episcopacy and liturgy established by law, by which they lost many of the subjects, calling in the Scots, proposing a covenant to the people upon high terms, and many other things, and all these without the King; nay, contrary to the King's command, who had so graciously condescended unto them, in granting many things unto them, prejudicial, as he thought, to his prerogatives and the ancient rights of his predecessors, especially the acts of Continuance and of the Triennial [Act of] Parliament. [...] For the militia it was alleged, the King promised it, and the lawyers and learned counsel informed them, that if the king in such a time should neglect it, they might take it and exercise it themselves without him; and it's reported, that the very same parties, who had given this advice to the Parliament, after they were come unto the king, did counsel him to set on foot the Commission of Array in opposition to the parliament's militia. [...] For seizing the navy, ports, and creating of officers, in a declaration of the Lords and Commons upon the treaty at Oxford [1643], is showed the necessity of doing so, and the antiquity of that practice: for they instance in many parliaments, which have done the like and more too. It was no new thing. And though his majesty affirmed these things were his by law, yet it was not his but by way of trust, for the defence, not the destruction of the kingdom. [...] For the Broad Seal, there was a necessity of making a new one, seeing that the former was surreptitiously against law and right carried and conveyed away. Neither had the King, as separate and divided from the Parliament, any right unto it. [...] The abolishing of episcopacy and liturgy, is conceived, might be justly charged upon the Scot, who when the King and so many great ones had deserted the Parliament, would not firmly adhere unto them but upon such terms. Otherwise the reformation of bishops and Book of Common Prayer was far more for the Protestant interest than Presbytery, which was rather inconsistent with it. [...] The calling of the Scots was said to be done in extremity, and grounded upon the National League, according to which they were bound of themselves to have assisted the Parliament, as some thought and judged. [...] The Covenant is said to be more from the Scot than the English [1643]:[43] and what the design of the first contrivers in it might be was known to few who took it. It proved to be of bad consequence (whether in respect of the nature of the Convenant, or some other cause may be doubted); for the Parliament of Scotland thought it a sufficient ground for [the] Duke [of] Hamilton to invade England [1648], and the English House of Commons judged them rebels and traitors, who should join with him or assist. Such is the frailty, inconstancy and depravity of men. [...] As for the high demands of the Parliament, it's alleged no king ever did such things, or gave occasion to make such demands, and he did but grant that which was reasonable, and necessary for the time, and less than former laws required; so that except, as separated from the Parliament, he was an absolute monarch, his denial of their demands was not consistent with the constitution of the kingdom.

21.

But after that the royal party was totally subdued, there falls out a subdivision amongst the anti-royalists. For they who could agree against a third party, could not agree amongst themselves. For they began to play Scotch and English first,[44] and then the Presbyterian (who much, though not in all things inclined to the Scot) and the Independent began to clash. So the state of the controversy seemed to be altered. For both these parties at the first professed themselves enemies only to popery and arbitrary government, which all true English Protestants were bound to oppose, and by the laws of the land might justly do it.[45] But neither Presbytery nor Independency could

---

[43] Lawson seems to be discussing the Solemn League and Convenant, 1643, rather than the Scottish National Covenant, 1638, signed in opposition to Charles's religious policies.

[44] A children's chasing game; the *OED* gives no usage earlier than 1802. The allusion may also be to the satirical tract *An Unhappy Game of Scotch and English* (Edinburgh?, 1646).

[45] The catch-cries of popery and arbitrary government were to remain central to polemics

be for our true interest, but rather against it. The truth is, they were
not unanimously resolved what they should build up, though they
agreed well enough in pulling down. And surely it's not wisdom to
pull down and raze to the ground an old house, which being repaired
might serve the turn, before they had a new one, and the same better,
ready to set up, or rather finished to their hands. Yet this was not all
the difference between the parties: but after the conquest of
Hamilton, and all the royal party rising and ready to join with him, yet
some of them, who were real and cordial, and did really join together,
laying aside for the time the difference of Presbytery and
Independency in subduing the adversary, were willing to join with the
King upon certain terms in the Isle of Wight [1647–8]. They thought
that such an agreement, if it might be made, was the only way to settle
us in peace. Others conceived, that such an agreement, if once made,
was destructive of all former designs and proceedings: and that if the
King was guilty of so much blood, and other crying sins, as the
Parliament, and especially the Kirk of Scotland had charged him withal, then to agree with him was to destroy the English interest, and
bring innocent blood upon themselves and the nation. Therefore in
an order for a solemn thanksgiving made by the Kirk, one particular
mercy to be remembered in that service, was, that the treaty with the
King in the Isle of Wight did not take effect. From this fearful guilt, if
justly charged upon the King and his party, some would dare to
conclude, that they who attempted to make an agreement with the
enemy so guilty, could not be so faithful as those, who refused all such
reconciliation, and endeavoured to take away all causes of future
danger. Yet if these latter, after a full and final ruin of the malignant
party, as they called them, should not proceed impartially to reduce
the government to the primitive constitution, and labour to settle the
Protestant religion for the substance, and the good laws of the commonwealth, they might prove more faithful in destroying, than in
building and laying the foundation of our future happiness. For to
pull down one arbitrary power to erect another, and neglecting the
substance of the Protestant religion, to protect sectaries, and erect
new models of their own brain, can be no act of fidelity. I will not
enter upon particulars, nor reflect upon any person or persons: for my

for the rest of the century on the grounds that Lawson outlines; cf. e.g. Andrew Marvell,
An Account of the Growth of Popery and Arbitrary Government (London, 1677).

intelligence is not so perfect as to know the secret designs and hidden motions of several parties; which if I did know, I might the better regulate mine own judgement in this point, though I could not satisfy others. Therefore I will leave all to the judgement of the eternal God, and pray for future peace, and humbly request him for to bless and prosper all such as with an upright heart have endeavoured, and do still labour to establish a wise and just government. And I further desire all those, whom God hath preserved and blessed with great success, to make a right use of God's mercies, least [lest] in the end they suffer the same or like judgements as God by them hath executed upon others for their sins. Though it be material to know who have been most faithful, and by whose means under God for the present we enjoy peace and the gospel, yet it may be of more moment, and also more useful, to take notice of the errors, mistakes and miscarriages both of Parliament and army from first to last. For by the knowledge hereof we gain some advantage, and wise men may easily understand how to avoid the like, and to prevent such miseries for time to come as we have suffered in time past. [It is necessary] to observe God's proceedings and the order which he hath observed in all our confusions, and the end, whereat he aims, and the duties he expects after so many judgements executed; [and] to consider what families and persons God hath punished in these sad times, and for what sins. And if we after so great success fall into the same sins, we must expect the like punishments: not to mention the great alterations in the dominions of Spain, Turkey, China of late days. Let's consider in brief, the strange works and proceedings of the Almighty with us in this corner of the world. To this end, let us take a short view of [1.] the wars, 2. the parliaments, 3. the King, 4. the civil government, 5. the church, 6. our present condition.

1. The wars are civil or foreign: civil in England, Ireland, Scotland. The royal standard of England marcheth into Scotland, where an army is ready to oppose. Yet no blow given; no blood shed. After this, we see two potent armies in England, and only a little skirmish at the first; a pacification is made, the National League concluded, both the armies disbanded. But after this, no man fearing it, a bloody massacre of two hundred thousand in the space of one month, besides many thousand slain and butchered, afterwards begins the tragedy in Ireland. Forces are sent to revenge that blood, and thousands of the bloody Irish are sacrificed to expiate the former murders. At length a

civil war is commenced in England, the same, very bloody, continues long, many thousands are slain, the sword rageth in every corner, the cry goes up to Heaven. The Parliament desiring not only to defend itself, but to relieve bleeding Ireland, is brought very low, is ready to submit, calls in the Scot, recovers, prevails, beats the King's party in the field, reduceth all their garrisons, and obtains a total victory in England. Ireland almost lost is recovered again, first in field battle, then by reducing all their garrisons. And in that kingdom from first to last, millions are slain, the ancient great families cut off, and the land for the greatest part made desolate; which was a dreadful judgement of the most just judge of Heaven and earth. Scotland, where the fire began to smoke at first, escaped long, at last felt the bottoms and cruelty of a bloody war managed against them by Montrose who at first was one of their covenanters. Yet this fire is quenched. They invade England twice, and are twice scornfully foiled and shattered to pieces in England, and at length wholly subdued by our English forces in Scotland, and remain subject to our power to this very day. Never so many fearful judgements executed, never so many bloody wars in so short a time can we read of in all our former histories. Before these wars are ended, they beat the Netherlanders, the most potent people by sea in the world.

2. Parliaments, which are the great bulwark of the kingdom, had been intermitted for sixteen years: at length, when no man did expect, one is called, but suddenly dissolved. Yet the Scots entered with a puissant army into the kingdom, made a necessity of calling a second, which is summoned, confirmed by an Act of Continuance, acts high, makes great demands, continues long. Yet it's deserted by the King and many of the members; opposed by an army, defends itself, undertakes the King in England, Scotland, Ireland. It makes a new Broad Seal, having formerly seized upon the navy and the ports, recruits itself by new elections. Then they fall out with their army, after that they are divided amongst themselves. In the end follows the seclusion of many of the members, and the remnant act, and by the army and the navy doth great things, but at last even this remnant by this army is totally routed and dissolved. This is that long-sitting parliament, which some say, might have been good physic, but proved bad diet. Never parliament of England varied more, never any more opposed; never any suffered more, never any acted higher, never any effected greater things. It made an end of kings, and new modelled the government.

3. The King deserting the Parliament, set up his royal standard, and is opposed, fought, beaten, finally and totally conquered, delivered by the Scots into the Parliament's hands, is confined, secured as a guilty person, tried, judged, condemned to death, executed. His family and children banished, and disinherited of the crown, wander in foreign countries, and many great ones suffered and fell with him. Many foreign states stood amazed, when they saw the potent prince and monarch of three kingdoms, reigning in great power and splendour than ever any of his predecessors, cast down so suddenly from the height of his excellency, laid in the dust and brought to nothing.

4. The civil government was much changed from the primitive constitution, neither could the Petition of Right [1628] help much, because the King and ministers of state would not observe it, but acted contrary unto it. So that it was arrived almost at the height of an absolute monarchy. But as the winding of a string too high is the breaking of it, so it fell out with monarchy. The Parliament first require an explication of that act for liberty, afterwards limit the regal power, curb it, assume it, exercise it, and in the end take it wholly away. Some indeed of the Lords and Commons declare, that they had no intention to change the fundamental government, by king, peers and commons, and perhaps really intended what they spake, yet they could not perform. For, that very frame was taken asunder and abolished, upon which followed several [three][46] models one after another. The first by the Act of Alteration [1649]; the second by the New Instrument [1653]; the third and last by the Humble Petition of Advice [1657], and yet we are not well settled.[47] So difficult it is after that a constitution is once dissolved, to establish a new frame. So that it may be truly said, that never king acted so much against a parliament, never parliament prevailed so much against a king. Some were for the state of Venice and that form of government as the most perfect model for England. Some intend levelling; some did judge it best, that the general should have continued only general for a while, and to head only the godly party: a strange fancy and conceit.

5. As for the church, many of the English began to look towards Rome, many came home unto the church and turned papists. Innovations were daily made in doctrine and discipline, and prelacy seemed

---

[46] As corrected in the second edition.

[47] This passage indicates that the revisions to an MS *c.* 1657 were not systematic.

to advance with the royal power. But this great Parliament puts a stay to all; begins to reform, and in reforming incline to an extreme. They take away episcopacy root and branch, abrogate the liturgy, make some alterations in the doctrine; compose a new confession of faith, a directory of worship, and begin to settle a Presbyterian discipline. Yet that in the very rise was opposed by the dissenting brethren, and never could be fully and universally so imposed, as to be received. Hereupon, contrary to promise, the golden reins of discipline were loosed, a general liberty taken, and swarms of sects appear, profess, and separate. Errors, heresies, blasphemies do almost darken this church, and over-spread the same. Never from the first receiving of Christianity in this nation was there so great a change in religion known to be made in so short a time.

6. Yet, after all these bloody wars, and greatest alterations in church and state, the substance of the Protestant religion continues; the universities stand, schools remain, learning flourisheth, sabbaths are observed, ministers maintained; never better sermons, never better books. The orthodox Christian is confirmed. Matters in religion, are not so much taken upon trust and tradition, as formerly. Arts and languages advance, the light of the gospel shines. The laws abide in force, justice is administered, peace enjoyed, the Protestant interest in foreign parts maintained. England is become a warlike nation, furnished with gallant men both for sea and land, is courted by great princes, is a terror to our enemies, a protection to our friends: and if we could agree amongst ourselves, it is a happy nation. Yet all this is from the wonderful wisdom of our God, who knows how to bring light out of darkness, good out of evil, and from his exceeding mercy, who hath heard the prayers of a remnant of his people in behalf of this nation, to which he intends good; if our sins do not hinder. And for my part, I will not cease to honour, and to pray for such, as from their hearts have endeavoured our good, and especially for such, which God hath made so eminently instrumental for our present happiness. Such as are trusted with great power, and employed in great business, are many times perplexed with great difficulties, and especially in distracted times. And if they do something amiss, we should not harshly censure, much less envy them, but rather pity them and pray for them: and remember our own frailty, and that if we had been in their place, we might have done worse.

22.

But to draw unto a conclusion of this long chapter, and not to offend the reader; let's consider what may be done to finish and perfect anything begun tending to our settlement. Far be it from me to presume to prescribe anything to wiser men, who have seriously considered of this very thing already. Yet I may be bold to deliver mine own opinion with humble submission to my betters; and if I err, I may have the greater hope of pardon, because I shall speak as one unbiased, and aiming with a sincere heart at the public good of the English church and state, which, though fearfully shaken and shattered, are not yet destroyed. And first, this is certain, that there are but two reasons of our unsettlement: [...] ignorance [and] wilfulness. For we either know not how to settle, and what the best means are, which most effectually conduce to that end. Or else, we are wilfully divided, and no way will serve the turn but our own. The first is the cause of our difference in judgement, the second of our disaffection: and without a unity of the whole, or at least of the major part, the business will hardly be effected. For, we are not in any immediate capacity of a general unity, till time hath wasted and consumed some of our divisions; and also the bitter enmity and rancour, which continues in the spirits of many to this day. Therefore, [first,] our settlement must begin in generals, and necessaries, and proceed by degrees. [Second], the foundation to be laid is [...] to find out the ancient constitution before it was corrupted too much, and understand the great wisdom of our ancestors, gained by long experience in the constitution of this our state. This may be done by some experienced statesmen, and antiquaries in law, and that as well, if not better out of parliament, than in parliament. For a parliament itself must have some foundation and certain rule of their very being, before they can act steadily and regularly, and not spend their time of every several parliament in moulding their government anew. It's a vain and presumptuous imagination, to think that we have attained to a greater measure of wisdom than our ancestors attained unto. And let us not undo what is already done, if it be consistent with the best model. [Third], let no man think that the public interest, either ecclesiastical or civil, of England is the interest of any one person or family, or any few persons or families, much less of any sect, party, faction. It cannot be denied, but whilst the succession of our kings was limited to a family, the succession was more certain. For so the next successor was more easily known, and competition, which in this case is so dangerous, was more easily avoided. Yet even this could not prevent the difference between the houses of York and Lancaster. And when the issue of Henry VIII failed, we had been in greater danger, if the King of Scots had not been a Protestant, and one who was conceived would prove firm to the English Protestant interest. But when this limited succession shall prove (as it may do) inconsistent with the public interest, it's not so much to be regarded. For, why should the honour or privilege of one family prejudice the universal safety of a nation[?] We know that vast empires and kingdoms have by an unlimited election continued long. And that which might help much in this case, is that policy of the German empire in the *Interregnum* to have an administrator general. [Fourth], in modelling the government, we must have a special eye unto the constitution, that it be such, as that it may, not only be consistent with, but effectually conduce to the promoting of peace and righteousness in the administration of the state, and also to the advancement of the Christian religion in the church. And I conceive our ancient government for these ends was excellent: and did also preserve and regulate the liberty of the people, and also wisely limit the supreme magistrate. [Fifth], the parliament being a general representative of the whole nation, and now of three, and trusted with our liberty, estates, lives, and in some measure with the religion we profess, should consist, and be made up of eminent and wise men. Therefore the election of them for the manner, should be more regular and orderly in respect of the electors, and better limited and more strictly tied to a right qualification of the persons elected, which should neither be unworthy nor unfit. It may indeed fall so out, that in these irregular, and sometimes tumultuous elections, some wise and eminent persons may be chosen, and the same may prove predominant and leading members in that great assembly; but this is but a chance, and no certainty, nor use of right reason in it. [Sixth], when a parliament is, once assembled and begins to act, if there be anything that concerns the preservation and continuance, either of the being of the state, or of the substance of the Protestant religion, that must be first dispatched, and the next the punishment of crying sins, which are the ruin of states. [Seventh], as for religion, so far as it concerns the state; it's fit that there be some general rule both of our profession and worship: but the rule of profession must be brief and grounded upon plain Scriptures, and so near to ancient confessions, as that no rational Christian, who acknowledged the Scriptures to be the word of God, could or would scruple. The rule of worship also must be plain and clear. Let nothing be imposed upon all, which any rational Christian as such, may not receive without scruple. As for discipline, as I have begun, so I will go on in the next chapter. But these things have been and will be considered by far wiser men, therefore I will not enlarge.

23.

I might have said something more of the manner of disposing sovereign power, and with Besoldus have observed, that as there may be two persons who make but one monarch, so there may be one king of two, or more distinct and several kingdoms.[48] This latter disposal was debated much in Calvin's case by the sage judges of the land: in which debate some of them, especially chancellor Egerton, did little less than make the King an absolute monarch, and the two kingdoms in effect one: but the Parliament was of another mind.[49] And the matter was far above their courts and cognizance; the union could not be determined, but by the Parliaments of both kingdoms, neither could this be done by them, if the union made any alteration in the constitution of either kingdom. In respect of mine intention, this chapter is very large, in respect of the matter very brief: and my desire is, that others would more seriously and impartially enquire into this subject, so far as it concerns our own constitution, which no doubt may be found out, and if it prove defective may be perfected, if men were peaceable and sought the public good.

---

[48] Besold, *De majestate*, ch. 3.3.
[49] Calvin's Case, 1608, concerned Robert Calvin's claim to immunity to the laws of the King of England because he claimed to be an alien (Scot). The judgement was that as he owned property in England a natural allegiance was due, or could be assumed; that the King's authority applied regardless, not least because if anything else were assumed, the administration of law in the three kingdoms, with but one monarch, would become impossible. Sir Edward Coke, *Reports*, pt. 7, fols. 583 ff. In more Lockean terms, Calvin was taken to accept tacitly the authority of the King because he enjoyed property under the King's protection.

CHAPTER 9

Of the disposition of ecclesiastical power: and first, whether it be due unto the bishop of Rome

I.

The most difficult point in politics is that of the *Jura Majestatis*, and the right disposal of them in a fit subject. And concerning the nature of civil power, the manner of acquiring and disposing of it, I have already spoken; and also of ecclesiastical power and the acquisition thereof. Now it remains, [that] I say something of the manner of disposing the Power of the Keys in the right subjects. This is a matter of great dispute in these our times. Therefore, when I expected to find all clear, because a *Jus divinum*, grounded on the Scriptures, was pretended on all hands, I found it otherwise. As, when one of our worthies had disemboked[1] the Magellanick Straits, and was entered into that sea, they call *Pacificum*, he found the word *Pacifick* really contradicted by violent storms. So it falls out here; I hoped to have landed in a region of perpetual peace, but I was found in a *Terra del Fuego*, a land of fire and smoke; like unto *Palma*, one of the seven Canary Islands, where, in September 1646, or thereabouts, a fire first raged fearfully in the bowels of the earth, and at length brake out, and ran in five several fiery, sulphurious streams into the main. In like manner, this Power of the Keys runs in five several channels, but very turbulently and impetuously. For the pope, the prince, the prelate, the presbyter, the plebeian rank, do every one of them severally challenge it; and nothing under a *Jus divinum* will serve the turn. Therefore I will,

1. Examine their several titles.
2. Deliver mine own judgement.
3. Add something of the extent of a particular church.

[1] To go from the mouth of a river into the sea.

2.

And this shall be my method, and the several heads of my ensuing treatise, before I enter upon the second part of the constitution of a commonwealth, which is *pars subdita*.

The first title is, that of the great Roman pontiff, who perhaps will storm, and that with indignation against any who shall presume to examine it. This bishop is the greatest prelate and clergyman in the world. And as old Rome from a poor beginning, and a few people became the imperial city of the world; so this prelate, from a poor persecuted minister of the gospel attained to this pitch of glory; and contrary to the example of Christ and his Apostles, lives in so great splendour, pomp and state terrene,[2] that the princes of the world cannot parallel him: and for the power, which he doth exercise and challenge, he is far above them. His court is very magnificent, and cannot be maintained without a vast revenue. Some say, that he is that second beast which came out of the earth, and had two horns of a lamb, but spake as a dragon, and exerciseth all the power of the first beast before him (Rev. 13.11, 12). His name is *Satanos*, his number twenty-five. He assumed the title of universal bishop about the year of our Lord, 666. So that his number in the name, in the radical sum, and in the time of his appearance, is 666. And for order's sake, I might [...] observe the power, relate the several reasons whereby the title to this power is confirmed, [and] examine whether they be sufficient or no. [First] the power, which is challenged is transcendent and very great, and that not only extensively, but intensively too, it's such as men never had and therefore could never give. And therefore, though he came out of the earth, yet he derives it from Heaven. To be the first patriarch of the imperial see will not serve the turn: neither will he be content to be a man and fallible, he must be infallible. Neither will this satisfy him, he must be the visible head of the universal church, universal bishop and monarch over all persons, all churches, in all causes ecclesiastical. Nay, this power is so extensive, that he must have something to do in Heaven, and much to do in Hell. He must be above all general councils. They cannot assemble, conclude, dissolve without his power. He must be president; all canons and judgements which they pass without him are of no force;

---

[2] Worldly splendour.

and only what he approves is valid. His very letters must be laws, and if he please, of universal obligation. His reservations and dispensations are very high, his judgements irreversible; he receives last appeals from all churches in the world; he judgeth all, is judged of none. His power to execute is strange, and his policy wonderful. He hath plenitude of power ecclesiastical. Yet this will not suffice him; he hath acquired temporal dominions, and is a secular prince. And because his territories are not large, he hath found out a way to possess himself of the Sword, and all temporal power *in ordine ad spiritualia*, must be his.

3.

But what are the reasons, whereupon this vast power is grounded? Surely they do build upon a rock, and not upon the sand.[3] Their reasons are taken from politics, from the ancient writers, and from Scriptures too. [...] From politics, they take this for granted, that amongst human governments, monarchy is the best; [...] that amongst monarchies despotical excels. This they dare not expressly affirm, yet the papal power which is challenged, is such. [Further they claim] that if monarchy be the best, then surely the government of the church is monarchical, for that being instituted from Heaven, must needs be the most perfect; [...] that the first monarch visible of the church was Peter, [and] that Peter was made such by Christ, and received a power to transmit it to others, and appoint his successors. [They hold] that he fixed his see at Rome, and made the bishop of that city his heir, so that he is *haeres ex asse*; [and] that so soon as any person is legally elected bishop of that see, he is *ipso facto*, the universal monarch, and the proper subject of plenitude of all ecclesiastical power. [Second], the epithets, the eulogies, the *Encomiums* of the bishop and the see of Rome, are collected out of ancient writers, and marshalled in order, and they make a goodly show: and who dare say anything against them. [Third] yet, because these are not of divine authority, therefore they search the holy Scriptures, and find it written that Peter was the only person and Apostle, to whom Christ gave the keys of Heaven's kingdom, and he must bind and loose on earth; and what shall so do on earth, shall be made good in Heaven. If this

[3] Matt. 7.25–6.

will not serve the turn, Christ saith to Peter, and to no other Apostles, 'If thou love me, feed my flock, my lambs, my sheep,' and to feed is to govern, and the flock, lambs, sheep, are the church.[4]

4.

Yet notwithstanding all these reasons, many rational men think, and they have reason for it, that this power is so great, that it's intolerable presumption for any person to challenge it, impossible for any man duly to manage it, but only Jesus Christ, who knew no sin, and was not only man, but the son of the living God. Besides, wise men do certainly know that the power was usurped and possessed by degrees first, and afterwards the greatest wits were set on work to invent a title: the usual way of all unjust usurpers. [...] As for their politics, they help them little: for in that reason from government, they presuppose all, and prove nothing from first to last, neither can any wit of man prove any of their supposals; yet all must be proved, and that demonstratively, and every one of them made evident, otherwise the vast mighty fabric falls to the ground. Many of themselves know in their conscience the invalidity and weakness of every one of them. As for these passages of ancient writers, which seem so much to honour and advance that church above others, many of them are hyperbolical and rhetorical strains, and far from being any ground either of logical or theological proofs. [...] Such as were proper might agree to that church for that time, when it was honoured with persons of eminent piety and learning, which were found in it as being the seat of the empire. And such things might be true of that church then, which do not agree unto it now. [...] It's found by the searching of the ancient manuscripts, that some things have been foisted into the books of these ancient authors in favour of that church. For they, who could (even before the fourth century was ended) corrupt the copy, if not the Latin original of the *Nicene* Council, and put in a canon for to warrant receiving appeals from Africa, which was not found in the Greek original, are not much to be trusted. [...] Suppose many or all of those ancient commendations, which were proper should be true, yet they will not amount to that plenitude of power, which in after-times was exercised, and to this is challenged by the bishops of that

[4]John 21.15–17.

see. [...] None of those honourable testimonies are of divine authority, or firmly grounded upon the Scriptures. And what the Scriptures give them, that we will not deny them. [...] As for their arguments from Scriptures, I have wondered that any rational man should ever use them, as they are by them applied to the pope. To argue, that because Christ said to Peter, 'to thee I give the keys of the kingdom of Heaven, and if thou lovest me, feed my sheep',[5] therefore the present bishop of Rome is the head and absolute monarch of the universal church, and invested with plenitude of power, is very irrational. There is such a vast distance between these Scriptures and the conclusion, and so many mediums to be used before they can come at it, and the same so uncertain, that no man, that will make use of his reason, can assent unto the conclusion; when all is said, that can be said, in behalf of this universal vicar from these texts. If we should maintain our cause against them by such arguments, they would reject us with scorn and indignation. Let his party plead and plead again, for his universal and transcendent power, I am sure of one thing, that if he loved Christ as Peter professed he did, and had a mind sincerely bent to feed his flock, he would never challenge, much less exercise such vast power. That Christ left a power sufficient to the church, we verily believe, but that he delegated so great a power, or delegated it unto him, we utterly deny, and have great reason for it. Yet, because we will not submit unto his papal majesty, we must be condemned as schismatics and heretics, deprived of all hope of salvation, as having no communion with that church, whereof he is head, and lodged in Hell, the Lowest Hell. And all this is done upon the weakest grounds that ever rational man did use. But we appeal to Heaven, where Christ will be our advocate, and plead our cause, and carry it too. If it were needful, I would single out the chiefest arguments used by them of Rome to maintain this title, and answer them distinctly. But this is done already by many worthy and learned men. Therefore I will take it for granted, as that which hath been made good and evident, that the pope is not the first and proper subject of the Power of the Keys.

[5] *Ibid.*, compounded with Matt. 16.19 (repeats information above).

CHAPTER 10

Whether the civil state have any good title to the Power of the Keys

I.

Yet if the pope cannot have and hold this power, yet the princes, sovereigns and civil states, especially Christian, will assume it, and they have the strongest, and the surest way of all others, if they once get possession for to keep it, and that's the Sword. King Henry VIII did not only refuse to submit unto the Roman supremacy, but took it to himself and became within his own dominions, over all persons, in all causes, as well ecclesiastical as civil supreme head and governor. So the priest by the prince was divested of a considerable part both of his power and also his revenue. But whether he could be the proper subject of his spiritual power, or make good his title to it, was much doubted, and that by many. As king, he was but *caput regni non ecclesia*: and as such, he might have some civil, but no ecclesiastical power at all. Yet though it was called ecclesiastical, yet it was not such [grammatically but rhetorically], not properly but by a trope, a metonymy of the adjunct for the subject *circa quod*. For the power of a state temporal is only civil, if properly and formally considered; yet the civil sovereign had always something to do in matters of religion, concerning which it may make laws, pass judgement, and execute the same. Yet, the laws, the judgements, the execution were civil, not strictly ecclesiastical. Therefore such as maintained the regal supremacy in ecclesiasticals, were so wise as to say, that it was but materially and objectively in the crown.[1] In which sense, it was always due to civil powers, as civil, as appears from Deuteronomy 13 and many other

[1] At this point the text carries two marginal Latin quotations, the second possibly from memory as it is abbreviated, misprinted and referenced to the wrong passage. ['The King cannot claim the Keys or (authority over) moral affairs except with respect to political externals'], Lancelot Andrewes, *Tortua Torti* (London, 1609). ['The supremacy suits the king in different ways not only in so far as he is a king but as he is a true and sincere Christian; objectively because he is a king and effectively because he is a Christian one. As a king because he has a principle of action, as a Christian one putting his authority into practice'], Francis Mason, *Vindiciae ecclesiae Anglicanae* (London, 1625), bk. 3, ch. 5, p. 312.

places of Scripture: as also from many examples, not only of the kings of Judah, but of Niniveh, Babylon and Persia. That many of these heathen princes, and also of the kings of Israel did abuse this power, for the establishment or exercise of a false religion and idolatry is no argument to prove they had it not, but that they did not use it aright. [To establish constraints about the sacred], did always belong, and that by divine institution to the civil higher powers.

2.

For the better understanding of this point, several things are to be observed. [First], that as there is no people so barbarous, but profess and practise some religion; so there is no state or orderly government, but acknowledgeth some deity or divine power, upon which they conceive their public peace, safety, prosperity, and good success doth depend: as we may by the very Scriptures, and also by other histories be informed. For every nation had their public gods, besides their family-tutelar deities. It's true, though by the light of nature, considering the glorious works of Heaven and earth, they might have known the true God, yet they changed the glory of God into a lie or false God, and conceived that to be a God, which was no such thing.

[Second], the supreme governors of these states, had a special care to order the matters of that religion which they publicly received. They made laws, appointed priests for the service and worship of their gods. This is also evident from Scripture, and from other histories too. This ordering of religion as public, was always held a right of the public power.

[Third], yet they had no power to establish, or observe any religion or worship, but that which God had instituted according to the laws of nature, or divine revelation; if they did, they abused their power. For that very power, as from God, was nothing but *jus ad recte agendum*, a right to do right in matters of religion. If they did otherwise, they abused their power, they lost it not. And if an heathen prince or state should become Christian, they acquire no new right, but are further engaged to exercise their power in abolishing idolatry, and establishing the true worship of the true God. This may be signified by the titles of Nursing-fathers of the Church, Defenders of the Faith, most Christian, most Catholic King: all which, as they signified their right, so they also pointed at their duty, which was to protect the true church, and maintain the true, Christian, catholic faith.

[Fourth], though regal and sacerdotal power were always distinct and different in themselves, yet they were often disposed and united in one person. Thus Melchizedek was both king and priest. Thus Romulus was prince, and the chief pontiff. For he is said ['to have reserved to the kingship supremacy in religious ceremonies and sacrifices and the conduct of everything regarding worship'].[2] The succeeding kings took the same place. After the regal power was abolished, it was an high office. When Rome became imperial, the emperors took the title of supreme pontiff, and some of them, after they became Christian, retained it. Yet still as the powers, so the acts were distinct. For Melchizedek as king, ruled his people in righteousness and peace; as priest officiated, received tithes, and blessed Abraham.[3] As they were sometimes united, so they were divided. For God entailed the sacerdotal power upon the house of Aaron, and afterwards, the regal power upon the family of David.[4] Neither did Christ nor his Apostles think it fit to make the ministers magistrates, or the magistrates ministers. Yet in this union and division you must know, that this sacerdotal and ministerial power, was not this civil power of religion, which always belonged to the civil governors, even then, when these two powers were divided.

[Fifth], if civil powers established religion and that by law, call synods, order them, ratify their canons, divest spiritual and ecclesiastical persons of their temporal privileges, or restore them, yet they do all this by their civil power, by which they cannot excommunicate, absolve, suspend, much less officiate and preach, and administer sacraments. In this respect, if the civil power make a civil law against idolatry, blasphemy, heresy or other scandal, they may by the same power justly punish the offenders by the Sword, and the church censure them by the Power of the Keys.

[Sixth], this *jus religionis ordinandae*, this power of ordering matters of religion, is not the power of the church, but of the state; not of the Keys, but of the Sword. The church hath nothing to do with the Sword, nor the state with the Keys. Christ did not say, tell the state,

---

[2] Dionysius of Halicarnassus, *Roman Antiquities*, bk. 2.14.1. Lawson quotes incompletely. The translation is adapted from the Loeb edition of Ernest Cary.

[3] Gen. 14.18; Ps. 110.4.   [4] Exod. 28; 2 Sam. 2.

and whatsoever ye bind on earth shall be bound in heaven, etc. Neither did he say of the church, that she beareth not the Sword in vain.[5] Therefore, he must needs be very ignorant or very partial, that shall conceive that the state is the [principal receiver] of the Power of the Keys.

3.

These things premised, give occasion to consider, how the Oath of Supremacy is to be understood, especially in these words, wherein the kings or queens of England were acknowledged (over all persons in all causes as well ecclesiastical as civil supreme head) and because that word head was so offensive, it was changed into governor. For the clearing hereof, it's to be observed, [first] that by these words, it was intended to exclude all foreign power both civil and ecclesiastical, especially that which the bishops of Rome did challenge, and also exercise within the dominions of the crown of England. [Second] that the kings and queens of England, had no power supreme in making laws and passing judgements without the parliament. Therefore by supreme governor, was meant supreme administrator, for the execution of the law; in the intervals of parliament. In this respect, the canons and injunctions made by the clergy, though confirmed by royal assent, without the parliament, have been judged of no force. [Third], that by ecclesiastical causes, are meant such causes as are materially ecclesiastical, yet properly civil, as before. For matters of religion, in respect of the outward profession and practice, and the parties professing and practising, are subject to the civil power. For by the outward part the state may be disturbed, put in danger of God's judgements, and the persons are punishable by the Sword, even for those crimes. Yet neither can the Sword reach the soul, nor rectify the conscience, except *per accidens*. That by ecclesiastical, is not meant spiritual in [the] proper sense, is clear, because the kings of England never took upon them to excommunicate or absolve; neither had those chancellors, that were only civilians, and not divines, power to perform such acts. Yet they received their power from the bishops, and it was counted ecclesiastical. [Fourth], in respect of these titles, those courts which were called spiritual and ecclesiastical, derived

---

[5] Matt. 18.17–18; Rom. 13.4.

their power from the crown. And the bishops did correct and punish, disquiet, disobedient criminous persons within their diocese, according to such authority as they had by God's word, and as to them was committed by the authority of this realm. These are the words of the Book of Ordination in the consecration of bishops. The words seem to imply, that they had a mixed, or at least a twofold power: one by the word, as trusted with the Power of the Keys, the other from the magistrate or crown, and that was civil. Such a mixed power they had indeed in the high commission. Yet though this may be implied, yet it may be, they understood that their power by the word of God, and from the crown were the same. The act of restoring the ancient jurisdiction to the crown [1559] doth make this further evident.[6] For it's an act of restoring the ancient jurisdiction in ecclesiasticals especially, to the crown; for that's the title. Where it must be observed, that the power was such, as the parliament did give. [...] They did not give it anew but restored it. [...] They could not [and] had no power to give it, if it belonged to the crown by the constitution, but to declare it to be due; upon which declaration the Queen might resume, that which the pope had usurped and exercised. [Further], it's remarkable, that not the Queen, but the Parliament, by that act did restore it: as the act of the Oath of Supremacy was made by a parliament, which by that act could not give the king any power at all, which was not formerly due. In respect of testament, temporal jurisdiction, dignities, privileges, titles as due unto the church by human constitution and donation, all ecclesiastical causes concerning these, were determinable by a civil power. How tithes are a lay-fee or divine right, hath been declared formerly. Hence it doth appear, that the Oath of Supremacy was not so easily understood, as it was easily taken by many: and the Oxford Convocation, I believe, but that they had already sworn, could have found as many reasons against it as against the covenant, especially if it had been new, as the covenant was. Many wise men at the first did scruple it, and some suffered death for refusal. Amongst the rest Sir Thomas More, a learned and a very prudent man, could not digest it; and though he might have an high conceit of the papal supremacy, yet that might not be the only reason of his refusal, but this, because he knew the crown had no ecclesiastical

---

[6] The Act of Supremacy, 1559, I Eliz., c. 1, which, with the Act of Uniformity, I Eliz., c. 2, was the basis of the Elizabethan Settlement.

power properly so called. Though this was not thought to be the true, but only the pretended cause of his death: For in his *Utopia*, he seems to dislike the indisputable prerogative, which was a *Noli me tangere*, and to touch it so roughly, as he did, might cost dear, as it did. Yet I have taken the Oath of Supremacy in that sense as our divines did understand it;[7] and I was, and am willing to give to Caesar, the things that are Caesar's.[8]

4.

That which hath been said in this point in brief is this: that though the civil powers have a right to order matters of religion in respect of the outward part, and so far as the Sword may reach it according to divine law, yet they have no Power of the Keys, which Christ committed to the church. For if we consider all the power exercised in matter of religion by David, Solomon, and the pious kings of Judah: by the Christian emperors and princes; by the kings of France and England, it was but civil. Neither is the power of our parliaments any other. For though they make acts concerning the public doctrine and discipline, yet these are but civil. They are not representatives of the church but of the state, whether the convocation was an essential part of the parliament, or a full representative of the church, I will not here debate. I find some great lawyers which deny both. And if their denial be true, then England had no general representative of the church in latter times. As for Erastians, and such as do give all ecclesiastical power of discipline to the state, and deny all power to the ministers, but that of dispensing word and sacraments: it's plain, they never understood the state of the question: and though a minister, as a minister have no power but that of word and sacraments: yet from thence it will not follow, that the church hath not a power spiritual, distinct from that of the state in matters of religion.

[7] The oath required of clerics by the Act of Supremacy, 1559, reiterating the requirements of the Act for the Submission of the Clergy, 1534, 25 Hen. VIII, c. 19.
[8] Matt. 22.21; Mark 12.17.

CHAPTER 11

Whether episcopacy be the primary subject of the Power of the Keys

1.

The prelate presumes that the Power of the Keys is his, and he thinks his title very good, and so good, that though he could not prove the institution, yet prescription will bear him out. For he hath had possession for a long time: and universality and antiquity seem to favour him very much. Yet I hope his title may be examined; and if upon examination it prove good, he hath no cause to be offended, except with this, that I of all others should meddle with it. But before anything can be said to purpose, we must first know the nature and institution of a bishop, which is the subject of the question. Secondly, put the reader in mind, that the question is not in this place, whether a bishop be an officer of the church, either by some special or some general divine precept, but whether he be [the principal receiver] the primary subject of the Power of the Keys. For he may be an officer and yet no such subject. Concerning a bishop, the subject of the question, two things are worthy our consideration; [...] what he is, [and] how instituted at the first. The definition and institution, seem rather to belong unto the second part of ecclesiastical politics, where I shall entreat of ecclesiastical officers; and the constitution of them. Yet I will here say something of both in order to [clarify] the question, though I be the briefer afterward.

2.

What a bishop is may be difficult to know, except we do distinguish, before we do define. For we find several sorts of bishops in the church Christian. There is a primitive, a prelatical or hierarchical, and an English bishop, distinct and different in some things from both the former for whom I reserve a place at the end of this chapter. The primitive bishop is twofold, [...] a presbyter [and] a president or superintendent. [...] A presbyter in the New Testament is bishop. For the elders of *Ephesus*, were made by the Holy Ghost bishop, or

superintendents over God's flock (Acts 20.28). And the qualification
of a bishop (1 Tim. 3.1, 2, 3, etc.) is the qualification of an elder
(Titus 1.5, 6, 7, etc.). For whatsoever some of late have said to the
contrary, yet presbyter and bishop were only two different words
signifying the same officer. And this is confessed by divers of the
ancients, who tell us that the word bishop was appropriated to one,
who was more than a presbyter, in after times.[1] [...] A bishop [also]
signified one that was above a presbyter in some respects, as a moderator of a classis, or president of a synod. But such a presbyter might
be only *pro tempore* for the time of the session; and after the assembly
dissolved, he might return to be a bare presbyter again. For to be a
moderator or president, was no constant place. The word in this sense
we find seldom used if at all. A president was a kind of superintendent
with a care and inspection, not only over the people, but [over] the
presbyters too within a certain precinct: and this was a constant place,
and the party called a bishop and by Ambrose and Augustine with
divers others, called *primus presbyterorum*; and these were such as had
no power, but with the presbytery jointly, and that without a negative
voice. And the presbytery might be a representative not only of the
presbyters strictly taken, but of the people too. For we may read in
Cyprian and other authors, that these bishops in more weighty matters of public concernment, did nothing without the counsel and
consent, not only of the presbyters but the people. This I call a
primitive bishop, not only because he is ancient, but also because the
place or office is agreeable to the rules of reason, of government, and
the general rules of the Apostles concerning order, decency, edification. There is also an hierarchical bishop, who may be only a bishop,
or an archbishop, and metropolitan or a patriarch; and these challenge the power of ordination and jurisdiction: and in jurisdiction
include and engross the power of making canons. This kind of episcopacy is ancient as the former. This last bishop is he, upon whom
Spalatensis and many others do fix:[2] and though they grant that he
should do nothing without the counsel of the presbytery, yet they give
him full power without the presbytery, which they join with him only
for advice. The English bishop is in something different from all
these, as shall be made evident hereafter. From these distinctions it's

[1] For example St Jerome, as cited in Marsilius of Padua, *Defensor pacis* (1324), ed. C. W.
Previté-Orton (Cambridge University Press, 1928), 1.12.4.
[2] M. A. de Dominis (1566–1624), see Biographical notes.

apparent, that the word bishop is equivocal, and must be defined several ways according to the several significations, which is easily done by that which hath been said already.

3.

For the first institution of episcopacy, there is as great difference in that, as in the former, and that not only in respect of the time when it was instituted, but also of the author of the institution. Those that are zealous for episcopacy, must needs have the institution to be divine; whosoever the author may be, whether Christ or his Apostles. Some learned and pious men make Christ the immediate author in that mission: [...] of the twelve Apostles [and] of the seventy disciples; in which mission, they observe an imparity between the twelve and the seventy, which imparity they say, continued in the bishops succeeding the Apostles, and the presbyters succeeding the disciples; but these will satisfy no considerate man. For though it be granted, that there was some imparity; yet, [...] the mission of both was immediately from Christ. [...] It was for the same work to preach the gospel, and do miracles in confirmation of the same. [...] They were limited and confined to the Jew; [...] there was no imparity of power and jurisdiction of the one over the other, both were immediately subject to Christ. [Further] that some of the ancients say, the bishops succeeded the Apostles, and presbyters, the seventy disciples can hardly be true, or any ways made good. Seeing therefore this mission of both was immediate, and for doctrine, and not for discipline, it cannot reach the power challenged and grounded upon it. The School of Sorbonne was of this mind, and say, it was a ground of the hierarchy.[3] But if it was a ground, it was but very infirm, for the hierarchy was but introduced [by human and not divine law] as may and will be made evident. Others waive this, and make the institution apostolical; yet in this they differ. For some say, it was from the Apostles, as Apostles, and immediately inspired, and in this particular, and then it is divine indeed. Others tell us, it was from them, as acting by an ordinary and ecclesiastical power. Again, it may be grounded upon some apostolic precept of divine, universal and perpetual obligation, or upon their

[3] Lawson has in mind (see below, sect. 4) the general statement *De ecclesiastica et politica potestate* (Paris, 1611), copy in More Library.

practice and example. The former, the Convocation at Oxford in their scruples against taking the covenant, dare not affirm; and indeed no such precept doth appear. Again, the precepts of the Apostles, were either general or special. And if there be not some special divine precept for this institution, it cannot be of perpetual obligation, nor necessary. Epiphanias confuting the heresy of Arius, if he be consistent with himself must needs be of this mind, because he affirms, that the business, of the church, may be fully dispatched and performed by presbyters and deacons without a bishop.[4] Jerome makes episcopacy a human constitution, and not divine. In this some excuse him: but Spalatensis saith, he cannot be excused.[5] Medina chargeth him, and other of the fathers with the Arian heresy.[6] As for those words of his: 'Quid facit Episcopus excepta ordinatione, quod non faciat Presbyter'; they may seem to reserve a power of ordination as proper to the bishop; and in this respect, episcopacy may be of a divine constitution. Yet Marsilius understands by ordination, the constitution of the church, not the ordination of ministers.[7] And there is great reason to think so, because otherwise his words are directly false, and known to be so, if meant of ordination of presbyters by imposition of hands. For long before his time, the bishops did many things which a presbyter could not do: neither could a bishop ordain without presbyters. If they had this power to themselves alone, and that by divine donation, Jerome must plainly contradict himself. If Jerome means the hierarchical episcopacy, which then in many places was the only episcopacy, then it's most certain, that that was not from God, but man; not from divine, but human constitution. And the hierarchical subordination, seems to be ordained directly to avoid schism, which that learned man [Marsilius] saith, was the occasion of that episcopacy.[8]

---

[4] St Epiphanius (315–403), *The Panarion or Refutation of all Heresies*. The Arian heresy denied the divinity of Christ, claiming that he was an instrument created by God.

[5] St Jerome (342–420) cited as Hierome, prolific and greatest of early Church scholars, responsible for the Vulgate Bible.

[6] Bartolomeo Medina (1586–1638), commentator on St Thomas Aquinas.

[7] *Defensor pacis*, 2.14, the most commonly cited point from Marsilius during the 17th century.

[8] *Defensor pacis*, 2.15.6. The status of episcopal ordination was to become a central and divisive one with the re-establishment of the Episcopalian Church of England in 1662. Lawson is supporting the arguments that would lead many to leave the Church. See also below, sect. 11. The concluding lines are prophetic.

4.

Though it would take up a full volume, to answer in particular all those who have asserted, and endeavoured to prove the divine right of this hierarchical prelate, invested with the power of ordination and jurisdiction (and therefore here I might be silent); yet, seeing the substance of all the rest may be read in Spalatensis, therefore I will single him out, and consider the force of his reasons, which are insisted upon by others to this day. And here we must observe, [...] that the bishop, which he maintaineth is hierarchical, and one invested with the power of ordination and jurisdiction; that his intention and design, is to prove him to be of divine institution; [and] to this purpose he allegeth several Scriptures, and he seems to find the fundamental charter in these words of our Saviour: 'As my Father sent me, so I send you', etc. (John 20.21, 23). Where I will observe, [...] his interpretation of the words, [...] his supposition of imparity between the twelve Apostles and seventy disciples; [and] examine whether the texts antecedent or consequent, or the words themselves do favour him. [First], therefore, he determines the agreement between his Father's mission of him, and his mission of them to be this: that as his Father gave him power to ordain, and constitute them in a superior rank of power and jurisdiction, and the seventy disciples of an inferior order: so he gave them power likewise to appoint them successors in a twofold rank, [namely] bishops with a full apostolical ordinary power [and] presbyters, without any such power of ordination and jurisdiction, for so he means.[9] [Second], in this exposition, he presupposeth an imparity of power, but very absurdly. For he gives the power of ordination and jurisdiction to the bishops alone, but none at all to the presbyters. And whereas imparity is a difference only in degrees, he makes the difference of the bishops and presbyters to be essential and specific. But of this before: and if any desire to see more, let them read the doctors of Sorbonne concerning this particular in their tract, *De ecclesiastica et politica potestate.*[10]

---

[9] M. A. de Dominis, *De respublica ecclesiastica, libri decem* (London, 1617), 1.1.3–9, pp. 159 ff. (marginal reference).

[10] *De ecclesiastica et politica potestate* (Paris, 1611). This was a late conciliar Gallican tract claiming theological supremacy for the representatives of the church over the papacy and general subjection of clerics to temporal authority.

5.

Thus you have heard [. . .] his exposition, [and] his supposition. Now
it follows we enquire, whether either of them have any warrant, or so
much as colour from the context, antecedent, or consequent. The
antecedent favours him not: for [John 20] verse 19, it's said, not that
the Apostles, but disciples were together: and the seventy are called
disciples, and some of them might be there, and his words directed to
them, and if this be so, the very foundation of the argument from this
place is razed. Neither doth the words following help him, but are
point-blank against him. For [John 20] verses 22, 23, it's said, 'He
breathed upon them, and saith unto them, receive ye the Holy Ghost,
whosoever sins ye remit, they are remitted,' etc. Where [. . .] many by
the Holy Ghost, understand spiritual power, or power of and from the
spirit. This power is not a power of ordination, or jurisdiction [in
external matters], but a power of remission and retention of sins,
[internally, in the court of penitence] as the schoolmen and casuists
speak. [. . .] They remit and retain sins by the word and sacraments.
Therefore in the ordination of presbyters, both in the pontifical of
Rome and our ordination book, these words are used, and after them
are added with some ceremony, this passage, 'Be thou a faithful
dispenser of the word of God, and his holy sacraments.' And again,
the Bible delivered into the hands of the party ordained, 'Take thou
authority to preach the word of God, and to administer the holy
sacraments.' This is the Power of the Keys promised (Matt. 16.19),
which place he himself understands of conversion by the word. [. . .]
This is the essential power of a presbyter, as a presbyter.

6.

In the third place, as neither the context, antecedent, nor consequent
help him; so neither do the words themselves. For except the
similitude and agreement between his Father's mission and his be
universal and adequate, or some ways specifically determined unto
this particular imparity of the twelve and seventy; and also of bishops
and presbyters, his exposition can never be made good. That it is not
universal is evident, and that by his own confession who tells us, that
the Father sent Christ to redeem, but Christ never sent the Apostles
to do any such thing. *As and so*, are notes of similitude indeed: and

therefore his Father's mission of him, and his mission of the Apostles must agree in something. And so they do – [...] he was sent, so were they; [...] he received the spirit, so did they; [...] he was sent to preach and do miracles, so were they; [...] his mission was extraordinary, so was theirs [in fact a sign is a similitude] and (as à Lapide saith) may signify *similitudinem officij, principij, finis, miraculorum et amoris*;[11] yet none of these can serve his turn. Therefore, saith Grotius, and that truly [a fair number of the similitudes for Kathos are not significant].[12] Gerard upon the same words, as used by our Saviour (John 17.18) multiplies the analogy, and makes these two missions agree in fifteen particulars: yet he never thought of this.[13] Christ, as he observes was sent, [...] to redeem [and] to preach the gospel; so they were sent not to redeem, but to preach, and did succeed him, not in his sacerdotal, but prophetical office; by the word and sacraments to apply the redemption, not as priests to expiate sins. Seeing therefore the analogy is not universal, nor any ways by the context, antecedent or consequent, or the text itself determined to this particular, but to another, as is apparent, therefore his exposition is frivolous, his supposition false, and the text no ground of an hierarchical episcopacy.

7.

Yet he proceeds to prove this imparity from examples. [First], of Peter and John sent to Samaria, that by imposition of hands, as of bishops, they whom Philip had converted, as a mere presbyter, might receive the Holy Ghost.[14] [Second], from Barnabas, sent as a bishop, as he takes for granted, to Antioch, to confirm the believing Jews, converted by the dispersed saints, in that faith they had received.[15] But will it follow, that Peter and John and Barnabas were bishops invested with

---

[11] Cornelius à Lapide (1567–1637), a biblical scholar with a strong taste for allegorical readings.

[12] Grotius, *Annotationes in libros evangelium, secondum Ioannem*, 17.18, *Opera omnia theologica* (1679 edn., facsimile, Stuttgart, 1972), 2.1, p. 559. Lawson's reference would be to the 1641 Amsterdam edition, two copies of which are listed in the Millington *Catalogus*. The word *kathos* ('as', or 'just as') is the first and key term in the simile 'As thou has sent me into this world, even so have I sent them into the world', John 17.18.

[13] Johann Gerhard? (1582–1637), Lutheran theologian and author of the much used *Loci theologici* (1610–22). [14] Acts 8.14.

[15] Acts 13.1 mentions Barnabas at Antioch among prophets (*prophetai*) and teachers (*didaskaloi*).

the power of ordination and jurisdiction, because they were sent by
the church of Jerusalem, not to ordain or make canons, or censure,
but by imposition of hands and prayer, give the Holy Ghost, and
confirm the new converts of Samaria and Antioch? How irrational and
absurd is this? [Third], he instanceth in Timothy, left by Paul at
Ephesus, and Titus left by him at Crete to ordain elders, and order
other matters of those churches, not fully constituted and perfected
for doctrine, worship and discipline.[16] But let it be granted, that they
had power of ordination and jurisdiction. Yet it will not follow from
hence, that because they had it, therefore presbyters had it not; nor
that they had it without presbyters, where presbyters had it not; nor
that they had it without presbyters, where presbyters might be had;
nor [. . .] that they had it as bishops, which is the very thing to be
proved. [. . .] The plain truth is, that they had it in those places and for
that time, as commissioned and trusted by the Apostle, to do many
things in that church, according to the canons sent them by the
Apostles, which they had no power to make themselves. Dr.
Andrewes taking all apostolical power to be divine, affirms episcopacy
to be a distinct order, and of divine institution, and grounds himself
upon the testimony of Irenaeus, Tertullian, Eusebius, Jerome,
Ambrose, Chrysostom, Epiphanius, and Theodoret: who all write,
that Ignatius, Polycarpus, Timothy, Titus, and others were made
bishops, and of a distinct order above presbyters by the Apostles
themselves.[17] Yet if he means by apostolical, whatsoever is done by
the Apostles, then many things apostolical are not divine, much less of
divine institution and obligation. For many things were done by them
in matters of the church by a mere ordinary power. [. . .] The
testimony of all these fathers is but human: and according to his own
rule cannot be believed, but with a human and fallible faith; [that
which by divine faith cannot be believed, cannot by divine faith be
done]. [. . .] If he meant, that those had power of ordination and
jurisdiction as bishops, he contradicts himself, affirming, that this
Power of the Keys, was given immediately by Christ not to Peter, not
to the Apostles, but to the church, and the church had it, to the
church it was ratified, the church doth exercise it, and transfer it upon
one or more [who thereafter would have the power of exercising it or

[16] 2 Tim. 1.18; Titus 1.5.
[17] Lancelot Andrewes, *Tortura Torti* (London, 1609).

ordering others to do so] (*Tortura Torti*, p. 42). So that none can have it, but as delegates of the church, not as bishops or officers.

8.[18]

The last instance from Scriptures, is in the angels of the seven churches of Asia: and he affirms these were bishops. But [first] so they might be, and yet only presbyters. Suppose [second] they were more than presbyters, and superintendents at least, it doth not follow they were hierarchical bishops: for if they were, it must appear from some divine record, or else how can I certainly believe it[?] [Third] let them be hierarchical prelates, yet it must be made evident by what warrant and institution, they became such. The institution must be grounded, either upon the practice or precepts of Christ or his Apostles: yet all these grounds have been formerly examined. But [fourth] doth any man think that these letters [and] messages were sent only to seven persons, who were bishops? It's evident and clear as the sun, they were directed to the whole churches to the ministers, which are called by the name of angels, and to the people. For the whole church of Ephesus, of Smyrna, and of the rest is commended, or reproved and charged with divers sins, and threatened with such punishments as must fall upon all. After all these proofs from Scripture, recourse is had to antiquity and universality, as sufficient grounds of a prescription, which is a good kind of title. But, [...] in divine things, especially such as are of ordinary and universal obligation, antiquity and universality, without a divine institution will not serve the turn. [...] The hierarchy prescribes as much, and as high as episcopacy, invested with power of ordination and jurisdiction, as proper to itself, yet it's confessed to be only of human institution. [...] What is it, how is it defined? What divine institution can be made evident of that, which they say is so universal and ancient? [...] Who are the witnesses, by whose testimony this antiquity and universality is proved? They are, besides some of later times but few, and all within the Roman empire, many of them bishops themselves, and some of them bitter enemies one against another. They are not one of a hundred amongst the bishops, not one of a thousand amongst others. Yet the church, in the Apostles' times, was enlarged to the ends of the earth. And as then, so

---

[18] Sections misnumbered in both editions.

now, there were in every century thousands that did never write, or if they did, they wrote not of episcopacy; and many of them might be as great scholars, as those whose books are extant. [Moreover], there was a special reason, why there might be bishops and the same hierarchical in the principal parts of the Roman territory, as shall be touched hereafter. [And], suppose these bishops to have the power of ordination and jurisdiction, yea, the whole Power of the Keys, which includes the legislative in making canons, can any man prove, that they had it always in all places: and if so, that they had it severally in their several precincts, and not jointly with their fellow bishops, as representatives in counsels, and also with presbyters and others too? It's well enough known, that other besides bishops had their suffrage in synods. Arles, President of the Council of Basle, proves stoutly that presbyters have their votes; and without them he could not have carried the cause against Panormitan and his faction.[19]

9.

After the primitive and the hierarchical episcopacy comes in the English, which hath something singular. He that will understand the nature of it more fully, must read Dr. Zouch, Dr. Mucket, Dr. Cosens the civilian his tables, with him (who calls himself Didoclavius) upon him.[20] By all whom we may understand, [that] it was not the primitive episcopacy; [...] it was clearly hierarchical (for we had bishops, and two archbishops of York and Canterbury, the one the metropolitan of England, the other of all England). The bishops took their oath of obedience to the archbishops, as appeareth by the book of ordination. They did arrogate the power of ordination to themselves, though presbyters did in the ordination impose hands with them, and some of them confessed, they had it only with the

---

[19] A marginal gloss cites the Archbishop of Arles as president of the Council of Basle (1431–49). The first president was Cardinal Julian Cesarini (1398–1444). The council, highly critical of the papacy, gave suffrage and even a majority to the lower orders over the bishops. Panormitan is presumably Abbas Modernus (Panormitanus), canonist (1386–1445), works in Millington, *Catalogus*.

[20] Richard Zouch, *Descriptio et judicii ecclesiastica ... Anglicanas* (Oxford, 1636); Richard Mocket, *Doctrina et politica ecclesia Anglicanae*, 1616; John Cosen, Bishop of Durham, possibly *A Collection of Private Devotions ... in ... the Ancient Church*, or *Regni Angliae religio catholica*, in *Works*, ed. J. H. Parker (Oxford University Press, 1843–55), vol. iv; Didoclavius, the fanciful pseudonym of the Scottish Presbyterian David Calderwood, d. 1650.

presbytery jointly. Yet we know how that by others is elected. [This is] not to say anything of their titles, dignity, revenue, baronies annexed to their sees, their place in the house of the peers in parliament, and their privilege. They had cast off in effect, not only the people, but presbytery. For though the presbytery had their clerks, both in the convocation at York, and also at London, if the parliament sat there; yet they took upon them in the end to nominate these clerks, and deprive the ministers of their right of election. As for the Deans and Chapters, which should have been eminent persons, and chosen by the presbytery in every diocese to represent them, they were degenerate from their original institution; and the bishops who should have done nothing but jointly with them, did all things without them. They in effect, though unjustly engrossed the whole power of administration. [. . .] Yet this is observable: that [first] they could make no canons but jointly in one assembly. [Second] that jointly among themselves, without the presbytery, they had not this power. [Third] that no canons were valid without the royal assent. [Fourth] neither by the constitution was the royal assent sufficient without the parliament. [Fifth] that they derived much of their ecclesiastical power from the crown. For by the Oath of Supremacy is declared, that the King of England is over all persons, even in ecclesiastical causes supreme governor; in which respect, all their secular power, revenue, dignity, and also their nomination and confirmation with their investiture is from him. He calls synods, confirms their canons, grants commissions to exercise jurisdiction purely ecclesiastical. In the first year of King Edward VI [1547], by a statute they were bound to use the king's name, not their own, even in their citations:[21] and as before, they must correct and punish offenders according to such authority as they had by the word of God, and as to them should be committed by the ordinance of this realm. So, that if the popish bishops derive their power from the pope, and the English from the king, neither of them could be *jure divino*. And by this, the title of most bishops in Europe is merely human, and that in two respects: [. . .] because it's hierarchical [and because it is] derived either from an higher ecclesiastical or an higher secular power.

---

[21] An Act for the Election of Bishops, Ed. VI, c. 2.

10.

Thus far I have enquired, though briefly and according to my poor ability, into the definition and institution of a bishop, the subject of the question, which is this, whether a bishop or bishops be the primary subject of the Keys? The meaning whereof is: whether they be the primary and adequate sole subject of the whole Power of the Keys, whereof the principal, though not all the branches, are making canons, and receiving last appeals, without any provocation from them? For they may be subjects, and not primary, they may be subjects of some part, and not of the whole power. [...] Whether they be such subjects of this power [concerning exterior things]. For [with respect to internal matters] the presbyters have as much as they. [...] Whether they be such subjects of such power [over externals in what manner when the episcopate is redoubled?] [...] Whether as such, they be such a subject by divine institution? For solution hereof, it's to be considered: [first] that except there be a universal consent, and the same clearly grounded upon Scripture, both what a bishop is; and [second] that made evident, that his title is of divine institution, the affirmative cannot be proved, [even] though a bishop could be clearly proved to have the power of ordination and jurisdiction, yet it will not follow from thence, that he is the primary subject of that power. For the negative, many things may be said: [...] neither the papal, nor the English bishop, so far as the one derives his power from the pope, and the other from the crown, can be the primary subject of this power; the secondary they may be. [...] For such as derive not their power from pope or prince, if they be the primary subject, they must be such, either severally everyone in his several diocese, or jointly in a synod. If severally, then everyone is a monarch in his diocese, and so the government of the church is monarchical: and every several bishop supreme and independent. And if so, where are our archbishops, metropolitans and patriarchs? And, why do we dispute against the monarchical government, and not grant to Bellarmine and others, that it is monarchical in general, though we deny the pope to be the sole monarch. If jointly in a synod, or council provincial, or national of one nation and several provinces, or several nations, or general: then they are not such as bishops, but either as members of the synod, or as delegates. If as members of the synod, and none can be members but bishops, as bishops, then the government of the church is purely aristocratical, and then it's worse than a pure monarchy, where there can be but one tyrant; whereas, in a pure aristocracy, there are usually many tyrants, or at least it proves an oligarchy. And in this respect, neither can a provincial council be subject to a national, nor a national to a general. If as delegates they have this power, as in general councils they are, then they cannot be the primary subject. And all these, if they will make their cause good, they must prove, which they can never do, that none but bishops have right of suffrage in councils. [...] If their title be good, it must be grounded either upon Scripture, or universal and perpetual custom: but from neither of these can it be proved, as shall appear hereafter. For by Scripture it's evident, that the church was made by Christ's institution the immediate and primary subject; and so confessed by bishops, by many great scholars, and by General Councils too. The first church, which was made such a subject, included the Apostles, who, in their ordinary capacity, were but parts and members though eminent members of the same. [...] If any shall say, that bishops as officers of the church, are the primary subject of this power, that implies a contradiction, because if the power of all officers, as officers, is derivative, and as the Apostles being officers of Christ, derived their apostolical power from Christ; so if bishops be officers of the church, they derive their power from the church, which is the primitive subject.

II.

Though both the definition, and the institution of a bishop be uncertain, and there is no universal consent in respect of either: yet I think, a constant superintendent trusted with an inspection; not only over the people, but the presbyters within a reasonable precinct, if he be duly qualified and rightly chosen, may be lawful, and the place agreeable to Scripture; yet, I do not conceive that this kind of episcopacy, is grounded upon any divine special precept of universal obligation, making it necessary for the being of a church, or essential constitution of presbyters. Neither is there any Scripture which determines the form, how such a bishop or any other may be made. Yet it may be grounded upon general precepts of Scripture concerning decency, unity, order and edification, but so, that order and decency may be observed by another way, and unity and edification obtained by other means. But there are many in these our days, which make episcopacy invested with power of ordination at least, of that necessity, that if ministers be not ordained by them, they are no ministers. They make the being of the ministry, and the power of the sacraments to depend on them: and they further add, that without a succession of these bishops, we cannot maintain our ministry against the church of Rome. But [...] where do they find in Scripture any special precept of universal and perpetual obligation, which doth determine that imposition of hands of the presbytery, doth essentially constitute a presbyter; and that the imposition of hands, if it did so, was invalid without an hierarchical bishop, or a certain constant superintendent with them? And if they will have their doctrine to stand good, such a precept they must produce, which they have not done, which I am confident they cannot do.[22] As for succession of such bishops, after so long a time, so many persecutions, and so great alterations in the churches of all nations, it's impossible to make it clear: Eusebius himself, doth so preface unto his catalogue of bishops, that no rational man can so much as yield a probable assent unto him in that particular.[23] But suppose it had been far clearer, yet it could not merit the force of a divine testimony; it would have been only human, and could not have been believed but with a probable faith. Nay, Irenaeus, Tertullian, Eusebius and others, do not agree in the first and immediate successors of the Apostles, no not of the Roman church.[24] For Irenaeus makes Clemens the third, whom Tertullian determines to be the first from the Apostles. Yet they all agree in this: that the succession of persons, without succession of the same doctrine was nothing. Tertullian confesseth, that there were many churches, which could not show the succession of persons, but of doctrine from the Apostles, and that was sufficient.[25] And the succession of persons is so uncertain, that whosoever shall make either the being of a church, or the ministry, or the power of the sacraments depend upon it, shall so offend Christ's little ones, and be guilty of such a scandal, as it were better for him, that a millstone were hanged about his neck, and he cast into the sea. The power of saving men's souls depends not upon succession of persons according to human

---

[22] Cf. the letter of Charles I to the Speaker of the House of Lords, Nov. 1647, affirming the *jure divino* status of bishops. S. R. Gardiner, *The Constitutional Documents of the Puritan Revolution, 1625–1660*, 3rd edn. (Oxford University Press, 1979), pp. 328 ff.

[23] Eusebius (260–340), Bishop of Caesarea; presumably a reference to his *Ecclesiastical History*, available in editions of 1554, 1659.

[24] St Irenaeus (130–200), *Adversus omnes haereses*, bk 3.4. (marginal reference).

[25] Tertullian (160–200), *De praescriptione haereticorum*.

institutions, but upon the apostolical doctrine, accompanied by the divine spirit. If upon the exercise of their ministerial power men are converted, find comfort in their doctrine, and the sacraments, and at their end deliver up their souls unto God their redeemer, and that with unspeakable joy, this is a divine confirmation of their ministry, and the same more real and manifest than any personal succession.[26] To maintain the ministry of England from their ordination by bishops, and the bishops by their consecration according to the canons of the council of Carthage, was a good argument *ad hominem*; yet it should be made good (as it may be) by far better arguments, and such as will serve the interest of other Protestant and reformed churches, who have sufficiently proved their ministry legal, and by experience, through God's blessing upon their labours, have found it effectual. But suppose the succession of our English episcopacy could be made good since the Reformation, it's to little purpose, except you can justify the popish succession up to the time of the Apostles, which few will undertake, none (I fear) will perform. Divers reasons persuade me to believe they cannot do anything in this particular to purpose, but amongst the rest this doth much sway with me, that there can be no succession without some distinct and determinate form of consecration and ordination, and except this form be determined by a special precept of Scripture, it cannot be of divine obligation. But any such special precept, which should prescribe the distinct forms of consecration and ordination we find not at all. We have some examples of constituting church officers by election, with the imposition of hands and prayer, yet this was common to all, even to deacons. So that the very forms of making bishops and presbyters, as we find them, both in the English book of ordination and the pontifical of Rome are merely arbitrary, as having no particular ground, but at the best only a general rule in Scripture, which leaves a liberty for several distinct forms. If any, notwithstanding all this, out of a high conceit of episcopacy, will refuse communion with such churches, which have no bishop, and yet are orthodox, or will account those no ministers, who are ordained by presbyters without a bishop; let such take heed, least [lest] they prove guilty of schisms. The substance of all this is: that bishops are not the primary subject of the Power of the Keys.

---

[26] Cf. William Perkins, *A Golden Chaine*, in *Works* (Cambridge, 1600), p. 494, who writes that 'succession of persons is nothing without succession of doctrine'. It is not clear how far the notions of real and personal are being evoked by Lawson.

CHAPTER 12

Whether presbytery or presbyters be the primary subject of the Power of the Keys

1.

In divers parts of Europe, where episcopacy hath been abolished, presbytery did succeed: and that (as it is asserted by many) upon such grounds, as will prove it as pure an aristocracy, as that of episcopacy was. The parties indeed have been changed, and instead of bishops we have presbyters: and though the former imparity be taken away, yet the form of government, which is aristocratic, remains. I have formerly heard many complain, that the bishops had cast off the presbyters: and now some do not like it well, that the presbyters have cast off the bishops, yet both do seem to agree to exclude the people, as distinct from the clergy, engrossing the whole power to themselves. These pure aristocratic forms have for the most part proved dangerous, especially in the church, because they do so much incline unto oligarchy, and usually degenerate into the same.

2.

But to observe some order; I will [first] examine what these presbyters are; [second] whether these being known, can according to Christ's institution be the primary subject of this power; [and] add something concerning our English presbytery. [...] These presbyters are of two sorts, [...] some are preaching, [and] some are not preaching, but only ruling presbyters or elders. The former are trusted with the dispensation of the word and sacraments, the latter are not. Both have the same name and are elders, yet differ much in respect of their ecclesiastical being. Of the preaching elder, I shall speak more at large in the second book in the chapter of ecclesiastical officers. This word elder, we do not find used either in the Old or New Testament in an ecclesiastical sense, before we read it in the Acts: and after that, we find it used about fifteen times in that kind of notion. The first place is Acts 11.30, the last, 1 Peter 5.1. Except we add that of 2 John 1. In many of these places, the word doth signify a preaching elder and minister of the gospel, and that most clearly and evidently; and if in any place it doth signify some other elder, it will be most difficult, if not impossible to define, what he should be. Yet this elder, which is presupposed to be distinct from the minister of the gospel, is said to be an officer of the church, which together with the preaching presbyter hath power of jurisdiction in ecclesiastical causes. To prove that there is such an elder, and that of divine institution, three places are principally insisted upon; and these I find discussed, and expounded, [...] in the London Divines[1] [and] before them in [George] Gillespie. Before him in Gerson, Bucerus, and they all go one way.[2] The first of these we read Romans 12.8. 'He that ruleth with diligence', that is, let him that ruleth, rule with diligence; where, he that ruleth, must be a ruling elder distinct from the preaching. But the word [*proistamenos*] doth not properly signify a governor, or ruler invested with power of command and jurisdiction, but a prime person set above, before, over others for inspection, guidance, and due ordering of persons, things, or actions. [Even] suppose in this place it should signify one invested with jurisdiction; how doth it appear that it is such a ruler ecclesiastical, as is distinct from a preaching elder? There is nothing in the place to evince it. [Further] seeing a minister of the gospel is a ruler in discipline, as is by themselves confessed, how may it be proved, that the person here meant is not the preaching elder, though not as a preaching elder but a pastor over a flock? For it must signify him alone, or him jointly with that other kind of elder. For if both be rulers, both must rule well. [Finally], it cannot be demonstrated, that the place speaks of discipline at all. For the place speaks of gifts, whereof one person may have many, and his duty is to exercise them all for the edification of the church.[3]

3.

The second place is, 1 Corinthians 12.28. Where the word translated governments, must signify this ruling officer, distinct from the

[1] *Jus divinum regiminis ecclesiastici ... by sundry ministers within the City of London* (London, 1646).
[2] George Gillespie (1613–48), Presbyterian theologian and one of the Scottish commissioners appointed to the Westminster Assembly, Martin Bucer and Jean Gerson (see Biographical notes).
[3] The root of the word under discussion was associated with giving, *proika*, freely given, *proiktes*, a beggar.

preaching elder. But [...] we find the word [*kubernetes*] taken for to signify a pilot, Acts 27.11,[4] and the same word in the Septuagint used in the same signification (Ezek. 27.28, 29 and Jonah 1.6) when the Hebrew word is *Chobel*. In them also I find *Tachbuloth*[5] fixed several times to signify counsels or wisdom, and translated in four of these places [*kubernesis*] (as Prov. 1.5: 11.14: 12.5: 21.30: 24.6: Job 37.12). And though it be true, that wisdom and counsel are necessarily required in a good governor invested with power, yet always they are essential   to   a good counsellor, and without them he cannot give good direction. [Moreover,] if we parallel the 28, 29, 30 verses, with the 8, 9, 10 verses of the same chapter, we shall find that governments signify such as have the gift of wisdom. [...] Let governments be governors, and the same ecclesiastical, will it follow that they were ruling elders distinct from preaching and ruling elders? Are there none other kind of governors but these? [Finally], this place doth not speak of external government and discipline, but of the gifts of the spirit, given for the good of the church. And I never knew rational and impartial scholars ground so great an office upon so weak a foundation, and argue from such an obscure place in respect of this eldership. It's far from proving any divine institution of such an office, as it doth not so much as imply it.

4.

The third place is, 1 Timothy 5.17. 'Let the elders that rule well, be counted worthy of double honour, especially those who labour in the word and doctrine.' From hence they infer that there are ruling elders, which labour in the word and doctrine, and others which do not. This presupposeth, that [*malista*] turned [as] 'especially' is taken here partitively. Yet that cannot be proved. For it may be added rather to signify the reason why, [than] the persons to whom, as distinct from other ruling elders, double honour is due. For in the [Westminster] Assembly it was alleged, that the participle in the original here, as in other places includes the cause. And then the sense is, 'Let the elders that rule well, be counted worthy of double honour, especially because they labour in the word and doctrine,' which seems to be the

---

[4] Acts 27.11 in fact refers to the master and owner of the ship.
[5] As Lawson transliterates I have omitted the original Hebrew.

genuine sense: and agrees with that, 'Esteem them very highly in love for their works' sake' (1 Thess. 5.13). [Further] 'Double honour', which is maintenance, is not due to ruling elders, who preach not the gospel. For the Lord ordained, that they which preach the gospel, should live of the gospel: they which do, not they which do not preach the gospel (1 Cor. 9.14). [Again] suppose it could be proved from this place, that they were ruling elders distinct from such as preach, how will it appear from thence, what their place was in the church, and what their power, and what their work? Yet, put all these places together, they cannot prove the divine institution of such an office, with the power of jurisdiction in causes ecclesiastical, for we do not find any special precept making this office universally and perpetually necessary, binding all Christian churches to observe it.

5.

But let us suppose such an officer, the question is, whether the elder with the preaching presbyter be the [principal receiver] of the Power of the Keys [in external matters]. That they are not the immediate subject is evident, [...] from the same reason why bishops are not. For Christ gave the power to the church, the whole church, as shall be manifest hereafter: but the elders are not the whole church. [Also] if they be the primary subject, then they are such as officers or representatives: but neither of these ways can they be such a subject. The disjunction is good, except they can give us another consideration, according to which they may have this power in this manner. The minor, which is, that neither as officers, nor as representatives can they be the primary subject, is thus proved: [...] not as officers, for the power of an officer, though universal, as these are but elders of particular congregations, is always derivative, and therefore he cannot be the first subject of that power, which is derived from a higher cause. Upon this ground, Mr. Hooker takes his advantage against Mr. Rutherford, and the seven dissenting brethren against the Assembly.[6] As for Mr. Hooker, he seems to take for granted, as he endeavours to prove, that jurisdiction belongs unto an officer as an officer. But this cannot be true, [first] because there are officers who have no jurisdiction,

---

[6] Thomas Hooker, *A Survey of the Summe of Church Discipline* (London, 1648), pt. 1, ch. 10, and esp. pt. 2.2–3; pt. 3.2.

as censors, sheriffs, constables, and many other in the state, and deacons in the church. [Second], suppose some officers have jurisdiction, yet they are not the first subject of it. [Third], he supposeth, as the dissenting brethren do, that every officer is fixed in, and related only unto a single congregation, whereas it's evident, and Mr. Parker confesseth it, that there may be officers which jointly take the charge of several congregations both for worship and discipline, as in the Netherlands, and this agreeable to the word of God.[7] Yet even these, much more such as are fixed to several particular congregations, can have no power out of those congregations, whereof they take charge, whether severally of one, or jointly of many. In this respect his argument is good against such as affirm, that power of jurisdiction belongs to officers as officers, and in particular to elders as elders. Yet both the Assembly and dissenting brethren confound, and that in the arguing, the power of the ministry, with the power of outward discipline, which ought not to be done. But the principal thing is, that officers, as such, cannot be the primary subject of power, for that belongs to them who make them officers.

6.

As they cannot have it as officers, so they cannot have it primarily as representatives. They may have power as officers, they may have it as representatives, yet not in this high manner or degree. For all representatives derive their power from the body represented. To clear this point, we must observe [the following: first], that many several congregations, which in respect of worship, are so many several bodies distinct, may associate and become one for discipline. [Second], when they are thus associate, the power is first in the whole, and derived from the whole unto the parts, and from the parts unto the whole: as in a single congregation, the power is in the whole, and every single member, even the officers are subject to the whole, which makes officers and gives them their power. [Third], that in this association of many congregations, when they act in a synod or representative, the parties, which make up the representative, do not act as officers, though they be officers in the several congregations but as representatives. Neither as representatives of several congrega-

[7] Robert Parker, *De politeia ecclesiastica, libri tres* (London, 1616), bk. 3, ch. 18?

tions, severally considered, but as jointly united in one body to represent the whole. As in a parliament many members are officers, yet do not act as officers, but all jointly act as one representative of the whole body. [Fourth], when many congregations united in one body for to set up one independent judicatory, do act by a representative, the whole body of these congregations, not the several congregations are [the primordial church] and the representative or synod is [the church as arisen]. [Fifth], that the power of discipline doth not issue from the power of teaching and administration of the sacraments. For then none but ministers should have the Power of the Keys, and not any could be joined with them, because they have their power by virtue of the ministerial office.

7.

Yet the authors of *Jus divinum regiminis ecclesiastici* do affirm, that ruling and preaching elders are the primary subject of this power and endeavour to prove it, and that by several arguments:[8] all [of] which may be answered by the very stating of the question. For they seem to me for to confound *Ecclesiam constituendum et constitutam*, officers ordinary and extraordinary; calling immediate and mediate; the government of the universal church, and particular churches *forum interius et exterius; Statum et exercitium*. Though the matter is clear enough, yet I will examine two of their arguments. The first is this:

> All those that have ecclesiastical power, and the exercise thereof immediately committed to them from Jesus Christ, are the immediate subject or receptacle of that power.
> But the church guides have ecclesiastical power, and the exercise thereof immediately committed unto them from Jesus Christ,
> Therefore they are the immediate subject or receptacle of that power.

For answer hereunto, we must understand what this power ecclesiastical in the question is; [...] what kind of subject is here meant; [...] what these church guides are; [...] what immediate commission from Christ may be; for that's the medium or third argument. [First], this ecclesiastical power is not that universal and supreme

---

[8] *Jus divinum ... by sundry ministers.*

power which is in Christ; nor the extraordinary power of extraordinary officers, as Apostles and others. It's an ordinary power of a particular church, and the same as universal and independent in respect of such a church. It's a power *in foro exteriori*, for outward government, it's a power supreme of making canons, constituting officers, and passing judgement without appeal, or from which there lies no appeal. [Second] the question is concerning the subject of this power, which subject may be primary or secondary, here the primary must be understood. [Third] church guides, as they understand them, are ruling and preaching elders. [Fourth] immediate commission from Christ, is, when Christ immediately gives power to any person, and by that donation designs him without any act of man intervening. Thus Paul was designed (Gal. 1.1) an Apostle, not of man, nor by man, but by Jesus Christ; this immediate commission is extraordinary. These things premised make it evident, [...] that the terms of the syllogism are more than three: because the words are so ambiguous. [Even], suppose the words to be clear and the terms but three, yet the minor [premise] is denied, [...] because by church guides are meant elders, who are ordinary officers of particular congregations, and therefore can have no immediate commission in proper sense; [and because] though they should be immediately commissioned, as they are not, yet the premises are insufficient to infer the conclusion. Their drift and design is, to prove that they have all their power from Christ alone, and not from the church. But they must know, that as they have their office, so they have their power. They have their office from the church immediately, from Christ *mediante Ecclesia*. For they are chosen, tried, approved by the church, and so designed to such an office by the church, and can exercise the power of discipline as officers in no church, but where they are officers. Again, the conclusion itself might be granted, if by ecclesiastical power they meant official power; and yet nothing to purpose, because the thing in question is not proved, nor so much as mentioned in the conclusion. Yet they endeavour to prove the minor from 2 Corinthians 10.8, where the Apostle speaks of the authority which the Lord had given them. But what authority was this? Interpreters say, it was apostolical, and so extraordinary. [...] Whether apostolical or not, yet it was their authority to preach the gospel, as appears in verse 16.[9] This is not the

---

[9] 2 Cor. 16, 'To preach the gospel in regions beyond you'.

power of discipline, the thing in question. The rest of the Scriptures alleged to prove the minor, speak either of the power of officers and power extraordinary, or of the power as ministers. Only Matthew 18.17, 18 is to be understood of the power of discipline, yet that place determines the church, not the elders to be the primary subject; and this is directly against them, as shall be showed hereafter.

8.

A second argument is this:

> All those, whose ecclesiastical officers for church government under the New Testament, are instituted by Christ before any formal visible Christian church was gathered or constituted, they are the first and immediate subject of the Power of the Keys from Jesus Christ.
> But the ecclesiastical officers of Christ's own officers were so instituted.
> Therefore they are the first subject of the Keys.
> Ch. 11, p. 183, of the second edition [1647].

Answer: [First] I find in this syllogism four terms. For in the major according to their own exposition, the officers were such, as that not only their offices were instituted, but that at the same instant made officers by Christ, before any Christian church had being or existence. These offices and officers were extraordinary (p. 184). In the minor, they include not only these offices and officers, but those of future times, which were not extraordinary. [Second] if they rectify the syllogism, and understand the minor only of such officers, as were actually in office before there was any Christian church, and then they argue [from species to genus] and infer a general from a particular; [then, third], how will they prove that ruling elders, distinct from preaching presbyters, were instituted by Christ or the Apostles, by virtue of a special precept of universal obligation? [Fourth] the question is, not of official power either ordinary or extraordinary. [Fifth] upon perusal of the Scriptures alleged to make good this argument, it will appear they confound officers and power extraordinary and ordinary, the church [to be made in future and in fact], power universal and particular.

9.

Hitherto I have enquired into the nature of presbytery, and examined, whether it can be the primary subject of church power [in external matters]; it remains I say something of the English presbytery, which was [. . .] intended [and] upon the advice of the [Westminster] Assembly modelled; [and is] now in some parts of the nation practised according to the Book of Discipline.[10] For this end we must observe:

[First] the nation was formerly and of old for civil government divided into counties, and the same division now retained for discipline. For the parliament thought it not good to follow the division of provinces and dioceses. The knights of the several counties chose certain ministers for the Assembly, who with some members of both Houses give their advice in matters of doctrine, worship and discipline: which was so far effectual as the parliament should approve. The discipline approved is made probationer for three years, declared and published in nine ordinances. The first whereof was agreed upon, about August 28, 1644. The last, August 28, 1646.

[Second] before this model could be finished, there was much debate and contention, especially between the dissenting brethren and the Assembly. For though by the [Solemn League and] Covenant[11] the discipline ought to be reformed according to the word of God, and the best reformed churches, yet there was not the agreement which ought to have been. For both parties pretended to make the Word of God the rule; yet some thought the government of the Kirk of Scotland, some that of New England to be the best and nearest to the word, and most conformable to that infallible rule: so that, though at the instance of our English commissioners, that clause (according to the Word of God) was inserted, yet it proved not effectual to determine the controversy, because their judgements were so different.

[Third] in this model, the first work is to make officers, and determine their power.

---

[10] Lawson's more detailed qualms about the Westminster Assembly and its Confession of Faith are in the Baxter Treatises, vol. ii, fols. 208–10, item 39(4), Dr Williams's Library, London. The Book of Discipline is presumably *The Form of Church Government to be used in the Church of England and Ireland* (London, 1648), but various volumes issued by the Assembly touched on discipline. The Presbyterian form of Church government was in operation in parts of Lancashire and Shropshire until after the Restoration.

[11] 1643, para. 1.

[Fourth] the first officers were called triers, who (upon the division of several counties into a certain number of precincts called classes; which consisted of certain secular and ecclesiastical persons, whose names were certified to the parliament) by the parliament were allowed, and from the parliament received their power.

[Fifth] these were extraordinary officers, and their first, and chiefest work was upon election, examination, and approbation to constitute congregational eldership.

[Sixth] these once constituted, were invested with power; for the exercise whereof, the parliament determines, [...] their courts; [...] the parties subject to their power; [...] the causes belonging to their cognizance; [...] the manner of proceeding; [...] the acts of jurisdiction.

[Seventh] as for their courts, [...] they make them to be congregational, classical, provincial, national; [...] define the number of the persons, how many must be of the quorum; [...] they subordinate the inferior to the superior, and all to the supreme, which was the parliament. [Further], they determine the times of their sessions, which of the inferior courts were more frequent, of the superior more seldom; [and] the order of appeals [is] from the inferior to the superior.

[Eighth] the parties subject to their jurisdiction, were all in their several precincts.

[Ninth] the causes were not civil or capital, but ecclesiastical, especially ignorance and scandal.[12]

[Tenth] their manner of proceeding was upon information, by summons, confession, conviction by witnesses.

[Eleventh] the acts of jurisdiction were suspension, removal from office or sacraments; receiving and restoring. The matter and substance of these ordinances, was enlarged and more distinctly and orderly declared in the Book of Discipline, 1648.

10.

This model, though imperfect, had something of the ancient primitive discipline; in many things was agreeable to the general rules of Scripture; and if exercised constantly by wise and pious men might have

---

[12] Made most explicit later in the Ordinance for the Ejection of Scandalous Ignorant and Insufficient Ministers and School Masters, 1654.

done much good, especially in preventing ignorance and scandal for time to come. Yet it had many enemies, as the prelatical and episcopal party, because it was not a reformation, but an abolition of episcopacy. The dissenting brethren liked it not, because it extended so far beyond the congregational bounds, took in whole parishes, did not require a sufficient qualification of the members, and subordinated congregations, and inferior assemblies to the superior and greater. The profane and ignorant were against it, because it called them to account, and required knowledge and a stricter kind of life; and this was a commendation of it. Some approved it not, because it was so like unto, and almost the same with the Kirk Discipline of Scotland. Many were offended with it, because of the ruling and lay elders as some call them. Besides, it was set up in the time of a bloody war, and without the King's consent, who was a great enemy unto it.[13] Neither were the statutes of the former discipline repealed. Though some did but assert the *Jus divinum* of it, yet that was not made so clear as to satisfy many, no not the parliament itself. Though the ordinances and the Book of Discipline require it to be generally put in practice, yet no man was eligible for an officer that had not taken the National Covenant, yet that was not generally imposed or taken: nor could any but a covenanter have any vote in the election. As the institution of it was an act of the civil power in the parliament without the being, so, it reserved the chiefest power unto itself, and to future parliaments: and it would not trust the ministry or the elders with it. And there might be several reasons for it. First, after the Reformation began, and ever since our separation from Rome, the ecclesiastical power was restored to the crown. [Second], in times of popery the church, and especially the pope and clergy, had encroached and entered too far upon the civil power. [Third], the general assemblies of Scotland were thought too much independent upon [of] the crown, and to have too great an influence upon the state. [Fourth], that seeing the church required the assistance of the state, it was judged necessary, that it should so far depend upon the state as it required the help of the state. Yet, if the discipline had been the pure and simple form instituted by Christ

[13] Lawson's reflections seem to be embracing the original attempts of the Long Parliament to establish something of a Presbyterian system of government with the Cromwellian alterations after its partial collapse. He was directly involved throughout this period in Shropshire. See Conal Condren, *George Lawson's* Politica *and the English Revolution* (Cambridge University Press, 1989), ch. 2.

162

and his Apostles, there had been no cause of these jealousies, no need of these policies. By all this it's evident, that the presbytery of England could not be the primary subject of the Power of the Keys, because they received their institution from the parliament, which reserved the chiefest power unto itself. It's true, that there was something ecclesiastical in it, yet even that depended upon the civil power more than upon an ecclesiastical assembly, or representative, though general.

CHAPTER 13

That the government of the church is not purely democratical, but like that of a free state, wherein the power is in the whole, not in any part, which is the author's judgement

1.

That the Power of the Keys is not primarily in the pope, nor in the civil sovereign; nor in the prelate; nor in the presbyter; nor in both jointly as in a pure aristocracy, hath been formerly declared. It remains, we examine the people's title as distinct from that of the bishop and the presbyter, as they are [pre-eminent citizens of the church], parts of a Christian community. The people and number of believers thus considered, are rather *plebs*, than *populus*. To understand this it's to be considered that in a Christian community there are neither *optimates* properly, nor *plebs*. There may be and are, as you heard before, such as are incomplete and virtual members, as women, children and other weak Christians, who are not fit to have any vote in the public affairs of the church, much more unfit to exercise and manage the Power of the Keys. There are also complete members, and amongst these some more eminent than the rest. To place the power in the inferior rank, or to make that party predominant, is to make the government democratic. And this opinion is not worth the confutation, because it's not only disagreeing with plain Scripture, but with the rules of right reason. In this regard they are generally rejected.

Some charge Morellius and the Brownists with this error, but I have not seen their books.[1] The learned Blondel may seem to be of this mind, because he placeth the power *in Plebe Ecclesiastica*.[2] But upon due examination, it will be found otherwise. Mr. Parker, who asserts the government in some respect to be democratic, rejects Morellius, yet he himself cannot be altogether excused. For he will have the government to be mixed, and partly democratic in the people, partly aristocratic in the officers or governors. He further explains himself, and saith, it's *Democraticum quoad Statum* for the constitution, *Aristocraticum quoad exercitium* for the administration and exercise of the power.[3] For he distinguisheth between the power, which is in the whole church and the dispensàtion or exercise thereof, which is in the governors or officers, who he saith, have not all the power of dispensation, because the church reserves so much as is convenient, and belonging to her dignity, authority, and liberty given her of Christ. But this is a mistake in politics and the general rules of government. For a state is mixed or pure in respect of the constitu-tion, not the administration: and the question is not concerning the secondary, but the primary subject of power, which the officers deriv-ing the power from the whole church cannot be, for they have it only at the second hand: as he himself confesseth. I will not examine his many arguments, because there is none of them *ad idem*, and to the purpose or point in hand: and they all and every one, as he misapplies them, presuppose an error. For they all should be limited to the fundamental power in constitution, but here power of constitution, and of administration are confounded; as also the power of the church with the power of officers.

2.

After the examination of all these titles, I proceed to deliver mine own judgement, and to make good the title of my mother the church. For I believe this to be the truth in this point: That the primary subject of

---

[1] The followers of Robert Brown (1550–1633); Jean Morel(?), *De ecclesia ab Antichristo* (London, 1589).

[2] David Blondel (1590–1655), *De la primauté en l'Eglise* (Geneva, 1641); and *De iure plebis in regimine ecclesiastica* (Paris, 1617).

[3] Robert Parker, *De politeia ecclesiastica, libri tres* (London, 1616) (marginal reference), bk. 3.7, p. 26.

the Power of the Keys is the whole church. For order's sake I will, [...] explain the proposition [and] confirm the same. In the explication I will inform the reader, [...] what I mean by the Power of [the] Keys, [...] by the whole church; [and] how, and in what manner I understand the whole church to be the primary subject of this power.

[First], this power is not the power of civil sovereigns, nor of officers, as officers, civil or ecclesiastical [in external matters], or of ministers, as ministers, nor the universal power of Christ, nor the extraordinary power of Apostles, or any other extraordinary officers; but it is an ordinary power of making canons, of constituting officers, of jurisdiction and other acts, which are necessary for the outward government of an ecclesiastical community, committed unto, and conveyed upon the church by Christ.

[Second], by the whole church, is not to be understood the universal church militant and triumphant, nor the whole church mystical, nor the whole church militant and visible of all times, nor of the visible church of all nations, existent in one time; but a whole particular church visible in some certain place and vicinity, that shall be fit to manage the Power of the Keys independently: as the church of Jerusalem, of Antioch, of Corinth, of Ephesus, of Smyrna, etc. Those who determine the series or order of appeals to ascend from a congregation, to a classis, from a classis to a provincial synod, from a provincial to a national, of one nation to a national of several nations, or from that unto an ecumenical or general council, extend the whole church far further than I do. As for the papal party, they presuppose all particular churches to make but one visible church, not only for doctrine and worship, but for outward discipline too; and the church of Rome must be the mother and queen of all other churches in the world. Yet they differ about the primary subject of the Power of the Keys. Some determine the pope as Peter's successor, to be the visible head and universal monarch of this church. Others, as the Councils of Constance and Basle, Cameracensis, Gerson, and the faculty of Paris, give this power to the whole church to be exercised in general councils.[4] Mr. Ellis doth charge some of our own, who affirmed this

---

[4] The Council of Constance (1414–18); of Basle (1431–49). Pierre d'Ailly, Cardinal Cameracensis, see *Questiones magistri Petri de Alliaco ... super libros sententiarum ... Lombardus ... et questionibus de potestate ecclesie in suis vesperiis disputatis* (Lyons, 1490, 1500); Jean Gerson, *Opera*, 2 vols. (Paris 1606), which also includes relevant consiliar theory by Alliaco, vol. i, pp. 896 ff.

power to be in the universal church with popery: and Mr. Hooker conceives he hath demonstrated learned and judicious Mr. Hudson to be guilty of the same, but he is mistaken, as since is made evident.[5] These two cannot possibly be reconciled whilst they proceed upon contrary principles. Mr. Hooker of New England understands by a visible church, such a church as is under a form of external discipline, and subject unto one independent judicatory; but neither Mr. Hudson, nor others of his mind understand any such thing. There is an universal visible militant church on earth: this church is truly *totum integrale*, and also an organical body; the head and monarch is Christ; all ministers officers, all believers, subjects: the word and sacrament privileges, and every Christian either by birth or baptism according to divine institution is first in order of nature a member of this universal or organical body, before he be a member of any particular church or congregation, and is so to be considered. And many, if not all the places of Scripture alleged by Mr. Hudson, are truly understood to speak of this universal church: though some of them seem to be affirmed only of the church mystical, as such, yet so that in divers respects they may agree to both. This cannot be popery, neither doth it presuppose any point of popery or other error. The grand error of the papist in this particular, is, to affirm that one church particular is above all churches in the world, not only in dignity but in power, so that all particular churches must be subject unto her, and her bishop invested with universal jurisdiction. To subject the universal church militant in one body to Christ, can have no affinity with this. And to subject every particular church to the universal, exercising her power in a representative, is no such error, nor so dangerous as that of the sovereignty of Rome. And though there be no such thing, because the distance is so great, that the association is impossible, yet the pope and his party did abhor to think of it. That question about visible and invisible is but a toy to this. The church therefore, which is the subject of the question is, a church, a particular church, a whole particular church. Yet there is a particular church primary and secondary: primary is the church considered as a community, and a secondary church [considered] by way of representation. The primary is the proper subject of real power, the representative of personal.

[5] John Ellis, *Arguments Produced by Mr. Hudson* (London, 1647); Thomas Hooker, *A Survey of the Summe of Church Discipline* (London, 1648), 1.15, pp. 250 ff.; Samuel Hudson, *The Essence and Unitie of the Church Catholick Visible* (London, 1645).

Whether this church be a congregational, or of larger extent shall be examined hereafter. [...] Thus you have heard, [...] what the power is [and] what the subject is. Now, [third] we must consider in what manner this power is in this primary subject. It's not in it monarchically, nor aristocratically, nor democratically, or any pure way of disposition; but in the whole, after the manner of a free state or polity. For there *Universi praesunt singulis, singuli subduntur universis*, so it is here; all jointly and the whole doth rule, every several person; though officer, though minister, though bishop, if there be any such, is subject to the whole, and to all jointly. And in this model the power is derived from the whole to the parts, not from the parts to the whole, though this community should consist of ten thousand congregations. This power is exercised in the highest degree by a representative general, in an inferior degree by officers or inferior assemblies: Upon this principle, though in another manner, the Councils of Basle and Constance did proceed against the Pope, as being but a part, though an eminent part, as the times were then of the church. Yet this proposition is not so to be understood, as though this church were the first fountain and original of this power, for she is not; she derives and receives it from Christ, as Christ from God. But she is the primary subject in respect of her parts and members.

3.

For the confirmation of this proposition, I will, [...] examine two places alleged by Mr. Parker and many others, for to manifest the original of church discipline, which I conceive are not so pertinent. [And], I will most of all insist upon the words of institution. [...] I will [also] enlarge upon those places, which speak of the exercise of this power; that from the manner of administration we may understand the constitution. The two places are Matthew 16.19 and John 20.22, 23. The first is concerning the promise, the second concerning the donation of the Power of the Keys, as they are by many expounded. The words of the promise are these, 'I will give unto thee the Keys of the Kingdom of Heaven, etc.' Many and different are the interpretations of this place, as given by writers, both ancient and modern; popish and Protestant. The difference is in two things especially; [...] what this power should be [and] to whom it was to be given. The power with many is the power of discipline [in external matters], with others the power of a minister, as a minister. [...] The person to whom this power is here promised no doubt is Peter; but under what notion Peter must be considered, is here the question. Some will have it to be Peter as a monarch and prince above the rest of the Apostles, including his successors, the monarchical bishop of Rome. Some will have Peter here considered as the mouth and representative of the Apostles, and in them, of all aristocratic bishops as their successors. Some will have him to represent the ministers, some the elders; some the church itself. And these again divide, and cannot agree, whether this church here [is] meant [to] be the universal church, or a particular; if universal, whether universal mystical, or visible: if visible, whether this be the church itself or a representative of the same; if representative, whether it must be represented by bishops only, or by bishops and presbyters, or by presbyters alone, or by bishops, presbyters and people. If a particular church, whether it be congregational, or diocesan, or some other: so that from this pronoun THEE, we have chemical extractions of all sorts of governments, ecclesiastical, pure and mixed; monarchic, aristocratic, democratic; of all kinds of churches, as universal, national, congregational; of all kind of governors, as popes, bishops, presbyters, the people. Yet I conceive this place is not meant of discipline, but rather of doctrine. The church is the universal, against which the gates of Hell shall not prevail; the Keys are the word and sacraments, accompanied with the power of the spirit. As building is conversion and edification, so binding and loosing admission into, or exclusion out of this church. The architect and chief master builder is Christ, as he is the principal agent in binding and loosing. His servants and co-workers are Apostles and ministers of the gospel, amongst whom Peter was most eminent amongst the Jews, Paul amongst the gentiles. For Christ used Peter first to convert the Jews (Acts 2), then convert the gentiles (Acts 10). And Paul laboured more abundantly than them all. The binding and loosing in Heaven, was the making of their ministry by the power of the divine spirit to be effectual. To this purpose Dr. Reynolds, Spalatensis, Casaubon, Cameron, Grotius with divers of the ancients, and Mr. Parker himself, who notwithstanding applies this, to the power of discipline, intending thereby to prove the Power of the Keys to be democratically in a congregational church.[6] Yet let it

[6] Probably John Rainolds (1549–1607), *De Romanae ecclesiae Idolatria* (Oxford, 1596), copies in Millington, *Catalogus*; M. A. de Dominis, *Papatus Romanus liber de origine*

be supposed that Peter, as receiving the Keys, doth represent the community of believers: or if as such he represent them, how will it appear that this church or community is a single congregation? Or if it be such a single congregation, how will it follow from hence that the power is in this congregation democratically? Mr. Parker should have considered that there is a great difference, between Peter, as professing that Christ was the son of the living God (for as such he was only a disciple admitted by Christ into his kingdom); and Peter receiving the Keys (for as such he was above a disciple, and hath power to admit others into this kingdom) not as a disciple, but as a minister of the gospel.[7]

4.

The place for actual donation and performance of the former promise, is said to be that of John 20.22, 23. The words of Christ, the donor are these, 'Receive ye the Holy Ghost, whosoever sins ye remit, they are remitted unto them, and whosoever sins ye retain, they are retained.' These have been alleged, as by [Parker], so by others to prove, [that] the Power of the Keys [in external matters] [...] is in the bishops alone; [and] that the priests have power upon auricular confession to absolve: and here they ground their sacrament of penance, and their sacerdotal power *in foro pœnitenciali*. From hence, some of ours have endeavoured to prove the parity of Apostles, and so of bishops against the pope's supremacy: for here they find the power promised only to Peter by name, given to all the Apostles. For to understand these words the better, we must observe in them a donation, and in it the donor, the donee, the power, the acts of the power [and] the ratification of these acts. The donor or person giving is Christ: the parties receiving this power immediately are Apostles, as extraordinary servants and officers: the thing given and received was the Holy Ghost, that is, ability and authority, divine and spiritual, necessary and requisite for the place. The acts were remitting and retaining, the same with binding and loosing (Matt. 16.19). The

(London, 1617); and more extensively, *De republica ecclesiastica* (London, 1617), copy in More Library; Isaac Casaubon (1559–1614), *De rebis sacris et ecclesiasticis* (London, 1614(?)); John Cameron, *An Examination of those Plausible Appearances which seeme most to Commend the Romish Church* (Oxford, 1626); Hugo Grotius, *Annotationes in evangelium, secundum Matthaeum*, 16.19; *Ioannem* 20.22–3, *Opera omnia theologica* (1679 edn., facsimile, Stuttgart, 1972), 2.1, pp. 163, 570.

[7] Parker, *De politeia*, bk. 3.

ratification of these acts, was the making them effectual by the concurrence of the divine spirit. For, these acts could not be spiritual and divine, and so powerful upon the immortal souls of men, nor the Apostles so much as ministerial and instrumental agents in this work, without a divine power and confirmation of the supreme judge making their sentence valid and executing the same. Hence that sweetest joy and admirable comfort of those who are remitted, and the terrors and torments of those that are condemned. These acts are performed by the word and sacraments, and the application of the promises or communications to particular persons, which application is made either more at large to a multitude at one time, or to single persons upon some evidence of their qualification. And it may be made infallibly so far as God shall direct infallibly, or fallibly, for want of clear evidence, in which case the sentence must be passed conditionally by man, though absolutely by God. All this is nothing to external discipline, or if it should extend so far, the party remitting and retaining is not the church, but the officers of the church and the officers of a church not under a form of outward government, but under another consideration. An ecclesiastical external commonwealth doth presuppose an ecclesiastical community, and the same consisting of believers, and the same united and associated for worship and divine performances tending to eternal salvation. And those thus associated may have communion in divine things and actions, and their pastors with their flocks, before any form of discipline be introduced or settled, and these believers may by word and sacraments receive heavenly comfort, and attain eternal life without such discipline, and before it can be established amongst them. And so, I hope, it is at this time in this nation with many faithful servants of God, who by the benefit of a good ministry, with God's blessing upon their labours, are truly converted, and continue, and go on in a state of salvation as happily, as many who are under a form of government. And here it is to be observed, that though the Apostles were extraordinary officers infallibly directed by the Holy Ghost, which Christ gave them; yet ordinary ministers lawfully called succeeding them, if they preach their doctrine truly, have a promise to convert and save the souls of sinful men. [Further] the work of these ordinary ministers, is not only to feed the flock of Christ already gathered, but to convert and gather sinners unto Christ; and this not by the rod of discipline, but the word of God, which is the power of God unto salvation. [. . .] This gaining souls to Christ is not the gathering of churches out of churches, and Christians out of Christians to make a party of their own, under pretence of a purer reformation, but it's a far more excellent work of another kind, tending directly to a higher end. [...] After a minister becomes a pastor of a flock, and hath relation unto them as his flock, and they to him as his people, he must needs have some power over them, and they must be subject unto him and obey him in the Lord, and he hath power to remit sins; to shut and open, and what he doth in this kind, according to his commission, will be made good in Heaven. Yet these acts of his are not acts of external discipline, but of his ministerial office, as he is a servant to Jesus Christ. This I speak not against discipline, which if agreeable to the Word of God is a great blessing; but against all such, who under pretence of this or that form of church-government, disturb the church, and discomfort and discourage many a precious saint of God. The end of this is to manifest, that these places of Scripture (Matt. 16.19, John 20.22, 23), are no grounds whereon to build church-government.

5.

Because former places are not so pertinent, I proceed in the next place to the words of institution of church discipline, you may read them (Matt. 18.17, 18). ['The foundation is upon jurisdiction in the external court and nowhere else.'] That's the only place for the institution and no other, saith Dr. Andrewes, in that most learned and exact piece far above his other works.[8] To understand this place we must observe [...] the parties subject to this tribunal; [and] the causes proper to that court. [Further] in what manner and order causes are brought in and prepared for judgement; [and] the judge. [Also we need to know] the acts of judgement upon evidence of the cause; [...] the ratification of these acts, and so of the power; [and] how this ratification is obtained, and the judgement made effectual. [First] the party subject to this tribunal is a brother. 'If thy brother offend thee' (verse 15). This may be explained from 1 Corinthians 5.11, 'But, now I have written unto you, not to keep company, if any man that is called a brother be a fornicator, or covetous, or an idolater, etc.' There are covetous persons and idolaters of the world (verse 10), and fornicators

---

[8] Lancelot Andrewes, *Tortura Torti* (London, 1609), p. 41 (marginal reference).

and idolaters which are called brethren: the former are without, the latter within the church. The former are subject to the judgement of God, but not of the church, the latter are subject to the judgement of the church, 'Do not thou judge them that are within.'[9] So that the subjects in this commonwealth are brethren, disciples, such as profess their faith in Christ.

[Second], the causes are spiritual and ecclesiastical, and must be considered under that notion. For it's a trespass, an offence committed by a brother, as a brother, against a brother as a brother; whether it be a wrong against a brother or a sin, whereby a brother is offended, grieved, displeased. For, if a brother be a fornicator, or idolater, etc., he must tell the church and not the state; he must be made as an heathen or publican. If he will not hear the church, this is no sentence of the state or civil judge, it's made good in Heaven, so is not the judgement of the civil magistrate. It must be the judgement of a brother as a brother within the church, which the church, as a church, must judge, and in the name of Christ, not of the civil sovereign, and the party offending must be delivered up to Satan, not to the Sword. Yet one and the same crime may make a person obnoxious, both to the temporal Sword of the magistrate, and the spiritual censure of the church, and may be justly punishable and punished by both; though some of our English lawyers have delivered the contrary, who might ground their opinion upon the ecclesiastical supremacy of the king. For though the laws of England might determine so, yet the laws of God and Christ do not.

[Third], the manner and order of proceeding, is [either] privately to admonish; and if that take effect, to proceed no further. [Or], if upon this the party will not reform, he must be charged and convinced before two or three witnesses; and if he shall persist impenitent, then he must be convented before the ecclesiastical tribunal upon information and accusation; and the same once made good, and evident, the cause is ripe and prepared for judgement.

6.

The judge in the fourth place is the church; 'Tell the church,' where we must know, what this church is. The word in the Greek is [*ecclesia*],

---

[9] 1 Cor. 5.12.

and we find it used in the Old Testament about seventy times by the Septuagint, who so often turn the Hebrew [*qhl*] by that name. Upon perusal of the places we shall find that it signifies assemblies, and of many kinds: as good, bad, holy, profane, greater, less, festival, civil, military, ecclesiastical and religious, occasional, standing, orderly, confused, ordinary, extraordinary. It's observable, that very seldom (some say but once, as Psalm 26.5), it signifies a wicked and profane society.[10] Sometimes, not often, it's a military body. But most of all by far (a few texts excepted) it notes an holy and religious convention or assembly. For sometimes it's the national polity of Israel under a sacred notion; and very often a religious assembly for prayer, fasting, dedications, renewing their covenant with God, praises, thanksgivings, and such like acts of worship. So that the word seems to be appropriate unto religious assemblies; and though it signify other societies, yet these most frequently and principally. And this is conformed from the New Testament, where it's used one hundred and eleven times at least, and in all these places signifies an assembly or society religious, except in Acts 19.32, 39, 41, where it signifies both a tumultuous, and also an orderly assembly or convention, as a civil court of judgement, which signification is here applied by our Saviour to a spiritual judicatory for spiritual causes. Though this be a special signification, yet it signifies the number and society of believers and disciples, who profess their faith in Christ exhibited, and this is this church-Christian, and the people of God. Yet it signifies this people under several notions, as sometimes the church of the Jews: sometimes of the gentiles, sometimes the universal church, sometimes particular churches; sometimes the militant church, either as visible or mystical; sometimes the church triumphant; sometimes a church before any form of government be introduced; sometimes under a form of government, so it's taken and supposed by our Saviour here. Grotius his conceit, that our Saviour in these words alludes to the manner of several sects and professions, as of Pharisees, Saducees, Essenes, who had their rules of discipline, and their assemblies and convention for the practice of them, may be probable.[11] Yet without any such allusion the place is plain enough from the context and other Scriptures. Erastus upon the place is intolerable,

---

[10] Ps. 26.5, 'I have hated the congregation of evil-doers...'.
[11] Grotius, *Annotationes in libros evangelium, secundum Matthaeum*, 18.17, 2.1, pp. 176–7.

and most woefully wrests it: so doth Bishop Bilson in his *Church-Government*, and is point-blank contrary to Dr. Andrewes, who in his *Tortura Torti*, doth most accurately examine, interpret and apply the words, and most effectually from thence confute Bellarmine.[12] One may truly say of that book, as he himself said of Augustine's treatise *De Civitate Dei*, it was [a work of winning excellence]. For civil, common, canon law, politics, history, school learning, the doctrine of the casuist's divinity, and other arts, whereof he makes use, it is one of the most learned and accurate of any put forth in our times. By his exposition of this text, he utterly overthrows the immediate *Jus divinum* of episcopacy in matters of discipline and ecclesiastical jurisdiction. He plainly and expressly makes the whole church the primary subject of the Power of the Keys [in external matters].[13] Therefore, suppose the bishops were officers by a divine right, as he endeavours to prove (though weakly) in his *Letters to Du Moulin*.[14] Yet at best, they can be but the church's delegates, for the exercise of that power and it's observable, that divers of our champions, when they oppose Bellarmine's monarchical government of the church, peremptorily affirm the Power of the Keys to be in the whole church, as the most effectual way to confute him, yet when they wrote against the Presbyterian and the antiprelatical party, they change their tone and tune. But to return unto the words of institution, [...] the word church here signifies an assembly; [...] this assembly is an assembly for religion; [...] the religion is Christian; [...] this assembly is under a form of external government; [...] this government presupposeth a community, and laws and officers ecclesiastical. These presupposed, it's a juridical assembly, or a court. [...] Because courts are inferior, superior, and supreme, it signifies all, especially supreme. [...] It determines no kind of government but that of a free state, as shall more appear hereafter. [...] Christ doth not say, *Dic regi*, tell the prince or state; nor *Dic Petro*, tell Peter or the pope, as though the government should be monarchical, either civil or ecclesiastical: nor *Dic*

---

[12] Thomas Erastus (1524–83); possibly a reference to his controversial *Explicatio gravissimae quaestionis* (London, 1589), trans. *The Nullity of Church Censures* (London, 1659); Bishop Thomas Bilson, *The Perpetual Government of Christ's Church*(?) (London, 1593), ch. 9, Lawson's own copy in More Library, annotated; Bellarmine St Robert, leading Catholic controversialist, 1542–1621.

[13] Andrewes, *Tortura Torti*, p. 41.

[14] Andrewes, *Of Episcopacy: Three Epistles of Peter Moulin ... Answered...* (London, 1647 edn.), pp. 14–19, 48 ff.

presbytero, tell the elders; nor *Dic apostolis et episcopis aut archiopiscopis*, that the government should be purely aristocratical; nor *Dic plebi*, that the government should be purely democratical; nor *Dic synodo*, tell the council general or particular. But it saith, tell the church, wherein there may be bishops, presbyters, some eminent persons neither bishops nor presbyters:[15] there may be synods, and all these either as officers or representatives of the church; and we may tell these, and these may judge, yet they hear and judge by a power derived and delegated from the church, and the church by them, as by her instruments, doth exercise her power. As the body sees by the eye, and hears by the ear, so it is in this particular; but so, that the similitude doth not run on four feet, nor must be stretched too far. This being the genuine sense favours no faction, yet admits any kind of order, which observed may reach the main end. For this we must know, and take special notice of, that Christ will never stand upon formalities, but requires the thing, which he commands, to be done in an orderly way. Yet it's necessary and his institution doth tend unto it, to reserve the chief powers in the whole body, otherwise if any party, as bishops, or presbyters, or any other part of the church be trusted with the power alone to themselves, they will so engross it, as that there will be no means, nor ordinary jurisdiction to reform them. Of this we have plain experience in the bishops of Rome, who being trusted at first with too much power, did at length arrogate as their own, and no ways derived from the church, and so refused to be judged. For if the church once make any party the primary subject of this power, then they cannot use it to reduce them. Therefore, as it is a point of wisdom in any state to reserve the chief power in the whole community, and single out the best and wisest to exercise it; so as, if the trustees do abuse their power, they may remove them or reform them: so it should be done in the church. If any begin to challenge either the whole or the supreme power as officers, many of these, nay the greater part of them may be unworthy or corrupted, and then the church is brought to straits and must needs suffer. Some tell us, that the King of England by the first constitution was only the supreme and universal magistrate of the kingdom, trusted with a sufficient power to govern and administer the state according to the laws: and his chief work was to see the laws executed. Yet in tract of time, they

---

[15] Andrewes, *Tortura Torti*, p. 41.

did challenge the power to themselves as their own, and refused to be judged. Yet in this institution, if Peter, if Paul, though Apostles, do offend, much more if patriarchs, metropolitans, bishops, presbyters do trespass, we must tell not Peter, not Paul, not an Apostle, not a bishop, not any other but the church. No wit of men or angels could have imagined a better way, not given a better expression to settle that which is good and just, and prevent all parties and factions, and yet leave a sufficient latitude for several orderly ways to attain the chief end.

7.

The judge being known, the judicial acts of this judge must be enquired into the fifth place, and these are two: the first is binding, the second loosing. For all judgement passed upon any person is either against him, and that is binding, or for him, and that is loosing. The former is called binding, because it more strictly doth bind him to suffer that punishment, to which he was liable upon the transgression of the law. There was an obligation upon him [...] to obedience. [...] Upon disobedience there follows a guilt, which is an obligation to punishment. [...] Judgement doth continue this obligation, and makes the punishment unavoidable:[16] The latter is a loosing, because upon some condition performed, it frees him from the punishment, and the bond of guilt. Of this binding there be several degrees. For as in a civil government, there be several degrees of punishment, according to the several degrees of the offences, so it's in the church. One of the highest punishments and degrees of binding, is to make one as a heathen and a publican. These words are differently understood, and expounded. Grotius thinks, that our Saviour in them did not intend excommunication.[17] Many take it for granted, that to be censured and judged a heathen and publican, is to be cast out of the church and excommunicated. And from these two words, heathen and publican, diverse, and amongst the rest [*Vignierus*], and Dr. Andrewes do observe a twofold excommunication.[18] The one is

---

[16] This reiterates a central theme of the 'Amica dissertatio', *c.* 1649, Baxter Treatises, vol. i, fols. 99–130b, item 9.
[17] Grotius, *Annotationes in libros evangelium, secondum Matthaeum*, 18.17, p. 177.
[18] Nicholas Vignier, *De venetorum excommunicatione* (Saumur, 1606). There is a marginal reference to Vignier. The text refers to *Quinquerclesiensis*, meaning the Hungarian diocese of Pécs. Andrewes, *Tortura Torti*, p. 41.

the greater, and that is to be as a heathen; the other the less, which is to be as a publican. The heathen was out of the church, the publican was not. The heathen might not, the publican might come into the temple; the heathen were strangers to the commonwealth of the Israelites, and were [*Lo-ammi*, Hos. 1.6–9]: the publican, being a Jew, was in the church, but like a scandalous brother. Whether this distinction be here intended or no, it's certain, [first] that there are degrees of ecclesiastical as well as civil penalties; [and] that by this being as a heathen and publican, is meant an ecclesiastical not a civil punishment in matter of religion: [...] both were deprived of ecclesiastical communion. In the text, 'If he will not hear the church, let him be to thee as a heathen and a publican.'[19] Three things are to be observed: [...] the penalty and the execution; [...] the sentence to be executed; [and] the crime or cause. The execution is to account him as a heathen and a publican, which is not to take away his house, lands, goods, civil liberty, life, but to separate from him, and have no communion with him in matter of religion and spiritual society, and to testify their dislike of him by shunning his company. [...] The sentence is the judgement of the church, whereupon this separation and non-communion is grounded. For, the church must judge and pass the sentence, before we can have any sufficient warrant for refusal of society. [...] The crime or cause must be made evident before the judge pass sentence: and it is not only the trespass or offence, but impenitence manifested to the ecclesiastical judge. Not to hear the church is for the guilty brother; not to confess and reform upon the church's public admonition. This puts him in an immediate capacity of condemnation and punishment. But more of ecclesiastical censures in the second book.

8.

The ratification of this sentence of the church, which is the sixth thing, followeth in these words, 'whatsoever ye shall bind on earth, shall be bound in Heaven, etc.' which are added, as Hilary saith well, *in terrorem metus maximi*, to strike a terror into the hearts of all such as shall make themselves liable to the censures of the church.[20] Yet they

---

[19] Matt. 18.17. Both Andrewes and Vignier draw explicitly from this *topos*.
[20] St Hilary of Poitiers? (*c.* 315–67).

are not only for terror, but for the sweetest consolation of the penitent absolved by the church; and so also for the encouragement of the church to proceed in discipline against the greatest. For though she hath not the Sword, nor any coactive force to imprison, fine, banish, put to death, and the profane and worldly wretches do not fear her censures, yet her censures shall be executed from Heaven, and be more terrible than any punishments inflicted by Sword of civil sovereigns. This ratification includes two things: [. . .] that when this judgement is once passed according to the rules of Christ, the supreme judge doth approve and decree it to be irrecoverable; [and] that he will by a divine and never failing power execute it; so that neither can any appeal, or complaint of a nullity make it void, nor any contrary strength or force hinder the execution. In this respect Hilary saith, it's *judicium immobile*, and cannot be reversed; Jerome, that it's corroborated and cannot be infringed. Tertullian, that it's *prejudicium ultimi judicii*, and stands good, as that ever shall.

9.

The means whereby this ratification is obtained, and the manner how it is effected, come in the last place to be observed. The means is their consent and prayer. For if two of them shall agree on earth, as touching anything that they shall ask, it shall be done for them by my Father which is in Heaven, which words do signify that they should agree upon the sentence, and pass the same with prayer. The manner how it comes to pass to be effected is, that when two or three of them are gathered together in Christ's name, he will be in the midst of them (verse 20). For it's not to be done in their own name, or by their own power, but they must assemble and proceed in Christ's name, and in his name give the definite sentence. According to this law the Apostle gave direction in Christ's name to gather together, and with the power of Jesus Christ to deliver the scandalous person to Satan (1 Cor. 5.4): so that Christ will be present with them, direct them, and assist them, and the work shall be more his, than theirs.

10.

Having [. . .] examined two places not pertinent, [and] enlarged upon the words of the institution, I will thirdly confirm the proposition from such places as treat of the exercise of this power. [...] These are such as speak of legislation; [...] of making officers; [and] of jurisdiction. The first of legislation and making of canons concerning matters controverted: As for canons, concerning things not controverted, we find single Apostles (especially Paul, and he most of all in his first epistle to Timothy) declaring and delivering them without any other joined with them. The exercise of this legislative power, we find in that famous synod held at Jerusalem (Acts 15). The difference of the interpretations of this text is no less than [that] of [the] former. For some question, whether it was a formal synod, having power to bind, or only an assembly for advice. Some make it, not only a synod invested with a binding force, but judge it to be a most excellent pattern for all synodical assemblies in time to come. Yet these are not certain, whether it was general in respect of all churches then extant. But let it be a synod having a binding force; it's doubted how the canons could bind other churches, who sent no delegates to represent them and act for them. Whether [they did] bind, because it was a General Council in some consideration, or because the Apostles were in it, and acted as extraordinary ministers of Christ invested with a universal power over all churches; or because they were received afterwards in every particular church; or because the matter was determined in Scripture, and out of it declared to be the mind of God, which seems to be implied in these words, 'It seemed good to the Holy Ghost and us' (verse 28). For all canons should be so made as to be clearly grounded upon some special or general precepts of Scripture, which were revealed by the Holy Ghost: for they should bind more in respect of the matter, and the reason upon which they are grounded, than in respect of the multitude of votes. For one good reason from the Scriptures is more binding than the consent of all general councils in the world. Another query there is, why this controversy should be determined at Jerusalem, and not at Antioch, or anywhere else. Whether it was, because that was the mother church; or because the Apostles were there at that time resident; or because other churches were not so fully constituted; or because there might be there representatives from all other churches. [Perhaps it was] because they, who sprang the controversy at Antioch, came from Jerusalem, and pretended the authority of the Apostles, and of the church; and because it was agreed at Antioch to refer the cause to the Apostles and elders at Jerusalem. Besides all these, there is another doubt concerning the members, which did constitute this synod; whether the Apostles only, or the Apostles with the elders; or besides these, the brethren as distinct from them; or whether if all these were of the synod, the elders and brethren had any decisive voice or no. But to leave these doubts, it's certain out of the text, [...] that upon controversy raised at Antioch by some, who came from Jerusalem, it could not be after much disputation there ended. [Further] that it was agreed that Paul and Barnabas with others of them should go unto Jerusalem to the Apostles and elders about this question. [...] When these delegates came to Jerusalem, they were received of the church, the Apostles and elders. [...] Upon this, and them acquainted with the controversy, the Apostles and elders came together to consider of this matter. [...] In this assembly, after much disputation, both Peter and James gave strong reasons, why circumcision and the ceremonies of the law should not be imposed upon the believing gentiles. [...] Upon these convincing reasons it pleased the Apostles and elders and the whole church to send special messengers and letters concerning the definitive sentence of the council unto Antioch. [Finally], the synodical letters, were written in the name of the Apostles, elders and brethren in this style, 'It pleased us' and 'seemed good unto us.' Divers particulars are here observable: [First], that we do not read that Paul acted anything as a judge in this controversy jointly with the rest of the synod, and perhaps the reason might be, because he was considered as a party: for no man not an Apostle should be judge and party in the same cause. [Second], that the Apostles did not act as immediately inspired in this particular, and according to any extraordinary, but an ordinary ecclesiastical power; for there was much disputation. [Third], they did not suddenly and instantly proceed to vote the matter: but they met to consider of it, and debated and disputed much before they determined. [Fourth], the determination was not grounded upon the multitude of votes, but upon divine revelation and Scripture, though not expressly, yet by way of consequence, as appears both from the words of Peter and of James. [Fifth], that which is the principal thing for which this text is alleged, is this, that the controversy is not referred to one Apostle, as to Paul alone, or Peter alone, or James alone, but to the Apostles jointly: and not to them alone, but to the elders, not to them and the elders alone, but to them with the brethren, and the whole church. [Sixth], that all these gave their consent; for it pleased the Apostles and elders, and the whole church. If Peter alone had been made judge, then the pope, if only the Apostles, then bishops; if the elders alone, then the presbytery; if the brethren alone, then the people would have challenged every one severally the legislative power in synods to themselves alone. Lastly, by this we learn upon what occasion, such great assemblies are requisite, if not necessary; we might add, that they convened by the permission, not commission of the civil power.

II.

By this you understand, how and by whom the legislative power was exercised. Of the exercise of the second branch of power in making officers we read (Acts 1.15). For, [...] upon the death of Judas, one of the sacred college of the Apostles, a place was void. This was the occasion [on which] Peter conceives, that another must be surrogated and succeed him in that place. [...] In an assembly of a hundred and twenty, as a chairman he proposeth the matter; [and] acquaints them with the occasion of a new election, and lets them understand the necessity of it, saying, there [must be one] ordained as a witness with us of Christ's resurrection. The reason he concludes from these words of Psalm 119.8. His office, charge, or bishopric let another take. By which words God signifies and commands that upon the death of Judas, another must take the charge with the rest of the Apostles. [...] Upon this the assembly proceeds without any *Congedeslier*,[21] or licence from any other to the election, and propose two, Justus and Matthias, both well qualified, and in that equality, that they knew not whether [which] to prefer. [...] Because they could not determine whether [which] was the fitter, nor upon a determination give a commission to make an Apostle, therefore by prayer and lot they refer and commit the cause to God, who choseth Matthias. In this election divers things are considerable, [first], that if Matthias and Justus were of the number of the seventy disciples (as it's very probable, if not certain), there was an imparity between the twelve Apostles and seventy disciples in respect of their place. Yet what this imparity was, and whether it should continue in the ordinary officers of the church succeeding them, is not here expressed. [Second], that

---

[21] Obsolete, to give authoritative leave; *Conge-dister*, second edn.

the election of the highest officer in the church, even of an Apostle was committed to this assembly, as fit to judge of his qualifications. [Third], that none should take upon them to elect a minister or officer of the church, who is not able to judge of his fitness for the place. [Fourth], that God gives none any power to elect or ordain, and constitute any a minister, officer, or representative of the church, who is not duly qualified for to do the work of the place, for which he was elected. Justus and Matthias must be able with the Apostles to bear witness of the resurrection of Christ. [Fifth], the principal thing for the point in hand to be observed, is, that neither Peter, nor any of the eleven, do take upon them to elect or design any person, or persons by themselves alone; but commit it to the whole assembly. And the whole assembly elected, prayed, cast lots. [Sixth], that though these persons [were] very eminent and full of the spirit, [they] could and might design the persons, but not give the power of Apostleship. To this head belongs the constitution of deacons (Acts 6), where we read of the occasion, and in some sort, of the necessity of this office. For [...] the Apostles knew there was a kind of necessity of such an officer as a deacon, and it was no ways fit to distract themselves in serving of tables, and neglect the great business of word and prayer; [and] that they call the multitude together. [Then] they propose the matter unto them, and signify what manner of persons deacons should be, and commit the election of persons amongst them rightly qualified to them. [...] They elect persons fit for the place; [...] they present these persons; [and] the Apostles pray and lay hands on them. Whether they used any form of words in this imposition of hands we do not read. The thing principally to be considered in this business, is, that the Apostles themselves alone do not take upon them to choose and constitute these deacons. To this may be added, that Paul doth not take upon him to send the charity and benevolence of the Corinthians, collected for the poor saints at Jerusalem, but refers it to themselves, to approve by letters such as they would use as their messengers (1 Cor. 16.3).

12.

The third branch of the Power of the Keys is, that of jurisdiction, which we find exercised in the church of Corinth, or rather a command of the Apostles binding them, as having that power to exercise it, reproving them in that they had not done it already in a particular case, and giving directions how it should be done. Out of the Apostles' directions (1 Cor. 5), we might pick a model of church-government; for there we have an ecclesiastical community under a form of government, and that is the whole church of Corinth. [...] We have [also] the members of this community, and they are the sanctified in Christ Jesus, and such are called to be saints. [...] We have the relation of these one to another, they are brethren, yet every particular brother subject to the whole church. [...] We have the power of jurisdiction, and the same in the whole body. [...] We have the power of excommunication, and by consequence of absolution and other ecclesiastical censures; and these in the whole church, which is reproved, because they did not exercise it upon so great an occasion, and for so great a cause. They are commanded to purge out the old leaven, and to cast out and put from amongst them that wicked person, because they had power to judge. [...] The persons subject to this jurisdiction, is everyone that is a brother of that church. [...] We have the causes, which make these persons and brethren of that church, liable to censure, and they are scandals, whereof we have a catalogue, whereby we may understand by analogy others not expressed. [...] We have the form of the sentence of excommunication, which must be solemnly passed in a public assembly convened, proceeding and passing judgement in the name of Christ. [...] In this judgement we have the Apostle passing and giving his vote by writing with the rest of that church. [...] We find that neither the Apostle, nor they can judge them that are without, but they are reserved to God's judgement. [Finally], we have the end of excommunication, which here is twofold: [...] in respect of the party excommunicated, [and] of the church and his fellow members. In respect of the person excommunicated, the destruction [is] of the flesh by some punishment for a time, that the spirit may be saved in the day of the Lord. In respect of the body of the church, the preservation [is] of the same from infection of the old leaven of malice and wickedness, that so, not only single persons, but the whole society may be continued pure. This is the rule of excommunication. The rules of absolution we find [in] (2 Cor. 2) where we may observe, first the person capable of it. And it is such a one [who] having been punished by many, the punishment prov[ing] sufficient, because by it he is grieved, humbled for his sin [and] in danger [of being] swallowed up with over-much sorrow, and by Satan to be tempted to despair. In a word, [there is absolution] when the party is penitent, and he appears really to be so. [Second] the nature of absolution, [...] is to forgive, and confirm our love unto him. [Third] this sentence of remission and reconciliation must be pronounced in the person of Christ. [Fourth] the persons, who must pass this sentence and see it executed are the same who excommunicated him: who here were Paul and the church of Corinth. [Fifth] the end of this act of judgement, which is to comfort and restore the party penitent; yet in this you must conceive all this is to be done in an orderly, and not in a confused and tumultuous manner both for the time, the place, the order of proceeding, and the persons who manage the business, and denounce the sentence. For these things must be committed to some eminent persons, who are fit for such a work. For though all must agree, yet some must exercise the power in the person of the church. We might further instance in the seven churches of Asia. For Ephesus, though reproved for her falling from her first love, yet is commended for her severity against the Nicolaitans (Rev. 2.6). The church of Pergamos is blamed for suffering such amongst them as taught the doctrine of Baalam, and the Nicolaitans: so is the church of Thyatira, because she suffered that woman Jezebel who, called herself a prophetess, to teach and seduce Christ's servants to commit fornication, and to eat things sacrificed to idols.[22] This was the remissness of discipline and neglect of the exercise of ecclesiastical jurisdiction; wherewith not only (though perhaps principally) the angels, but the whole church are charged.

13.

The total sum of all these particulars is this: that the primary subject of the Power of the Keys, is the whole church:

> [This appears from the institution, according to which we must tell the church; the church must bind and loose; and her judgement shall be ratified in Heaven. This also appears from the exercise of the Power of the Keys by the whole church with respect to legislation, the constitution of officers and jurisdiction.]

If any shall say, that the power is in the Apostles or bishops, or

[22] Rev. 2.20.

superintendents lawfully constituted, it's true: if that it's in the presbyters, it's so: if that it's in the brethren or people, it cannot be denied. Yet if any will argue from these places, that it's in the bishops alone; or in the presbyters alone; or in the brethren alone; or in the officers or representatives of the whole church primarily, it cannot be true. If any say it's in the whole church primarily, in the officers and representatives secondarily for exercise, that's the undoubted truth, and must needs be granted. In all the former examples of the exercise of this power, it's very remarkable, and specially to be noted, that where there was a church, with which the Apostles (who were far, and very far above all others who did succeed them) might act, they would not act alone, but jointly with the elders, multitude, brethren; and the reasons hereof are obvious, [...] because they would follow and observe Christ's institution; [...] give example for future times; [and] they know that, as they, when their faith was weak, did strive amongst themselves for priority and superiority, so there would [come many] after them, who would contend what person, or persons, or party should be greatest. Yet notwithstanding all this it's certain, that where the government of a church is not regular, or a form of discipline is not settled, God in his infinite mercy supplies these defects by an orthodox, pious, faithful, painful ministry, which is the fundamental office of Christ, and the means of conversion and salvation of men's souls. And though we have certain clear rules for the generals and necessaries of discipline; yet, as in extraordinary cases the Apostles did not observe them: so neither in the like cases are we strictly bound to do otherwise. If any desire the testimony of former times and the practise of ancient days, fathers, councils, histories might be alleged, as they have been by many learned men of latter times; but of any one person Blondel hath done most.[23] Dr. Andrewes is punctual and peremptory in this right disposal of this power in the proper subject. For, after that he had spoken first of the institution, then of the exercise, he thus concludes, and that most pithily, ['in short this very power is given to the church and the church may then confer it on one or many, who thereafter would have the power of exercising it or ordering others to do so']. For this also he allegeth the Council of Constance, Cameracensis, Cusanus, Gerson, and the school of

---

[23] David Blondel, *Apologia pro sententia Hieronymi de presbyteris et episcopis* (Amsterdam, 1646).

185

Sorbonne.[24] The congregational party must needs acknowledge this in general. For this is it which Mr. Parker, which Mr. Hooker of New England go about to prove; but their way is certainly too democratical, though Mr. Parker grants, that their government in respect of the exercise is aristocratical: yet that expression is no ways good.[25] For if in proper sense any state ecclesiastical or civil be aristocratical, then the optimates, or such as answer unto them must needs be the primary subject, and the rest, even officers, are subjects, and derive their power from the aristocratical party. But perhaps he means, that the whole church, which he considers as democratical, singles out the best and fittest to be governors, and trusts them with the exercise of the power, and from them the government is denominated aristocratical. But in this sense all states should be aristocratical.

14.

For the more full and perfect understanding of this government and discipline ecclesiastical, we must know and remember, [...] that there are certain general rules of government, which God himself observes in his government, both temporal and spiritual of the world, and especially in the ordering of men and angels. [...] These general rules, are observed by all well-ordered states in the world, and in the constitution and administration of them we may easily find them, and without them, we cannot well or fully understand their model. [...] All those are found in many places of the Scriptures, neither without them can be Scriptures be well understood. [...] Besides the fundamental and essential rules of government, there are many accidentals, according to which all particular polities may differ one from another. [...] Church government, as here handled, is nothing else but the application of these general and essential rules to a particular community and society of Christians, whereby they may be continued in unity, piety and peace, and mutually further one another in the way to Heaven. [...] These ends may be attained by a faithful

---

[24] Andrewes, *Tortura Torti*, p. 42. I have slightly abbreviated the quotation, which substantially repeats what Lawson has said and which had been used by him above, ch. 11.3. To Cameracensis (de Alliaco/d'Ailly) Lawson adds the name of another major conciliar theorist, Nicholas of Cusa (1400–64); see his *De concordia Catholica* (completed 1433; Paris, 1514).

[25] Robert Parker, *De politeia*; Thomas Hooker, *A Survey*. Lawson is repeating the points made above.

godly diligent ministry, without any form of outward discipline. [...]
Yet a form of discipline established will much further, help and
strengthen the ministry in this work, and effectually conduce to the
attaining of these ends, keep Christian societies closer together, and
make them far more permanent, firm and powerful. [...] Every
Christian in any society ecclesiastical is bound by his very baptism,
without any further federation, to submit unto these general and
essential rules once applied. [...] In erecting a church discipline,
there must be a special care taken of two things chiefly, [...] of the
constitution, that it be agreeable, especially in essentials, to Christ's
institution, otherwise men may refuse, and that justly to submit unto
it; [and] of the administration, that it be committed to the wisest and
the best, who are most fit to manage it. [...] Because many of the
ministers are not qualified for this business, and there are many, no
ministers, of eminent piety, learning and wisdom, I see no reason why
only the clergy or ministry, and every one of that profession, should
alone be trusted with the power of administration, and these eminent
persons excluded. Where do we find the spirit promised only unto
ministers and bishops? Do we not know, and by experience, that
excellent gifts, and amongst others the spirit of wisdom and government are given to others, as well as to some of them? Nay, how many
unworthy and unfit persons do we find entered into the ministry? And
with us besides others, the causes thereof are, because presentations,
and admissions are granted for carnal relations, favour, gifts, good
turns; and also because that parishes are not fitly united and divided,
and the maintenance in many places of great charge is very poor.
Otherwise I know no reason, why the congregational party should so
much exclaim against parishes. For the work of ministers is not only
to edify believers, but also to endeavour the conversion of heathens
and publicans, especially in their particular assignations. For, if these
divisions parochial were duly made, parishes might be very fit assignations for the work and maintenance of the several ministers, and the
same agreeable to the general rule of decency and order. In the
constitution and administration of particular churches, neither the
practice of Christ nor his Apostles, much less of primitive times can
be any binding rule. [...] For Christ and the Apostles did many
extraordinary things, which we neither may, nor can do. [...] Divine
precepts, either general or special, are the only rule which we are
bound to follow. [...] They did many things as the present times, and

the conditions of persons and places required, which may not be done by us or any other, except we have the same power, and in the like case. [...] In the constitution of a church, or in the reformation of the same, much and dangerously corrupted, many things may be lawfully done, which under a well-settled government will prove very unlawful. For though, where there is no outward form of ordinary vocation and ordination established, that which Volkelius maintains against Zwingli, for one that is [of a blameless life sufficient for teaching] to take upon him the charge of a minister, and do Christ what service he is able, may be lawful.[26] Yet to do so, where there is a eutaxy in a settled church must be unjust, because amongst other things, such a one shall transgress the rule of decency and order. [...] Though Christ and his Apostles did deliver unto us all the essential and fundamental rules of church-government, and we find them in the Scripture, yet many accidentals were left to sanctified reason to be directed to the general rules. And in this respect, we must make use of our Christian prudence, both in modelling and reforming of Christian churches. But if we stand upon these rules of prudence in accidentals and circumstantials, as of divine institution and obligation, we cannot be excused. [...] Though there may be several orderly ways and means to attain the chief end of church discipline, yet those are the best, which most observe the essentials of government, and the general rules, and are most effectually conducing to that end. [...] Seeing therefore, there may be several and different means in respect of accidentals, and they severally may attain and reach the end, it's the duty of us all [...] to unite ourselves in the bond of charity; [and to] observe the fundamental and essential rules of government, which are clearly known. [And], with a meek, humble and pure heart seek out such particulars, as are not yet made clear unto us, and wherein we may differ for the present, till at length we may satisfy one another.

---

[26] Ulrich Zwingli (1484–1531) but 'Swinglius' in the text may be a misprint for Smiglecius, whom Johann Volkelius is in fact attacking, *Responsio ad unam refutationem dissolutionis nodi Gordii a Martino Smiglecio nexi* (Racow, 1618); and *De vera religione libri quinque* (Racow, 1630), bk. 6 (*sic*), chs. 12–13.

CHAPTER 14

Of the extent of a particular church

1.

After the examination of the several titles of such as challenge the supreme Power of the Keys, and the declaration of mine own judgement, the third thing proposed was the extent of a particular church. That there is a supreme Power of the Keys; that there is a primary subject of this power, that this power is in the church; that it's disposed in this church in a certain order and manner in one or more, purely or mixedly, few, if any, will deny. But that it is disposed in the whole church after the manner of a free state, so that every particular Christian community, is the primary subject of it, is not so easily granted, though I conceive it, as many other worthy and excellent men do, to be truth delivered unto us by Christ and his Apostles. Yet let this be agreed upon, yet there is another difference concerning the bound and extent of this church. This is not the proper place, I confess, to handle this particular, for extent presupposeth a church constituted and in being, and it's an accident of the same. Therefore *pars subdita*, which is the second integral part, as of a state, so of a church, should first have been spoken of. In this point I find a threefold difference: for some extend this church, which is the primary subject of the Power of the Keys, very far, and make it to be the universal church of all nations. Others confine it to be a single congregation. A third party will admit of a diocese, or a province, or a nation, and be contented to stay there. This question, if we understand it, presupposeth union and communion. There is a union and also a communion in profession and worship, a union mystical, a union in government external, which we call discipline. A union in profession and worship there is and ought to be of all orthodox Christians in the world. For they all profess the same faith, and worship the same God in Christ, hear the same word, celebrate the same sacraments. It's true, they do not, neither can they so meet in one place, as to partake of the same individual ordinances, for there is no necessity of any such thing. Yet, whosoever shall refuse to join in the same individual worship of the same God in Christ according to the gospel, when it may be done (as when one converseth with Christians in some remote parts) he cannot be free from schism. For all refusal of communion with Christ's saints and servants, without just and sufficient cause is a schism. So if any party or persons shall not admit of other Christians only upon this account, because they agree not with them in some accidentals, which are neither necessary, nor in themselves considered, conducing to salvation, they must needs be schismatics. For any separation, which hath not sufficient and evident warrant from some divine precept, is unlawful. There is a mystical union of all true believers; for, there is 'one body, one spirit, one hope of calling, one Lord, one faith, one baptism, one God and father of all, who is above all, through all, in all' (Eph. 4.4, 5, 6,). There is a union for government external, of this the question is to be understood. And this union is so necessary in every commonwealth, whether civil or ecclesiastical, that it's no commonwealth, if it be not one, and so one, that every particular person, especially in a church, be subject to one and the same supreme independent judicatory. Concerning the universal extent there are, as you heard before, two opinions: They first make one church, the church of Rome, to have power over all other churches, and invest the bishop of that church with a universal power of legislation and jurisdiction, this is a popish error indeed. The second opinion subjects all particular churches to the universal, whereof they are but parts: this is no popery, nor do the present popes and church of Rome like it. This universal church cannot act but by a general representative, and such a general representative there yet never was, since the church was enlarged from sea to sea, and from the river unto the world's end.[1] Such a general council and court either standing, or occasional, few, I think, do expect. As for the councils of Nice, Chalcedon, Ephesus, Constantinople, they were no such councils, not general in proper sense.[2] They were confined within the Roman empire; and, if well examined, they left out several parts of that too. The meaning therefore of some, who submit particular churches to the universal, is this: That so many several parts and particular churches, as can combine in one synod, may in some extraordinary cases, and difficulties, especially, if they be of general concernment, submit unto such a synod, as being of greater

---

[1] *Contra* Baxter? *The Grotian Religion Discovered* (London, 1658).
[2] Nicaea, first council 325; Chalcedon 451; Constantinople 381; Ephesus 431.

authority and ability, if rightly constituted. Yet, if these particular churches have their proper independent judicatories, this submission is but a voluntary act, and rather like a reference or transaction, than any appeal. When, and in what cases such references are fit to be made, I will not here enquire. Besides these universalists, if we may so call them, who extend the bounds of this church too far, there are others who confine it to a too narrow compass, as many do conceive; they determine it to be a congregation. Of this judgement was Mr. Parker, a learned man in the reign of King James;[3] in our times the dissenting brethren and their party, which follow their principles, and put them in practice to this day. They were called the dissenting brethren, because in the assembly of divines [Westminster Assembly] for advice, they dissented from the Presbyterian party. Afterwards, they were called the congregationals, because they confined the church to a congregation; and independents, because in their single congregations they erected an independent judicatory, and challenged an independent Power of the Keys, as due by the institution of Christ, to every several congregation gathered by them. But let their names be what they will, and the reason of their names what they shall please, let's consider the thing itself. And before the question can be discussed to purpose, we must enquire, [...] what their congregation is; [...] how they are gathered; [and] whether this narrow compass be grounded upon Scripture or no. For the nature of a congregation, as they seem to take it, Mr. Parker gives in a clear account. For with him, [...] a congregation is a multitude of Christians, which may ordinarily and conveniently assemble in one place to communicate in the ordinances of God.[4] [...] He confesseth that the essence thereof doth not consist in the act of assembling: for then upon every dissolution and parting of the company assembled, it would cease to be a church. Yet Mr. Hooker prevents this caution as needless, for he makes those, whom Mr. Parker calls Christians, and himself visible saints, to be the matter and confederation, either explicit or implicit to be the form: and this federation ties them together, not only when they assemble, but at other times too. This is that which Mr. Parker calls union by convention.[5] Yet, [...] he adds, that though they ought to be no more numerous, than may ordinarily assemble in one place, yet they may

---

[3] Robert Parker, *De politeia ecclesiastica, libri tres* (London, 1616).
[4] *Ibid.*, bk. 1.1; bk. 3, chs. 16–17.   [5] *Ibid.*, bk. 3.17.

and sometimes do meet severally, and have several ministers, who severally officiate in several assemblies, and take charge of the whole church in common. But [...] they have but one consistory. He instanceth for this last in the German churches, and the cities of Holland (*Polit. eccles. lib. 3*, sect. 3 [ch. 17]). Whether this be the notion of a church with the present congregational party or no, I know not. I have much desired to have seen something, wherein all that party agrees in, made public, to satisfy such as desire to know their minds. By this definition, they exclude parishes or parochial churches, which are united under one minister; diocesan churches united under one bishop; provincial churches united under one archbishop and metropolitan. Yet both of them Mr. Parker, and Mr. Hooker[6] might easily have known [...] that neither the parochial, nor diocesan, nor provincial church was accounted the primary subject of the Power of the Keys, as they affirm their congregation to be. [Further], that a parish is not now, nor with understanding men ever was taken for a congregation Christian, as a parish in a civil notion. For therein may be heathens, Jews, Mahometans, schismatics, heretics, apostates. But, it's called a church or congregation ecclesiastical in respect of the minister, and those Christians of that precinct, who ordinarily assemble to perform the acts of divine worship. [...] If the name church may be given to a few Christians in one family and house, as it is (Philem. 2, Col. 4.15), I know no reason but it may be given to a number and society of Christians in one parish, where, by reason of vicinity and cohabitation, they may ordinarily and conveniently meet together for divine service, which some of their congregations cannot do.

2.

The manner of gathering these congregations is not in the same vicinity or elsewhere to convert heathens, or Jews, or Mahometans, or papists to make them Christians. Though no doubt some of them, being pious and learned men, if providence give them occasion, would endeavour to do it. But they gather Christians, Protestant Christians from amongst Christians; and such as they find fitted to their own hand without any pains of theirs, but by the sweat and

---

[6] Thomas Hooker, *A Survey of Church Discipline* (London, 1648), bk. 1.2–4; bk. 2.3.

labour and care and prayers of some other faithful pastors and ministers of Christ, under whose hands they formerly have been to whose charge they have been committed, and under whose ministry God hath prospered them. These amongst others, they either persuade to be of their congregations, or if they offer themselves voluntarily, they admit them, and this to the great grief of their own faithful pastors. When they accept of these, they neither teach them any new article of faith, which formerly they professed not; nor press upon them any new duty according to the commandments of Christ, which is either necessary or conducing to salvation. There is no essential of Christianity, which they can superadd to what they had before. Only, if ceasing to be episcopal, or Presbyterian, or parochial, they are willing to confederate with them, to walk after their manner, and be of their party, they are willing to receive them. If this be their manner of gathering churches, as it's well known it is with some, I dare say they have no example, much less any precept in the Scripture for it. They admit indeed of some, which are very unworthy, and such as many Presbyterians would not accept, with hope that upon their solemn covenanting they will prove better. I do not write this out of partiality, or prejudice; for some of that party are my special friends, and I dearly love them; some are pious, prudent and learned, and I honour them much. Yet I desire them seriously to consider what they do, and also so far as they can to forecast, what is likely to be the issue, if they do not unite more firmly amongst themselves, and combine with other pious ministers, and people of God both in worship and discipline. For they may make perhaps five hundred, or increase to a thousand independent congregations; and can any wise man imagine that these can continue long without some subordination, and certain rules of a former union? And can this be consistent with the interest of any Christian civil state? If they be searching out some better way, according to the rules of Christ, with a sincere resolution to fix upon it, when it's once found, as some of them do intimate they are, their proceedings are more tolerable. God hath fearfully punished divers of their congregations, and they have been divided amongst themselves, and some of their members fallen off, and have proved far worse than ever they were, whilst they continued under their own pious ministers.

3.

But to come to the principal thing, which is their congregational extent; for to that narrow compass they confine that church, which must be the primary subject of this power. The question is not whether some congregations, in some cases, may be the subject of this power in this degree; nor, whether every well-constituted congregation may not have and exercise discipline within themselves, for some particulars. For this will be granted them. For both the Presbyterian, and also the parochial congregations and vestries did so under the bishops; but, whether their congregations gathered in their manner be this primary subject, and this according to any precept of Christ. Or, if we leave out that restriction of *being gathered in their manner*, [the question is] whether by any institution and precept of Christ the independent power of discipline doth [generally originate in] primarily belong unto a congregation. For if it do, then it belongs in this manner to them, and them alone as single congregations, and to no other association of Christians. And if any other association do assume it, they transgress a precept of Christ, which is of universal and perpetual obligation. For to prove the affirmative, Mr. Parker makes use of the words *synagoga* and *ecclesia*, as most commonly taken in Scripture. And the dissenting brethren instance [...][7] the first apostolical churches. Mr. Parker's first argument is taken from the signification of the words *ecclesia* and *synagoga* in Scripture. And, [...] he presupposeth that these signify a congregation; [...] that a congregation is an assembly meeting in one place; [...] hence he infers that [there is no first church which is not a congregation]. His meaning is, that if the people of any precinct, as of a diocese, or province exceed the bounds of a congregation, so that they cannot conveniently and ordinarily meet in one place, they are not that first church to which the Power of the Keys doth primarily and originally agree. And he allegeth for this purpose Dr. Reynolds, saying, that in every place of the Old and New Testaments, *synagoga ecclesia est*, and as well *synagoga* as *ecclesia*, when they are said to speak of a congregation political, signify only an assembly meeting in one place (*Polit. eccles. lib. 3*, sect. 3).[8] For answer hereunto, it will be sufficient to examine the signification of these words, as used in the Scripture; and by what we shall see

---

[7] Both editions have 'in'.   [8] Parker, *De politeia*, bk. 3.17, pp. 192–3.

whether the argument from the signification of the word be good or no. To this end it may be observed, that the word *synagoga* is used by the Septuagint one hundred and seventy times, if not above in the Old Testament, under [*ᶜedâ*] we find it one hundred and twenty times: and in the first eight places, it signifies the congregation of all Israel, which consisted of six hundred thousand fighting men, besides women and children (as Exod. 12.3, 6, 19, 47: 16.1, 2, 9, 10. Judges 20.12). It's an assembly of four hundred thousand at least. The word [*qhl*] is thirty-seven times turned [synagogue], a congregation; and in the three first places an assembly or congregation of nations: (as Gen. 28.3, 35.11, 48.4). Cyrus his army gathered out of many nations, is, *Kahal Synagoga* (Jer. 50.9). So the vast army of Gog and Magog is, *synagoga* a congregation (Ezek. 38.4). Again, as *synagoga* may signify a congregation of many thousands, and a far greater number than Mr. Parker's congregation, so the word *ecclesia* is used under the word *Kahal* seventy times, as formerly upon another occasion was noted [ch. 13.6]: and in the first place it signifies the congregation of all Israel, both in Leviticus 8.3 and also Deuteronomy 18.16. It many times signifies the assembly of Israel, sometimes a general representative. In the New Testament (Heb. 12.23) it's the 'general assembly of the first born, which are written in Heaven' (Eph. 4.22); it's that body, 'whereof Christ is head';[9] and ch. 2.20, that 'building, whereof the Apostles and prophets are the foundation, and Christ the chief corner stone'. From all this it's clear, that the words *ecclesia* and *synagoga* signify, besides civil and military, ecclesiastical assemblies, and the same either political or local: and the place is either particular, or special, or general; in which sense a whole region and vast country may be one place. So that one fallacy, [...] is in the word 'place'; [...] another in the word 'assembly' meeting in one place: For, [...] the assembly and meeting may be rare and extraordinary, as the words do divers times signify, as is evident; and this cannot agree to Mr. Parker's ordinary and convenient meeting. [Moreover,] they signify assemblies meeting in far greater numbers than in his congregation. For the number of persons which made up divers of these assemblies, were thousands, nay hundreds of thousands: as four hundred thousand, five hundred thousand, nay millions and whole nations. And if so, then they who stand for a national church, will desire no

---

[9] Misquotation and citation of Eph. 5.23?

more; the provincial and diocesan party will be content with fewer. Again, the words sometimes signify a political society, consisting of such persons, as shall never meet together in one place, except at Christ's right hand, and in the place of glory. So that, if the former distinction used in stating the question be remembered, and the question be understood thus, that some congregations, such as Mr. Parker describes the church to be, may sometimes in some respects be the subject of an independent Power of the Keys, then these places are not much against him. But if he understand it so, that if any church exceed the bounds of his congregation, of so many as may ordinarily and conveniently meet together, it's not of Christ's institution, nor can be the primary subject of this power, then his argument, a *nomine ad rem*, from the word to the thing, is no argument. But, suppose the words should always signify one congregation, which may ordinarily meet in one place, which yet they do not, how will it follow from any of those places, that such a congregation and none other is this primary subject?

4.[10]

His second argument is taken from the description of the church as represented to John the Divine (Rev. 4). For he takes it for granted, that the church there mentioned, consisting of twenty-four elders, and the four beasts, was a congregational church; or rather that the church there, was a congregation in his sense. Answer: But, [first] let it be granted that there is a description of a church, and the same Christian visible, yet it will no ways agree to his congregation. For [...] there is an allusion made to the congregation of Israel, pitching in four squadrons under four several ensigns, as the ensign of Judah was a lion, and three tribes under every ensign with the priests and Levites, encamping next [to] the Ark between it and the squadrons. This was a congregation, as you heard before of six hundred thousand men besides women and children. [Second] this congregation of the four beasts and twenty-four elders sing a song of praise unto the Lamb Christ, and acknowledge that he was slain, and had 'redeemed them to God by his blood out of every kindred, and tongue and people, and nation' (Rev. 5.8, 9). This is a congregation gathered out of every nation. This can be none of Mr. Parker's congregation.

---

[10] Misnumbered as 5 in both editions.

5.[11]

His third argument is taken from Matthew 17.18 and from 1 Corinthians 5. In the first place, [...] Christ saith, 'Tell the church.' [...] This church is the primary subject of the Power of the Keys. But [...] he doth not say, this church is congregational in his sense, neither can any wit of man prove it out of that place. [...] The word church in that place is indefinite, and signifies first a Christian community without any determination of the number of persons, greater or less. [...] Though this community and whole body be principally meant, yet it's here signified as exercising her judicial power by her representatives, who may easily meet in one place, when the whole body cannot; and that place may be capacious enough to receive them, yet far too narrow to contain the whole church and all the members, and every one of them represented in that place. As for 1 Corinthians 5.4, which is the second place quoted by him, he argues from those words, 'when ye are gathered together', that a church is a congregation, consisting of so many as may ordinarily meet in one place. Answer: [...] It's granted, that according to the Apostles' directions, the incestuous person must be excommunicated in a public assembly of persons meeting in one place. But the church may assemble personally or virtually in their own persons, or by and in their representatives. That this church did meet virtually in her representatives, as least no man can doubt; but that all and every one of that church were personally present in that assembly, no man can prove; for, it was a meeting, as he confesseth, for the exercise of power of jurisdiction. [Even] suppose all the church of Corinth could and did meet in that assembly, how will it follow, that every other church, as that of Jerusalem, could do so too: or that if any church was so numerous, that they could not ordinarily meet but in several places: will it follow, that therefore it could not be the primary subject of this power? But something more to this hereafter.

6.

To reserve his fourth argument to the last, I proceed unto his fifth: which is drawn from communion in word, prayer, sacraments, and his

---

[11] Sect. 10 in first edition.

sixth in watching one over another. In that of communion he con-
founds worship and the exercise of discipline, which are two very
different things, and also he grossly equivocates in the matter of
identity, which even freshmen know to be threefold, [in genus, species and individual number]. For he conceives there can be no communion but amongst those, who meet in one place to exercise those
heavenly duties. Answer: It's true, that if the number of persons in
one church exceed, they cannot all be edified, and enjoy a sufficient
communion in worship by one man, officiating at one time in one
place, where they cannot all assemble. But what's this to purpose? It's
nothing to government. Communion in worship is one thing, in
government another. The communion of one particular church in this
latter respect is political, and consists in this, that they have the same
supreme and independent judicatory according to certain laws, as
they are subject to the same independent judicatory in the same
precinct. Communion in word, prayer and sacraments is rather moral
than political, and may be had, and is enjoyed many times, in many
places, where there is no external discipline settled or exercised. The
end of word and prayer is first to make Christians, and then to edify
them, and these are no sooner made and multiplied, but they must
hear, pray, [and] participate [in] the sacraments, before any form of
discipline be instituted; and if every one would constantly do his duty
in these things both privately and publicly, there would be no need of
discipline. [...] Whereas he conceiveth, that there can be no such
communion and edification, but one and the same individual assembly, he is much mistaken, and besides his words are very ambiguous.
For the better understanding hereof, we must know that the end of
communion in word, prayer, sacraments is conversion and edification,
as before. [...] These ends may be attained, as well in several congregations under one supreme judicatory for discipline, as in one congregation independent, or several congregations having their several
supreme judicatories. For both of them depend upon the ministry as
instrumental, and upon the spirit as the principal agent, which *caeteris
paribus* may be as effectual in several congregations not independent;
and every one of them severally (as in one, though independent), and
at the same time. And though discipline may further edification in a
congregation, yet it may be furthered as much, when it's exercised by
one independent power over several congregations, as when it's
exercised by one supreme power of one congregation over itself.

Experience doth clearly evince this, and might satisfy us. But I have wondered at the design of some men, who go about to bind men to the individual participation in the same ordinances, if they will be of the same church, as though that could be no church, where all the members could not, or did not thus individually participate. For few of their own congregations are so ordered, as that all the members communicate at one time; but some at one time before the rest, some at another after the rest. That which is required of all Christians is no such thing, but that they all worship God both in private and public, according to the same general rules of the gospel. As for mutual watching one over another, that's the duty of all Christians, as Christians, and as fellow subjects and brethren under the same God and Lord Jesus Christ, though there never were any discipline settled. And this is done far better by them, who cohabit, and constantly, or for the most part converse one with another, than by them who live ten, twenty, thirty miles distant one from another as some of the congregationals do. Nay, members of one and the same congregation bound to this watching one over another, live one at London, another at York; one in Ireland, another in Scotland, and their pastor and most of their brethren in England.

7.

To return unto his fourth argument from the form of apostolical churches – as of Jerusalem, Antioch, Ephesus, Corinth, etc., which is the same which the dissenting brethren insisted upon in the [Westminster] Assembly, I might refer him and them to what the Assembly hath learnedly answered. The argument is to this purpose: *The first apostolical churches were only congregational, yet the primary subject of the Power of the Keys. Therefore all other churches should be congregational, and as such they are the primary subject of the Power of the Keys.* Whether this be that which is intended, let every one judge, who is acquainted with the controversy. The argument is that of induction taken from example, that which they assume, as clear out of Scripture to them is, that all and every one of the first apostolical churches were congregational and only congregational, and none of them parochial, or classical, or synodical, or diocesan, or national, or had any presbytery above a presbytery. That which they would hence infer is, that only a congregational is the first church agreeable to the first institution, and the first subject of the Power of the Keys. The argument in form may be this: All rightly constituted churches ought to be like the first apostolical churches; but all the first apostolical churches were congregational. Therefore all rightly constituted churches are congregational. The major [premise] is very doubtful and admits of many restrictions. The minor is denied. The conclusion as inferred from these premises is not to [the] purpose. [...] The major presupposeth that all good examples are to be followed, and that they are equivalent to a binding precept. But this is certain, whatsoever they or others may say, that examples, as examples, though good, do not bind to imitation: for they only bind by virtue of some precept or divine institution. The Apostles in the first plantation of churches did many good things, which we cannot imitate, and if we could, yet, if their practice in those things was not grounded upon a precept of universal and perpetual obligation, it doth not bind us. They did many things by virtue of some particular precept binding them as Apostles, and no ways else; and some things in extraordinary cases, upon extraordinary occasions. In this respect the first churches planted by them, might differ in many things from all other churches in future times. Therefore, if the major should be to purpose, it must be understood so, that all churches rightly constituted, are bound and that by some divine precept of universal obligation, and perpetual force to be like unto the apostolical first churches in all things, and especially in this, that they were congregational. How they will prove this I know not: and if they prove it not clearly they do nothing to [the] purpose. [...] The minor is denied both by the episcopal and Presbyterian, and in particular by the divines of the [Westminster] Assembly, who more particularly and distinctly answer all the proofs brought by them to affirm it. Their proof is by way of induction: as the church of Jerusalem, Samaria, Damascus, Antioch, and so of the rest were congregational. Where [first] the term congregational must be understood; [then] we must enquire, whether the induction be sufficient or no. [...] A church may be said to be congregational in respect of worship or discipline. In respect of worship two ways, [...] of prayer and word; [and] of the administration of the sacraments, either of baptism or the Lord's Supper, as the Assembly doth well distinguish. Now, how will they [congregationalists] prove, that the whole church of Jerusalem with all the members thereof, did constantly meet in one place to administer and receive the Lord's Supper? Where is the text that expressly or by consequence saith any such thing? Again, a congregational church may be in respect of discipline, and that several ways. For [...] a congregation may signify a community of Christians as the primary subject of the Power of the Keys; [...] this community exercising this power, and that either by a representative of the whole or some part. If they understand them to be congregational in respect of the exercise of discipline, so that their representatives of part, or the whole, might all of them congregate and meet at one time in one place, as ordinary or extraordinary occasion should require; [then] in this sense it will be granted, that even the church of Jerusalem, in its greatest extent, was congregational. But this is not their sense. For, they mean by congregational, such a community and vicinity of Christians, as that all and every one of the members may ordinarily and conveniently meet at one and the same time, in one and the same place, not only for discipline, but worship: and so, that if any multitude of Christians exceed this proportion, they must divide and erect a new independent judicatory; and they were bound so to do, if they did not, they ceased to be such churches as Christ did institute, and could not be the primary subject of the power of discipline. How they should prove the minor in this sense, I do not understand. They, who first took up this congregational notion, perhaps had a design to overthrow diocesan bishops, and this was thought an effectual means for that end; and if this conceit had not first possessed their minds, they would never have imagined any such thing to be so much as implied in these examples. But suppose some such thing to be implied at least, for expressed it is not in these places; the induction may be said to be imperfect. For there were many churches planted by the Apostles, and far more than are mentioned in the Acts of the Apostles. For Paul upon his conversion went into Arabia, and then returned again to Damascus (Gal. 1.17). Other of the Apostles no doubt went into Egypt, Ethiopia, India, Persia, Armenia, Spain, France, Germany. Yet none of these churches are mentioned in the Scripture history. Therefore it might be said, there is not a sufficient enumeration of particulars to make up a general.[12] But suppose these churches to have been congregational at first; it's certain, they enlarged and multiplied to far greater numbers in after-times: and though this be

---

[12] This moves towards an almost Popperian scepticism about induction. The remarks may be an echo of the extreme scepticism about inference and causation developed by Nicholas of Autrecourt.

certain, yet it's no ways certain that upon this multiplication, they did divide into independent congregations, and erected independent judicatories in every particular congregation, and were bound so to do, and that by a divine precept. And I wonder much at Mr. Parker that he should argue so much against a diocesan church, and yet grant, that all Israel, consisting, as he himself confesseth, of many myriads, should be but one congregation, which was of a far greater extent than a diocese. Whether this congregation was as now it is by many managed amongst us, be not formally schism, as it is charged by some learned men, I will not here debate. But this I must needs say, that such congregationals, as by this notion, go about to unchurch all other churches, which are not cast in the same mould, must needs be guilty of some such crime. It was first set up to oppose diocesan churches, and now to oppose Presbyterian classes. But there is another thing, which I wish all wise and judicious men to consider: whether this doth not tend unto or at least give occasion of schism, and also to inform themselves, what effects it hath had hitherto, yet so as to distinguish between these effects of it, which are *per se*, and flow from the nature of it, and such as are *per accidens*. Yet in the meantime, charity, meekness, humility, pity of weak brethren becomes us all, who profess ourselves Christians; and we ought to stand well affected towards all, who seem to us to look towards Heaven. Let us further consider how far rational and pious men agree, and according to those things, let us keep communion and heartily serve our God, humbly imploring his divine majesty in the name of Christ to open our eyes, and sanctify our hearts, that at length we may be united in the same judgement and affection, and with one mind, and one mouth glorify God even the father of our Lord Jesus Christ.

8.

After the consideration of a congregational extent as too narrow, and of a universal, as too large, I proceed to say something of a national extent as a mean between. The congregationalist will censure it too great by far; the universalist as too little by much. Yet I shall willingly, as in other things, refer myself to the judgement of moderate, pious, judicious, impartial men: Let them condemn me or acquit me, as they shall see just cause. First it must be remembered, that the subject of this whole treatise, is the government of men by men under God and

Jesus Christ our blessed Saviour. Of God's more immediate government I have spoken in my *Divine Politics*:[13] where I show it's monarchical, supreme, universal, and cannot be bounded to any part of
the whole universe. For he being immense, and not only virtually, but
actually present in all places, at all times, is only fit to govern all
nations, and the whole world as the universal sovereign; but this is far
above the power not only of men but of angels. Therefore, whatsoever
he doth in Heaven, we know, that when through his blessing mankind
was multiplied, and especially after the flood, and had replenished the
earth, they were divided into several societies, and were subject to
several independent tribunals. We never find them under one: neither
do we in his word or works read of a catholic king over all nations, nor
of a universal bishop over all churches. Howsoever some have
pretended such a title, yet they could never show their patent subs-
cribed by the hand of Heaven. But, suppose they could have acquired
the possession of the whole earth, which never any did; yet no one
man, no one council, no one consistory had been able sufficiently to
manage so vast a power, and in any tolerable manner to govern all
mankind at one time living upon the earth. It seemed good indeed, to
our wise God, both in former and latter times to enlarge the power of
some states, and especially that of the Romans. Yet that very empire
of so large extent, took in but a little part of the whole earth: and this
appears plainly now since by navigation, some of the remote parts of
the globe, and both the hemispheres thereof have been discovered.
Yet in the greatest extent it was thought by some of their wisest
princes the best policy, *Cogere terminos Imperii*, to limit and bound it,
because they thought the body of too big a bulk, to be well ordered
either by prince, or senate, or people, or by all together. But to return
to the matter in hand: the question is, whether a national community
of Christians may not lawfully be subjected to one supreme judicatory
ecclesiastical. To understand the question the better, it's to be
observed, [...] that a community of Christians may be said to be
national several ways, or in several respects: As [...] when all the
Christians of one and the same nation, do associate and unite in one
body; [...] when these Christians are the major part of the people;
[...] when the whole nation, or the generality thereof have received
and do profess the same Christian faith. I will here suppose the major

---

[13] *Theo-politica* (London, 1659).

part or generality to be Christians, and the association and incorporation to be made by a tacit or explicit consent, which sometimes may be confirmed by the laws of the supreme power. Yet this generality may be so understood, as that there may in the same nation, be found Turks or Mahometans, pagans, atheists, Jews, which cannot be of this body; and that also there may be some schisms and separations amongst such as profess themselves Christians, and sometimes there may be none. This in my sense is a national community of Christians, and a church confident before any form of external discipline be introduced. [Further], when I speak of subjection, I do not say, that they are always in all nations bound by any divine precept to be so; but that they may, and that lawfully according unto the Scriptures. I [also] understand this subjection, so as that every several member be subject not to one man, or one party, but to the whole; and that either properly taken or virtually for a representative of the whole, which shall have power in the name of the whole body to make canons, and in judgement to receive last appeals. [. . .] I understand the question of nations indefinitely taken, for if any be of so vast extent, as that one independent court may be either insufficient or inconvenient, I rather exclude than include such. For, suppose all Tartary should be counted one nation, or all China, I conceive, they are too large. [Finally], I mention only a national community; for if that be granted, the classical and provincial must needs come in. The congregational party, I know, holds the negative. And here upon the by I will take the liberty for to answer Mr. Parker's seventh argument, for his congregational way. It's taken from politics, and is to this purpose: That as little states are more easily and better governed than great ones, so is a congregational church, which is but of a narrow compass, than a classical, diocesan, or provincial, or national, which is far greater. Answer: Though less communities may be better governed, than one too great, yet a great one of moderate extent may be better governed and defended than one that is too little. For God's own peculiar people and nation, which was first under judges, then under kings, was subject to one supreme tribunal for a long time, above five hundred years; and afterwards it was divided into two. Yet it was better governed under one, than under two; when subject to one individual tribunal, than when to two, but of this more hereafter.

9.

For the confirmation of this, we must note, that there is no divine precept in the New Testament, which particularly determines either the extent of place or number of persons, to which a particular independent church is confined: we do not find there either the *minimum* or *maximum quod sic*. Therefore some latitude must needs be granted. [Also ...] the history of the New Testament doth not reach those times, wherein it pleased God to fulfil those prophesies, which promised, 'That kings should become nursing-fathers, and queens nursing-mothers of the church' (Isa. 49.23), and she should suck the breasts of kings, who should come unto her light. [...] When one should become a thousand, and a small one a strong nation; 'I (saith the Lord) will hasten in it its time' (Isa. 60.16, 22): where, one saith, he alludes to the creation, which he finished in six days, hastening, and could not rest and keep his sabbath till all was ended, and man was made. [...] 'When nations, who knew not Christ, should come unto him' (Isa. 55.5).[14] These, I say, were not fulfilled in the Apostles' times. [...] Many of the primitive Christians, after their conversion continued for a certain time without any set form of external government, or perfect rules of New Testament worship, except to word and prayer, were settled. Hence those words of the Apostle, 'The rest will I set in order when I come' (1 Cor. 11.34). [...] Even within the compass of that time which the Scripture history reacheth, there was a great inequality in the apostolical churches for the number of the persons, which was far greater in one church than in another, and in the same church fewer at the plantation, and far more numerous afterward. For the kingdom of God was like leaven, which did spread and diffuse itself; and to a grain of mustard seed, which did grow mightily.[15] [...] After many of these became formal polities, they increased so much, that without divisions and subdivisions, they could not be well ordered, so as that every part should be subjected to the whole. This ecclesiastical history testifies [...] that the inequality of the first churches, planted by the Apostles, was so great in the former respects; [and] that some of them were incomplete, not fully formed, not grown up to their full stature. [...] Most of them did mightily increase and enlarge afterwards; [and] the

---

[14] Misreferenced both editions.   [15] Matt. 13.31.

prophesies of the glorious enlargement of the church began but to be fulfilled in the times of the Apostles; therefore those first churches, as in the Apostles' times, could be no obligatory examples to us for matter of extent, except with admission of some great latitude. From all this it follows, that the rules, whereby this controversy must be decided, must be the generals of decency and order, so far as they may prove most efficaciously conducent unto the preservation and edification of the body. Yet we must have a special care to observe the institution and the examples agreeable thereunto. And that church, which is ordered according to these rules, and most effectually tends unto these ends, is the best and most approved of Christ. He doth not respect and value churches as they are congregational, Presbyterian or episcopal, nor as of more narrow and larger compass; nor as of less or greater number; but as so ordered, as to discover false brethren, reject heretics, purge out the old leaven, cast out scandalous persons, free from the doctrine of Nicolaitans and Jezebel, and keep themselves in unity and purity.[16] And surely, as our Christian profession is disgraced, so is God highly displeased; because we so miserably distract God's people, and urge upon them such accidentals with so great importunity, though they be neither essential, nor necessary to good government.

IO.

I might instance [the following:] in the church of Israel, which no doubt was national from the times of Moses till the reign of Jeroboam; all which time it continued entire in one body, adequate to the state, and was never divided into independent congregations. This example is not to be sleighted, as it is by some. For this church was modelled, enlarged and confined by God himself. Neither was it in this particular any type or shadow of something to come, which upon the coming of Christ, and the revelation of the gospel was to vanish. And this at least it will prove, that a national church under one supreme judicatory is not unlawful in itself. [...] I might add, that it's nowhere prohibited in the New Testament; [...] that it's agreeable to the rules of decency and order; [...] that it's not contrary to the institution. [...] If the state be Christian, it may have much help, and many advantages

---

[16] Rev. 2.6, 20.

from the state, especially when the divisions of church and state are the same. But [further], if a congregational church may be lawful, then a national may be so too. And the reason of the consequence is, because a national may be as easily and as well, nay, more easily and better governed than a single congregation, much more than thousands of independent congregations in one and the same state. That the multitude of Christians in one nation associating and uniting in one body, and subjecting itself to one supreme judicatory, may be better ordered than many independent congregations in the same nation, is evident. For [...] they may be far more firmly united, and far more free from schisms and separations. [...] Order, which is the life of government, may far more easily be established and observed. [...] It will be far stronger to preserve itself from all opposition both within and without. [...] It will be furnished with far more excellent persons endued with excellent qualities for to make officers and representatives. [...] It will be of far more authority. [...] It will be far more able to reform and reduce into order the greater multitudes and whole congregations, and the greatest persons. [...] It will be far more able to receive appeals, to make canons, give advice, hear and determine the most difficult causes, and to execute their highest judgements. One reason of all this is, because so many gifts of the spirit may be united in one. To clear this more fully, we may consider a difference, [first], between a single congregation independent, and a national community under one and the same Power of the Keys. [Second], between a multitude of these independent congregations, supposing all the Christians of a nation made up their several polities, and all the congregations of a nation united severally for worship, and some acts of discipline, yet all subject to one supreme judicatory ecclesiastical. For the first difference, it's twofold: in the number of persons; [and] in the distance of place, in respect of the parts and members of these bodies; both which, if they be too great, are thought to be impediments of government. As for the number of persons: [...] they must not be too many, as they ought not to be too few. [...] They are far more for number in a national than in a congregational church. [...] As for this great multitude of a nation, if not too vast, reason, and the same confirmed by experience will tell us, that by distinction and a wise division, with a co-ordination of parts equal, and a subordination of the less to the greater, and all the several parts unto the whole, a multitude, though of millions, may be united into one organical body, and governed as one man. And by the way, we may take notice of a mistake in Mr. Hooker of New England, who thinks that a church or community of Christians cannot be an organical body till officers be made; whereas the making of officers is an act of administration, and presupposeth the constitution, whereby it's properly and formally organical, before any act of administration.[17] But to return, that whereby so many are made one is order, which unites Heaven and earth, and all things therein in one body: much more a petty multitude of Christians of one nation. This is apparent in all bodies politic; as universities, corporations, counties, armies and commonwealths. This is God's way of government, which the wisest governors did always imitate. Thus Moses chose able men out of all Israel, and made them rulers over the people, rulers of thousands, rulers of hundreds, rulers of fifties, and rulers of tens. And they judged the people at all seasons: the hard causes they brought to Moses, but every small matter they judged themselves (Exod. 8.25, 26). In this text considered with the antecedent, many things as proper to government are observable: [...] there must be laws, officers, [and] courts according to the *tria Jura Majestatis* of legislation, making officers and jurisdiction. These presuppose a community, and a constitution. [...] There must be a power of making laws, that belongs to the sovereign; [...] laws by this power must be made for administration, which without them must needs be arbitrary and irregular. [...] Those laws once enacted must be promulgated that they may be known. [...] Once known, they must regulate both the people's obedience, and the acts of officers, and judgements of the judges. After laws once established, they must be executed: and that cannot be orderly and effectually done without a division of the people. For [...] they must be numbered, divided into tens, fifties, hundreds, thousands, tribes. [...] They must be co-ordinate and equally poised, tens with tens, fifties with fifties; hundreds with hundreds; thousands with thousands. [...] They must be subordinate, ten to fifty, fifty to a hundred: and hundreds to thousands, and all unto the whole. When this is done, officers, by whom these laws must be executed, must be made. These must first be well qualified. [Second] the people must choose them (Deut. 1.13). [Next] Moses must appoint them their places, assign them their circuits, give them their charge. [Finally], they must have their courts

---

[17] Hooker, *A Survey*, pt. 2. pp. 1 ff.

and sessions, judge, execute the laws, and be subordinate, the lesser courts to the superior, and all to the supreme. For their causes, especially if difficult, must ascend till they came to Moses, and he brought them to God, who was their sovereign; this was extraordinary. But afterwards they had their Sanhedrin and court of appeals. This subordination seems to be implied in those words of our Saviour (Matt. 5.22). 'But I say unto you, that whosoever is angry with his brother without a cause, shall be in danger of the judgement; and whosoever shall say unto his brother Raca [conceited ass], shall be in danger of the council, but whosoever shall say, thou fool, shall be in danger of Hell fire.' One thing in all this is considerable; that Moses did not make every division, not every court severally independent, but subordinated all unto one supreme consistory. A multitude, though national, therefore is no impediment to good government, especially when they are numbered, divided, co-ordinated, and subordinated, and so by a certain and fixed order made one.[18]

I I.

As a multitude is no hindrance, so neither is a national distance of parts. For if we should enquire into the constitution of the Chaldean, or the Persian empires, of both which we might learn much out of the holy Scriptures, especially in the books of Ezra, both first and second (called Nehemiah) and Esther and Daniel; most of all we should find, [first] that the extent of them was far more than national, and the distance of the parts far greater. [Second], that these were divided, subordinated, not only in the parts less to the greater, but also in their officers both for war and peace, the revenue, and the administration of justice, and so by order united under one head. The empire of Rome (the parts whereof were severed at a very great distance, as from the River Euphrates in the east, to the ocean upon the west of France, and from Egypt southward to the north of the lesser Asia) was according to their principles of policy, as well governed as any European petty state at this time is. The Turkish seigniory, though of great extent, is as well ordered as divers several kingdoms Christian, confined to a far more narrow compass. Their order is good, their

---

[18] Cf. John Eliot, *The Christian Commonwealth* (London, 1659), who explicitly believed that the Mosaic numbering of Britain was the key to a settlement.

strength great, their counsel, which doth manage it, politic, their laws for administration of justice certain, their divisions, from matters of religion, few or none: and their internal strength must needs be firm, and the continuance of their dominion hath been long. Some attribute the excellency of their government to their severity in punishments, and their bounty in rewards: yet though these add something, yet these are but the least part. The dominions of Spain are many, and scattered at a very great distance round about the globe on both sides [of] the line, within and without the tropics, yet all these are subjected to one supreme judicatory, and are tolerably governed, and by a great deal of policy have been kept together till of late. France indeed is stronger, because divided into thirty provinces, it's united in one vicinity, and subject to one monarch. Yet in these vast dominions and great empires, the union of their many parts so distant did depend, not only upon ordinary means, but some extraordinary acts of divine providence. From all this it's evident that by division, co-ordination, subordination, the supreme power of one nation, nay of many nations, may be diffused through the whole body, so as to animate it, and reach every part, even the remotest.

12.

Yet it may be objected that all the members of a national church can never meet together in one place and assembly. It's true, they cannot, neither is it needful. Joshua called and assembled all Israel, when yet none but their elders, their heads, their officers, their judges were called and convented (Josh. 23.2), upon which place Masius thus comments: [Therefore from his calling all Israel in convocation it is then deduced that the whole body of the people was represented.] So that all Israel met in their representative.[19] Thus David, thus Solomon did use to convocate all Israel. As our state hath its *Wittena Gemot* [Witan Moot], the parliament, which Camden calls *Pananglium*, so a national church may have a general assembly to represent the whole.[20] And this may be so composed, as to be an abridgement, and contrac-

---

[19] Andrea Masio, *Josua imperatoris historia* (Antwerp, 1574), ch. 23, pp. 327–8. The quotation has been slightly shortened, but includes the beginning of Masio's sentence, which Lawson omitted. Masio's work was regarded as authoritative until the 18th century, see Henry Owen, *Critical Disquisitions* (London, 1734).

[20] William Camden, *Britannia* (London, 1586), *tribunalia Angliae*, p. 63.

tion of the quintessence of the wisdom, piety and learning of a national church; this is a most excellent way for a community to act by. This may be both the *terminus a quo et ad quem*, of all these public acts, which are of weight and general concernment. By this the nomothetical power is exercised: to this by appeal the highest causes are brought, and finally determined; yet, here it's to be observed, that a representative of the whole, is not the whole properly, but synecdochically, and an instrument, whereby the whole doth so act; yet if any thing be done amiss in a former particular assembly, the whole may correct it by a latter. [Moreover], if the constitution of a general representative be right, and the members thereof duly qualified, and act according to their qualification, there will be so much reason and wisdom in their determinations, as that they will bind more by virtue of the matter than the authority and votes of their persons. We might add that in these independent congregations, there is neither any conveniency, nor necessity, that all the members should meet either for juridical or legislative acts, though it be expedient that all should know what is done. They call women and children together for worship, but not for matters of judgement and discipline. It's sufficient if such as are rational and judicious have suffrage in the same matters. Marsilius in his *Defensor pacis* determines the power of legislation to be [in the people or the whole body of citizens]. Yet he grants that the laws may be made [by the weightier part], or their trustees: and that what is so done by them, is done by all. But in this particular he excludes women, children, servants, strangers, though inhabitants, if not incorporated;[21] likewise Mr. Parker, who gives the whole and independent Power of the Keys into a congregation under a democratical form, yet will have the exercise of this power in the officers in an aristocratical mode.[22] Seeing therefore that neither multitude of persons, nor distance of place, nor impossibility of a virtual and sufficient convention of all the members, being the differences between a national and a congregational church, and conceived to be the impediments of good government, are no impediments; I know no reason but that all the Christians of a nation may be as well governed by a subjection to one supreme judicatory, as a congregation independent.

[21] Marsilius of Padua, *Defensor pacis* (1324), ed. C. W. Previté-Orton (Cambridge University Press, 1928), 1.12.4.
[22] Robert Parker, *De politeia*, bk. 3.7.

13.

But let us oppose this national community under one supreme tribunal to a thousand or more independent congregations, as hitherto we have compared it with one single congregation; and then that which was affirmed will be more apparent. For, [...] national community Christian may have the same members, the same gifted men, the same officers, and the like assemblies for worship, as subjected unto one tribunal, which the same number of Christians in the same nature, divided into a thousand or more independent polities may have. And the same gifted men and officers may act more effectually for the good of the whole when they are thus united, than when scattered and divided like the vital spirits in so many several bodies. For [unity is strength], and the being more firmly, orderly, and regularly united, may more easily animate and effectually move and direct one body, though great, than so many bodies independent one upon another and severed, though little. [...] Again in this national body every congregation, classis, province may act, order, hear and determine matters belonging to their cognizance, and within their precincts, without troubling any general representative, except in the highest, most difficult businesses of general concernment, which with all extraordinary matters are reserved for that highest assembly: And all this is done according to the rules of government allowed by God, and practised by the best polities in the world. [...] The congregationals grant, that any of their single congregations independent, in a difficult point, or business may take the advice of twenty, thirty, forty other congregations or more. Yet if the major part of them or all should agree and give their judgement, that one congregation shall not be bound by their advice, but shall have power to judge against it, or subscribe unto it. Seeing in this case no Scripture binds this or other congregations to be independent, nor perhaps allow any such thing, except in some extraordinary cases, it were worth the serious consideration of wise men, whether it be more agreeable to the rules of good government, and the general precepts of church discipline, that one of these congregations alone should have the power to determine, and that finally, this difficult cause, and all the rest only to advise, than that jointly with this one, all the rest and most of them as good, and some perhaps better, should have power, not only to advise, but determine. And whether this determination of all jointly were not

likely to prove better, and more effectual, and more conducing to the
end of discipline, than that determination of one. But against this two
things may be said, [first], that all those other congregations may err,
but this is but to suppose, and to suppose a thing both unlikely and
extraordinary, that forty well-constituted churches may err, and that
one be free from error. [Second], by this it seems to follow, that in
some difficult cases one national church may not only take the advice
of many others, but subject themselves unto them. But [...] we are
bound only to submit unto the word of God made clear unto us,
though it be very likely that many seeking God and making right use
of the means, are more likely to find out the truth, and understand the
word of God better than one. [...] I stayed [stopped] at a national
church, and did not expatiate further, because experience hath taught
us how prejudicial it hath been even to this state to suffer appeals to
be made, either unto foreign churches, or states. Neither is it fit in
respect of the civil sovereign Christian, that the church within this
state should any ways depend upon any other church whatsoever.

14.

I had said before, that a national multitude of Christians associated
into one body, and subjected to one supreme Power of the Keys, may
be as easily and as well governed and edified, as if they were divided
into many several communities and independent congregations. Now
I add, that in divers cases they may be more easily and better governed
and edified. This might be made manifest, [first] from the many
inconveniences, which will follow from the multiplication of
independencies in a national church and Christian state, all [of]
which by an internal connexion and subordination may be avoided.
Histories read with attention and understanding will manifest this,
and the experience of these times in our church and nation. [Second,
it is clear] from the disproportion, and also the difference between the
church and state in respect of the extent, and the multitude of
independent polities ecclesiastical, within the bowels of one entire
civil commonwealth Christian. I do not mean, that the constitution of
the church and state should be the same, so that if the state be
monarchical, the church should be such too; or if aristocratical, it
should be aristocratical. For, though God hath determined the model
of the church, yet he hath not so particularly defined the constitution

of the state. Neither do I affirm, that the church by any divine precept is bound to be co-adequate to the state. Only this I say, it will be convenient, advantageous to the church, and agreeable to the general rules of decency and order, that it be co-adequate to the state. [...] That there be but one independent church in one national state, except there be some special impediment. But not to insist so much upon these, a third and greater reason to prove this, is taken from the insufficiency of a congregation to govern and order itself in divers cases, not so incident to a national church well ordered. Amongst others, there be four acknowledged and reckoned up by Mr. Parker himself. The first is, when one and the same cause may concern, not only one single congregation, but divers several other neighbouring churches. The second, is the inability of the eldership of an independent congregation. The third, is maladministration. The fourth, is appeal upon maladministration presumed. Concerning these four cases I observe, [...] that no single congregation doth continue long, but some of these cases, if not all, will fall out; [and] that in these cases there can hardly be any redress. [Further] that a national church is ordinarily furnished with sufficient remedies against these evils. Upon all this it follows, that in some cases a national church is of a better constitution, than a congregational. Whereas Mr. Parker, in the case of maladministration grants appeals, in that very concession he divests his congregation of her independent power, and makes it to be no polity at all. For, if (as he saith) a congregational church be, and that by divine institution, the primary subject of the Power of the Keys, how can it be subject to another church or churches, as if it appeal, it must needs be? [An equal among equals has no power] is a certain rule. For, [offence from an obligation] will not here take place.[23] To be independent and dependent cannot agree to the same church at the same time. And is it likely that Christ denieth the Power of the Keys to that church, which in all the forementioned cases was sufficiently furnished with effectual means of redress, and give it to that which is in itself insufficient? There be several kinds and degrees of communion between particular churches independent, and that for mutual help and edification: yet all those kinds and degrees of communion are but extrinsical, and the communion is but like that of leagues and friendship between state and

---

[23] *Contra* Parker, *ibid.*

state, which can no ways reach appeals. And as it is in several distinct states, so it's in several distinct churches. [The argument] of Dr. Jackson is very remarkable and worthy consideration.[24] That the best union that can be expected between visible churches, seated in several kingdoms or commonwealths independent one upon another, is the unity of league or friendship; and this union may be as strict as it shall please such commonwealths and churches to make it, and to subject such a church in such a case unto another, is to build a Babel or seat for Antichrist.[25] This implies that a church may be national, and he gives a good reason why it should be no more. And according to this rule, Mr. Parker, by granting in this case appeals, doth no better than build a Babel and so I fear many others do by making every congregation independent.

15.

But to say no more in this place of appeals (the power of receiving whereof is a branch of majesty, and the exercise of this power belongs to administration, and comes under the head of jurisdiction, where they are to be handled at large). I further do conceive, that the condition of these independent congregations, is no better than that of petty states, as those of the Netherlands, and the cantons of Switzerland. These cannot subsist without a strict confederation, or a foreign protection: and both are dangerous, and sometimes, if not often, prove prejudicial. Though the States-General of the Low Countries have their commission from the several republics, and with this clause, *salva cujusque populi Majestate*; yet they are ready many times to usurp and exercise more power than is due unto them. But foreign protection sometimes proves a supreme power. But the danger of our independent churches, as with us, is far greater: because they are so petty and far less bodies, and no ways by any certain rules firmly united. From all this discourse a rational reader will conceive that a national church in my sense is far more agreeable to the rules of government, which we find in Scripture, than so many independent polities ecclesiastical in one nation. Some still do conceive, and they have reason for it, that as this notion of an

[24] Dr Thomas Jackson, *A Treatise of the Holy Catholic Faith* (London, 1627), ch. 8, p. 63 (marginal reference), in *Works*, 3 vols. (London, 1673), vol. iii, p. 837. First edn. in More Library.   [25] *Ibid.*; Lawson is partially quoting.

independent congregation was at first invented to oppose the diocesan bishop; so the dissenting brethren pitched upon it in opposition to the Scottish Kirk, and the English Scotified Presbyterian. And as in the reign of Queen Elizabeth, some great ones, and counsellors of state protected the new conformist, and made use of him to poise the bishop; so in our days there were statists, who knew how to make the congregational party subservient to their civil interest, not only to poise, but to beat down the Presbyterian, and which they far more aimed at, their party both in England, in the parliament and army, and also in Scotland, which in the end was done to some purpose. For at last the independent became predominant, had great friends, was much favoured, obtained good maintenance, and some of them were put in the best places, and enjoyed the best preferments in the city, universities and country.[26] Nay, some of them do not scruple plurality of places, as though the word pluralist were only unlawful, and plurality, the thing itself legal and just enough. Some of them do much mislike the parochial divisions, yet like parochial benefices well enough; and are unwilling, once possessed of them, to part with them. Yet this power and profit is made not only by them, but others, the great interest; few seek a real reformation with sincerity of heart.

16.

To draw near a conclusion, not only of this chapter, but of this discourse of the party supremely governing in church and state; it's the duty of us all in the best manner, and by the best means to endeavour; and make it our chief design to reform and unite this divided and distracted church of ours. For this end, we should first lay aside our divisions, as they proceed either from ignorance or error, or disaffection; and let us see and try how far we may agree in the general and clear truths of Scripture, revealed for to direct us in the right ordering of a Christian society, and 'put on charity, which is the bond of perfection, and let the peace of God rule in our hearts, to which we are called in one body' (Col. 3.14, 15). For if we do not 'hold the truth in love' (Eph. 4.15),[27] no good thing will be done. These are the only and effectual means, whereby the foundation of

---

[26] The cap may be intended to fit Cromwell's chaplain Dr John Owen, 1616–83.
[27] Eph. 4.15 reads 'speaking' for 'hold'.

our church happiness can be laid. [...] Let no person or party assume any power, but what Christ hath given him or them upon a clear title. [...] Let us give every one their due: As for the Pope, we must leave him to God, who will in his due time take order with him. Let civil sovereigns have their right in matters of religion. Let the bishop be reduced to his ancient superintendency and inspection. Let the presbyters be contented to be officers, or at the best representatives, and not challenge to themselves alone the original Power of the Keys. Let the people not be wronged or any ways deprived of that right, which is theirs by the rules of the gospel. [...] Let us make our Christian associations, neither greater nor less than Christ allows us, and which may be fittest for a good administration. [...] Let's not impose upon others any form or model of church-government, which is not agreeable to Christ's institution; nor assert those things to be of divine authority, which are not clearly grounded upon some divine precept. [...] In things not necessary, either to salvation, or the good of the church, or not plainly conducing to the edification thereof, let's grant a latitude. And in such things, though we may differ in judgement, yet let's agree in affection, and in charity bear one with another, till we be better informed. [...] Let the nation continue divided into counties as it is, and the divisions of the church be made accordingly, or some other way, if any better may be found out. [...] Let the primary subject of the Power of the Keys be the whole, and exercised by the best in every precinct: but let the highest causes and the most difficult cases, with the nomothetical part be reserved for the general representative. In all this the assistance of the state is to be implored: and we must do nothing to the prejudice of their just power, nor give them any causes of jealousies or suspicions. [...] Some special care must be taken, not only for the edification of the more knowing and professing Christians, but also for the instruction of the ignorant, and reformation of the profane and scandalous; and this latter is the more difficult work. This cannot be done so well by itinerants, as by fit persons fixed in their several charges. [...] The chief interest of the nation, as Christian, is, as you formerly heard, the substance of the Protestant religion: which consists not in Episcopacy, or Presbytery, or Independency, nor merely in a separation from the church of Rome as corrupt, and parted from the purity and simplicity of the gospel (for this is but negative); but in certain positives of doctrine, worship and discipline clearly agreeable to the gospel. Neither need we go to lay a new foundation, but consider what the former doctrine, worship, and discipline was, and retain the best, reject the superfluous, rectify that which was amiss, and supply and perfect the defects. When all this is done, it were good that some forms of these established by authority may be made public, yet so, that all these may be plain and clear and consonant to the gospel. By doing thus we might testify to the world, that we continue Protestants and reformed Christians, and that our design was reformation and not confusion and abolition of saving truth amongst us. The sum of this discourse is: *Christ hath given the Power of the Keys, the church to which it's given is the primary subject, and is bound to exercise it by her officers and representatives for the church's good. For as the apostolical, so this power was 'given for edification, not destruction'* (2 Cor. 10.8).

CHAPTER 15

Of subjection in general, and the subjects of a civil state

I.

In the former part I have, according to my poor ability, declared, [...] what the act of government is. [...] That the subject of it being a commonwealth both civil and ecclesiastical, it hath two parts: [...] the constitution [and] the administration of the same. [I have argued] that the matter of a commonwealth is the community, and the form, an order of superiority and subjection; [...] that there are two integral parts of a commonwealth, [...] *pars imperans*, the sovereign, [and] *pars subdita*, the subject. [I have declared] what the power of a sovereign is, how it is acquired, how disposed, and that both in a civil state and church. Now according to order comes in *pars subdita*, to be considered both in a civil and an ecclesiastical notion. What a subject in a civil state is cannot be known in particular, except we know the nature of subjection in general. The word in Greek, which signifies to be subject is [*hypotassesthai*] to be subordinate. For subjection presupposeth order, not physical and local, but moral of superior and inferior. That which makes a superior is power, and power over another, which is not invested with it; in which respect he is inferior in relation to him that hath power over him. And so soon as God hath made one superior to another instantly, the party inferior is bound to subjection, which is a thing due unto this superior. God hath set him in a place under, not above, nor in the same rank; and by this very placing of him, he is made a subject by divine ordination. And this is the first degree of subjection, from which follows an obligation to active and voluntary submission. And this obligation ariseth not only from this that the power over him is God's, not as he is creator merely and the author of nature, as Suarez doth express it,[1] nor only as he is a supreme Lord by creation and preservation, committing some measure of his power to man, but also from this, that he commandeth man to submit. Actual subjection is an acknowledgement of this power in such a person, and a voluntary submission. This voluntary submission is a duty, and that which God requires in the word honour in the fifth commandment, and the Apostle from God, when he saith, 'Let every soul be subject to the higher power.'[2] This submission is, [...] a resigning up of their own understanding, will and power unto the understanding, will and power of his superior, so far as God hath made him superior. By this submission he becomes his vassal and servant, and renounceth other lords and masters in that kind. Upon this submission follows either an obligation to obey just commands, or to suffer upon disobedience. There are several kinds and also degrees of this subjection: there is a subjection of children to parents, servants to masters, wives to husbands, scholars to their teachers, soldiers to their commanders, people to their sovereigns, and of all unto God. And because he is supreme, and we are wholly both in his power and under it alone, therefore subjection in the highest degree, and a total and an absolute resignation of ourselves unto him, and him alone is due. And the truth is, no submission or subjection is due to any other, but all to him. For, when we submit to other higher and lower lawful powers, we submit unto him in them, who participate some portion of his power, not of their own. For, there is no power but of God,[3] nay, there is no power but which is God's. This subjection is not merely to

---

[1] Francisco Suarez; see e.g. *Prima pars summae theologiae de Deo uno et Trino* (Lyons, 1617), bk. 2.12, pp. 58–9; or at length *Tractatus de legibus* (Coimbra, 1612), e.g. bk. 2.6, p. 124.
[2] Rom. 13.1.   [3] *Ibid.*

be under the predominant force and strength, but also under the
directing wisdom, and the justly commanding will of another. Thus
far of subjection in general.

2.

The subjection in this place is subjection to a public power, and the
same is, [...] civil [or] ecclesiastical. [...] Civil subjection will be best
known, if I first define a subject, [then] consider how many degrees
and distinctions of subjects there be. Bodin taking *civis* and *subditas*
for the same, saith that [a citizen is a free man (homo) having power
over another].[4] Arnisaeus is more exact, for thus he defines subjects,
[subjects are the parts of a commonwealth, by whose powers in
respect of all things they are obliged; for whom in recompense rights
and privileges flourish].[5] As for Bodin, he mistakes much by con-
founding *civis et subditus*. For though every subject be *civis*, yet every
civis is not a subject. A person is said to be *civis* as a member of a
community, before any form of government be introduced. A subject
presupposeth a supreme power determined, and thereupon being
under that power becomes a subject. The one is a member of a
community, the other of a commonwealth. In the latter definition we
may observe, [...] the general [and] the special nature and difference
of a subject. The general nature is, that subjects are a part of the
commonwealth. For, as you heard before, a commonwealth hath two
parts, [...] the sovereign [and] the subject. By parts, are meant members or integral parts, which united, constitute and make up the body
of a state; wherein none can be found, but they are either subjects or
sovereign.[6] In this that they are parts they differ not from the
sovereign, who is also a part, though the most eminent and principal.
In the special nature thereof we may observe two things: [...] the duty
of a subject [and] the benefit. The duty is implied in the obligation,

---

[4] The context makes it clear that, as Lawson claims, Bodin does not see a significant
difference between subject and citizen. The English translation of Richard Knolles, *The
Six Books of the Commonwealth* (London, 1606), p. 47, refers to the citizen as a free
subject. The original French has *le citoyen* as 'le franc subject tenant de la souveraineté
d'antruy', *Les Six Livres de la république* (Paris, 1583), 1.6, p. 68.

[5] Henningus Arnisaeus, *De republica constituenda*, 12, in *Opera politica omnia* (Strasburg,
1648), p. 115, Latin in both editions is misprinted.

[6] Cf. Hobbes, *Leviathan*, pt. 2, ch. 18, 'And he that carrieth this person, is called
SOVEREIGN and is said to have *sovereign power*; and every one besides, his SUBJECT.'

the benefit in the enjoyment of some advantages. In the duty we may observe three things: [...] an obligation; [...] the party to whom subjects are obliged; [and] the measure of their obligation. The obligation, as I said formerly, follows upon a subjection, and the subjection upon the designing of a sovereign. For, in a designation of a sovereign by a general consent, according to reason and God's ordination, men deprive themselves of that unlimited liberty, which they had as members of a community, and bind themselves to a certain rule and order of inferiority. They divest themselves of some power, and take a lower place, and resign themselves up unto a superior will. Upon this resignation, and from it, they become subject, and by their very place are bound to submit. So that this obligation follows a kind of former subjection. But neither of the former authors [Bodin or Arnisaeus] tell us, what the act or thing is, to which they stand obliged, though both of them do imply it. And it is a constant submission and fidelity, and both voluntary. And though they may perhaps refuse to give this submission and fidelity, yet they are bound to yield it. This is the obligation. [...] The party to whom they are bound is the sovereign, and they mean the civil sovereign. And because they are bound unto this sovereign in respect of his power, they express the power, and imply the party invested with this power. And he cannot be a sovereign, except his power be supreme and universal in respect of the whole body of the community; therefore they say subjects are bound to the supreme power; for though they are under the power of officers and inferior rulers, yet the power of such is but the power of the sovereign trusted in their hands for the exercise thereof. This sovereign, as you heard before, may be either real, as the whole community, reserving the chief and radical power to themselves; or personal, as a general representative, or a chief and universal magistrate.[7] The measure is *quoad omnia*, in respect of all things, as their goods, persons, lives, actions in reference to the public good.[8] Yet this obligation must be legal as the power is legal, regular and rightly bounded. For absolute submission is due to God alone, according to the first commandment of the first table; a limited submission is only due to man according to the first commandment of the

---

[7] This specification of real majesty runs counter to the original account. The change seems to hinge on Lawson's ambivalent understanding of representation.
[8] Glossing Arnisaeus, *De republica*, ch. 12, p. 115.

second table.[9] For man is first bound to God, and then to man in an inferior degree; and every subject as bound to man, is first bound to real majesty, and to seek the good of the whole, then to personal majesty, so far as it extends to the benefit of the whole, and no further: for as *salus populi*, the good of the people is the chief end whereat all power should aim, so it's also the chief end of subjection. And according to the measure of the power is the measure of subjection: they must be commensurable and co-adequate, neither less nor greater. As power must be just and conformable to the laws of God, so subjection must be too, and we cannot be bound to submit in anything that is unjust and unreasonable; neither ought we, neither is it wisdom to give too great, or an absolute power unto any, so as to destroy our propriety and just liberty. This is the duty.

3.

The benefit follows, for no subjection but should aim at some good, and it's either unjust, or vain, if no benefit rebound from it. The benefits here mentioned are rights and privileges.[10] In every well-constituted and well-ordered state there are certain general rights, and also privileges both real and personal, which are not due unto strangers. No rational people will subject themselves but upon condition of protection both from wrongs within the state, and from violence of foreigners; and so to better their estate. For power being ordained of God, was intended for the good of the parties to be governed; for the Sword is put by God into the hands of higher powers, for to punish the unjust, and protect the just in their rights and due. As for privileges, he [Arnisaeus] understands them in an unusual sense; for privileges being reckoned amongst laws, which were favourable, as opposed to such are called odious, and bring grievances, and charges upon the subject, are usually made for the benefit of some single persons: For if they were general, as here they are taken, they were not privileges properly, except in respect of strangers of other states, which in that particular state none but the subjects could enjoy. From this subjection it follows, that if the

---

[9] Deut. 4.13. The Ten Commandments: 'He wrote them on tablets of stone,' referring to the first and fifth commandments. The second edition carries the marginal gloss 'Personal measure of subjection rightly bounded.'
[10] Arnisaeus, *De republica*, ch. 12, p. 115.

sovereign require fealty and homage, he acknowledging his power must solemnly testify it; and if it be demanded, confirm it by oath. For as princes and personal sovereigns swear to the people, so the people are bound to engage themselves to them again. And by this oath of fealty they renounce all other powers, not only foreign but domestic too. For upon what reason can protection be due, if the persons protected be not faithful, and loyal according to the constitution of the state? By this subjection, if the sovereign make laws, the subject is bound to obey or suffer. And if the command be unjust, he is not bound to obey, because he subjected himself according to the laws of wisdom and justice. Yet in such cases he being a subject, as a subject, must be willing to suffer and not resist the power; for though the power be just, and we are bound to submit, yet we are not bound to obey the unjust laws of a just power. The Apostles would not obey the unjust commands of their rulers, yet they did not resist their power, but rather suffered, though unjustly persecuted. By this subjection, the subject is bound to maintain their higher powers for the public good and safety. 'For this cause therefore (saith the Apostle) pay you tribute also, for they are God's ministers, attending continually upon this [very] thing' (Rom. 13.6). By this subjection he is further bound to hazard, not only his estate, but his life and person for the sovereign, and the state in a time of public danger. And all this must be done not for fear but conscience sake. For subjection is a duty required by the moral law of God, and must be performed out of love, and in obedience unto God: and cannot be performed by any so fully as by a sincere Christian. And though we must pray for all men, yet especially must we pray for them (1 Tim. 2.1). And in praying for them, we pray for ourselves, and for our own peace. Honour also is due from subjects to their sovereigns by reason of their eminent dignity, which ariseth from their power. Contrary to these are dishonouring, reviling, or vilifying the higher power; disobedience to their just laws, denying of tribute and other dues; refusing to hazard person or estate for the public safety; revolting and infidelity, keeping intelligence with enemies; open rebellion and resistance of their power; secret treasons and conspiracies against their person, or other ways directly or indirectly. And the greatest treason and rebellion, and infidelity is that against the state itself and real majesty; the next is that against personal majesty in the general representative of the whole community; the next to that, is that against the person or persons, upon whose safety the peace and happiness of the people much depends. And that which is against government in general, is far greater than that which is only against this, or that form in particular. Treason against laws is more heinous than treason against persons: and treason against the fundamental laws, than treason against laws for administration. This treason against the fundamentals was charged upon the Earl of Strafford; and the personal commands of the King could no ways excuse him.[11] Yet it was not thought fit that the judgement passed upon him, should be made a precedent for inferior courts because none but a parliament could judge of and declare the constitution, and what was against it, and what not.

4.

And here I might take occasion to speak of subjection unto usurped power, and acting under it, of the continuance of this obligation unto subjection, and the dissolution of it; of the obligation, of the Oaths of Supremacy and Allegiance [1559], the Protestation [1641], the Covenant [1643] and Engagement [1649, 1650] in respect of such as have taken them. Of the civil wars of late, how far they tended unto the dissolution of the government, and how far they did actually dissolve it. Whether the warlike resistance made by the Parliament against the King's commissions and his party was rebellion: and whether there was any legal certain power that could justly challenge subjection, or induce an obligation to it, since the commencement of the war: or whether the power continued in the Parliament till the members thereof were secluded: whether the Act of Alteration [1649][12] was a sufficient ground of obligation or whether any of the alterations made since, can be sufficient for that purpose. But the distinct discussion hereof would require a great volume, which I intend not. Neither if I should presume to deliver my judgement in these particulars, is there any probable hope of giving satisfaction, seeing so many men of eminent parts and learning do so much differ in them. I can, and I shall pray that God would open our eyes to see

---

[11] Thomas Wentworth (1593–1641), attainted for treason by the Long Parliament. The Act of Attainder is printed in R. S. Gardiner, *The Constitutional Documents of the Puritan Revolution, 1625–1660*, 3rd edn. (Oxford University Press, 1979), pp. 156 ff.

[12] Presumably the Acts of May 1649 abolishing the monarchy and the House of Lords, and declaring Britain to be a 'free state'.

the truth, and unite our hearts in love one towards another. [As] for usurpation, few do distinguish between the usurpation and manner of acquisition, and the power itself. For power is God's, and is always just, though it may be both acquired and exercised unjustly. There are also several kinds of usurpation, whereof some may be apparently unjust, and some doubtful: and there is scarcely any power now in the kingdoms and states of this world, but were usurped, either by the present possessors, or some of their predecessors. Neither can the tract of time make them lawful without some rational consent either tacit or express, and something of divine providence besides. For supreme power personal cannot be usurped and possessed by any man without the will of God, not only permitting, but acting and giving it too: not that he approves man's sin, or can do anything unjust, but for reasons just and good, known many times only to himself and not to us. For God hath made use of usurpers for to execute his judgements, and to do as much justice, as many lawful successors or possessors, and may bless them temporally for their good service, and yet punish them for their ambition and unjust manner of seeking power. By this he no ways doth warrant or encourage, or give the least liberty to anyone to usurp power unlawfully. We must in this point put a great difference between those usurpations which are contrary to the moral laws of God, and such as are only disagreeing with human institutions, which many times may be unjust. Suppose we desire to have a usurper or usurpers removed, yet we must consider, whether removal may not do a far greater mischief than our submission can possibly do. When we do submit, we must not so much look upon the unjust manner of acquiring the power, as at the power itself, which is from God; and we must consider the necessity, which divine providence hath brought us into, seeing he gives us no power, or opportunity to right ourselves in respect of human titles, or free ourselves from such as we conceive usurpers, under whom he many times gives us protection, peace, justice, and the gospel. It's no wisdom to be so ready and rash as to call everyone usurper, which doth not obtain his power according to the fancies and ideas of our own brain; and to deny all power, when as they know, that if there should not be power, and in the hands of some, and the same exercised too, all would come to ruin, and they themselves could not escape. It may be observed, that the greatest usurpers themselves are readiest to charge those with usurpation which have justly dispossessed them. Yet for all this we must not justify usurpation that is truly and really usurpation, neither must we swallow gudgeons,[13] comply with every party, and sail with every wind, as some are ready to do. Yet on the other hand, we must not be too scrupulous and pretend conscience, and yet make our fancy or some human constitutions our rule, and adhere unto them, as though they were divine institutions. For some, whilst they refuse either to submit or act under a power in their conceit usurped, they become guilty of more heinous sin; and when they presume they are faithful to some personal majesty, they prove unfaithful to real, and their own dear country, preferring the interest of some person, or family or persons before the good of the whole body of the people, to whom they owe more than to any other. And, whosoever will not be faithful unto his own country, cannot be faithful to any form of government or personal governors. Yet, whosoever will handle this point accurately, must first define what usurpation in general is. [Further, consider] how many kinds and differences of usurpation there be; [...] what the particular usurpation is against which he argues; and [...] state the particular case with all the circumstance.

5·

The continuance and dissolution of a legal power is also to be observed. As for real majesty it always continues, whilst the community remains a community; and subjection to this is due till it be destroyed.[14] Subjection to personal majesty in a representative cannot in just things be denied, till a latter representative make their power void. The personal majesty of a king with us requires subjection, whilst he lives, and governeth according to law; but upon his death, or upon tyranny in exercise, or acting to the dissolution of the fundamental constitution, he ceaseth to be a sovereign, and the obligation as to him ceaseth. A parliament turning into a faction, acting above their sphere, wronging king or people, cannot justly require, nor rationally expect for subjection. And though private persons cannot, yet the people by a latter and well-ordered parliament may both judge them,

---

[13] Small freshwater fish, bony and muddy in flavour, hence swallow gudgeons, swallow anything. Walton's *Compleat Angler* gives advice on preparation.

[14] This seems to contradict previous understandings of a community in which, *per se*, there is no subjection.

and call the exorbitant members to account. When a personal sovereign cannot protect his subjects, because their lives, persons, estates, are in the power of another, he cannot rationally require subjection, but for the time at least he should be willing to free them from allegiance: and to let them make the best terms they can for themselves. But voluntary revolt or rebellion cannot free them from this obligation to their lawful sovereign. In a word, so many ways as majesty and sovereignty may be lost, so many ways this obligation may be dissolved. Yet in all these dissolutions subjects must remember, that their obligation to God and their country doth continue, when not only personal sovereigns, but also the forms of government are altered. There are just causes and reasons of the dissolution of this obligation, and there are also unjust pretences and grounds of denying subjection. If any out of an innovating humour or desire of alteration, or discontent with their present governors, or conceits of false titles, or an intention to advance some of their own party, or a belief, that any foreign prince or priest can absolve them from their allegiance; or that their sovereigns are wicked, or do not administer justly, or are tyrants, when they are not, or in any such like case, shall seek to cast off the yoke, and think themselves free, they must needs be guilty, and cannot be excused. Those are the greatest offenders, who are enemies to government itself under pretence of liberty, or impunity in their crimes, veiled under the notion of self-preservation, or a reformation of some things amiss.

6.

The oaths of Allegiance and Supremacy, could alter nothing in the constitution: and both did presuppose our allegiance due to England, according to the fundamental laws, and could neither take it away nor add anything unto it. The parliament by them might declare what was the duty of every subject. The occasion of them both are well known: the end was to exclude all foreign power in matter of religion and civil right, in both which the pope had usurped formerly, and might do so for future times, especially, seeing many subjects did incline so much unto the see of Rome. They seemed to bind the subjects, taking them not only to the present kings or queens, but their heirs and successors. For the king might have heirs and successors: and he might have no heirs, and yet have successors. For Queen Elizabeth had no

heir or heirs, but a successor she had. Yet, because the crown is not
entailed by common law, and the fundamental rule, as some tell us,
therefore none is a successor till he be designed, and actually invested
and acknowledged, and till then the oaths were not administered to be
taken by any particular subject. The oath taken to the former prince,
if once removed by death or some other way, though it expressed
heirs and successors, was not thought sufficient. It must be taken
anew unto the present successor by name. Yet, if the crown had been
entailed, or the king's proper fee by inheritance, this seems to be
needless. One reason of these words inserted[15] seems to be this, that
seeing succession and election was usually in a line, it was intended by
them to exclude pretenders, and all power of the pope, or any other to
dispose of the crown when the former possessor was removed or
deceased. Yet they did not so tie us to be faithful unto the power of
England, to be exercised by king, peers, and commons, as that it were
unlawful to be true and faithful unto the community of England,
though under another form. The obligation to our country was far
higher, and fidelity to it was due by the laws of God and nature, so
that we must seek the good thereof, though the government was
altered. Fidelity unto the community is first due; fidelity to it under
some form of government was the second: fidelity unto it as under
that form by king, peers and commons, was the third; fidelity unto the
person of the king is the last, and presupposeth the former.
Whosoever understands and takes them otherwise, perverts the true
meaning, and makes them unlawful. The Protestation and Covenant
were made in a time of danger and distraction, and did include or
presuppose the former obligations:[16] yet the Protestation superadded
something concerning the Protestant doctrine of the Church of England to be maintained, and the Covenant something of discipline as to
be performed, and both extended to the preservation of the peace and
union of the three kingdoms. Neither of them did allow any unlawful
means to compass these ends. Neither of them could take away our
obligation to our country, and destroy our English primary interest,
but it remains entire: and since all the alterations made afterwards, we

[15] i.e. the oath of Allegiance in the Act of Supremacy, 1599, specifying allegiance to
Elizabeth, 'her heirs and lawful successors'.
[16] The Protestation, 3 May 1641. See Gardiner, *The Constitutional Documents of the Puritan Revolution*, pp. 155 ff. The Solemn League and Covenant, 25 Sept. 1643, *ibid.*, p. 267. These, like the Act of Supremacy, involved oath-taking.

are as much as ever bound to seek and promote the same; and whosoever will refuse to do so, upon pretence of these oaths, the Protestation and the Covenant, he is traitor to the common good of the nation. For as there is a positive, so there is a negative infidelity. For though such did not use any means positive to destroy it, yet they neglect it, and if everyone should do as they do, sit still and look on, and do nothing, it would certainly come to ruin, and fall into the hands of those who are their mortal enemies.

7.

The late civil wars in England did not only tend unto the dissolution of the government, but actually for that time dissolve[d] it. For, if the first supreme power personal was in king, peers, and commons jointly, then it follows, that when the King forsook the Parliament, and refused to act jointly with them, it was dissolved, much more when he set up his standard, and granted the Commission of Array and fought against them. For then there were two contrary powers and supreme commands, and subjects in strict sense were not bound to obey either. And the Parliament did declare, that *whensoever the King should make war upon them, it was a breach of the trust reposed in him by his people, contrary to his oath, and tended to the dissolution of the government.*[17] If the government was dissolved, it will follow that the subjects were freed from their allegiance. Yet the allegiance due to the community of England did continue; and everyone was bound to adhere to the just party according to the laws of God, though in doing so, they could not observe the laws of men. And whosoever did oppose that just party, did render themselves for ever uncapable of the benefit of the English protection, and were *ipso facto* enemies to their own country, their own peace and safety. Yet the Parliament did not declare, that upon a war made upon them, the government was actually dissolved; because though that war tended to the dissolution thereof, yet they conceived that the form did remain still in king, peers, and commons; and a considerable party of the Lords and Commons remained in the place, whither they were summoned by the King, and by virtue of the Act of Continuance continued a

---

[17] This compresses the opening paragraph of the 'Sentence of the High Court of Justice upon the King', 1648–9, in Gardiner, *The Constitutional Documents of the Puritan Revolution*, p. 337.

parliament, and that the King's power was virtually in the two houses:
yet in this, they passed above the letter of the law, and followed the rules
of equity and reason; and perhaps they had some hopes of rectifying the
King, and had no intention to alter the form, if they could preserve it,
and keep it up.[18] But all their wisdom and endeavours could not prevent
the judgements, that God intended to execute.

8.

[The question here is] whether the warlike resistance made by the
Parliament against the King, against his commissions, against his
party, was a rebellion? The King did declare it to be rebellion, and
proclaimed the Parliament party rebels and traitors, yet he did not
declare the Parliament to be rebellious.[19] For so to have done had
been offensive to his own party, and he had a considerable party
perhaps in both the Houses: and if he did acknowledge it to be a
parliament, in condemning them he must have condemned himself,
because he was an essential member of the same. Neither did the
Parliament profess they fought against, but for the King.[20] Yet, if they
fought against such as were commissioned by the King, they fought
against the King, and, if the King declared the Parliament's party to
be rebels and traitors, he must needs judge the Parliament guilty;
because as he in his war was the principal agent, so they on their side
were too. This gave occasion of curious distinctions. For, men did
distinguish between Charles Stuart and the King, between his regal
and his personal capacity: and on the other side, between the Parliament and a party in the Parliament, though the whole Parliament did
commission and arm. Thus they found a difference between the King
and himself, and the Parliament and itself. These distinctions were
not altogether false: yet though Charles Stuart and the King, and so
the Parliament, and a party in the Parliament, might be distinguished,
yet they could not be separated. And woe unto the people that is

[18] The Act against Dissolving the Parliament?, 10 May 1641, in Gardiner, *The Constitutional Documents of the Puritan Revolution*, p. 158.
[19] See e.g. 'The Impeachment of one Member of the House of Lords and Five Members
of the House of Commons', in Gardiner, *The Constitutional Documents of the Puritan
Revolution*, p. 236.
[20] 'Decaration of the Houses in Defence of the Militia Ordinance', 6 June 1642; 'The
Votes of the Houses for Raising an Army', 12 July 1642, in Gardiner, *The Constitutional
Documents of the Puritan Revolution*, pp. 254–61. Lawson is also descanting on the
surrounding pamphlet literature.

brought into such straits and perplexities. For, if they kill Charles Stuart, they kill the King; and, if the King destroy that party in the Parliament, he destroys the Parliament.[21] But to return unto the question; it's one thing to be rebellion, another to be judged rebellion. For that may be judged rebellion, which is not such, and the same thing may be justified by one and condemned by another. Arnisaeus handles this matter at large, and makes the question in general to be this: 'Whether upon any cause whatsoever, it is lawful for the subjects to resist, or take up arms against their lawful sovereign?'[22] When he hath stated the question, he determines upon the negative, and proves it. In stating the question, he seems to define a subject to be one, who hath given his allegiance to his lawful prince. But what he means *per fidem datam*, is not made so clear. Then he distinguisheth of [between] princes. For, [...] there are *regna pactionaes*, where princes are made upon condition. [...] There are *regna absoluta*, where the princes are absolute; [...] there are tyrants, and that of two sorts; [...] in title, as usurpers; [and] in exercise. These distinctions being made, he grants, that princes upon condition may be resisted for their ill-administration; [...] that tyrants in title, before the subjects bind themselves unto them, may be opposed; [...] that tyrants in exercise may be deposed, and that by their tyranny, *excidunt jure suo et si haereditario*, divest themselves of their power, though hereditary.[23] [Finally he holds] that absolute sovereigns who have [who hold transferred not delegated power], cannot be resisted lawfully, though they be vicious, and their administration impious, and unjust, if it reach not tyranny, which is directly against the laws and rules of government, and tends to the destruction of the commonwealth. But in all this discourse, he doth not produce any authentical record, or fundamental charter for these absolute sovereigns, which have [all power in all ways transfused from the people].[24] As for that Roman transfusion of power upon the

---

[21] The difficulty of sustaining plausibility in doctrines of office is central to the constitutional debates throughout the period. Confusions over doctrines of office are found also in the tracts of Henry Parker, and in Philip Hunton's *A Treatise of Monarchy* (London, 1643). For discussion see Conal Condren, *George Lawson's Politica and the English Revolution* (Cambridge University Press, 1989), pp. 112 ff., 130 ff.

[22] Arnisaeus, *De auctoritate principum* (Strasburg, 1635), bound in with *De jure majestatis* (Strasburg, 1635), pp. 3–4. See also *Opera politica omnia*; the question is the third of four headings prefacing the volume.

[23] *De auctoritate*, pp. 5–6; ch. 4, 12.15; also *De jure majestatis*, bk. 2.1, pp. 159 ff.

[24] Lawson is paraphrasing here. Arnisaeus's account is full of examples when authority is still at issue. (See above, ch. 5 n. 33.)

emperors, it's an uncertain thing: *lex regia* doth nowhere appear, it's doubted of many, as it is denied by many. And, suppose that people should be so unwise, what's that to others? He seems to contradict his own definition of a subject, which I formerly explained, he mistakes most grossly the constitution of some states, wherein he instanceth, *whosoever will determine this controversy, or debate it to purpose, he must, 1. define subjection, and declare the several degrees of it, according to the several constitutions of commonwealth. 2. If he instance in a particular state, he must certainly know the fundamental laws thereof, and truly express them. He must put the case aright, and state the question hic et nunc et rebus sic stantibus.*[25] This resistance, if rebellion must be an act of a subject, as a subject; and that cannot be but against his sovereign, as his lawful sovereign according to the laws of God and just laws of men.[26] And no man is able to justify the resistance of a subject, as a subject. The question is therefore, *whether he that is a sovereign may not be in some case resisted by the people, and if he may, in what case a resistance is lawful and free from the guilt of rebellion?* Our case in England is extraordinary, and not easily known by many of our own, much less by strangers not acquainted with our government. The resistance in the late wars, was not the first that was made against the kings of England, by the people of England, though it differed from all the former. The difference was between the King and Parliament, whereof he was a part, yet severing himself from the whole body. And the Parliament was no subject, considered as a parliament, for then the King himself being an essential part thereof should be a subject. As he was divided willingly or wilfully from it, he could be no king, no sovereign. For, if the power was in King and Parliament jointly, it could not be in him alone. Besides, when there is no parliament, we know he is a king by law, and the kingdom is *Regnum pactionatum non absolutum*. If he make himself absolute, by that very act he makes himself no King of England. For the common and fundamental law knows no such king. Yet this was all either he or his party could say to justify themselves. If he say, the militia was his, the Parliament will say, it's theirs as well as his, and except he be absolute, it must needs be so. For, if the supreme power be in king, peers and commons jointly, the militia, which is an essential part of this power, could not be his alone. The

---

[25] *De auctoritate*, ch. 1.
[26] *Ibid.*, 3.1 assumes only the categories of subject and sovereign.

Parliament conceived that when he left them he left his power with them, and if that could be made good by the fundamental constitution, then all England was bound to subject to them for the time, and obey their just commands. And, if it were not so, how could all such as took up arms with the King against them be adjudged traitors, as they were. If these things be so, there could be no rebellion upon the Parliament's side because according to these rules the Parliament was no subject; the King then, separated from the Parliament, refusing to act with them, acting and warring against them, was no sovereign. The question in the time of those bloody and unnatural dissensions, was stated several ways: as, whether it was rebellion in subjects commissioned by the Parliament to resist evil counsellors, agents, ministers of state, and delinquents, sheltering themselves under the King as divided from the Parliament, and acting against the laws by his commissions? Or, whether the Parliament of England lawfully assembled, where the King virtually is, may by arms defend the religion established by the same power, together with the laws and liberties of the nation, against delinquents, detaining with them the King's seduced person?[27] Or, whether the Parliament might not grant a commission to the Earl of Essex by a force to apprehend delinquents about the King to bring them to a due trial, and this even against the personal will of the King? Or, whether after the Parliament had passed a judgement against the King, they might not lawfully give commission to General Fairfax, to apprehend the King's person, and bring him to the Parliament?[28] Or, supposing the King to be an absolute monarch, whether any of these things could be done by any commission from the Parliament, as the condition of the kingdom stood at that time? Thus, and several ways was the question then stated and debated. But the truth is, that if the fundamental government be by king, peers, and commons jointly, and that neither the Parliament, consisting of these three states, nor the Parliament as distinct from the King, nor the King as divided from the Parliament could alter this constitution, nor lawfully act anything contrary unto it, then so soon as the Commission of Array on one side, and of the

---

[27] Belief in conspiracy against the king or a conspiracy *topos* was central to the debates of the early 1640s.
[28] 'The Votes of the Houses for Raising an Army', 12 July 1642; 'The Act Erecting a High Court of Justice for the King's Trial', 6 Jan. 1648–9, in Gardiner, *The Constitutional Documents of the Puritan Revolution*, pp. 261 and 357–8.

militia on the other were issued out, and were put in execution, the subjects in strict sense were freed from their allegiance. And if they acted upon either side, their actings were just or unjust, as they were agreeable or disagreeable to the fundamental laws, and the general and principal end of government. For even then their subjection to the laws of God and fundamental constitution of the kingdom did continue: and they were even then most of all bound to endeavour with all their power the good and preservation of their country bleeding, and conflicting with the pangs of death. And in that cause no man was bound too scrupulously to observe the petty rules of our ordinary administration, which were proper for a time of peace, which could not help but hinder her recovery. In such an extraordinary case, many extraordinary things, if not in themselves unjust, might have been done to prevent her ruin. And if the Parliament had gone at first far higher than they did, they had prevented the ruin of the King, the disinherition [disinheritance] of his children, and very much effusion of blood, which followed afterwards.[29] The business then was easy, which afterwards became difficult and could not be effected but with the loss of many thousands, and the hazard of themselves: for their cause at first was well resented [*sic*, presented/received] and had many advantages, but was much prejudicial by too much intermeddling with religion, and making some alterations in the church before the time.

9.

The next question is, whether since the commencement of the war, there was any certain ordinary legal power, which could induce an obligation, or if there was any such power after the war was begun, it continued after the war was ended till the secluding of the members, and upon that seclusion ceased.[30] The answer unto these two questions seems not to be difficult. For there neither was, nor could be any such certain ordinary legal power, which could in the strict letter of

---

[29] This is directly analogous to Hobbes's view that had Charles not been persuaded to compromise, there would have been no war. This reason of State parallels Lawson's earlier expressed reason of Church, but seems to contradict his belief that evil acts destroy a good cause.

[30] Pride's Purge of the Long Parliament, 1648; see David Underdown, *Pride's Purge, Politics in the Puritan Revolution* (Oxford University Press, 1971).

the law bind all English subjects to subjection. For, during a parliament, this binding power is in king, peers, and commons jointly: in the intervals of parliament, it's in the king acting according to the laws of administration. But all this while, nay to this day, there is no such parliament, no such king. And both in the time of the wars and after, both King and Parliament acted not only above but contrary to many of our laws, which in the time of peace are ordinarily observed. Neither of them could give us any precedent for many things done by them: and those few precedents alleged for some of their actions were extraordinary, and acts of extraordinary times. If the counties and people of England had not been ignorant and divided, the division of King and Parliament did give them far greater power than they, or their forefathers had for many years. But it did not seem good to the eternal wise and just providence to make them so happy. Punished we must be, that was his sentence, and punished we have been; yet few of us receive correction, or return to him that smote us. Some think an ordinary power continued on foot till the members were secluded, yet there was no such thing; for the two Houses could not according to ordinary rules exercise the ordinary power of the King, though they might use his name, and did so contrary unto his consent. If they should allege that his power was forfeited and did devolve upon them, that would be hard to prove. We know well enough, if it be not in him, where it is: it could no ways be in them but for the exercise, and in them for that end it was an extraordinary way. Some would say, that if the King was dead either naturally or in law a Parliament must instantly dissolve and be no parliament, because there was wanting an essential part. The Act of Continuance could not help them in this case, for it presupposed all the three essential parts. Neither could any particular parliament enact, that there should be a parliament without all the three essential members. If they should make any such act, by a following parliament it may be repealed, and the parties in the name of the people of England, called to account for altering the fundamental government. For we must not favour one particular parliament, so as to wrong all England, or suffer any ill example to be given. Yet, if ever any parliament did deserve not only to be pardoned, if they did some things amiss, but to be rewarded for their service, surely this parliament did: for never any suffered more even from him who summoned them, and from them who chose the particular members: Never any was brought into the like straits: I mean, that this respect was to be had to the upright party. But, if there was no ordinary power, what must the people do in such a case and distracted condition? In this I will give mine opinion in that which follows.

10.

Whether could the Act of Alteration, which required the Engagement or any of the alterations, which followed, introduce an obligation to subjection?[31] The answer is, they could not in any ordinary way do any such thing. For if the constitution was dissolved, and the personal majesty forfeited, it must devolve unto the people, and no parliament, nor part of a parliament, or any other person but the people could neither alter the former government nor model a new one. For, according to the general principles of government, the right of constitution, alteration, abolition, reformation is the right of real majesty; if it be not their right, then the people may be bound to subjection without their consent. [First,] a parliament may declare it, but some make a question whether their declaration be binding, if they who required the Engagement did intend to exclude a king, who should separate from them, or refuse to act with them, or challenge an absolute power. [Second, is it binding if they] abolish the House of Lords, as distinct from that of the Commons with a negative voice in legislation, and of such lords as were lords by writ or patent only? [Third], to declare that upon a dissolution the power was devolved to the people, it was the more tolerable, yet who gave them power to do this, or declare this? When I mention the people of England as the primary subject of power, and the heir of real majesty, I mean the rational judicial party; for no consent of people, that is not rational and agreeable to the laws of God, is of any force. And I exclude not only such as are barely members virtually, but all rebels, traitors, and malignant persons. For in the midst of these bloody distractions, and perplexity of minds, there was a *sanior pars*, a rational judicious party that unfeignedly desired the peace, welfare, and happiness of England. And, when many members of a community are insufficient of themselves to judge, what is just and good, and many of them

---

[31] The Engagement, 1648–9, required of all men over 18 years, following the Act declaring England a Commonwealth, see Gardiner, *The Constitutional Documents of the Puritan Revolution*, pp. 388, 391; Blair Worden, *The Rump Parliament* (Cambridge University Press, 1977), introduction, for the uncertain status of the Rump.

perverted, the power remains in [the rational part, or that which is weightier]; and in those, who upon right information shall consent with them.[32] For many who are not able of themselves to judge, yet when they are rightly informed, are willing to consent. But to return unto the former question: Seeing there was no ordinary power, which could introduce any strict obligation, what must the people do in such a case? What's their duty? The answer is, that though there was no ordinary, yet there was an extraordinary power ever since the wars were ended to this day, which they were bound to obey. For, [first], seeing the community of England did remain, and in the same a better party, real majesty did continue. [Second], the fundamental government could not be dissolved by one king and one parliament, though they both had agreed to do it. For, though as to them it was actually dissolved, yet the right might remain virtually in the community; I mean, a right to continue it, if they pleased. [Third], as the case now is, and was since the wars were ended, this fundamental government could not be so restored as to act. [Fourth], all parties did agree that there should be a government and a power for protection, and administration of justice; but the difference was, what the model should be, and most of all, who should exercise this power. Some did challenge and seek it for themselves, some for their friends, whom they conceived to favour their party and interest. For many of the royalists were for the late King's eldest son, not so much for the public good, as for their private interests and many other parties were guilty of the very same crime. [Fifth], government itself for the substance is more material, than this or that form, and the exercise of power, than the exercise by such or such particular persons. For, if there be not a governing power, and some to exercise it, and the rest to submit, there can be no protection from enemies, no justice, no order, but a mere anarchy, upon which a ruin instantly and unavoidably will follow.[33] For prevention whereof much may be done, which in a time of safety would be utterly unlawful. The people may submit to any, whom they shall conceive shall be able to protect them, and willing to preserve the laws for administration of justice. They need not stand upon doubtful titles, nor quiddities in law, but may do what

[32] The Latin here does not imply a disjunction between rational and weightier; it strongly echoes Marsilius of Padua, *Defensor pacis* (1324), 1.12 and his notion of the *valentior pars* or weightier part of the whole citizen body.
[33] Cf. Hobbes, *Leviathan*, ch. 13.

they can do, so that it be not unjust by the moral laws of God. [Sixth], seeing some particular government was necessary, and all rational men did agree in this, therefore there was an obligation to subjection, and every particular person was bound to submit unto the present power, under which they enjoyed the benefit of the laws, and protection both from public enemies and private injustice. This is not so to be understood, as though everyone or any ought to rest in this extraordinary condition; but to desire and endeavour to restore the first constitution freed from corruption, or some part or degrees of it, and proceed by little and little, as God in divine providence shall prepare the people for it, and enable us to introduce it and settle it. But still we must prefer the public good before any particular form of government, and seriously consider, what is best to be done for the present. For, when we cannot do what we will, we must be willing to do what we can: whosoever will not submit in such a case, nay, and act too for the public good and interest of his dear country, must needs be guilty before God, as not loving God, and his public neighbour as they are bound to do. It was a just resolution and profession of some, who returned to act in parliament, after the members were secluded, and the King put to death, and said, though they did not like and approve of some things already done, yet they would join cordially with the rest to promote the public good for future times. So likewise the judges, after another great alteration was made, debating what to do, they unanimously agreed to act, because there was a necessity that justice should be administered unto the people, and the laws kept in force. They did not think it fit to demur and delay till the names of king and parliament should be put in their commission; they knew they were not essential to justice, or necessary, or so much as conducing to the administration thereof, as the case then was. Neither did they scruple to undertake the work, because of the former oaths, Protestation, Covenant, Engagement: for, if these did tie their hands from doing God and their country service, they knew they must be [chains of injustice], but so they did not understand them. The sum is, there was an extraordinary power, besides the allegiance due unto God and our country, and therefore subjection was due from all Englishmen. Let us suppose an *inter-regnum*, as there hath been, is and in part will be till we be more fully settled, and the power ordinary brought into a constant channel, will any man doubt or fear to submit and act, because he conceives things are not ordered according to his mind?

And shall there be no government, no submission till he be satisfied, and his idea established? Suppose all should do so, especially such as are of parts and ability, what will become of us all? Let wise men consider what would be the consequents thereof. It's true, no party should engross the power to the prejudice of our liberty and the public good; yet we must stay God's time, and use such means as may stand with the public safety. Some kinds of remedies may at some times help, which at another may do mischief, not cure, but kill. We should remember that it's not committed to man but reserved by God unto himself to dispose of the kingdoms and states of the world. It's not in our power to have and choose what government and governors we will. That we, after such bloody wars and bitter dissensions have not a settled state, it's God's judgements upon us for our sins; that for the present we enjoy peace and the gospel, it's his unspeakable mercy. 'Let every soul therefore be subject to the higher powers, for there is no power but of God: the powers that be, are ordained of God. Let us submit ourselves to every ordinance of man for the Lord's sake, whether to the king as supreme, or unto governors, as unto them, who are sent by him for the punishment of evil doers, and the praise of them that do well.'[34] Where, amongst other things these are observable, that governors, and government are of God; [. . .] that the end of government is the punishment of evil doers, and the praise and protection of them that do well. [Also], that governors are supreme or subordinate. For by [*ktisis anthropine*], turned ordinance of man, is meant, civil government moulded by man, and governors designed and created by man to rule over man. [Further] that subjection to these is due by divine law and ordination. These things I thought good to deliver, and to express my mind briefly in the matter of subjection, and so humbly in this (as in all the rest) submit to wiser men. And my intention is peace, and my end the public good; which I with a single heart desire to promote, without any inclination to a faction or party.

II.

The authors of politics speak of the distinction, division, and education of subjects;[35] and though some of these belong to a community,

---

[34] Rom. 13.1–2.

[35] Lawson probably has post-Bodinian continental public law theorists in mind, but possibly the Jesuit Adam Contzen in particular, whose name surfaces below, n. 50.

or are presupposed before a community can be complete, some of them are reducible to administration, the second part of this art. Yet I will briefly handle them in this place, because they are accidents to *pars subdita*, [and] because they prepare the subject for government, and so facilitate administration [. . .].[36] Seeing the principal subject of my discourse is ecclesiastical government, and for the more particular and distinct knowledge hereof, I refer the reader to other authors, who have written more at large concerning these particulars. Yet not to be altogether silent, let us speak first of strangers: then secondly, of complete subjects.

[Incomplete and imperfect subjects are either resident or temporary.]

Strangers are such as either only sojourn, or such as fix their habitation in another commonwealth, where they are neither perfect members of the community, nor complete subjects of the commonwealth. Such as only sojourn or travel out of their own state, are called *Peregrini*, in Greek [*apodemoi kai parapidemoi*], and sometimes [*Xenoi*]. In Hebrew [*twsbym*], this is their name when they are in another commonwealth. There may be many reasons and causes of sojourning and peregrination. Abraham by God's special command forsook his own country, and sojourned in the land of Canaan, so did Isaac and Jacob.[37] Some are persecuted and fly from their own country for safety and shelter; some guilty persons fly for to avoid punishment; some sojourn for succour in a time of famine, as Israel in Egypt;[38] some live in foreign nations for traffic; some for to improve their knowledge and gain experience in several kinds of professions. To such we owe much of our skill in trades, several workmanships, in learning, in geography, in the nature of their soil, buildings, military art; the manners and customs of several nations, the disposition and nature of the inhabitants, in the model of states, in the manner of administrations. Some converse in other states to learn fashions, or wickedness; some as spies and intelligencers. The ends and the events are therefore several. Some are good and beneficial to themselves, to their country, to other nations. The issue of some men's

---

[36] The substantial diagram taking up the rest of the page is omitted here. Lawson claims it is 'not accurate though sufficient for my design', p. 228, and its headings are repeated and discussed in the following pages.

[37] Gen. 12.1; 37.1. [38] *Ibid.*, 47.27.

travel is vanity, or vice, or mischief. There are strangers, who do not merely travel and sojourn, but also fix their habitation in other states; these are called *Advena, incola,* and in Greek [*hiereis*],[39] in Hebrew [*crym*], though the word be used for pilgrims and sojourners. Neither of these are properly subjects of that state, where they live, yet they ought to carry themselves fairly and not do anything to the prejudice of the laws or government of the places where they do converse: and according to their good carriage they are to be used civilly. It was God's charge to Israel to use strangers well, because they themselves had been strangers in the land of Egypt. For strangers are used strangely, and in foreign countries exposed to many abuses and dangers. But special kindness is to be shown to such as are miserable, and flee for religion, or for protection. The magistrate of every commonwealth should have a special eye upon these strangers, and enquire into their carriage and their practice. To receive too great multitudes of them, may be dangerous, and some may do mischief, either by corrupting the subjects, or seeking to betray the state. Neither is it safe to naturalize many of them, much less to advance them to places of power and trust, which must needs offend the subjects and natives, especially when these are favoured and preferred, and the other are neglected. The judgement of God upon the Jew in this respect is very heavy; for they are commonly hated in all places, and not suffered to inhabit in many nations, and where they are permitted to dwell and trade, hard terms are put upon them.

12.

[*Those fully subjects are so by birth or adoption*]

There are besides strangers such as are properly and completely subjects, who according to their subjection enjoy the benefit of protection, the rights and privileges of subjects. Yet there is a great difference amongst these, according to the several constitutions of states. For, some are far more free and enjoy far greater privileges, as the Roman subjects did, as is evident in Paul, who said to the Centurion, 'Is it lawful for you to scourge a man that is a Roman and

---

[39] 'Priests', wrongly set?; the word appears properly below, sect. 13; *allo-genes/daros* would fit better here.

uncondemned?' (Acts 22.25). For a Roman could neither be condemned unheard, nor scourged, if not condemned. These had divers other privileges, which the provincial subjects had not before they were enfranchised. The subjects of England, if they enjoy their right, are more free than the subjects of France or Spain, and divers other countries. Some are little better than slaves, especially such as live under despotical sovereigns. The right and privileges of subjects are acquired several ways, which may be reduced to two: For some are such by birth, which are called *cives originarii*, some by allection [attraction, adoption]. This distinction is the same with natural and naturalized, as you heard in the doctrine of a community. This distinction is implied in those words of the chief Captain Lysias, saying, 'With a great sum obtained I this freedom'; and of Paul, who answered, 'But I was freeborn' (Acts 22.28). These as subjects were essentially the same, and if either should as such be preferred, the native subject *caeteris paribus* had the priority. Subjects also as subjects are equal, though in divers other respects accidental unto them, they may be very unequal; some may have special privileges; some may be officers, and by virtue of their office have their privileges. Here some take occasion to speak of the multitude and paucity of subjects in the same territory and state. If they be few, they may receive fugitives and adopt strangers, as Romulus did. If they be too many, they may send out colonies, and make new plantations. If the multitude be not too great, it's the honour of the sovereign and safety of the state; if [they are] too few, it's the weakness of a nation, and a danger of destruction. For, in the multitude of people is the king's honour, but in the want of people is the destruction of the prince (Prov. 14.28). Yet this is to be understood of a multitude well qualified and ordered by a good prince. For, tyrants and oppressors waste and destroy their people to their own ruin.

13.

There is another distinction of subjects, for they are [clerical or laity].

By ecclesiastical persons are understood, such as are indeed subjects, yet their office and work is in matters of religion; they act between God and man, as messengers, and mediators between them. They deliver God's mind to men, and offer men's prayers and gifts to God. They officiate in divine services, and that's their chiefest work.

They are singled out from amongst men to direct others unto eternal life. These anciently were called priests, and their place was honourable: yet there was an imparity amongst themselves. In the New Testament, these ecclesiastical persons are never called [*hiereis*], priests, but ministers of the gospel, or presbyters, under which words are signified all Apostles, prophets, evangelists, pastors and teachers. So that the word priest was given only to Christ or Melchizedek; or the Levitical pontiffs and ministers, or some heathenish sacrificer.[40] Yet in after-times, because the sacrament of the eucharist was a commemoration of the sacrifice of Christ, therefore in respect thereof the table was called an altar, and the minister a priest. At length, the church of Rome turned the sacrament into a sacrifice, properly so called, and the minister into a priest. And this was the original of the mass. This ecclesiastical function was instituted by God, and very honourable both in that respect, and also because their work is so excellent and necessary: for upon it under God, religion and the benefits of religion both private and public, temporal and eternal do much depend. To these by divine commands maintenance is due from the people, and they have been much honoured in well-constituted states with many privileges and immunities. But their own unworthiness, and the profaneness of the people have much debased them. Yet, good ministers with good people will be much esteemed to the world's end: and when the chief shepherd shall appear, 'they shall receive a crown of glory, which fadeth not away' (1 Pet. 5.4). These were accounted as a distinct and eminent order of subjects, as they were solemnly ordained. The rest of the subjects and the sovereign in respect of these have the name of seculars, and the subjects are called laics or lay people. This distinction is not so to be understood, as though the rest of the people had nothing to do with religion. For they are bound to serve their God, and seek eternal life, which that they might attain, this spiritual office was ordained from Heaven. And every sanctified person is a priest to offer spiritual sacrifice to God. Yet, this doth not make any such person a minister and public officer of Christ, who must sequester himself from worldly business more than other men to tend his calling, to which he is consecrated and solemnly devoted. With this distinction agrees that of clergy and laity. Whence the name *clerus*, the clergy for the ministry, should have its

----

[40] e.g. Ps. 110.4; Heb. 5.6, 10.

243

original, is uncertain. The people of Israel sanctified and consecrated unto God, were called [*kleros*], the lot or inheritance of God, and the priests and ministers were the eminent party of this lot and people. For the people as distinct from the pastors are called the clergy, lot, or heritage of God (1 Pet. 5.3), in which it cannot be proper to the ministers. It's true, that the first officer made by the church after that Christ was glorified, was made by lot, 'For the lot, that is (*Cleros*) fell upon Matthias' (Acts 1.26). From whence some think the system of presbyters and deacons, were called the clergy [*klerotes*], and [*klerotos*], signify one made an officer by lot. As for laity, we find often in the Old Testament, the people as distinct from the priests and Levites, called [*laos*], the laity. The Apostle and seventy disciples were distinguished from the rest of the disciples and believers. The Apostles, prophets, evangelists, pastors and teachers, were different orders from the rest of the church. The twenty-four elders, which signify the priests and Levites divided into orders by lot, were distinct from the four beasts, that is the main body of the church: but these are days of confusion and disorder. Everyone will be a prophet and a teacher, either presuming upon their gifts, yet scorning to engage themselves for the service of Christ in the poor and much despised ministry; or pretending blasphemously to the spirit, which God never gave them.

There is another distinction of subjects [between nobles and commoners].

Some are noble, some of a lower form and rank, *Nobilis* is any gentleman well descended. Yet there is a difference [between nobility and nobility of character]. For though [all true gentlemen are noble, yet not all born noble are gentlemen], because [a gentleman], is not only one well born, but also one virtuous. In this respect, the word of a gentleman is more than the word of a nobleman, nay, than the word of a king. Yet nobility with us is taken more strictly, and is given to none under a baron and peer of the kingdom, which hath right of suffrage in parliament, as one of the House of Lords. The ancient nobility of England is much diminished and decayed, and many of their estates alienated. And the late barons created by patent do much obscure them: and if these as barons have their suffrage in the House of Lords by virtue of their honour, and not their virtue and wisdom, I do not see how the parliament should be *Wittena Gemot* [Witan Moot]; the meeting of wise men. It were wisdom by some strict law to limit [the right of nobility] unto virtue and wisdom. For, honours should be conferred rarely, and upon merit and worth; for they have great privileges, which should not be made so common and prostituted to the lust and ambition of everyone that can pay for them. The subjects of lower rank, if freeholders, have also their privileges, and one principal, is a power to elect the knights of the county to represent in parliaments. There be other accidental differences of less moment, which I pass by.

14.

After these distinctions, follows a division of the whole body of the subjects into parts: and this is necessary, especially in respect of the administration. For without an orderly division the subjects cannot be well governed. Israel was divided into tribes; tribes into families; families into households; households into persons. Thus they were divided, and according to this order Achan was discovered (Josh. 7.16, 17, 18), and they had their [*pilarchous*] heads of their tribes: and their [*demarchous*] heads of their hundreds, as Masius upon the place observes.[41] The Romans were also divided, *in Tribus, et Tribus in Curias*; and after these we read of *centurias* and *decurias*. We read that Alfred divided England into counties, counties into hundreds, the hundreds into allotments. In some counties we find ridings and wapentakes; yet Sir Henry Spelman under the word hundreds, understands by wapentake a hundred, which in the Welsh is called *cantreda*, where he adds, that the counties were divided into tithings, rapes, and lathes: and hundreds were divided into tithings and friberges.[42] Upon this division made, it's said, that justice was administered with that ease, exactness and severity, that any man's goods, might at any time be secure in any place. Yea, they might hang golden bracelets in the highway side, and in open view, and none durst meddle with them. To this head, belongs the numbering of the people by poll, enrolling their names and estates, without which taxations cannot be justly imposed. The end of this distribution was to reduce the people into a certain order, according to which the equal parts were co-ordinate one with another, as counties with counties, hundreds with hundreds, so that one had no jurisdiction over another.

[41] Masius, *Josuae imperatoris historia* (Antwerp, 1574), ch. 7, p. 132.
[42] Sir Henry Spelman, *Glossarium archaiologicum* (London, 1687 edn.), p. 302; see also 'Of the Ancient Government of England', in *The English Works*, ed. Edmund, Bishop of London (1727 edn.), pt. 2, pp. 50–1; and above, ch. 8 n. 38.

The unequal were less or greater, and were subordinate over another. The unequal were less or greater, and were subordinate the less to the greater, which had jurisdiction over the less, and all the parts were subject to the whole. This was necessary for judicial proceedings, that actions in law might proceed according to the subordination of courts.[43] For anciently with us actions did commence in the courts, held by the lords of the manors: if the cause were too high, or could not there be determined, or justice had, appeal was made to the hundred court, from thence to the county court, from thence to the king's court. In the word *comitatus* Sir Henry Spelman observes this was the ancient order, and thinks it an abuse and great disorder, that in our days, every petty business and cause is brought into the king's court at Westminster.[44] What the division of this nation was under the Romans is not so well known, except we may conjecture of it by the ancient division of the provinces, and cathedral sees and dioceses, which much differed from these of latter times. Camden finds some divisions of England in the time of the Romans, yet they are not clear and certain. Under the Saxons he finds several divisions: [...] some according to certain proportions of lands; [and] he makes the heptarchian argument that it was divided into seven parts. At length, he concludes his political division with that of counties, which he, as Sir Henry Spelman, ascribes to the King Alfred.[45] But I have read, that it was thus divided before his time, and this is more probable, because *The Mirrour* informs us of counties, and of counties before there were any Saxon kings.[46]

---

[43] Spelman, *Glossarium archaiologicum*, pp. 302–3. In 'Of the Ancient Government of England' Spelman calls the Anglo-Saxon government, comparatively speaking, a utopia, p. 49.

[44] Spelman, *Glossarium archaiologicum*, pp. 138–43.

[45] William Camden, *Britannia*, 'Britannia divisio' (London, 1586), pp. 52 ff. expanded in Camden's *Britannia*, trans. Philemon Holland (London, 1637), pp. 154–9.

[46] Andrew Horne, *The Mirrour of Justices*, trans. 1642 (London); the context indicates Lawson is citing from memory, and getting it wrong. *The Mirrour* is quite explicit that county divisions post-date the Saxon invasions, ch. 1.2. Immediately before, however, Horne refers to the Saxons coming from the surrounding countries. The semantic and phonetic proximity of county and country may have caused the lapse. Nevertheless, Lawson's scepticism about Alfred's responsibility for county divisions seems well founded.

15.

[As subjects may be divided and distinguished so may education into noble or mundane modes]

After the division and distinction of subjects follows education, and in the very constitution of a state, some special care must be taken of this. There is some education in a family, but more perfect in a community, but the best and most perfect is found in a well-con-stituted and ordered state, which in laying the very foundation, pro-vides for the better institution of the subjects. The end hereof is the good of the people, and preparing for the preservation of the com-munity, and the better and more easy administration and government of the commonwealth. There are few, to whom God in the creation of their immortal souls, and their mortal bodies hath not given some special power, disposition, and propension to something more than another. The work of education is to improve those principles and powers, so as to bring them to a greater perfection. And for such as have the care of education, it's an excellent piece of wisdom, to discover what the genius and disposition even of children is, and what they seem to be made for: and so by instruction and example, draw it to the height and utmost pitch it's capable of. How many excellent sparks are raked up in the ashes of sloth and negligence, or else utterly quenched or at least made useless by a diversion of them to other things, to which God did not dispose. Great is the ignorance, imprudence and negligence of parents, masters, and others in this particular. This education is either more noble and excellent, or less and inferior. The more noble is that which improves man's know-ledge either in human or divine learning. Human learning, both in parts and languages is useful for the state, and beneficial to the church. By reason man excels a beast, and by learning he excels other men, and by divine learning he is made like unto angels, and to God his creator. For this end wise and good men, being of a public spirit, and intending the general good, erect schools, colleges and universi-ties, and endow them with competent maintenance, for to encourage such as shall take the care of them. Of the original and progress of these societies, we may read in Hospinian.[47] Yet, much more we may

---

[47] Rudolphus Hospinianus, *Festa Christianorum* (Zurich, 1612 edn.). Copy in More Library.

find, than he hath written of them. Schools strictly taken as with us, are only for the entering of children, and teaching the rudiments of some arts and some languages. Colleges and universities, serve for higher improvement, neither are they limited to some particular arts or languages, but according to the clause in their charter, *licentia generalis studi*, they may enlarge to all learning, all languages. Yet, this general study is usually confined to philosophy, law, medicine, theology. The principal design of them should be to breed gentlemen for the state, and ministers for the church: but, there is not any due care taken to furnish the nation with either of these. Some by their constant and diligent pains do much improve themselves. Such as are idle and negligent lose the opportunity, their time, and their very school learning, misspend their days in vanity, and learn iniquity; and the sons of the nobility, gentry and rich men, are much guilty in this respect. It's [a] pity that such noble foundations should through our ignorance be so little beneficial: and it's a great sin, which God will punish, that they are so much abused. These places for learning are great blessings of God, if we would make right use of them, we should find it to be so. But it is a sad thing to consider how both instruction is neglected and discipline remitted. In this kind of education the Jesuits are said to excel, and to single out the best capacities to direct them orderly in learning both languages and arts, till they have made them general scholars, teaching them how to make use of their learning. And their discipline is strict, but it's [a] pity, that all this improvement should be made subservient to a wrong end. There is hardly any intelligent people or state, that doth not provide some, that should be skilful in religion, and know how to officiate in religious services; and for these they provide a sufficient maintenance. These were anciently priests, and many of them great scholars, and such as did instruct others, who should succeed them, and direct the people in the worship of a deity, upon whose favour they conceived, the public weal and happiness did much depend. Yet many of the heathen priests had familiarity with the devil, and were great magicians.

16.

There is an inferior kind of education, [necessary for the commonwealth; it comprises husbandry and manufacture, defence, and commerce].

The first is for the preservation of the commonwealth, without which the subjects cannot, live or the commonwealth subsist. Husbandry and trade, and manufactures tend to this end. And though this may seem to be an institution proper to families, yet families make a commonwealth; and the governors should take special care of ordering these aright, so that the state may have sufficient commodities both of growth, and manufacture, not only for itself, but for exportation to bring in what the country wants most. Under husbandry, we may comrpise not only the tillage and manuring of the ground, but also the ordering of cattle. These were the first professions in the world: for Adam brought up his children to this purpose. Abel was a keeper of cattle, and Cain a tiller of the ground (Gen. 4.2). And Noah planted a vineyard: for he began after the flood to be a husbandman, and planted a vineyard (Gen. 9.20). These are so generally necessary, that the wise man saith, 'the profit of the earth is for all, the king himself is saved [served] by the field' (Eccles. 5.9). There are certain manual trades without which a people cannot well subsist, as clothing, and all such works as belong thereunto, which are many. Next, are such as are for building, as masons and carpenters; for a man must have house and harbour; for this end also such, as Tubal-Cain,[48] who work in iron and brass, are useful, and are subservient to [serve] many professions. Amongst these some are for curious workmanship, as Bezaleel;[49] some professions are not much useful and rather hurtful than beneficial for a state, as being subservient only to vanities, pride, and unlawful pleasures. Therefore the magistrates should have a special care to order these, to cast out all idle people, all lazy beggars, and set the poor on work. None that can work should be idle, but take upon them some honest profession, and no professions or persons should be suffered, who bring detriment unto the commonwealth.

17.

These professions of husbandry, keeping of cattle, manufactures and mechanic[al] trades, if well ordered, tend much unto the preservation of the state, for without them it cannot well subsist. Yet there is another institution, and the same noble, and necessary to the defence.

---

[48] Tubal-Cain, seventh-generation direct descendant of Cain, Gen. 4.22.
[49] Bezaleel made the Ark, Exod. 37.1.

For there may be raised rebellions, and seditions within, and there may be invasions from without. From both these there is great danger to the commonwealth: therefore as everything is armed with some power to defend itself, so a sufficient strength is required in every political body for to continue the safety thereof. And this is a sword, not only of justice but of war. This sword of war especially cannot be well managed without a sufficient skill, which cannot be had without instruction, exercise and experience. Hence the art military is not only useful but necessary in every well-ordered state. One thing especially requisite in this profession, is to have good commanders, men of valour and prudence, able to lead and instruct others. God himself would have Israel his own people a warlike nation. Therefore, after that he had given them possession of the land of Canaan, he left some certain nations unsubdued, only that the generations of the children of Israel, might know to teach them war, at least, such as knew nothing before of it (Judg. 3.1, 2). Those who lived in the times of Joshua were well experienced, but the generation following had no experience, neither could they learn any without some enemies constantly to exercise them. Therefore, though wars be heavy judgements, yet it's the will of God, there should be warlike dissensions, and that for many ends: [...] to punish the wickedness of the world; [...] to let men know, how sweet a blessing peace is; [...] to be a nursery and school of breeding gallant men, especially, when he by them intends to do some great work. In consideration of these things, it's good that any state in time of peace, not only choose captains, train soldiers, provide arms: but also send some into foreign wars to learn experience. Of this part of institution, as also of that of learning, you may read at large in Contzen.[50] Of the laws of war Grotius may be consulted.[51] That some wars are lawful, especially such as are necessary and undertaken for our defence, there's no doubt: and not only defensive but offensive arms may be justified out of the holy Scriptures, and from the example of Abraham, Joshua, many of the judges, and David, who were excellent commanders, under whom many gallant men served. When God intended to ruin Judah, he threaten[ed] to take away the mighty man (Isa. 3.2). It's a sad presage, when the gentry and nobility of a nation become vicious and effeminate: and

---

[50] Adam Contzen, *Politicorum, libri decem* (Mentz, 1620, 1627), bk. 4 on education, bk. 10 on war.
[51] Hugo Grotius, *De jure belli ac pacis* (Paris, 1625) and various editions prior to 1660.

this was one cause of that heavy judgement of God which many of them suffered in the late wars, wherein England gained great skill and experience both by sea and land, yet with the woeful expense of much of her own blood. And how happy had we been, if so much valour had been manifested in the ruin of the enemies of Christ and his gospel. Whosoever desires to understand more of this subject, as belonging to politics, let him read military books. If this be so necessary for the defence and safety of an earthly state; how much more is the spiritual militia necessary for the defence of our souls?

18.

There is another profession, and the same useful for many things, but in particular, for to enrich the state: it's that of merchandise and traffic. These merchants are of several sorts: some deal in petty commodities, and sell by parcels; some are for wholesale; but the chiefest are such as are great adventurers, and trade by sea, and traffic with all nations. These are the great monied men of the world who have great princes and whole states their debtors. These furnish us with rarities and varieties of the earth, and enrich us with the com-modities of east and west, south and north, and the remotest parts of the world. These make new discoveries, and might furnish us with many rare inventions, books, and arts. But most intend rather private gain than public good. It were to be wished, that our luxurious and wicked expenses were turned another and better way, to maintain scholars in those countries, where they maintain factors, for the improvement of learning and the propagation of religion. The king of Spain and the Jesuits are the only politicians in this kind: though it be a question, whether this profession be not derogatory to nobility. Yet King Solomon and Jehosaphat were adventurers in corporations;[52] and [in] great cities, these tradesman and merchants have their several companies and their orders, and are called by some systems, which cannot be well regulated, without some laws of the sovereign power.

---

[52] 1 Kgs. 10.15; 2 Chr. 17.13.

CHAPTER 16

Of subjects in an ecclesiastical polity

1.

Of subjection in general, and subjection to a civil power, I have spoken; and because there is an ecclesiastical power and subjection due unto it, therefore order requires, that I conclude the first part of politics with the explication of the nature of spiritual subjection and subjects. This spiritual relation and duty arising from it presupposeth subjection [...] absolute to God as creator and preserver; [...] to him as redeemer, [and] to Christ as head and universal administrator of the church. [It is owed] to him [also] as having instituted an ecclesiastical discipline, and promising to every particular church, using the Keys aright in their judicial proceedings, to be with them so, as to make their judgement effectual; and that what they bind on earth shall be bound in Heaven, and what they loose on earth shall be loosed in Heaven. So that this subjection is due to the power of Christ in every particular visible church. For, when a multitude of Christians associate, and according to the rules of Christ erect an independent judicatory, it's the duty of everyone in that association to submit unto it, if he will be a member of the same, and enjoy the benefit of that external government: and by the very institution of Christ, though there be no solemn confederation, they are bound so to do. This subjection is different from that, which is due from the people to their proper pastors. The power external of the Keys, as you heard, is [...] in the whole church particular, according to the extent, as the primary subject of the same; [...] in the representative exercising this power; [and] in the officers. The representative is either general, to which every particular person must submit, or particular, to which the particular members of that association and division are bound to submit, and none else. Submission is due unto the officers according to their intensive and extensive power, and no further. The rule and measure of this subjection, are the special or general precepts of Christ and his Apostles, and if a church, or its representatives, or officers transgress these precepts, they cannot justly challenge any submission as due unto them. In this respect it's necessary, there should be canons to regulate both the fundamental, and also the derivative power, and the same agreeable to the gospel. The want of these and the observation thereof may be an occasion, if not a cause of separation, whereof the church itself may be guilty, and will prove so to be. This subjection ariseth from this, that they are members of such a church: for every single member is subject to the whole. Here is no exemption of any, though they should be bishops, metropolitans, patriarchs. The patriarch of Rome may challenge a transcendent power to be above all laws, and all judgements; he will command all; judge all, will be commanded, will be judged by none. But all this is but an unjust and insolent usurpation. For Christ's institution in those words, 'Tell the church,' excludes such powers, dethrones such persons. He that will sit in the church of God, as God, must needs be the son of perdition. From this subjection ariseth an obligation to acknowledge the just power of the church to be faithful unto it, and by all means to seek the good thereof, to obey the laws, and submit unto the just judgement of the same.

2.

This being the brief explication of subjection, whence a Christian is denominated a subject of a particular church under a form of government; the next thing to be done is, to enquire, who are subjects, how they may be distinguished: and how they may be divided, and how educated. [...][1]

[...] They are distinguished both from others, and also among themselves; from others they are differenced; for some are within, some without, some are brethren, some not: This is implied by the Apostle, when he saith, 'If any man that is called a brother'; and 'what have I to do to judge them that are without? Do not ye judge them that are within?' (1 Cor. 5.11, 12). Therefore there are such as are not brethren, such as are without and cannot be judged by the church; these are no subjects. There are brethren, such as are within, and may be judged: these are subjects. By this distinction, Mahometans, pagans, unbelieving Jews are excluded. For, none can be a member of a church Christian, but a Christian, who by baptism is solemnly admitted to be a subject of God the Father, Son and Holy Ghost, and

[1]Diagram omitted to avoid repetition.

a member of the universal church. And whosoever shall be such, may be a member, and so a subject of a particular visible church. Yet one may be a member of one particular church, and not of another; for as in civil politics, none can be a subject of two several states civil at one time, so in ecclesiastical government, no person can be a subject of two particular independent churches at the same time. Therefore, when the Apostle saith, 'Do not ye judge them within?' is to be understood of the members of that particular church of Corinth. For they could not judge them of the church of Rome, of Ephesus, of Jerusalem or any other but their own: yet here is to be observed, that manifest apostates, though they have been Christians, cannot be received into a Christian church; nor such as have been members of an heretical, superstitious, idolatrous church, till they have renounced their heresy, superstition, idolatry. Neither must any subject himself to any such church, nor continue in it, if formerly he hath been a member: for all sinful communion is unlawful. Yet, wherein there is no such thing, and God in his providence casts him upon another church, he may subject and also continue. As in a civil state there are sojourners, and strangers, and also plenary subjects, so there may be in a particular church. For, all such as are members and subjects of one church, and yet either sojourn or inhabit in another for less or longer time, they are not subjects till they be incorporate, yet they are subjects of the Catholic church in any part of the world. And, upon letters testimonial, or any other sufficient information, they may be admitted to communion in word, prayer, and sacraments: for these are privileges of the universal church, and common to all Christians of age, as Christians. But these doth not render them members of that particular church, for discipline without submission and admission. Only, if they do offend against the just canons of that church where they are strangers: the rule of *delictum in alieno territorio*, etc. holds good, and they may be censured, where the offence is committed, and where the scandal is committed. Of plenary subjects, some are such by birth, some by election. Those by birth are like the native Jew, those by election are like the proselite.[2] Yet this is to be observed, that as one who was a heathen, might be made both a proselite and a member of that church of Israel at the same time, and the same act, so one that was of no church, as being no Christian, may be made a

---

[2] Exod. 12.48; Acts 2.10.

Christian, and a member of a particular church visible at once. Therefore, we must distinguish of such as are incorporated into a church [...] (Eph. 2.11, 12). There were such, who were gentiles, and so none of God's people, and aliens from the commonwealth of Israel, and strangers to the covenants of promise, who afterwards (verse 19), where no more strangers and foreigners; but fellow citizens with the saints, and of the household of God, and so of no people made a people, and more, of no Christians made Christians. There be others who formerly were Christians, and that which is more, subjects of some one particular church, which are made subjects of another. This is so to be understood, as that to be a Christian, or a member of a particular church is not merely from birth, but from birth of Christian parents, who are members of the church universal, and sometimes, nay often of a particular church under a form of government. Neither doth this birth without divine ordination incorporate us into the one or other. For to be a Christian is not from nature, but from God's gracious ordination. [This] requires that even those who are born in the bosom of the church and baptized too, should, when they come to age be instructed in the covenant, and also own their baptism by profession of their faith, and promise for to keep the covenant. The neglect of this is the cause, why many congregations have such unworthy members: yet it's not necessary by any divine precept that all should be excluded whom we do not certainly know to be real saints. And here I will take occasion to debate of two things much controverted in these times: [...] of the qualification of a member of the church; [and] of separation from a church.

3.

For the qualification of a church member it's agreed, that visible saints, though not real may be members of a church. But the question is, what a visible saint is? By visible, the congregational party, in particular Mr. Hooker of New England understands, one that shall appear to such, as should admit him to be a saint. This saintship is, as he informs us, in knowledge and practice: and he grants a latitude in both.[3] This visibility is that, whereby they appear to us to be saints in

---

[3] Thomas Hooker, *A Survey of the Summe of Church Discipline* (London, 1648), pt. 1, ch. 2, pp. 14–15.

respect of their knowledge and practice. And thus they appear and may be represented to us, either immediately by examination of their knowledge, and knowledge of their practice, either from our own sight, or their expressions mediately by the testimony of others who are judged by us to be credible. By this, the grossly ignorant, and such as trade and constantly live in sin, and are obstinate and refuse to be reformed, are excluded. To these must be added, such as are grossly erroneous, and blasphemers, and such as deny plain and saving truth with divers others. For, all these may have sufficient knowledge, and for their lives may be blameless, and for their outward carriage eminently just, honest, holy. But that which makes the question difficult is, the difference between such as never were born in the church, nor baptized, nor admitted for Christians, and those who have been either born in the church, baptized, lived, and continued Christians by profession; or such as upon their profession and promise, when they were at age were baptized and admitted. Shall their birth give them right to baptism, and their baptism right to membership, and the gross ignorance of them born in the church and baptized make them no members, or deprive them of their native and baptismal right? Or shall it not? But, suppose they have some knowledge of Christ, and the principles of Christianity, and yet be idolaters, covetous, drunkards, railers, incestuous persons. For one that is called a brother, and a real member of a particular church may be such, as is evident, from 1 Corinthians 5.11, 12. Besides, such a brother may deny to hear the church, as implied in Matthew 18.17. Yet these may own their baptism, profess their faith in Christ, and utterly renounce all other religions. The question therefore is, whether these and such like are not members of a church Christian. If they be not, how can the church censure, judge them, cast them out? Yet such owning their baptism, and the faith whereinto they were baptized, may be censured; and if they will not hear the church, may be cast out. These are neither pagans, nor Mahometans, nor unbelieving Jews, they will abhor them, God will judge them as Christians, as being baptized, as having heard the gospel, as owning Christ, and professing their hope to be saved by him; though he will say unto them, 'Depart from me ye workers of iniquity.'[4] These, if cast forth, do not cease to be brethren, till they renounce Christianity. These associate with Christians,

---

[4] Matt. 7.23.

frequent Christian assemblies for divine worship, and usually are under the ministry, and if there be any external government, by their very baptism owned are subjects to the Power of the Keys. Many as bad as these and some worse were in the church of the Jews, and yet not *Lo-ammi*, but reckoned amongst the people of God, till God took away both his word and spirit from them.[5] The Nicolaitans and the disciples of Jezebel were as bad as these, yet they were members of the churches where they lived: how else could they be cast out, as Christ commands.[6] The Valentinians, and many of the gnostics were worse than these, and yet many of them were in and of some Christian church visible.[7] These must be either without or within, except we can find a third place for them, as they of the church of Rome have invented purgatory for such as were not good enough for Heaven, or bad enough for Hell. They, as I conceive, do far better, who enclose them within the pale of the visible church, and seek to reform them, than they who place them in the outward court, and leave them amongst the gentiles. It were but reasonable, that they who are so pure and strict in their new invented way, would declare in proper terms their [minimum requirements], and make the same evident out of the Scriptures. But this they have not done: they seem to us, whatsoever they are amongst themselves, to be sceptics.

4.

As there is a controversy about qualification, so there is about separation. Separation presupposeth union and communion ecclesiastical: for, as in nature there can be no separation but of things some way as joined and united, so it is in government both civil and ecclesiastical. For, there cannot in [a] proper sense be any separation from the church, but of such as have been in a church, members of a Christian community, or subjects of an ecclesiastical visible polity. This communion is either with the whole as the party governing, or with the members amongst themselves as fellow subjects, if a discipline be settled; and it is in doctrine and profession, or in worship, or in discipline, or in some of these, or all. But the communion with the church in general, and with God the Father and Jesus Christ the Son

---

[5] Hos. 1.9. [6] Rev. 2.6, 15, 20–2.
[7] Followers of the gnostic Valentinus, 2nd century AD.

is of a higher kind. Communion presupposeth this separation is either passive, or active and voluntary. Passive is, when any is separated either justly or unjustly from a Christian society, and this may be negative or positive. Negative, is a non-admission after they had been formerly admitted: and this may be done upon sufficient reason, or without any just and sufficient cause. Positive, is a plain ejection of such as are in the church. Separation active, is that which is voluntary; and as the former, so this may be just or unjust, and may admit of several degrees, according as the union and communion is. For, some separation may be total, some partial, and of partial, some may be greater, some less. The reason why I take occasion to speak of this subject is, because these are times of separation: and it were good to know, what may be justly done, what not, either in separating others by non-admission, or ejection, or in separating ourselves. And this is a certain rule, that all union and communion instituted commanded, or approved of God ought to be observed: and whosoever shall violate this must needs be guilty, there can be no just or sufficient cause to do so. The Church of England was formerly a true Protestant and reformed church, and had the same public doctrine, the same form of public worship, the same public discipline. Yet, because the first reformation was judged imperfect, and many abuses and corruptions entered in afterward, which did alter it for the worst, therefore a further and a new reformation was thought to be at least expedient, if not necessary. That the first reformation in respect of discipline was imperfect is evident, first from *The Book of Common Prayer* in the rubric of the Commination [litany of divine threat], which plainly implies, that the ancient discipline was not, and as it seems, could not, at that time be restored, and till the restoring of it the Commination must be used. Yet it was never restored, neither did any seem to seek it. Again, the imperfection thereof appears by that book made by the commissioners in the latter end of the reign of Edward VI which is called *Reformatio legum ecclesiasticarum*. Yet that though imperfect was never established, nor by the bishops put in practice.[8] The latter abuses, innovation, superstitions brought in by the bishops, and as some say, at the King's command, and that without law and authority of parliament, were confessed by many, and exclaimed against

---

[8] The *Reformatio* (1553) (printed 1571) was the result of an Act of Parliament, 1549, and the deliberations of thirty-two ecclesiastical advisers to Edward VI; it was an attempt to compile a corpus of ecclesiastical law.

generally: and divers charged the bishops as guilty of usurpation; and how could they be less, when they imposed the reading of *The Book of Sports and Recreations on the Lord's Day*, and punished divers ministers refusing to read it? And, which was not tolerable, the rule of their proceedings in the exercise of their power were canons never allowed by parliament, besides the business of altars, and bowing towards them, which had no colour of law.[9] Many began to set up images in their churches, and innovate in doctrine. In consideration of all these things, a reformation, if it might be had, was thought necessary, not only for the perfection of the first, but also for to cut off the late introduced corruptions, and prevent the like for the future. An opportunity seemed to be put into the hands of a parliament with an Assembly of Divines for advice to do this. A reformation they promise, begin to act in the way, and the expectation was great. But, instead of perfecting the former reformation, they cause a new [Westminter] Confession of Faith, and new catechisms to be made, instead of the former liturgy and set form of worship, a new directory is composed and allowed.[10] For discipline the episcopal power is abolished, and the former government dissolved, the Presbyterian way, and that very near to that of Scotland is agreed upon. So, that whatsoever was formerly determined by law is null and void. In the end, all that was done in doctrine, worship, and discipline in a time of war, without and against the mind of the King, did vanish, was rejected by many, and received by few, and such an indulgence under pretence of favouring tender consciences, was granted, that every one seemed to be left at liberty. Hence sprang so many separations and divisions, that England, since she became Christian, never saw the like. There were divisions in doctrine so many as could not be numbered, and men were in their judgements not only different, but contrary. And the former errors pretended to be great, were few in number, far less noxious in quality to these latter, which were very many and some of them blasphemous and abominable. All the old damned heresies

---

[9] *The Book of Sports* (1617, reissued 1633), listing the games and sports permissible on Sundays. See R.S. Gardiner, *The Constitutional Documents of the Puritan Revolution, 1625–1660*, 3rd edn. (Oxford University Press, 1979), pp. 99–103. It was burnt by Parliament in 1643.

[10] See *ibid.*, for the Root and Branch Petition, Dec. 1640, pp. 137 ff.; the Declaration of the Houses on Church Reform, Apr. 1642, pp. 247 ff.; the Nineteen Propositions, 8 June 1642, pp. 249 ff.; Lawson's more theological problems with the Westminster Assembly and its Confession of Faith are in the Baxter Treatises, see above, ch. 12 n. 10.

seemed to be revived and raked out of Hell; and the more vain or blasphemous an opinion was, it was by some the more admired. For worship instead of some ceremonies or superstitions, at the worst all kind of abominations brake out of the bottomless pit. Some professed high attainments and dispensations to the contempt of sabbaths, sacraments, and Scripture itself. Some turned Ranters, as though the old abominable gnostics had been conjured up from Hell. Some became Seekers, till they lost all religion. Some were Quakers, and most rude, uncivil, inhuman wretches, deadly enemies to the ministry, and most violent opposers, of the truth; and some no ways ill-affected, but otherwise well-disposed people seemed to be suddenly bewitched, as the Galatians were, and could give no reason nor Scripture for the separation and alterations.[11] To be Anabaptists seemed to be no offence in comparison of the former. For discipline, some adhered to the prelatical form, and refused communion with the Presbyterian party, who with the Scottish Kirk thought their way to be the pattern in the mount. The congregational was of another mind, and stood at as far a distance from them on one hand, as the rigid prelatical party did on another. Yet in all this God preserved an orthodox party, who retained the substance of the Protestant religion with moderation, and these are they whom God will bless and make victorious in the end. For, all these came to pass and were ordered by divine providence, to discover the frailty of all, the wickedness of some, the hypocrisy of others, to manifest the approved, to confirm the sincere, and let men know what a blessing, order and government in church and state must needs be. Here are many separations, some passive, but many active. As for the Quakers, Seekers, above-ordinance-men [antinomians], Ranters, their separation under pretence of great purity, is abominable: the Antipedobaptists and the Catabaptists cannot justify themselves: and in the end it will appear.[12] The dissenting brethren and congregational party after they began to gather churches, with the rigid prelatists and Presbyterian cannot be excused. They, who actually concurred to procure a liberty and indulgence, especially the zealots in that work, who had a design to promote their own way, have much to answer for, and their account will be heavy. And surely they are no ways innocent, who took away

---

[11] Gal. 3.1.
[12] Those hostile to infant baptism and those insisting on complete immersion, respectively.

the former laws and government before they had better, and in their own power, effectually to establish them. And whosoever departed from the former legal doctrine, worship and discipline in any thing, wherein it was agreeable to the word of God, must needs be worthy [of] blame; as also those who took an ill course to introduce that which was better. They, who will not communicate with others, or refuse to admit unto communion with themselves in all parts of worship, such as are orthodox and not chargeable with scandal, are offenders, and cannot be free from schism in some degree. The usurpations of the bishops, and the innovations made by them and their party, together with their negligence and remissness in the more material parts of discipline, gave no little cause of divisions and separations. To be hasty, high, rigid in reformation is a cause of many and great mischiefs. This Church of England upon the first reformation within a few years brought forth to God, even under that imperfect reformation many precious saints and glorious martyrs. And after the persecution how did she multiply, and yield as many able and godly ministers and gracious servants of God as any church in the world of that compass. And all those good children were begotten, nursed, and increased, whilst under one supreme independent national judicatory. And though the first reformation was imperfect, and the church in some things corrupted, and many members of the same without sufficient cause persecuted by some of the ungodly and unworthy bishops: yet, for any of the subjects and members to separate from her without some weighty cause must needs be a sin. A reformation might have been made without pulling down the whole frame, and opening a way to the ensuing divisions. Imperfection is no sufficient cause to separate from that church, wherein any person receives his Christian being, or continuance, or growth of that being; neither is every kind of corruption. No church but hath some defects, but hath some corruptions, and no man should depart from any Christian society, further than that society is departed from God. To depart and divide upon conceits of greater purity and perfection, or out of a spirit of innovation; or in anything which is approved of God, and not contrary to his word, cannot be lawful. Let every one therefore reflect upon the former divisions, and consider the present distractions, and examine himself how far he either is, or hath been guilty, and confess his sin to God desiring pardon, and for time to come endeavour peace, and supply the defects of understanding,

which in some things is the cause of difference in judgement with the
greater measure of charity. For, though we had less knowledge than
we have, and yet more charity, the breaches of the church easily be
made up. Thus far I have digressed, and enlarged upon this subject,
out of a desire to persuade every member of a particular church to
submit unto the lawful power thereof, and continue united in the
same body, till God shall give a command and commission to come
out or separate.

5.

The end of this discourse concerning the distinction of the subjects of
the same church, is, to show the nature and measure of subjection,
and the manner how we become subjects, and what the duties of such
subjects are. Something might be added concerning the manner of
admission, which Mr. Parker, and so many of the congregational way
do think was not good and allowable.[13] His and their exceptions I will
not here mention, but will with them confess, [...] that as they be
born in such a parish, or forced by the magistrate, they could not be
members of the church; [...] that baptism, without instruction of such
as are capable, is not sufficient. [Further] that it's fit that everyone
when they are instructed, so as to understand the substance of the
covenant, should publicly in their own persons profess their faith and
make their vow. [And] that when this is done, some care should be
taken of their lives, that it may be known, whether they walk according
to their profession and their promise. Yet this may be said, that by
good ministers something to this purpose was done, and though by
others it was neglected. And the church even from the first reformation required and intended this in the strict command of catechizing,
and in confirmation. For though confirmation was no sacrament, nor
proper to a diocesan bishop by divine institution, yet the end was
good, and the effect might have been happy, if it had been duly
observed. For, it would have so qualified the members of the church,
that we should not have had so many ignorant, so many scandalous in
every parochial precinct. But it was either neglected or abused. But
because to be a right qualified member of a visible church is not
sufficient, let every one remember that it's his duty to be a citizen and

[13] Robert Parker, *De politeia ecclesiastica* (London, 1616).

subject of Heaven, and to live accordingly. For, as the Apostle saith (Phil. 3.20), 'Our conversation is in Heaven,' so we turn it, though there may be more in the original. For, [*politeuma*] may be turned, [the law of the municipality, city or town]; as Jerome, Tertullian, and Sidonius understands it,[14] with Beza, à Lapide, Musculus, Heinsius.[15] The sense is, that we are burgesses, denizens and subjects of Heaven, and incorporated into a heavenly polity. Therefore let our life be holy and heavenly, and let us converse most and chiefly with God, and remember that we are but pilgrims and strangers upon earth, and by the observation of the laws of this heavenly kingdom, we tend to our abiding mansions above. And if our lives and carriage be such, though men may persecute us, cast us out, separate from us, refuse to admit us; yet we know our God approves us, we have fellowship with him, and with Jesus Christ his son, whilst we walk in the light, as he is light, and in the end we shall be happy, and our joy will be full.

6.

As the subjects must be divided and subordinated in a civil state, so must they be in a church. The people of Israel were three times numbered and divided: the first numbering was by tens, hundreds and thousands, that Moses might make officers and judges for the civil government (Exod. 18). The second which was most exact and purely ecclesiastical as you may read in the four first chapters of the book Numbers, which was so entitled by the Septuagint, because of this numeration and division of the people. They were also numbered the third time (Num. 26). The end of that second numbering was, that they might, according to an excellent order, encamp about the tabernacle, and also march in order before and after it. The first division upon the numeration was of the whole body of Israel into two parts; [...] that of the Levites, which was subdivided into four parts; [and] the second of the other twelve tribes in one body first separated from the Levites, and this was subdivided into four squadrons, and in

---

[14] St Jerome (*c.* 342–420); Tertullian (*c.* 160–220); St Sidonius (*c.* 432–80).
[15] Theodore Beza, Calvinist reformer (1519–1605); Cornelius à Lapide (1567–1637), biblical scholar; possibly Andraeus, Bartholomaeus, Valentinus or most likely Wolfgang Musculus, all biblical scholars, *fl.* 15th–16th centuries; possibly Daniel Heinsius, late 16th century.

every squadron three tribes, which according to their ensigns quartered at a distance, east, west, north, south of the tabernacle, the Levites being within them. The description of the universal church (Rev. 4), as learned men have observed, alludes to this order. And both these Scriptures teach us, that without numeration, division, and subordination, there can be no order in the worship of God, or the government of the church. And the first thing done upon this division according to God's command, was the removing of the lepers and unclean out of the camp, which was the more orderly and easily done upon the former division, and doth teach what must be done in the constitution of a church, and exercise of discipline.

7.

Of the division either of particular churches of one city and the territories thereunto belonging, or of several churches in one province, according to the cities of the several provinces we read nothing at all in the Scripture. Neither can any such thing be evidently and certainly proved from the seven angles of the seven churches of Asia the less, now called Anatolia. As for the divisions made afterwards in the Roman empire, I shall say something anon. The Church of England, if we may believe Mr. Brerewood, was anciently divided into three provinces, according to the three provincial cities of York, London, Cacruske in Monmouthshire; though after that we find Valentia and Flavis Cesariensis added to make five: of which divisions we find something in Camden.[16] Yet afterwards we find another division of the whole island into two provinces, York and Canterbury. These were divided into several dioceses, the dioceses into archdeaconries, the archdeaconries into so many rural deaneries, the rural deaneries into parishes. This was an orderly way, and did facilitate government much. The Church of Scotland was divided into provinces and shires, and upon the reformation, as some tell us, these shires into classical presbyteries: but afterwards reduced in our times under a certain number of bishops. Yet Archbishop Spoteswood informs us out of their public records, that from the first reformation they had superintendents.[17] In the reformation intended in England,

---

[16] Edward Brerewood, *The Patriarchal Government of the Ancient Church* (Oxford, 1641).
[17] John Spoteswood, *The History of the Church of Scotland* (London, 1655).

when episcopacy was taken out of the way, and the presbytery introduced, they divided the church according to the counties, the counties into classes, the classes into congregations. The subordination was of congregations to a classis, of the classis to a provincial synod of a county; of these provincial synods to a general assembly.

8.

Of the division of the church within the Roman empire, we may read in several histories both civil and ecclesiastical, and in the acts and canons of several councils. And from this division the hierarchy, which is ancient derives its original. To understand this you must know, that hierarchy presupposeth episcopacy: for before there were bishops there could be no subordination of inferior unto superior bishops. What these bishops were, and how they did first arise, and what their power was, the Scripture saith nothing, much less gives any divine precept special for the institution of them, or the manner of their consecration. That of Timothy, Titus, and the angels of the churches, will not evince any such thing, as hath been said before. That there were bishops anciently and betimes in the Christian church within the Roman empire cannot be doubted, if human story be of any force. After these bishops (whom the general rule of decency and order, together with the light of reason might manifest to be convenient) were multiplied, and according to the number of the cities, wherein Christian churches were planted, set up in these cities, and these cities subordinated unto others in the same province, these bishops began to be subordinate to the archbishops. For, as a bishop is one above a multitude of presbyters, so, an archbishop is one above a multitude of bishops. The bishop of the chief city and metropolis in a province was called a metropolitan. The bishop of the chief city of a diocese of the Roman empire was called a primate, or patriarch. By diocese, you must not understand an episcopal diocese, but a far greater compass. For the Roman empire was first divided into dioceses, the principal whereof were three: one in Asia, another in Africa, as now we understand it, another in Europe. These greater circuits were divided into provinces, as we read the empire of Persia was parted into one hundred and twenty-seven provinces in the reign of Ahasuerus. And some tell us, that the provinces of the Roman empire were at first one hundred and twenty. The chief city of the

Asian diocese was Antioch, of the Egyptian and African, Alexandria, of the European, Rome. According to these three cities, where the great officers of the empire kept their residence, were set up three patriarchs: one of Rome, one of Alexandria, one of Antioch, and all the city bishops and provincial metropolitans were under these, if they were within that division, as there were several provinces out of these dioceses; as that of Carthage in Africa, of York in Britain; Justiana Prima in Dacia. To the three patriarchates in after-time were added [an]other two: as that of Constantinople or new Rome, and that of Jerusalem. The first division and subordination of the church was made about the time of the second century, and followed the division of the empire that then was, and as then divided. Yet it did not reach the whole empire, though there might be Christians in all the parts thereof, and many more far beyond the bounds thereof. That there was such a hierarchical order before the great council of Nicaea [325], is evident from divers canons of the same, and continued after, as appears by the council of Chalcedon [451], and Constantinople [381], and others. What the limits and bounds of the first three patriarchates were, we may read in some authors. But you must know, that this division of the empire was several times altered by divers of the emperors, even by Constantine himself, so that the ecclesiastical division and model could not be always exactly conformable unto it. Of this model Spalatensis [M. A. de Dominis] saith but little, Mr. Brerewood a little more, Dr. Reynolds is very brief, Dr. Ussher is a little more large in his Lydian or Proconsular Asia.[18] Yet far more might be discovered of these particulars, both out of human and also ecclesiastical histories.

9.

This little may give us some light in the matter of the ecclesiastical hierarchy. Observe therefore first, that supposing bishops some ways in a large sense to be *jure divino* above the presbyters; yet as Spalatensis affirmeth, they by divine law are equal amongst themselves. For, if they succeed the Apostles, though some grant *primatum ordinis*, yet there is no primacy of jurisdiction of one above another. For Peter's

---

[18] M. A. de Dominis, *Papatus Romanus, liber de origine* (London, 1617); the other authors mentioned are anthologized in *The Original of Bishops and Metropolitans Briefly Laid Down* (Oxford, 1641).

supremacy, asserted by the Romans, can have no sufficient ground in Scripture.[19] Ignatius[20] in his *Palma Christiana*, doth maintain the title of archbishop, and goes about, though very weakly, to prove even out of the Scriptures, that primates are *jure divino*, yet he seems to understand by primacy, that only of order; but he is hardly worth the taking notice of. [...] Yet before the Nicene Council, there was a hierarchy of the church in some parts of the Roman empire. For there were bishops, metropolitans, patriarchs. [...] This hierarchy was a conforming of the church in division and subordination to the civil state of the empire. For, as the state was divided first into greater parts, called dioceses, and the dioceses into provinces, and the provinces into cities, and their territories; so the church was divided. As the cities and their officers were subordinate to the provincial officer, who did reside in the metropolis of the province, and the officers provincial were under the power of the chief officer, who kept his residence in the chief city of the diocese; so the city bishops were subject to the metropolitan of the province, and the metropolitans of the provinces to the patriarch, residing in his patriarchal city. [...] Though this was a prudential order and good for administration, yet it was but human in the state, and also human in the church. For in neither was it of divine institution. For, if it had been such, they could not justly have altered it, as they did afterwards in several places. [...] Therefore, the episcopal hierarchy, though ancient and of long continuance, yet is not of divine authority; neither do we find any divine ordination for it. [...] Therefore, the argument from episcopacy to hierarchy is not good and valid: but to confound episcopacy and hierarchy is gross. For a bishop was before a metropolitan or patriarch: and though some kind of bishop should be of divine institution, yet a hierarchical bishop may be, and is a human invention. [...] It was not thought good to erect one supreme independent judicatory ecclesiastical in the whole Roman empire. For they made three patriarchates independent one upon another: and if they had all been put in one, yet many parts of that empire and of the church within it had been without those bounds. [...] Whether the patriarchs at first had

---

[19] De Dominis, *Papatus Romanus*, ch. 1, pp. 1 ff.

[20] I have found no such text attributed to any Ignatius, although the sentiments would fit St Ignatius Loyola; and the Ignatian Epistles are replete with injunctions to respect bishops. The Epistle to the Trallians asserts that without bishops there is no church (St Ignatius, *Epistles*, Loeb edn. (London, Heinemann, 1912)), 1.2.6.

jurisdiction over the metropolitans, and the metropolitans over the bishops, and they over the presbyters is very uncertain. And, if they had no jurisdiction according to the metropolitan, nor from the metropolitan to the patriarch. It's likely that the power was in synods, and men might appeal from an inferior to a provincial synod, and from the provincial to the patriarchal, which was the highest court, except the Christian emperors call a general council. And, that was said to be a general council, which extended beyond the bounds of one patriarchate, especially if it included all. After these patriarchates began to be such eminent places, many ambitiously sought them, and there was great contention amongst themselves, who should be greatest and have the precedency. Neither could general councils by their determinations prevent them for time to come. [...] The patriarch of Rome, though but at first one of the three, and afterwards of the five, and according to some, of the seven, if you take in Justiniana Prima with Carthage, did challenge the precedency and pre-eminency of them all. And though the council of Chalcedon gave the Constantinopolitan see equal privileges with his, yet he would not stand to their determination, but afterward challenged greater power than was due, began to receive appeals from transmarine parts beyond the bounds of his diocese, and to colour his usurpation, alleged a canon of the Nicene Council, which was not found in the Greek original. He will be president in all general councils; no canons must be valid without his approbation. His ambition aspires higher, when the title of universal bishop had been denied the patriarch of Constantinople by Gregory the Great. Boniface his successor assumes it.[21] And by degrees, they who follow him usurp the power, and at length the civil supremacy is arrogated, and the Roman pontiff must dispose of kingdoms and empires, and will depose and advance whom he pleaseth. And is not he the man of sin and the son of perdition, 'who opposeth and exalteth himself above all that is called God, or that is worshipped, so that he as God sitteth in the temple of God, showing himself that he is God?' (2 Thess. 2.3, 4). From all which words, he that goes under the name of M. Camill[u]s, defines Antichrist in this manner, [Antichrist is the supreme pontiff raised as a pretended substitute in opposition to Christ] (lib. 1, c. 3 *de Anti-Christo*).[22] As the Roman state subdued and subjected unto them-

---

[21] St Gregory the Great, 669–731, pope from 715; St Boniface, 680–754.
[22] M. Camillus, *De Anti-Christo*; beyond this untraceable, but see E. Millington, *Catalogus librarum* (London, 1681), p. 28, where the work is listed, n.p., n.d.

selves the former empires and monarchies of the world, and this in themselves, after that became vassals and servants unto one absolute imperial monarch, and by him Rome-heathen reigned over the kings of the earth (Rev. 17.18). So in tract of time, Rome Christian usurped jurisdiction ecclesiastical over all churches, and her patriarch swallowing up all the power of the former patriarchs, became universal monarch and visible head of the universal church. The occasions, true causes of this usurpation, and the means whereby he by degrees aspired to this transcendent power are well enough known. Some will tell us, that episcopacy or rather prelacy was the occasion at least of the hierarchy, and the hierarchy of the papacy.[23] For, if there had not been a bishop invested with power in himself, and a provincial jurisdiction given to one metropolitan, and many metropolitans subjected to one patriarch, the bishop of Rome could have had no advantage nor colour for his usurpation. This makes many prudent men jealous of episcopacy, especially as many understand a bishop to be one invested with the power of ordination and jurisdiction, and that by divine law without the presbytery. Division and subordination, which are essential to government, could be no proper cause of the papal supremacy. But, the trusting of power ecclesiastical in one man, extending and enlarging the bounds of one particular church and independent judicatory too far, and subordinating the people and presbyters to the monarchical jurisdiction of one bishop, the several bishops to one metropolitan, the several metropolitans to one patriarch, and several patriarchs to one Roman pontiff did much promote, and effectually conduce to the advancement of one man to the universal vicarage. At the first institution of the hierarchy, neither the people nor presbytery were excluded; the patriarchates were of a reasonable extent, the patriarchs independent one upon another, and the end intended was unity, and prevention of schism; and the subordination seemed to be made out of mature deliberation. Yet human wisdom, though never so profound, if it swerve from the rules of divine institution, proves folly in the end. Let not all this discourage any ecclesiastical community, or dissuade them from division, co-ordination, subordination, if so be they keep the power in themselves as in the primary subject, and reserve it to the whole, and not communicate it to a part, and keep themselves within a reasonable

---

[23] A marginal gloss to the second edition, p. 442, is more direct: 'Prelacy the occasion of Hierarchy, and that of Papacy'.

compass. From all this we may conclude, that a secession from Rome, and the rejection of his ecclesiastical supremacy, if so be we retain the true doctrine and pure worship of God, is no schism, especially in England. For [first], there were many provinces out of the great patriarchate, and no ways subject to any of them, but they had their own proper primates and superintendents. Amongst these England was one, and by the canon of Nicaea had her own jurisdiction, and was under no patriarch, but a primate of her own. [Second], the bishop of Rome was at first confined to that city, and after he was made patriarch, he had but the ten *suburbicarian* provinces, and the rest of the provinces of Italy had Milan for their metropolis.[24] [Third], that after the conversion of the Saxons, that that bishop should exercise any power in England, was a mere usurpation. And to cast off a usurped power, and the same tyrannical, could be no schism at all. There is a book printed at Oxford, in the year 1641, wherein we find several parcels of several authors bound up in one. The first author is Dr. Andrewes, the second Bucer, the third Dr. Reynolds, the fourth Bishop Ussher, the fifth Mr. Brerewood, the sixth Mr. Dury, the seventh Mr. Francis Mason.[25] The design of the whole is to maintain episcopacy, and in part to prove the hierarchy. [First], some of the forementioned authors do grant with Jerome, that the church was first governed by the common advice of presbyters, though this position in strict sense is not true, as hath been formerly proved. [Second], some grant, that at the first institution of bishops, a bishop was nothing else but a president or moderator in presbyterial meetings. [Third, some grant that] afterwards these were constant and standing, with a power of superintendency, not only over the people, but the presbyters within a city and the territory thereof. [Fourth, some grant], that when a church was extended to a province, in the metropolis thereof they placed a chief bishop, called a metropolitan, who had the precedency of all the other city bishops. [Fifth], that these bishops could do no common act, binding the whole circuit without the presbytery. [Some accept also] that there were such bishops and metropolitans in the Apostles' times. Thus Dr. Ussher doth affirm, and he quotes Ignatius to this purpose. [Some accept] that there was an imparity both in the state and church of Israel under the

---

[24] The *suburbicarium* dioceses were the seven immediately surrounding Rome, each headed by a cardinal bishop.
[25] *The Original of Bishops and Metropolitans Briefly Laid Down.*

Old Testament, and so likewise of the ministers in the church of the New Testament – thus Dr. Andrewes. [Finally, some accept] that most reformed churches have bishops, or superintendents, and something answerable to bishops. The design of all this seems to be this, to prove that episcopacy and hierarchy are apostolical and universal. Yet none of these produce any clear divine testimony for this, much less any divine precept to make this regiment to be of perpetual and universal obligation. Neither doth any of them all tell us distinctly what the power of bishops, of metropolitans, of patriarchs was: nor whether they exercised their power as officers, or representatives, or by an immediate *jus divinum* derived from Christ unto them. All that can be made clear, is, that some kind of bishops may be lawful and have been ancient, and of good use, though of no necessity.[26] As for the hierarchy, it's merely human, and being at first intended for unity, was in the end the cause of the most bloody schisms that ever were in the church; and an occasion of intolerable ambition, emulation and contention.

10.

Subjects ecclesiastical being distinguished and divided must be educated: and so I come to education and institution. Though spiritual education be far more useful and necessary, yet we find most men more careful to improve their children for this world than the world to come. The reason is, they seek these earthly things more than God's kingdom, love the world more than God, and prefer their bodies before their souls: we should provide for both, yet for the one far more than the other. For, what will it avail us to be temporally rich and spiritually poor: to gain the world and lose our souls? This therefore is a special work of the church to educate her children, and nurse them up for Heaven: and the magistrate Christian is bound to further her in this work. Adam, though lord of the whole earth, and one who might give his children far greater estates in land than any man ever could, yet brought them up, not in idleness, but honest labour. But his principal care was to teach them how to serve their God, and when they were at age, to bring their offerings before him. God saith of Abraham, 'I know him, that he will command his children and his household after him, and they shall keep the way of the

---

[26] The second edition converts these last two phrases into a marginal gloss, p. 446.

Lord to do justice and judgement: that the Lord may bring upon Abraham, that which he hath spoken of him' (Gen. 18.19). Joshua saith, 'as for me and mine house we will serve the Lord' (Josh. 24.15). It was the command of God, that Israel should diligently teach their children the words of God, and 'talk of them when they sit in their houses, and when they went abroad, and at their lying down and rising up' (Deut. 6.7). How often doth Solomon exhort to this duty, and earnestly persuade all, especially children, to hearken unto, understand, remember, and constantly follow the instruction of their parents and their teachers?[27] This was the care of Moses, of Joshua, the judges and good kings of Judah. For this end the priests, Levites and scribes were ordained of God, and the schools of the prophets were erected for this work. This was one prime work of the Levite, to teach Jacob God's judgements, and Israel his laws (Deut. 33.10). This same commandment of spiritual education is repeated in the New Testament. Parents must bring up their children in the nurture and admonition of the Lord. This was the great work of Apostles, prophets, evangelists, pastors and teachers. For, they must not only pray, but teach, and labour, not only for conversion, but the edification of the church's children. Every Christian should help and further one another in this work. As parents in their families should have knowledge, and be able to instruct their children; so all schools should have a care to instruct the scholars, not only in languages and human learning, but also in the saving doctrine of salvation. This was the reason, why by the canons of the church they were bound to catechize the children committed to their charge. The universities and colleges were bound to this likewise, and were seminaries, not only for lawyers, philosophers and physicians, but especially for divines, who, though they improved their knowledge in arts and languages, yet it was in subordination to their diviner and more excellent profession. To this head belongs correction, good example, and prayer. For the principal teacher is the spirit, who must write God's truth in the heart, and make all means of education effectual. The public and principal officers, trusted by Christ with this work, are the ministers of the gospel: whose work is not merely and only to preach and expound, but to catechize. In these works we are either very negligent or imprudent. For, we should plant and water, and pray

---

[27] Prov. 2–4.

272

to God for the increase: we should lay the foundation and build thereon; yet some will do neither, some will preposterously water before they plant, and build before they lay the foundation, and so do Christ little service, and the church little good. Some take upon them the charge, and are insufficient. Men may teach by word or writing. By word first, the principles should methodically according to the ancient creeds and confessions be taught: this is the foundation. Without this sermons, expositions, reading of Scriptures, and books of piety will not be so profitable, and edifying as they might be. People should be taught to believe the saving and necessary truths of the gospel, obey his commands, pray for all blessings and mercies, and especially for the spirit, that their faith may be effectual, their obedience sincere, and also to receive the sacrament aright, and make right use of their baptism. Expositions should be plain and clear, that the people may not only hear, but understand, and be moved by the truth understood. Sermons should be so ordered, as that the texts proposed, and the doctrines and divine axioms thereof may be cleared, understood according to the drift and scope of the spirit. And the application should be pertinent, to inform the understanding with the truth and remove errors, and when that is done, to work effectually upon the heart, and make it sensible of sin past, and pertinent by the precepts, the comminations and the promises, to comfort and raise up the soul dejected; and this especially by the promises of the gospel, and upon motives to exhort to duty and upon reasons restrain from sin. This ordinance and means of divine institution is much abused many ways, by instilling of erroneous and novel opinions, with which the people are much taken, if delivered with good language by impertinencies, digressions, quaint terms and formalities. But of these things I have spoken in my *Divine Politics*.[28] This institution is so necessary, that without it the church cannot subsist, nor the government thereof be effectual.

11.

Thus you have heard, that the subject, or as some call it, the object of politics is a commonwealth, the subject whereof is a community, and the parts the sovereign and the subject. According to this method,

---

[28] *Theo-politica* (London, 1659), bk. 1, ch. 2, pp. 9–12; cf. also Epistle to the Reader.

though mine ability be not much, I have spoken of a community both civil and ecclesiastical, and of a commonwealth, [first] civil, then [...] ecclesiastical. In both the first part is the sovereign, where I enquire [...] into his power civil, and then into the spiritual Power of the Keys in the church. [Then], I proceed to declare how the civil sovereign acquires, or loseth his power, and how the church derives her power, or is deprived of it. [...] The next thing is, the several ways of disposing the power civil in a certain subject, whence arise the several forms of government civil, and the disposal of the Power of the Keys; the primary subject whereof is not the pope, or prince, or prelate, or presbyter, or people, as distinct from presbyters, but the whole particular church, which hath it in the manner of a free state. Here something is said of the extent of the church. After all this comes in *pars subdita*, both civil and ecclesiastical, where I speak of the nature of subjection, and of the distinction, division and education of the subjects, both of the state and church. All this is done with some special reference both to the state and Church of England, desiring peace and reformation. If any require a reason, why I do not handle ecclesiastical government and civil distinctly by themselves without this mixture, the reasons are especially two: [First], that it might be known, that the general rules of government are the same both in church and state: for both have the same common principles, which by the light of reason, observation and experience may be easily known, but especially by the Scriptures, from which an intelligent reader may easily collect them. Therefore, it's in vain to write of church-government, without the knowledge of the rules of government in general, and the same orderly digested. The ignorance of these is the cause why so many write at random of discipline, and neither satisfy others, nor bring the controversies concerning the same unto an issue. [Second], by this joint handling of them, the difference between church and state, civil and ecclesiastical government; the Power of the Sword and the Keys is, more clearly, as being laid together, apparent. For this is the nature of [differentia, they are elucidated by juxtaposition]. This is against Erastus, and such as cannot distinguish between the power of ordering religion for the external part, which belongs unto the civl sovereigns of all states, and the Power of the Keys, which is proper to the church, as a church. Yet, if these two reasons will not satisfy, and some reader may desire and wish they had been handled distinctly, he may read them as distinct and several even in this book. I myself had some debate within myself, what way I should handle them, yet upon these reasons I resolved to do as I have done.

12.

A commonwealth once constituted is not immortal, but is subject to corruptions, conversion and subversion. The authors of politics following the Philosopher, make these accidents the last part of their political systems and some speak of them more briefly, some at large; and declare the causes, and prescribe the remedies, both for prevention and recovery. Corruption is from the bad constitution, or the maladministration; and both sovereign and subject may be, and many times are guilty. The conversion and woeful changes, and also the subversion and ruin is from God as the supreme governor and just judge of mankind, who punisheth not only single and private persons and families, but whole nations and commonwealths. Of these things the Scripture, human stories and our own experience do fully inform us. But of them, if it may be useful, I shall speak more particularly and fully in the second book, the subject whereof in general is, administration; in particular [it is about] laws and canons; officers of the state and of the church, and jurisdiction both civil and ecclesiastical. The reasons why I desire to publish this first, and severally from the latter part, are partly, because, though the first draft of that latter part was finished above half a year ago, yet I intend to enlarge upon the particulars: partly because I desire to know, what entertainment this first part may meet withal. For if it be good, I shall be the more encouraged to go forward; but chiefly, because the most material heads and controversies are handled in this, which is far more difficult. The latter will be more easy, yet profitable and useful, especially if some of greater ability would undertake it. The God of truth and peace give us humility, patience, charity, and the knowledge of his truth; that holding the truth in love, we may grow up unto him in all things, which is the head, even Christ, to whom be honour, glory and thanks for ever, Amen.

FINIS

Index

References to persons and books of the Bible

Footnotes have not been separately indexed where they occur on the same page as a main entry.

Proper names of persons (excluding Biblical references)

Personal names are frequently given by Lawson in a Latinate or referential form and may be misspelt or conflated with those of other writers. Where it has been possible to trace the reference the name is given in the correct spelling. Where references are obscure or unknown, we have indicated this by inserting (?) in the index entry. Charles I of England is so consistently treated by Lawson in terms of his office that he appears in the *Index of subjects* as 'the King'.

Modern commentators and authors mentioned in the footnotes have not been indexed – see Bibliographical guide. Footnotes have not been separately indexed where they appear on the same page as a main entry.

Index

Index

Subjects and areas of argument

Lawson's argument is both tightly and sequentially structured. In addition, following normal preaching practice, he summarises his argument as a preamble to the exposition of his text: 'the most effectual means . . . to promote the public good (that) only such as fear God may have cause to rejoice' (p. 5). This summary, 'The arguments of the several chapters' (pp. 8–14), should be used in conjunction with this index, as it has not been felt necessary to insert index entries which would merely duplicate the guidance which he saw fit to provide.

Footnotes have not been indexed where they occur on the same page as a main entry.

281

Index

also the argument of chapters 2,
3, 13, 14
Confession of Faith, The, 259
congregationalism: see
    Independency; non-conformist
    sects; Parker, Robert; the
    argument of chapters 13, 14
consent, xx, 18, 23, 24–5, 28, 34, 35,
    36, 47–8, 52, 81, 100, 105, 106,
    138, 148, 149, 178, 179, 180,
    204, 220, 221, 225, 235, 236–7
Constitutional Documents, 105, 150,
    160, 161–2, 224, 229–33, 259
Coronation Oath, 59, 63, 72, 73,
    100, 108 109
covenant, 37–9, 106, 116, 135, 140,
    173, 255, 262: see also Solemn
    League and Covenant

discipline, 32, 35, 40, 80, 85–6, 121,
    125, 136, 139, 144, 153–63,
    165–78, 184–8, 189, 193, 194,
    198, 200–1, 204, 207, 211,
    212–13, 218, 228, 248, 252,
    254, 257–62, 264, 274
dissolution (of government form), 28,
    30, 46, 48, 56, 57, 69, 113, 224,
    226–7, 229–34, 236–9: see also
    the argument of chapters 5, 8

education (as one of God's
    blessings), 247–8
Edwardian Reformation, Statutes of,
    147, 258
Eikon Basilike, 3n, 111n
Elizabethan Settlement, Statutes of,
    135–6, 228
Engagement, xxii, xxiii, 65n, 224,
    236–9: see also the argument of
    chapter 8
Erastianism, xi, xix, xx, 136: see also
    the argument of chapters 10, 16
European states (as examples of
    government forms), 28, 55, 57,
    62, 73, 90, 92, 94–5, 98, 119,
    121, 124, 128, 156, 215, 251
exclusion/separation/excommunica-
    tion from a church, 16, 40, 51,
    78, 81, 122, 133, 134, 168,
    176–8, 183–4, 187, 197, 211,
    236, 255, 256, 262, 269: see
    also the argument of chapter 14

family/hereditary rule, xxi, 26, 34,
    58, 59, 61, 62, 64, 66, 69, 74,
    77, 85, 90, 123–4, 133, 192,
    236, 245–6, 247, 264
fundamental constitution/law, xvi,
    xviii, 48, 52, 56, 67, 69, 74, 99,
    113, 124, 164, 186–8, 224, 226,
    227–8, 231–3, 235, 237, 252–3
government forms (pure and mixed),
    xi, xii, xvi, xxii: see also
    European states; the argument
    of chapters 8, 14
Grand Remonstrance, The, xxii,
    113n

Henrician Reformation, Statutes of,
    136
His Majesty's Answer to the
    Nineteen Propositions, 115
Humble Petition and Advice, The,
    121

Independency xi, xiv, 55, 112, 117–
    18, 191–218: see also non-
    conformist sects.
Instrument of Government, 121
Isle of Wight Treaty, 118

jews: see non-christians

Keys, Power of the, xi, xvi, xxv: see
    also the arguments of chapters
    10–13
King, the (Charles 1), xv, xvii, xxii–
    iii, xxiv, 67–8, 69, 111–22, 125,
    162, 224, 229–38, 258, 259
kingship of England, origin and
    powers of, 56, 57, 100–10, 131,
    147, 226: see also the argument
    of chapters 8, 15

law, xi, xvi, xix, xxvi, xxviii, 65, 92,
    93, 102–3, 107, 114, 117, 222–
    4, 228; see also fundamental
    law; God
loyalty, hierarchy of, xxiii
Magna Charta, 62
majesty/sovereignty; x, xii, xix, xx,
    xxii–iii, xxv: see also the
    argument of chapters 4, 5, 8,
    10, 15
Modus tenendi, 110

282

Index

CAMBRIDGE TEXTS IN THE HISTORY OF POLITICAL THOUGHT
Titles published in the series thus far

Heterick Memorial Library
Ohio Northern University

	DUE	RETURNED		DUE	RETURNED
1.			13.		
2.			14.		
3.			15.		
4.			16.		
5.			17.		
6.			18.		
7.			19.		
8.			20.		
9.			21.		
10.			22.		
11.			23.		
12.			24.		

Heterick Memorial Library
Ohio Northern University
Ada, Ohio 45810